The Princeton Review®

Cracking the

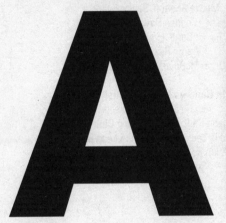AP®

WORLD HISTORY EXAM

2019 Edition

The Staff of The Princeton Review

PrincetonReview.com

Penguin
Random
House

The Princeton Review
110 East 42nd St, 7th Floor
New York, NY 10017
Email: editorialsupport@review.com

Published in the United States by Penguin Random House LLC, New York, and in Canada by Random House of Canada, a division of Penguin Random House Ltd., Toronto.

Terms of Service: The Princeton Review Online Companion Tools ("Student Tools") for retail books are available for only the two most recent editions of that book. Student Tools may be activated only once per eligible book purchased, for a total of 24 months of access. Activation of Student Tools more than once per book is in direct violation of these Terms of Service and may result in discontinuation of access to Student Tools Services.

ISBN: 978-1-5247-5818-9
eBook ISBN: 978-1-5247-5850-9
ISSN: 1546-9077

AP is a trademark registered and owned by the College Board, which is not affiliated with, and does not endorse, this product.

The Princeton Review is not affiliated with Princeton University.

Editor: Colleen Day
Production Editors: Lee Elder and Harmony Quiroz
Production Artist: Craig Patches
Content Contributor: Kevin Kelly

Printed in the United States of America on partially recycled paper.

10   9   8   7   6   5   4   3   2   1

2019 Edition

Editorial
Robert Franek, Editor-in-Chief
Casey Cornelius, Chief Product Officer
Mary Beth Garrick, Executive Director of Production
Craig Patches, Production Design Manager
Selena Coppock, Managing Editor
Meave Shelton, Senior Editor
Colleen Day, Editor
Sarah Litt, Editor
Aaron Riccio, Editor
Orion McBean, Associate Editor

Penguin Random House Publishing Team
Tom Russell, VP, Publisher
Alison Stoltzfus, Publishing Director
Amanda Yee, Associate Managing Editor
Ellen Reed, Production Manager
Suzanne Lee, Designer

Acknowledgments

The Princeton Review would like to extend special thanks to Kevin Kelly for his valuable contributions to the 2019 edition of this book. We are also, as always, very appreciative of the time and attention given to each page by Lee Elder, Harmony Quiroz, and Craig Patches.

Contents

Get More (Free) Content

1 Go to **PrincetonReview.com/cracking.**

2 Enter the following ISBN for your book: 9781524758189.

3 Answer a few simple questions to set up an exclusive Princeton Review account. (If you already have one, you can just log in.)

4 Click the "Student Tools" button, also found under "My Account" from the top toolbar. You're all set to access your bonus content!

Need to report a potential **content** issue?

Contact **EditorialSupport@review.com.**
Include:

- full title of the book
- ISBN number
- page number

Need to report a **technical** issue?

Contact **TPRStudentTech@review.com** and provide:

- your full name
- email address used to register the book
- full book title and ISBN
- computer OS (Mac/PC) and browser (Firefox, Safari, etc.)

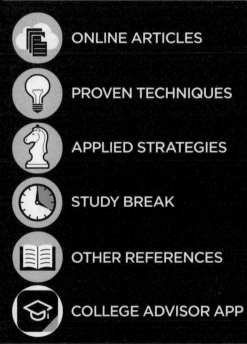

The Princeton Review®

Once you've registered, you can...

- Access comprehensive study guides and a variety of printable resources, including bubble sheets for the practice tests in the book and lists of need-to-know World History terms

- Get valuable advice about the college application process, including tips for writing a great essay and where to apply for financial aid

- If you're still choosing between colleges, use our searchable rankings of *The Best 384 Colleges* to find out more information about your dream school.

- Check to see if there have been any corrections or updates to this edition

- Get our take on any recent or pending updates to the AP World History Exam

Look For These Icons Throughout The Book

ONLINE ARTICLES

PROVEN TECHNIQUES

APPLIED STRATEGIES

STUDY BREAK

OTHER REFERENCES

COLLEGE ADVISOR APP

Part I
Using This
Book to Improve
Your AP Score

- Preview: Your Knowledge, Your Expectations
- Your Guide to Using This Book
- How to Begin

PREVIEW: YOUR KNOWLEDGE, YOUR EXPECTATIONS

Your route to a high score on the AP World History Exam depends a lot how you plan to use this book. Start thinking about your plan by responding to the following questions.

1. Rate your level of confidence about your knowledge of the content tested by the AP World History Exam:

   A. Very confident—I know it all
   B. I'm pretty confident, but there are topics for which I could use help
   C. Not confident—I need quite a bit of support
   D. I'm not sure

2. If you have a goal score in mind, circle your goal score for the AP World History Exam:

   5   4   3   2   1   I'm not sure yet

3. What do you expect to learn from this book? Circle all that apply to you.

   A. A general overview of the test and what to expect
   B. Strategies for how to approach the test
   C. The content tested by this exam
   D. I'm not sure yet

YOUR GUIDE TO USING THIS BOOK

This book is organized to provide as much—or as little—support as you need, so you can use this book in whatever way will be most helpful to improving your score on the AP World History Exam.

- The remainder of **Part I** will provide guidance on how to use this book and help you determine your strengths and weaknesses

- **Part II** of this book contains Practice Test 1 and its answers and explanations. We recommend that you take this test before going any further in order to realistically determine
  o your starting point right now
  o which question types you're ready for and which you might need to practice
  o which content topics you are familiar with and which you will want to carefully review

Once you have nailed down your strengths and weaknesses with regard to this exam, you can focus your test preparation, build a study plan, and be efficient with your time.

- **Part III** of this book will
  - provide information about the structure, scoring, and content of the AP World History Exam
  - help you to make a study plan
  - point you towards additional resources

- **Part IV** of this book will explore various strategies such as
  - how to attack multiple-choice questions
  - how to write effective essays
  - how to manage your time to maximize the number of points available to you

- **Part V** of this book covers the content you need for the AP World History Exam.

- **Part VI** of this book contains Practice Test 2, along with its answers and explanations. If you skipped Practice Test 1, we recommend that you take both tests (with at least a day or two between them) so that you can measure your progress. Additionally, taking these tests will help to identify any external issues: if you get a certain type of question wrong more than once, you probably need to review it. If you only got it wrong once, you may have run out of time or been distracted by something. In either case, reviewing your practice test results will allow you to focus on the factors that caused the discrepancy in scores and to be as prepared as possible on the day of the test.

You may choose to use some parts of this book over others, or you may work through the entire book. The ways in which you use this book will depend on your needs and how much time you have. Now let's look at how to make this determination.

HOW TO BEGIN

Got Bubble Sheets?
We provide a bubble sheet for each practice test in the book. You can also download one from your Student Tools if you need extra copies.

1. **Take Practice Test 1**

   Before you can decide how to use this book, you need to take a practice test. Doing so will give you insight into your strengths and weaknesses, and the test will also help you make an effective study plan. If you're feeling test-phobic, remind yourself that a practice test is a tool for diagnosing yourself—it's not how well you do that matters but how you use information gleaned from your performance to guide your preparation.

   So, before you read further, take Practice Test 1 starting at page 9 of this book. Be sure to do so in one sitting, following the instructions that appear before the test.

2. **Check Your Answers**

   Using the answer key on page 51, count how many multiple-choice questions you got right and how many you missed. Don't worry about the explanations for now, and don't worry about why you missed questions. We'll get to that soon.

3. **Reflect on the Test**

   After you take your first test, respond to the following questions:

   - How much time did you spend on the multiple-choice questions?

   - How much time did you spend on the short answers and essays?

   - How many multiple-choice questions did you miss?

   - Do you feel you had the knowledge to address the subject matter of the short answers and essays?

   - Do you feel you wrote well-organized, thoughtful short-answer responses and essays?

4. **Read Part III of this Book and Complete the Self-Evaluation**

   Part III will provide information about how the test is structured and scored. It will also set out areas of content that are tested.

   As you read Part III, re-evaluate your answers to the questions above. At the end of Part III, you will revisit and refine the questions you answer above. You will then be able to make a study plan, based on your needs and time available, that will allow you to use this book most effectively.

5. **Engage with Parts IV and V as Needed**

   Notice the word *engage*. You'll get more out of this book if you use it intentionally than if you read it passively, hoping for an improved score through osmosis.

   Strategy chapters will help you think about your approach to the question types on this exam. Part IV will open with a reminder to think about how you approach questions now and then close with a reflection section asking you to think about how or whether you will change your approach in the future.

   Content chapters are designed to provide a review of the content tested on the AP World History Exam, including the level of detail you need to know and how the content is tested. You will have the opportunity to assess your mastery of the content of each chapter through test-appropriate questions and a reflection section.

6. **Take Another Test and Assess Your Performance**

   Once you feel you have developed the strategies you need and gained the knowledge you lacked, you should take Practice Test 2, which starts on page 403. You should do so in one sitting, following the instructions at the beginning of the test.

   When you are done, check your answers to the multiple-choice sections. Ask a teacher to read your essays and provide feedback.

7. **Keep Working**

   In addition to this book and its online Student Tools, there are other resources available to you, including a wealth of information on AP Students, the official site of the AP Exams. You can continue to explore areas that can stand to improve and engage in those areas right up to the day of the test. For updates and information on the AP World History Exam, as well as free practice, check out its home page: **https://apstudent. collegeboard.org/apcourse/ap-world-history/about-the-exam.**

Need Some Guidance?
If you're looking for a way to get the most out of your studying, check out our free study guide for this exam, which you can access via your Student Tools. See the Get More (Free) Content page for step-by-step instructions for downloading your bonus materials.

AP Students
The AP Students home page is **https://apstudent. collegeboard.org/home.**

Part II
Practice Test 1

- Practice Test 1
- Practice Test 1: Answers and Explanations

Practice Test 1

The Princeton Review®

Completely darken bubbles with a No. 2 pencil. If you make a mistake, be sure to erase mark completely. Erase all stray marks.

1.

YOUR NAME: _____
(Print)　　　　　Last　　　　　　　　　　First　　　　　　　　　　M.I.

SIGNATURE: _____ DATE: ____ / ____ / ____

HOME ADDRESS: _____
(Print)　　　　　　　　　　Number and Street

_____
City　　　　　　　　　　State　　　　　　　　Zip Code

PHONE NO.: _____

IMPORTANT: Please fill in these boxes exactly as shown on the back cover of your test book.

5. YOUR NAME

First 4 letters of last name				FIRST INIT	MID INIT
Ⓐ	Ⓐ	Ⓐ	Ⓐ	Ⓐ	Ⓐ
Ⓑ	Ⓑ	Ⓑ	Ⓑ	Ⓑ	Ⓑ
Ⓒ	Ⓒ	Ⓒ	Ⓒ	Ⓒ	Ⓒ
Ⓓ	Ⓓ	Ⓓ	Ⓓ	Ⓓ	Ⓓ
Ⓔ	Ⓔ	Ⓔ	Ⓔ	Ⓔ	Ⓔ
Ⓕ	Ⓕ	Ⓕ	Ⓕ	Ⓕ	Ⓕ
Ⓖ	Ⓖ	Ⓖ	Ⓖ	Ⓖ	Ⓖ
Ⓗ	Ⓗ	Ⓗ	Ⓗ	Ⓗ	Ⓗ
Ⓘ	Ⓘ	Ⓘ	Ⓘ	Ⓘ	Ⓘ
Ⓙ	Ⓙ	Ⓙ	Ⓙ	Ⓙ	Ⓙ
Ⓚ	Ⓚ	Ⓚ	Ⓚ	Ⓚ	Ⓚ
Ⓛ	Ⓛ	Ⓛ	Ⓛ	Ⓛ	Ⓛ
Ⓜ	Ⓜ	Ⓜ	Ⓜ	Ⓜ	Ⓜ
Ⓝ	Ⓝ	Ⓝ	Ⓝ	Ⓝ	Ⓝ
Ⓞ	Ⓞ	Ⓞ	Ⓞ	Ⓞ	Ⓞ
Ⓟ	Ⓟ	Ⓟ	Ⓟ	Ⓟ	Ⓟ
Ⓠ	Ⓠ	Ⓠ	Ⓠ	Ⓠ	Ⓠ
Ⓡ	Ⓡ	Ⓡ	Ⓡ	Ⓡ	Ⓡ
Ⓢ	Ⓢ	Ⓢ	Ⓢ	Ⓢ	Ⓢ
Ⓣ	Ⓣ	Ⓣ	Ⓣ	Ⓣ	Ⓣ
Ⓤ	Ⓤ	Ⓤ	Ⓤ	Ⓤ	Ⓤ
Ⓥ	Ⓥ	Ⓥ	Ⓥ	Ⓥ	Ⓥ
Ⓦ	Ⓦ	Ⓦ	Ⓦ	Ⓦ	Ⓦ
Ⓧ	Ⓧ	Ⓧ	Ⓧ	Ⓧ	Ⓧ
Ⓨ	Ⓨ	Ⓨ	Ⓨ	Ⓨ	Ⓨ
Ⓩ	Ⓩ	Ⓩ	Ⓩ	Ⓩ	Ⓩ

2. TEST FORM

_____

3. TEST CODE　　4. REGISTRATION NUMBER

⓪	Ⓐ	Ⓙ	⓪	⓪	⓪	⓪	⓪	⓪	⓪	⓪
①	Ⓑ	Ⓚ	①	①	①	①	①	①	①	①
②	Ⓒ	Ⓛ	②	②	②	②	②	②	②	②
③	Ⓓ	Ⓜ	③	③	③	③	③	③	③	③
④	Ⓔ	Ⓝ	④	④	④	④	④	④	④	④
⑤	Ⓕ	Ⓞ	⑤	⑤	⑤	⑤	⑤	⑤	⑤	⑤
⑥	Ⓖ	Ⓟ	⑥	⑥	⑥	⑥	⑥	⑥	⑥	⑥
⑦	Ⓗ	Ⓠ	⑦	⑦	⑦	⑦	⑦	⑦	⑦	⑦
⑧	Ⓘ	Ⓡ	⑧	⑧	⑧	⑧	⑧	⑧	⑧	⑧
⑨			⑨	⑨	⑨	⑨	⑨	⑨	⑨	⑨

6. DATE OF BIRTH

Month		Day		Year	
◯ JAN					
◯ FEB	⓪	⓪	⓪	⓪	
◯ MAR	①	①	①	①	
◯ APR	②	②	②	②	
◯ MAY	③	③	③	③	
◯ JUN		④	④	④	
◯ JUL		⑤	⑤	⑤	
◯ AUG		⑥	⑥	⑥	
◯ SEP		⑦	⑦	⑦	
◯ OCT		⑧	⑧	⑧	
◯ NOV		⑨	⑨	⑨	
◯ DEC					

7. GENDER

◯ MALE
◯ FEMALE

The Princeton Review®

1. Ⓐ Ⓑ Ⓒ Ⓓ
2. Ⓐ Ⓑ Ⓒ Ⓓ
3. Ⓐ Ⓑ Ⓒ Ⓓ
4. Ⓐ Ⓑ Ⓒ Ⓓ
5. Ⓐ Ⓑ Ⓒ Ⓓ
6. Ⓐ Ⓑ Ⓒ Ⓓ
7. Ⓐ Ⓑ Ⓒ Ⓓ
8. Ⓐ Ⓑ Ⓒ Ⓓ
9. Ⓐ Ⓑ Ⓒ Ⓓ
10. Ⓐ Ⓑ Ⓒ Ⓓ
11. Ⓐ Ⓑ Ⓒ Ⓓ
12. Ⓐ Ⓑ Ⓒ Ⓓ
13. Ⓐ Ⓑ Ⓒ Ⓓ
14. Ⓐ Ⓑ Ⓒ Ⓓ
15. Ⓐ Ⓑ Ⓒ Ⓓ

16. Ⓐ Ⓑ Ⓒ Ⓓ
17. Ⓐ Ⓑ Ⓒ Ⓓ
18. Ⓐ Ⓑ Ⓒ Ⓓ
19. Ⓐ Ⓑ Ⓒ Ⓓ
20. Ⓐ Ⓑ Ⓒ Ⓓ
21. Ⓐ Ⓑ Ⓒ Ⓓ
22. Ⓐ Ⓑ Ⓒ Ⓓ
23. Ⓐ Ⓑ Ⓒ Ⓓ
24. Ⓐ Ⓑ Ⓒ Ⓓ
25. Ⓐ Ⓑ Ⓒ Ⓓ
26. Ⓐ Ⓑ Ⓒ Ⓓ
27. Ⓐ Ⓑ Ⓒ Ⓓ
28. Ⓐ Ⓑ Ⓒ Ⓓ
29. Ⓐ Ⓑ Ⓒ Ⓓ
30. Ⓐ Ⓑ Ⓒ Ⓓ

31. Ⓐ Ⓑ Ⓒ Ⓓ
32. Ⓐ Ⓑ Ⓒ Ⓓ
33. Ⓐ Ⓑ Ⓒ Ⓓ
34. Ⓐ Ⓑ Ⓒ Ⓓ
35. Ⓐ Ⓑ Ⓒ Ⓓ
36. Ⓐ Ⓑ Ⓒ Ⓓ
37. Ⓐ Ⓑ Ⓒ Ⓓ
38. Ⓐ Ⓑ Ⓒ Ⓓ
39. Ⓐ Ⓑ Ⓒ Ⓓ
40. Ⓐ Ⓑ Ⓒ Ⓓ
41. Ⓐ Ⓑ Ⓒ Ⓓ
42. Ⓐ Ⓑ Ⓒ Ⓓ
43. Ⓐ Ⓑ Ⓒ Ⓓ
44. Ⓐ Ⓑ Ⓒ Ⓓ
45. Ⓐ Ⓑ Ⓒ Ⓓ

46. Ⓐ Ⓑ Ⓒ Ⓓ
47. Ⓐ Ⓑ Ⓒ Ⓓ
48. Ⓐ Ⓑ Ⓒ Ⓓ
49. Ⓐ Ⓑ Ⓒ Ⓓ
50. Ⓐ Ⓑ Ⓒ Ⓓ
51. Ⓐ Ⓑ Ⓒ Ⓓ
52. Ⓐ Ⓑ Ⓒ Ⓓ
53. Ⓐ Ⓑ Ⓒ Ⓓ
54. Ⓐ Ⓑ Ⓒ Ⓓ
55. Ⓐ Ⓑ Ⓒ Ⓓ

AP® World History Exam

DO NOT OPEN THIS BOOKLET UNTIL YOU ARE TOLD TO DO SO.

At a Glance

Time
55 minutes
Number of Questions
55
Percent of Total Score
40%
Writing Instrument
Pencil required

Instructions

Section I, Part A of this exam contains 55 multiple-choice questions. Fill in only the ovals for numbers 1 through 55 on your answer sheet.

Indicate all of your answers to the multiple-choice questions on the answer sheet. No credit will be given for anything written in this exam booklet, but you may use the booklet for notes or scratch work. After you have decided which of the suggested answers is best, completely fill in the corresponding oval on the answer sheet. Give only one answer to each question. If you change an answer, be sure that the previous mark is erased completely. Here is a sample question and answer.

Sample Question   Sample Answer

Chicago is a   (A) ● (C) (D)
(A) state
(B) city
(C) country
(D) continent

Use your time effectively, working as quickly as you can without losing accuracy. Do not spend too much time on any one question. Go on to other questions and come back to the ones you have not answered if you have time. It is not expected that everyone will know the answers to all the multiple-choice questions.

Your total score on the multiple-choice section is based only on the number of questions answered correctly. Points are not deducted for incorrect answers or unanswered questions.

At a Glance

Time
40 minutes
Number of Questions
3 (Questions 1 and 2 are required. Then, choose EITHER Question 3 or Question 4.)
Percent of Total Score
20%
Writing Instrument
Pen with black or dark blue ink

Instructions

Section I, Part B of this exam consists of 4 short-answer questions, of which you will answer 3. Answer all parts of Questions 1 and 2, and then choose to answer EITHER Question 3 or Question 4. Write your responses on a separate sheet of paper.

After the exam, you must apply the label that corresponds to the last short-essay question you answered—Question 3 or 4. For example, if you answered Question 3, apply the label ③ . Failure to do so may delay your score.

WORLD HISTORY

Section I, Part A

Time—55 minutes

55 Questions

Directions: Each of the questions or incomplete statements below is followed by either four suggested answers or completions. Select the one that is best in each case and then fill in the appropriate letter in the corresponding space on the answer sheet.

Questions 1–3 refer to the image below.

Cuneiform tablet containing an administrative account of barley distribution, ca. 3100–2900 B.C.E.

1. The writing form depicted in the image above illustrates which of the following advances in human civilization?

   (A) The ability of the Sumerians to create published texts that were widely available to the masses

   (B) The ability of the Sumerians to organize their society more effectively by keeping written records of economic transactions

   (C) The ability of the Sumerians to travel to other parts of the world using advanced wagon-wheel technology

   (D) The ability of the Sumerians to domesticate wild animals for human use

2. Which of the following changes most directly accompanied the increase in grain production during the time period of the cuneiform tablet shown above?

   (A) An increase in hunter-gatherer lifestyles

   (B) An increase in monotheistic belief systems

   (C) An increase in economic equality between men and women

   (D) An increase in urban populations and organized communities

3. Which of the following geographic features was a primary factor that enabled the Sumerians to farm crops, such as the barley mentioned in the administrative account shown above?

   (A) The river valleys of the Tigris and Euphrates

   (B) The mountains of the Hindu Kush

   (C) The Nile Delta

   (D) The deserts of the Arabian peninsula

GO ON TO THE NEXT PAGE.

Questions 4–6 refer to the passage below.

"Our constitution does not copy the laws of neighboring states; we are rather a pattern to others than imitators ourselves. Its administration favors the many instead of the few; this is why it is called a democracy. If we look to the laws, they afford equal justice to all in their private differences; if no social standing, advancement in public life falls to reputation for capacity, class considerations not being allowed to interfere with merit; nor again does poverty bar the way, if a man is able to serve the state, he is not hindered by the obscurity of his condition. The freedom which we enjoy in our government extends also to our ordinary life. There, far from exercising a jealous surveillance over each other, we do not feel called upon to be angry with our neighbor for doing what he likes, or even to indulge in those injurious looks which cannot fail to be offensive, although they inflict no positive penalty. But all this ease in our private relations does not make us lawless as citizens. Against this fear is our chief safeguard, teaching us to obey the magistrates and the laws, particularly such as regard the protection of the injured, whether they are actually on the statute book, or belong to that code which, although unwritten, yet cannot be broken without acknowledged disgrace."

Thucydides, *History of the Peloponnesian War*, circa 415 B.C.E.

4. According to the passage, which of the following is a characteristic of classical Greek democracy?

   (A) The weighing of individual accomplishment above financial status

   (B) The imitation of neighboring states' laws and principles

   (C) The ability of average people to overthrow leaders with whom they disagree

   (D) The justice system's protection of the injured only through explicitly written legal codes

5. During the time period in which this text was written, who was allowed to participate in the Greek democratic process?

   (A) All adult men born within the geographic boundaries of the state

   (B) All adult men and women born within the geographic boundaries of the state

   (C) All adult men who were citizens of the state by birth

   (D) All adult men and women who were citizens of the state by birth

6. Which of the following correctly describes one of the primary reasons that Greek culture was disseminated widely around the Mediterranean region during the time period represented by the passage?

   (A) The geography of Greece contains many natural resources that facilitated a profitable mining industry.

   (B) The geography of Greece contains numerous freshwater lakes that facilitated a successful fishing industry.

   (C) The geography of Greece contains prominent river valleys that facilitated widespread agriculture.

   (D) The geography of Greece contains many natural harbors that facilitated trade and commerce.

GO ON TO THE NEXT PAGE.

Questions 7–10 refer to the map and passage below.

<u>Source 1</u>

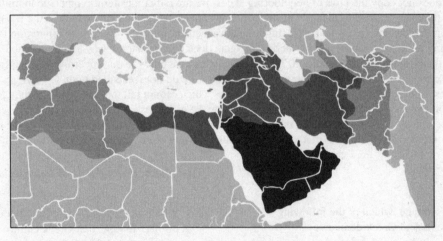

Map of the Mediterranean and Arab world, circa 600–750 C.E. (with modern countries superimposed)

<u>Source 2</u>

"After fighting three battles with the Romans, the Muslims conquered them. So when the chief men of the city saw these things, they went to Amr, and received a certificate of security for the city, that it might not be plundered. This kind of treaty which Muhammad, the chief of the Arabs, taught them, they called the Law; and he says with regard to it: "As for the province of Egypt and any city that agrees with its inhabitants to pay the land-tax to you and to submit to your authority, make a treaty with them, and do them no injury. But plunder and take as prisoners those that will not consent to this and resist you." For this reason the Muslims kept their hands off the province and its inhabitants, but destroyed the nation of the Romans, and their general who was named Marianus. And those of the Romans who escaped fled to Alexandria, and shut its gates upon the Arabs, and fortified themselves within the city."

"And in the year 360 of Diocletian [i.e., 644 C.E.], in the month of December, three years after Amr had taken possession of Memphis, the Muslims captured the city of Alexandria, and destroyed its walls, and burnt many churches with fire. And they burnt the church of Saint Mark, which was built by the sea, where his body was laid; and this was the place to which the father and patriarch, Peter the Martyr, went before his martyrdom, and blessed Saint Mark, and committed to him his reasonable flock, as he had received it. So they burnt this place and the monasteries around it...."

Sawirus ibn al-Muqaffa, *History of the Patriarchs of the Coptic Church of Alexandria*, circa 1080 C.E.

7. The shaded portions of the map shown in <u>Source 1</u> indicate which of the following?

   (A) The extent of the Roman Empire during its peak geographic reach

   (B) The extent of the Byzantine Empire during the years of the Crusades

   (C) The extent of the Arab conquest during the years during and after the life of Muhammad

   (D) The extent of Sassanid-controlled territory during Persia's peak geographic reach

8. The text in <u>Source 2</u> reflects which of the following policies commonly employed by Muslim leaders in conquered lands?

   (A) The death penalty for those who refused to convert to Islam and submit to the authority of the conquerors

   (B) Taxation on those who refused to convert to Islam and submit to the authority of the conquerors

   (C) Forced exile for those who refused to convert to Islam and submit to the authority of the conquerors

   (D) No penalty for those who refused to convert to Islam and submit to the authority of the conquerors

GO ON TO THE NEXT PAGE.

9. Which of the following best characterizes the split between Sunni and Shia Muslims during the time period after the death of Muhammad?

    (A) A disagreement about the rightful successor to Muhammad's rule

    (B) A disagreement about the best location for pilgrimage activities in Mecca

    (C) A disagreement about the legal status of women within Islam

    (D) A disagreement about the Muslim theological understanding of God

10. Which of the following is a major difference between early Christian and early Muslim beliefs?

    (A) A belief in one god

    (B) A belief in the divinity of Jesus

    (C) A belief in proselytization

    (D) A belief in the importance of charity

GO ON TO THE NEXT PAGE.

Questions 11–12 refer to the passage below.

"Upon their arrival they were honorably and graciously received by the grand Khan, in a full assembly of his principal officers. When they drew nigh to his person, they paid their respects by prostrating themselves on the floor. He immediately commanded them to rise, and to relate to him the circumstances of their travels, with all that had taken place in their negotiation with his holiness the pope. To their narrative, which they gave in the regular order of events, and delivered in perspicuous language, he listened with attentive silence. The letters and the presents from pope Gregory were then laid before him, and, upon hearing the former read, he bestowed much commendation on the fidelity, the zeal, and the diligence of his ambassadors; and receiving with due reverence the oil from the holy sepulchre, he gave directions that it should be preserved with religious care. Upon his observing Marco Polo, and inquiring who he was, Nicolo made answer, This is your servant, and my son; upon which the grand Khan replied, "He is welcome, and it pleases me much," and he caused him to be enrolled amongst his attendants of honor. And on account of their return he made a great feast and rejoicing; and as long as the said brothers and Marco remained in the court of the grand Khan, they were honored even above his own courtiers. Marco was held in high estimation and respect by all belonging to the court. He learnt in a short time and adopted the manners of the Tartars, and acquired a proficiency in four different languages, which he became qualified to read and write."

Marco Polo's Travels, circa 1300 C.E.

11. The encounter described in the account above illustrates which of the following?

   (A) The economic dominance of the Ottoman Empire

   (B) The influence of Middle Eastern religious beliefs on the peoples of South Asia

   (C) The lack of cooperation among major political groups in the High Middle Ages

   (D) Amiable cultural exchange between Europe and Asia

12. Which of the following best characterizes one way in which the Mongol Empire was very different from the other major empires of the ancient and medieval worlds?

   (A) The Mongols generally ignored or assimilated to the cultural identities of the people whom they conquered.

   (B) The Mongols often took over territory without major destruction or bloodshed.

   (C) The Mongols imposed their religious beliefs on the people whom they conquered.

   (D) The Mongols had little interest in trading with their geographic neighbors.

GO ON TO THE NEXT PAGE.

Questions 13–15 refer to the image and passage below.

<u>Source 1</u>

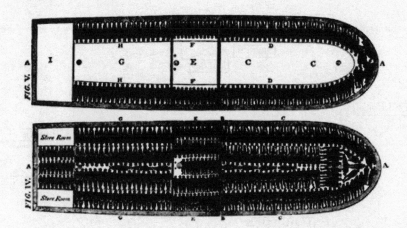

Diagram of a slave ship from the transatlantic slave trade, circa 1790

<u>Source 2</u>

"Are you *a man?* Then you should have an *human* heart. But have you indeed? What is your heart made of? Is there no such principle as compassion there? Do you never *feel* another's pain? Have you no sympathy? No sense of human woe? No pity for the miserable? When you saw the flowing eyes, the heaving breasts, the bleeding sides and tortured limbs of your fellow-creatures, was you a stone, or a brute? Did you look upon them with the eyes of a tiger? When you squeezed the agonizing creatures down in the ship, or when you threw their poor mangled remains into the sea, had you no relenting? Did not one tear drop from your eye, one sigh escape from your breast? Do you feel no relenting *now?* If you do not, you must go on, till the measure of your iniquities is full. Then will the great GOD deal with *you*, as you have dealt with *them*, and require all their blood at your hands."

Excerpt courtesy of the Rare Book Collection, Wilson Special Collections Library, UNC-Chapel Hill.

John Wesley, *Thoughts Upon Slavery*, 1774

13. The sentiment exhibited in <u>Source 2</u> reflects the concerns of which of the following groups?

    (A) The Puritans
    (B) The Freemasons
    (C) The Evangelicals
    (D) The Mormons

14. Which of the following most accurately depicts the historical context of the movements of goods and people during the centuries of transatlantic trade?

    (A) Slaves to the Americas; cotton, sugar, and tobacco to Europe; textiles, rum, and raw goods to Africa
    (B) Slaves to Africa; cotton, sugar, and tobacco to Europe; textiles, rum, and raw goods to the Americas
    (C) Cotton, sugar, and tobacco to the Americas; slaves to Europe; textiles, rum, and raw goods to Africa
    (D) Slaves to the Americas; cotton, sugar, and tobacco to Africa; textiles, rum, and raw goods to Europe

15. Which of the following correctly characterizes one consequence of the layout of transatlantic slave ships, as shown in <u>Source 1</u>?

    (A) Many slaves died of disease in the crowded hulls of tightly packed ships.
    (B) Slave ships often sank due to overcrowding and imbalanced weight allotment.
    (C) Slaves were forced to assist in the rowing of the slave ships.
    (D) Slave ships carried approximately equal numbers of slaves as crewmembers.

GO ON TO THE NEXT PAGE.

Questions 16–18 refer to the map and passage below.

Source 1

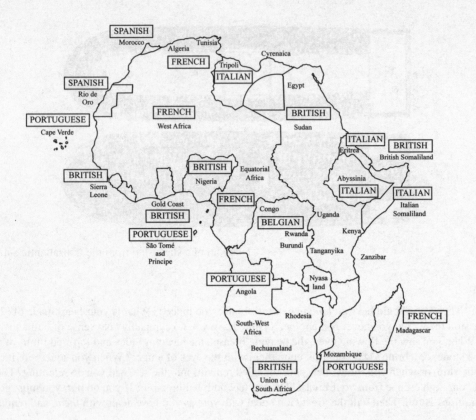

Map of European colonies in Africa, early twentieth century

Source 2

"I repeat, that the superior races have a right because they have a duty. They have the duty to civilize the inferior races....In the history of earlier centuries these duties, gentlemen, have often been misunderstood; and certainly when the Spanish soldiers and explorers introduced slavery into Central America, they did not fulfill their duty as men of a higher race....But, in our time, I maintain that European nations acquit themselves with generosity, with grandeur, and with sincerity of this superior civilizing duty.

I say that French colonial policy, the policy of colonial expansion, the policy that has taken us under the Empire [the Second Empire, of Napoleon], to Saigon, to Indochina [Vietnam], that has led us to Tunisia, to Madagascar-I say that this policy of colonial expansion was inspired by...the fact that a navy such as ours cannot do without safe harbors, defenses, supply centers on the high seas....Are you unaware of this? Look at a map of the world."

Reprinted with permission of the Brooklyn College Department of History.

Jules Ferry, *On French Colonial Expansion*, 1884

16. The boundary lines on the map (Source 1) reflect which of the following?

   (A) Natural barriers such as rivers and mountain ranges
   (B) Traditional tribal divisions within African societies
   (C) Linguistic differences
   (D) European economic and political concerns

GO ON TO THE NEXT PAGE.

17. The reference in <u>Source 2</u> to "superior races" and "inferior races" reflect which of the following attitudes?

    (A) The idea that the colonization of Africa would be profitable for European nations

    (B) The idea that European navies needed use of African ports

    (C) The idea that African peoples would benefit from European cultural influence

    (D) The idea that Africans and Europeans would have mutually beneficial cultural exchanges

18. Which of the following describes a negative short-term effect of the European colonization of Africa?

    (A) Famines occurred when African farmers were forced to grow crops for export.

    (B) Europeans built infrastructure such as roads and railways in the lands that they colonized.

    (C) Missionaries from Europe built schools for native populations.

    (D) Africa experienced a general improvement in medical care under European rule.

GO ON TO THE NEXT PAGE.

Questions 19–20 refer to the two passages below.

<u>Source 1</u>

"The case of a broken thigh is analogous to that of the arm, but in particular, a fractured thigh is mostly deranged forwards and outwards, for the bone is naturally flattened on those sides. It is to be set by the hands, with ligatures, and even cords applied, the one above and the other below the fracture. When the fracture takes place at one end, if at the head of the thigh, the middle part of a thong wrapped round with wool, so that it may not cut the parts there, is to be applied to the perineum, and the ends of it brought up to the head and given to an assistant to hold, and applying a ligature below the fracture, we give the ends of it to another assistant to make extension. If it is fractured near the knee, we apply the ligature immediately above the fracture, and give the ends to an assistant, with which to make extension upwards; and while we put a ligature round the knee to secure it, and while the patient lies thus, with his leg extended, we arrange the fracture."

Paul of Aegina, *Epitome: On the Fracture of the Thigh and Nose*, late seventh century C.E.

<u>Source 2</u>

"Medicine considers the human body as to the means by which it is cured and by which it is driven away from health. The knowledge of anything, since all things have causes, is not acquired or complete unless it is known by its causes. Therefore in medicine we ought to know the causes of sickness and health. And because health and sickness and their causes are sometimes manifest, and sometimes hidden and not to be comprehended except by the study of symptoms, we must also study the symptoms of health and disease. Now it is established in the sciences that no knowledge is acquired save through the study of its causes and beginnings, if it has had causes and beginnings; nor completed except by knowledge of its accidents and accompanying essentials."

Ibn Sina (Avicenna), *On Medicine*, circa 1020 C.E.

19. The two passages on medicine illustrate which of the following cultural exchanges that occurred in the period 600–1450 C.E.?

   (A) The influence of Mesoamerican science on Europeans through systems of trade and navigation

   (B) The influence of Chinese science on Islamic civilizations through European immigration to Islamic lands

   (C) The influence of Egyptian science on the Byzantines through European scholars

   (D) The influence of Greek science on Europeans through Byzantine and Islamic scholars

20. Which of the following characterizes both of the passages?

   (A) A reliance upon supernatural understandings of physical phenomena

   (B) A reliance upon reason and rationalistic understandings of physical phenomena

   (C) A reliance upon abstract philosophical understandings of physical phenomena

   (D) A reliance upon astrological understandings of physical phenomena

GO ON TO THE NEXT PAGE.

Questions 21–24 refer to the image and passage below.

Source 1

Reconstruction of the Aztec Great Temple of Tenochtitlan

Source 2

"This great city contains a large number of temples, or houses, for their idols, very handsome edifices, which are situated in the different districts and the suburbs; in the principal ones religious persons of each particular sect are constantly residing, for whose use, besides the houses containing the idols, there are other convenient habitations. All these persons dress in black, and never cut or comb their hair from the time they enter the priesthood until they leave it; and all the sons of the principal inhabitants, both nobles and respectable citizens, are placed in the temples and wear the same dress from the age of seven or eight years until they are taken out to be married; which occurs more frequently with the first-born who inherit estates than with the others. The priests are debarred from female society, nor is any woman permitted to enter the religious houses. They also abstain from eating certain kinds of food, more at some seasons of the year than others.

Among these temples there is one which far surpasses all the rest, whose grandeur of architectural details no human tongue is able to describe; for within its precincts, surrounded by a lofty wall, there is room enough for a town of five hundred families. Around the interior of the enclosure there are handsome edifices, containing large halls and corridors, in which the religious persons attached to the temple reside. There are fully forty towers, which are lofty and well built, the largest of which has fifty steps leading to its main body, and is higher than the tower of the principal tower of the church at Seville. The stone and wood of which they are constructed are so well wrought in every part, that nothing could be better done, for the interior of the chapels containing the idols consists of curious imagery, wrought in stone, with plaster ceilings, and wood-work carved in relief, and painted with figures of monsters and other objects. All these towers are the burial places of the nobles, and every chapel in them is dedicated to a particular idol, to which they pay their devotions."

Hernan Cortés, *Second Letter to Charles V*, circa 1520

GO ON TO THE NEXT PAGE.

21. Which of the following was an Aztec practice that took place at temples, such as that depicted in <u>Source 1</u>, and highly disturbed the Spanish conquistadors?

    (A) Human sacrifice
    (B) Grain storage
    (C) Burial rites
    (D) Trade and commerce

22. Which of the following describes the primary motivation of the Spanish conquest of the Aztec empire?

    (A) A desire to convert native populations to European cultural practices
    (B) A desire to establish trade networks in South America
    (C) A desire to establish permanent agricultural lands
    (D) A desire to acquire gold and spices

23. The description of Tenochtitlan's temples in <u>Source 2</u> indicates that which of the following was true of Aztec society in the sixteenth century?

    (A) It was outward-focused and relied upon networks of ocean trade.
    (B) It was highly complex and contained large numbers of skilled artisans.
    (C) It was egalitarian in its treatment of women.
    (D) It had largely peaceful relations with neighboring civilizations.

24. Cortés' numerous references to "idols" in <u>Source 2</u> illustrates which of the following conflicts between the Spanish conquistadors and the peoples of the New World?

    (A) Spanish monotheism versus Aztec polytheism
    (B) Spanish capitalism versus Aztec communalism
    (C) Spanish authoritarianism versus Aztec ethnocentrism
    (D) Spanish hedonism versus Aztec intellectualism

GO ON TO THE NEXT PAGE.

Questions 25–29 refer to the two charts below.

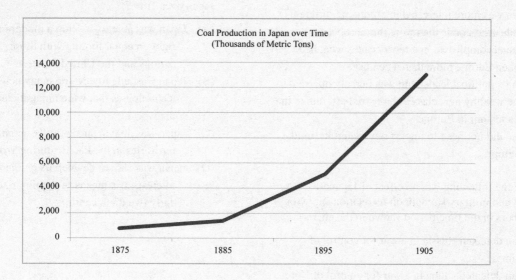

Coal Production in Japan over Time
(Thousands of Metric Tons)

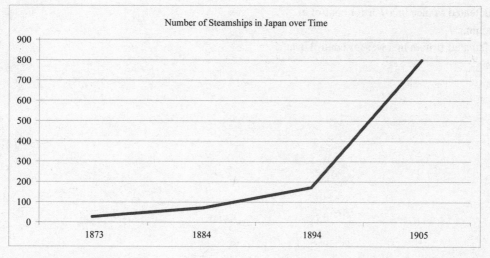

Number of Steamships in Japan over Time

25. Which of the following political eras in Japan best contextualizes the dramatic increases shown in the charts above?

(A) The Tokugawa Shogunate
(B) The Heian Era
(C) The Meiji Restoration
(D) The Showa Era

26. As an effect of the increased industrialization shown in the charts above, which of the following occurred in Japan in the late nineteenth century?

(A) The increased aggression of Japan toward the United States
(B) The weakening of Japanese imperial traditions
(C) The decrease in cultural creativity
(D) The abolition of the samurai warrior class

GO ON TO THE NEXT PAGE.

27. Based on the charts and your knowledge of world history, how was industrialization in Japan different from industrialization in Europe?

(A) Japan was more interested in producing different industrial goods than were the Europeans.

(B) Japan accomplished in a few decades what had taken Europe more than a century.

(C) Japan's political leadership was fiercely opposed to the wealthy new class of industrialists, unlike the leadership in Europe.

(D) Japan did not need to import raw materials, unlike Europe.

28. Which of the following was an effect of Japanese industrial and military strength on its relationship with its neighbors in the time period shown in the charts?

(A) Japan defeated Russia in a war for control of Siberia.

(B) Japan defeated China in a war for control of Korea.

(C) Japan defeated France in a war for control of Indochina.

(D) Japan defeated Britain in a war for control over Burma.

29. Which of the following was a long-term effect of the rapid growth of Japanese shipbuilding capability illustrated in the second chart ("Number of Steamships in Japan over Time")?

(A) Japan was able to develop a modern navy that could fight on equal footing with those of European nations and the United States.

(B) Japan was able to develop many new naval technologies that were unparalleled elsewhere in the world.

(C) Japan was able to successfully defend German territories in the Pacific during World War I.

(D) Japan was able to develop its civilian maritime interests as a means of demilitarization in the early twentieth century.

GO ON TO THE NEXT PAGE.

Questions 30–31 refer to the two passages below.

<u>Source 1</u>

"In the days of a great struggle against a foreign enemy who has been endeavoring for three years to enslave our country, it pleased God to send Russia a further painful trial. Internal troubles threatened to have a fatal effect on the further progress of this obstinate war. The destinies of Russia, the honor of her heroic Army, the happiness of the people, and the whole future of our beloved country demand that the war should be conducted at all costs to a victorious end.

The cruel enemy is making his last efforts and the moment is near when our valiant Army, in concert with our glorious Allies, will finally overthrow the enemy. In these decisive days in the life of Russia we have thought that we owed to our people the close union and organization of all its forces for the realization of a rapid victory; for which reason, in agreement with the Imperial Duma, we have recognized that it is for the good of the country that we should abdicate the Crown of the Russian State and lay down the Supreme Power."

Tsar Nicholas II, *Abdication*, March 15, 1917

<u>Source 2</u>

"History will not forgive revolutionaries for procrastinating when they could be victorious today (and they certainly will be victorious today), while they risk losing much tomorrow, in fact, the risk losing everything.

If we seize power today, we seize it not in opposition to the Soviets but on their behalf. The seizure of power is the business of the uprising; its political purpose will become clear after the seizure....

It would be an infinite crime on the part of the revolutionaries were they to let the chance slip, knowing that the salvation of the revolution, the offer of peace, the salvation of Petrograd, salvation from famine, the transfer of the land to the peasants depend upon them.

The government is tottering. It must be given the death-blow at all costs."

Vladimir Illyich Lenin, *Call to Power*, October 24, 1917

30. Czar Nicholas II's declaration of abdication in <u>Source 1</u> is best understood in light of which of the following?

    (A) Economic prosperity that fostered dislike of the aristocracy

    (B) Widespread dislike of Nicholas' tolerance of political dissidents

    (C) Large-scale military losses and resentment of the working classes

    (D) Persecution of religious minorities

31. What was the principal philosophical underpinning of Lenin's call to power in <u>Source 2</u>?

    (A) Capitalism

    (B) Mercantilism

    (C) Fascism

    (D) Marxism

GO ON TO THE NEXT PAGE.

Questions 32–33 refer to the object shown in the following image.

The Discus Thrower, second century C.E.

32. The statue in the photograph displays the artistic influence of which of the following civilizations?

    (A) Egyptian
    (B) Greek
    (C) Olmec
    (D) Berber

33. Which of the following artistic themes can be seen in the object in the image?

    (A) An emphasis on realistic depiction of the human body
    (B) An emphasis on abstract ideas and expressions
    (C) An emphasis on allegory and religious themes
    (D) An emphasis on symbolism and political protest

GO ON TO THE NEXT PAGE.

Questions 34–36 refer to the map below.

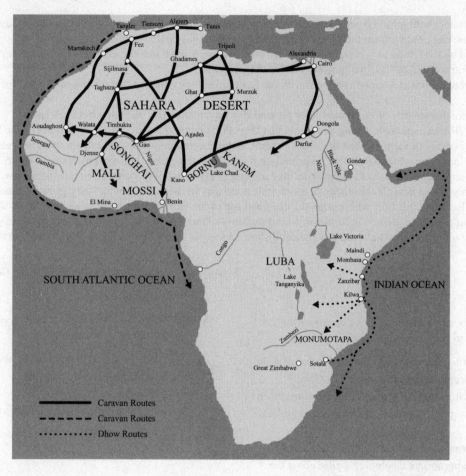

Trade map of Africa, circa fifteenth century C.E.

34. Who were the primary groups traversing the Sahara Desert to reach West Africa along the trade routes shown on the map?

   (A) Islamic traders
   (B) European traders
   (C) Chinese traders
   (D) Mongol traders

35. What was one significant effect of the Indian Ocean trade shown on the east side of the map?

   (A) The emigration of large numbers of Africans to southern Asia
   (B) The development of the Swahili language
   (C) The conversion of most of the coastal parts of eastern Africa to Christianity
   (D) The importation of gold from Arabia

36. What is the main reason that there were no significant trade routes in the central portion of the map?

   (A) The hostility of local tribes discouraged outsiders from entering.
   (B) The central part of Africa has no significant resources.
   (C) Linguistic barriers made trade difficult.
   (D) The harshness of the terrain made travel practically impossible.

GO ON TO THE NEXT PAGE.

Questions 37–38 refer to the passage below.

"The Romanists have, with great adroitness, drawn three walls round themselves, with which they have hitherto protected themselves, so that no one could reform them, whereby all Christendom has fallen terribly.

Firstly, if pressed by the temporal power, they have affirmed and maintained that the temporal power has no jurisdiction over them, but, on the contrary, that the spiritual power is above the temporal.

Secondly, if it were proposed to admonish them with the Scriptures, they objected that no one may interpret the Scriptures but the Pope.

Thirdly, if they are threatened with a council, they pretend that no one may call a council but the Pope…

…The second wall is even more tottering and weak: that they alone pretend to be considered masters of the Scriptures; although they learn nothing of them all their life. They assume authority, and juggle before us with impudent words, saying that the Pope cannot err in matters of faith, whether he be evil or good, albeit they cannot prove it by a single letter. That is why the canon law contains so many heretical and unchristian, nay unnatural, laws; but of these we need not speak now. For whereas they imagine the Holy Ghost never leaves them, however unlearned and wicked they may be, they grow bold enough to decree whatever they like. But were this true, where were the need and use of the Holy Scriptures? Let us burn them, and content ourselves with the unlearned gentlemen at Rome, in whom the Holy Ghost dwells, who, however, can dwell in pious souls only. If I had not read it, I could never have believed that the devil should have put forth such follies at Rome and find a following."

Martin Luther, *Address to the Nobility of the German Nation*, 1520

37. When the author of the passage above discusses the "second wall," to what is he referring?

(A) The differing views of Catholics and Reformers on the appropriate definition of "Holy Ghost"

(B) The differing views of Catholics and Reformers on the appropriate use and interpretation of biblical texts

(C) The differing views of Catholics and Reformers on the appropriate theological belief about the divinity of Jesus

(D) The differing views of Catholics and Reformers on the appropriate method of baptism

38. How is the "temporal power" mentioned in the passage best understood contextually?

(A) A clerical or ecclesiastical authority

(B) A legal or scholarly authority

(C) A state or secular authority

(D) A business or economic authority

GO ON TO THE NEXT PAGE.

Questions 39–41 refer to the passage below.

"We are not Europeans; we are not Indians; we are but a mixed species of aborigines and Spaniards. Americans by birth and Europeans by law, we find ourselves engaged in a dual conflict: we are disputing with the natives for titles of ownership, and at the same time we are struggling to maintain ourselves in the country that gave us birth against the opposition of the invaders. Thus our position is most extraordinary and complicated. But there is more. As our role has always been strictly passive and political existence nil, we find that our quest for liberty is now even more difficult of accomplishment; for we, having been placed in a state lower than slavery, had been robbed not only of our freedom but also of the right to exercise an active domestic tyranny… We have been ruled more by deceit than by force, and we have been degraded more by vice than by superstition. Slavery is the daughter of darkness: an ignorant people is a blind instrument of its own destruction. Ambition and intrigue abuses the credulity and experience of men lacking all political, economic, and civic knowledge; they adopt pure illusion as reality; they take license for liberty, treachery for patriotism, and vengeance for justice. If a people, perverted by their training, succeed in achieving their liberty, they will soon lose it, for it would be of no avail to endeavor to explain to them that happiness consists in the practice of virtue; that the rule of law is more powerful than the rule of tyrants, because, as the laws are more inflexible, every one should submit to their beneficent austerity; that proper morals, and not force, are the bases of law; and that to practice justice is to practice liberty."

Simón de Bolívar, *Message to the Congress of Angostura*, 1819

39. The passage is best understood in the context of which of the following political movements?

   (A) The fight for workers' rights in Central America
   (B) The fight for independence in South America
   (C) The fight for economic justice in the Caribbean
   (D) The fight for political autonomy in the Philippines

40. The author of this text expresses a belief in which of the following as requirements for a properly functioning legal system?

   (A) Truth and religion
   (B) Freedom and democracy
   (C) Intelligence and order
   (D) Morality and justice

41. Simón de Bolívar, the author of the passage, accomplished which of the following?

   (A) The first union of independent Latin American states
   (B) The first military victory of the War of 1812
   (C) The first military victory of the Spanish-American War
   (D) The first political coup by someone of mixed-race descent

GO ON TO THE NEXT PAGE.

Questions 42–45 refer to the two passages below.

<u>Source 1</u>

"We, men and women, who hereby constitute ourselves as the National Organization for Women, believe that the time has come for a new movement toward true equality for all women in America, and toward a fully equal partnership of the sexes, as part of the world-wide revolution of human rights now taking place within and beyond our national borders.

The purpose of NOW is to take action to bring women into full participation in the mainstream of American society now, exercising all the privileges and responsibilities thereof in truly equal partnership with men.

We believe the time has come to move beyond the abstract argument, discussion and symposia over the status and special nature of women which has raged in America in recent years; the time has come to confront, with concrete action, the conditions that now prevent women from enjoying the equality of opportunity and freedom of which is their right, as individual Americans, and as human beings."

National Organization for Women, Statement of Purpose, 1966

<u>Source 2</u>

"The long-term goal of Gay Liberation, which inevitably brings us into conflict with the institutionalized sexism of this society, is to rid society of the gender-role system which is at the root of our oppression. This can only be achieved by eliminating the social pressures on men and women to conform to narrowly defined gender roles. It is particularly important that children and young people be encouraged to develop their own talents and interests and to express their own individuality rather than act out stereotyped parts alien to their nature.

As we cannot carry out this revolutionary change alone, and as the abolition of gender rotes is also a necessary condition of women's liberation, we will work to form a strategic alliance with the women's liberation movement, aiming to develop our ideas and our practice in close inter-relation. In order to build this alliance, the brothers in gay liberation will have to be prepared to sacrifice that degree of male chauvinism and male privilege that they still all possess."

Gay Liberation Front, Manifesto, 1971

42. <u>Source 2</u> endorses which of the following as the most important way to achieve the goals discussed in the passage?

   (A) Lessening the pressures of gender conformity

   (B) Forming a strategic alliance with the Women's Liberation Movement

   (C) Sacrificing chauvinism and privilege

   (D) Encouraging youth to expand their individuality

43. <u>Source 1</u> suggests that which of the following was true about the women's movement in 1966?

   (A) It had succeeded in achieving all of its goals.

   (B) It was ready for more abstract discussions.

   (C) It was not a movement supported by men.

   (D) It had not achieved full equality for all segments of society.

44. According to the text, the authors of <u>Source 2</u> see which of the following as an obstacle to achieving Gay Liberation?

   (A) Rigid societal gender roles

   (B) Conflicts with the women's rights movement

   (C) Societal privileging of some races over others

   (D) Inequity in pay scales

45. Which of the following do both <u>Source 1</u> AND <u>Source 2</u> identify as obstacles to their aims?

   (A) The lack of concrete action

   (B) Inequality between the sexes

   (C) Male chauvinism and privilege

   (D) New movement sand alliances for equality

GO ON TO THE NEXT PAGE.

Questions 46–48 refer to the passage below.

"Let a woman retire late to bed, but rise early to duties; let her nor dread tasks by day or by night. Let her not refuse to perform domestic duties whether easy or difficult. That which must be done, let her finish completely, tidily, and systematically, When a woman follows such rules as these, then she may be said to be industrious.

Let a woman be correct in manner and upright in character in order to serve her husband. Let her live in purity and quietness of spirit, and attend to her own affairs. Let her love not gossip and silly laughter. Let her cleanse and purify and arrange in order the wine and the food for the offerings to the ancestors. When a woman observes such principles as these, then she may be said to continue ancestral worship.

No woman who observes these three fundamentals of life has ever had a bad reputation or has fallen into disgrace. If a woman fail to observe them, how can her name be honored; how can she but bring disgrace upon herself?"

© The East Asian Library and the Gest Collection, Princeton University.

Ban Zhao, *Lessons for a Woman,* circa 80 C.E.

46. Which of the following is an expectation for women in ancient China, according to the passage?

   (A) That they obediently fulfill their obligations within the home

   (B) That they collaborate with their husbands on domestic tasks

   (C) That they pursue education in order to find meaningful employment

   (D) That they speak their minds boldly

47. Which theme in the passage was common in patriarchal ancient societies?

   (A) The importance of attending to the affairs of others

   (B) The importance of ancestor worship

   (C) The importance of systematically arranging wine

   (D) The importance of female purity

48. In what way were women's lives in the period 600 B.C.E. to 600 C.E. generally more restricted than women's lives had been globally before the advent of sedentary societies?

   (A) Women were increasingly thought of as primary earners for the family.

   (B) Women were increasingly responsible for the care of their children.

   (C) Women's power was increasingly confined to the private sphere.

   (D) Women's power was increasingly confined to the public sphere.

GO ON TO THE NEXT PAGE.

Questions 49–50 refer to the two passages below.

<u>Source 1</u>

"We proclaim Him also by our senses on all sides, and we sanctify the noblest sense, which is that of sight. The image is a memorial, just what words are to a listening ear. What a book is to the literate, that an image is to the illiterate. The image speaks to the sight as words to the ear; it brings us understanding."

John of Damascus, *Apologia Against Those Who Decry Holy Images*, circa 730 C.E.

<u>Source 2</u>

"To make our confession short, we keep unchanged all the ecclesiastical traditions handed down to us, whether in writing or verbally, one of which is the making of pictorial representations, agreeable to the history of the preaching of the Gospel, a tradition useful in many respects, but especially in this, that so the incarnation of the Word of God is shown forth as real and not merely fantastic, for these have mutual indications and without doubt have also mutual significations."

Decree of the Second Council of Nicaea, 787 C.E.

49. The late eighth-century religious debate in Byzantium that occasioned the writing of the passages is best understood in the context of which of the following?

   (A) Disagreement about the true nature of divinity
   (B) Disagreement about the role of the priesthood
   (C) Disagreement about the appropriate use of religious iconography
   (D) Disagreement about the best form of ascetic practice

50. Which of the following religious movements was ideologically opposed to the sentiments about the use of holy images reflected in the passages?

   (A) Sunni Islam
   (B) Buddhism
   (C) Zoroastrianism
   (D) Jainism

GO ON TO THE NEXT PAGE.

Questions 51–53 refer to the passage below.

"Upon this a question arises: whether it be better to be loved than feared or feared than loved? It may be answered that one should wish to be both, but, because it is difficult to unite them in one person, it is much safer to be feared than loved, when, of the two, either must be dispensed with. Because this is to be asserted in general of men, that they are ungrateful, fickle, false, cowardly, covetous, and as long as you succeed they are yours entirely; they will offer you their blood, property, life, and children, as is said above, when the need is far distant; but when it approaches they turn against you. And that prince who, relying entirely on their promises, has neglected other precautions, is ruined; because friendships that are obtained by payments, and not by greatness or nobility of mind, may indeed be earned, but they are not secured, and in time of need cannot be relied upon; and men have less scruple in offending one who is beloved than one who is feared, for love is preserved by the link of obligation which, owing to the baseness of men, is broken at every opportunity for their advantage; but fear preserves you by a dread of punishment which never fails."

Nicolo Machiavelli, *The Prince*, circa 1513 C.E.

51. Which of the following best characterizes the author's attitude in the passage?

    (A) Cynicism about the loyalty of a ruler's subjects
    (B) Optimism about the fair-mindedness of political leaders
    (C) Criticism of the religious establishment
    (D) Ambivalence about the future of his economic prospects

52. Machiavelli's treatise is best understood in the context of which of the following?

    (A) A time of burgeoning economic prosperity among the lower classes of Italian society
    (B) A time of increasing religious devotion among the elite Italian scholars
    (C) A time of intense political conflict among warring Italian city-states and other factions
    (D) A time of collegial cooperation between scholars and ecclesiastical authorities in Italy

53. The political philosophy espoused in the text above is different from those of the medieval period in which of the following ways?

    (A) It accepted the notion that monarchs were justified in asserting their authority.
    (B) It was a pragmatic rather than an ethical or religious ideology.
    (C) It stressed the importance of looking back to the classical past.
    (D) It did not rely upon strong concepts of equality across class boundaries.

GO ON TO THE NEXT PAGE.

Questions 54–55 refer to the two passages below.

<u>Source 1</u>

"It is impossible to demand that an impossible position should be cleared up by peaceful revision and at the same time constantly reject peaceful revision. It is also impossible to say that he who undertakes to carry out these revisions for himself transgresses a law, since the Versailles "Diktat" is not law to us. A signature was forced out of us with pistols at our head and with the threat of hunger for millions of people. And then this document, with our signature, obtained by force, was proclaimed as a solemn law."

Adolf Hitler, speech to the Reichstag, September 1, 1939

<u>Source 2</u>

"We shall not flag or fail. We shall go on to the end. We shall fight in France, we shall fight on the seas and the oceans, we shall fight with growing confidence and growing strength in the air, we shall defend our island, whatever the cost may be. We shall fight on the beaches, we shall fight on the landing grounds, we shall fight in the fields and in the streets, we shall fight in the hills; we shall never surrender."

Winston Churchill, speech before Parliament, June 4, 1940

54. What is the historical background for Adolf Hitler's condemnation of the Treaty of Versailles mentioned in <u>Source 1</u>?

   (A) Hitler's belief that Poland's territorial borders should not be violated
   (B) A rising intolerance of ethnic and political minority groups
   (C) A widespread belief in Germany that it had been unfairly treated at the end of World War I
   (D) Hitler's attempted collaboration with Italian leader Benito Mussolini

55. Winston Churchill's speech in <u>Source 2</u> is best understood in the context of which of the following?

   (A) British support for growing resistance movements in Eastern Europe
   (B) British trade deals with American manufacturers of military hardware
   (C) British appeasement of the Axis powers
   (D) British fears about a possible invasion attempt by Nazi Germany

GO ON TO THE NEXT PAGE.

WORLD HISTORY

SECTION I, Part B

Time—40 minutes

3 Questions

Directions: Answer all parts of Questions 1 and 2, and then choose to answer EITHER Question 3 or Question 4. Read each question carefully and write your responses on a separate sheet of paper.

Use complete sentences; an outline or bulleted list alone is not acceptable. On test day, you will be able to plan your answers in the exam booklet, but only your responses in the corresponding boxes on the free-response answer sheet will be scored.

1. **Use the image below to answer all parts of the question that follows.**

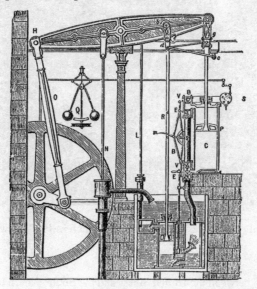

Illustration of James Watt's mechanical steam engine

a) Identify TWO specific technological advances that benefited from the development of the Watt engine.
b) Explain ONE specific long-term effect of the introduction of the Watt engine on each of the technological advances you identified in part (a).

GO ON TO THE NEXT PAGE.

2. Use the image below to answer all parts of the question that follows.

The above poster celebrates the tenth anniversary of the Sputnik launch in 1957, in which the Soviet Union successfully launched a satellite into space.

a) Identify how the "space race" between the United States and the Soviet Union had its origins in the Cold War nuclear arms race.

b) Using TWO specific examples, explain how the end of communism changed the relationship between the United States and the former Soviet Union.

GO ON TO THE NEXT PAGE.

Choose EITHER Question 3 OR Question 4.

3. **Answer all parts of the question that follows.**

   a) Explain TWO factors that led to the emergence of Rome as a Mediterranean power.

   b) Identify and explain TWO specific ways in which the Romans assimilated Greek culture during the period 100 B.C.E. to 600 C.E.

GO ON TO THE NEXT PAGE.

4. Use the passage below to answer all parts of the question that follows.

"The greatest improvement in the productive powers of labor, and the greater part of the skill, dexterity, and judgment with which it is anywhere directed, or applied, seem to have been the effects of the division of labor....To take an example, therefore, the trade of the pin-maker; a workman not educated to this business, nor acquainted with the use of the machinery employed in it, could scarce, perhaps, with his utmost industry, make one pin in a day, and certainly could not make twenty. But in the way in which this business is now carried on, not only the whole work is a peculiar trade, but it is divided into a number of branches, of which the greater part are likewise peculiar trades. One man draws out the wire, another straights it, a third cuts it, a fourth points it, a fifth grinds it at the top for receiving, the head; to make the head requires two or three distinct operations; to put it on is a peculiar business, to whiten the pins is another; it is even a trade by itself to put them into the paper; and the important business of making a pin is, in this manner, divided into about eighteen distinct operations, which, in some factories, are all performed by distinct hands, though in others the same man will sometimes perform two or three of them."

Adam Smith, *The Wealth of Nations*, 1776

a)   Identify and describe TWO specific historical examples from 1750 to the present day that illustrate the benefits of the division of labor as described in the text.

b)   Identify and describe ONE critique of Adam Smith's view of labor.

STOP
END OF SECTION I
IF YOU FINISH BEFORE TIME IS CALLED, YOU MAY CHECK YOUR WORK ON THIS SECTION.
DO NOT GO ON TO SECTION II UNTIL YOU ARE TOLD TO DO SO.

The Exam

AP® World History Exam

DO NOT OPEN THIS BOOKLET UNTIL YOU ARE TOLD TO DO SO.

At a Glance

Total Time
1 hour, 40 minutes
Number of Questions
2
Percent of Total Score
40%
Writing Instrument
Pen with black or dark blue ink

Question 1 (DBQ): Mandatory
Suggested Reading and Writing Time
60 minutes
Percent of Total Score
25%

Question 2, 3, or 4 (Long Essay): Choose ONE Question
Answer either Question 2, 3, or 4
Suggested Time
40 minutes
Percent of Total Score
15%

Instructions

The questions for Section II are printed in the Questions and Documents booklet. You may use that booklet to organize your answers and for scratch work, but you must write your answers in this Section II: Free Response booklet. No credit will be given for any work written in the Questions and Documents booklet.

The proctor will announce the beginning and end of the reading period. You are advised to spend the 15-minute period reading the question and planning your answer to Question 1, the document-based question. If you have time, you may also read Questions 2, 3, and 4.

Section II of this exam requires answers in essay form. Write clearly and legibly. Circle the number of the question you are answering at the top of each page in this booklet. Begin each answer on a new page. Do not skip lines. Cross out any errors you make; crossed-out work will not be scored.

Manage your time carefully. The proctor will announce the suggested time for each part, but you may proceed freely from one part to the next. Go on to the long essay question if you finish Question 1 early. You may review your responses if you finish before the end of the exam is announced.

After the exam, you must apply the label that corresponds to the long-essay question you answered—Question 2, 3, or 4. For example, if you answered Question 2, apply the label ② . Failure to do so may delay your score.

WORLD HISTORY

SECTION II

Total Time—1 hour, 40 minutes

Question 1 (Document-Based Question)

Suggested reading period: 15 minutes

Suggested writing time: 45 minutes

<u>Note:</u> You may begin writing your response before the reading period is over.

Directions: Question 1 is based on the accompanying documents. The documents have been edited for the purpose of this exercise.

In your response you should do the following.

- **<u>Thesis/Claim:</u>** Respond to the prompt with a historically defensible claim that establishes a line of reasoning.

- **<u>Contextualization:</u>** Describe a historical context relevant to the prompt.

- **<u>Evidence:</u>** Support an argument in response to the prompt using at least **six** documents. Use at least one additional piece of specific historical evidence (beyond that found in the documents) relevant to an argument about the prompt.

- **<u>Analysis and Reasoning:</u>** For at least **three** documents, explain how or why the document's point of view, purpose, historical situation, and/or audience is relevant to an argument. Demonstrate an understanding of the historical development that is the focus of the prompt, using evidence to support or modify an argument that addresses the question.

GO ON TO THE NEXT PAGE.

Question 1: Using the documents and your knowledge of world history, evaluate how governments and international organizations responded to the consequences of World War II after it ended in 1945.

Document 1

Source: Preamble to the Charter of the United Nations, 1945.

WE THE PEOPLES OF THE UNITED NATIONS DETERMINED

- to save succeeding generations from the scourge of war, which twice in our lifetime has brought untold sorrow to mankind, and

- to reaffirm faith in fundamental human rights, in the dignity and worth of the human person, in the equal rights of men and women and of nations large and small, and

- to establish conditions under which justice and respect for the obligations arising from treaties and other sources of international law can be maintained, and

- to promote social progress and better standards of life in larger freedom,

AND FOR THESE ENDS

- to practice tolerance and live together in peace with one another as good neighbours, and

- to unite our strength to maintain intertnational peace and security, and

- to ensure, by the acceptance of principles and the institution of methods, that armed force shall not be used, save in the common interest, and

- to employ international machinery for the promotion of economic and social advancement of all peoples,

HAVE RESOLVED TO COMBINE OUR EFFORTS TO ACCOMPLISH THESE AIMS

Accordingly, our respective Governments, through representatives assembled in the city of San Francisco, who have exhibited their full powers found to be in good and due form, have agreed to the present Charter of the United Nations and do hereby establish an international organization to be known as the United Nations.

GO ON TO THE NEXT PAGE.

Document 2

Source: Preamble to the Constitution of Japan, 1946.

We, the Japanese people, acting through our duly elected representatives in the National Diet, determined that we shall secure for ourselves and our posterity the fruits of peaceful cooperation with all nations and the blessings of liberty throughout this land, and resolved that never again shall we be visited with the horrors of war through the action of government, do proclaim that sovereign power resides with the people and do firmly establish this Constitution. Government is a sacred trust of the people, the authority for which is derived from the people, the powers of which are exercised by representatives of the people, and the benefits of which are enjoyed by the people. This is a universal principle of mankind upon which this Constitution is founded. We reject and revoke all constitutions, laws, ordinances, and rescripts in conflict herewith. We, the Japanese people, desire peace for all time and are deeply conscious of the high ideals controlling human relationship and we have determined to preserve our security and existence, trusting in the justice and faith of the peace-loving peoples of the world. We desire to occupy an honored place in an international society striving for the preservation of peace, and the banishment of tyranny and slavery, oppression and intolerance for all time from the earth. We recognize that all peoples of the world have the right to live in peace, free from fear and want. We believe that no nation is responsible to itself alone, but that laws of political morality are universal; and that obedience to such laws is incumbent upon all nations who would sustain their own sovereignty and justify their sovereign relationship with other nations. We, the Japanese people, pledge our national honor to accomplish these high ideals and purposes with all our resources.

Document 3

Source: Preamble to the Constitution of India, 1949.

We, the people of India, having solemnly resolved to constitute India into a sovereign socialist secular democratic republic and to secure to all its citizens:

JUSTICE, social, economic and political;

LIBERTY of thought, expression, belief, faith and worship;

EQUALITY of status and of opportunity; and to promote among them all FRATERNITY assuring the dignity of the individual and the unity and integrity of the Nation;

In our constituent assembly this twenty-sixth day of November, 1949, do hereby adopt, enact, and give to ourselves this constitution.

GO ON TO THE NEXT PAGE.

Document 4

Source: Preamble to the Constitution of France, 1958.

The French people hereby solemnly proclaim their dedication to the Rights of Man and the principle of national sovereignty as defined by the Declaration of 1789, reaffirmed and complemented by the Preamble to the 1946 Constitution.

By virtue of these principles and that of the free determination of peoples, the Republic offers to the Overseas Territories that express the will to adhere to them new institutions based on the common ideal of liberty, equality, and fraternity and conceived with a view to their democratic evolution.

Document 5

Source: Vietnamese Declaration of Independence, 1945.

… for more than eighty years, the French imperialists, abusing the standard of Liberty, Equality, and Fraternity, have violated our Fatherland and oppressed our fellow citizens. They have acted contrary to the ideals of humanity and justice. In the field of politics, they have deprived our people of every democratic liberty…

For these reasons, we, members of the Provisional Government, representing the whole Vietnamese people, declare that from now on we break off all relations of a colonial character with France; we repeal all the international obligations that France has so far subscribed to on behalf of Vietnam and we abolish all the special rights the French have unlawfully acquired in our Fatherland. The whole Vietnamese people, animated by a common purpose, are determined to fight to the bitter end against any attempt by the French colonialists to reconquer their country. We are convinced that the Allied nations, which at Tehran and San Francisco have acknowledged the principles of self-determination and equality of nations, will not refuse to acknowledge the independence of Vietnam. A people who have courageously opposed French domination for more than eight years, a people who have fought side by side with the Allies against the Fascists during these last years, such a people must be free and independent. For these reasons, we, members of the Provisional Government of the Democratic Republic of Vietnam, solemnly declare to the world that Vietnam has the right to be a free and independent country—and in fact is so already. The entire Vietnamese people are determined to mobilize all their physical and mental strength, to sacrifice their lives and property in order to safeguard their independence and liberty.

GO ON TO THE NEXT PAGE.

Document 6

Source: Universal Declaration of Human Rights, 1948.

Article 1.
All human beings are born free and equal in dignity and rights. They are endowed with reason and conscience and should act towards one another in a spirit of brotherhood.

Article 2.
Everyone is entitled to all the rights and freedoms set forth in this Declaration, without distinction of any kind, such as race, colour, sex, language, religion, political or other opinion, national or social origin, property, birth or other status. Furthermore, no distinction shall be made on the basis of the political, jurisdictional or international status of the country or territory to which a person belongs, whether it be independent, trust, non-self-governing or under any other limitation of sovereignty.

Article 3.
Everyone has the right to life, liberty and security of person.

Article 4.
No one shall be held in slavery or servitude; slavery and the slave trade shall be prohibited in all their forms.

Article 5.
No one shall be subjected to torture or to cruel, inhuman or degrading treatment or punishment.

Article 6.
Everyone has the right to recognition everywhere as a person before the law.

Document 7

Source: Final Report to the Secretary of the Army on the Nuremberg War Crimes Trials United States, 1949.

The documents and testimony of the Nuremberg record can be of the greatest value in showing the Germans the truth about the recent past, quite apart from the judgments and sentences pronounced on individual defendants. The judgments, and the principles of law on which they were based, must obviously be considered in a world setting, and not in a purely German context. There is little chance that the judgments and principles of Nuremberg will be of much benefit in Germany if they fail to win more than lip-service in the world at large.

GO ON TO THE NEXT PAGE.

Question 2, Question 3, or Question 4 (Long-Essay Question)

Suggested writing time: 40 minutes

Directions: Choose ONE of EITHER Questions 2, 3, or 4.

In your response you should do the following.

- **Thesis/Claim:** Respond to the prompt with a historically defensible thesis/claim that establishes a line of reasoning.

- **Contextualization:** Describe a broader historical context relevant to the prompt.

- **Evidence:** Support an argument in response to the prompt using specific and relevant examples of evidence.

- **Analysis and Reasoning:** Demonstrate an understanding of the historical development that is the focus of the prompt, using evidence to support or modify an argument that addresses the question.

Question 2: Evaluate the extent to which the emergence of Christianity in the first century C.E. can be considered a pivotal point in the history of the Mediterranean region. In the development of your argument, consider what changed and what stayed the same after the emergence of Christianity as a world religion.

Question 3: Evaluate the extent to which the split between the Roman Catholic and Eastern Orthodox churches in the eleventh century C.E. can be considered a pivotal point in the history of Christianity. In the development of your argument, consider what changed and what stayed the same after the split between these two Christian factions.

Question 4: Compare and contrast the effectiveness of two anti-colonial movements in the late nineteenth and twentieth centuries. In the development of your argument, explain what was similar about the effectiveness of the two movements and what was different.

STOP
END OF EXAMINATION

Practice Test 1:
Answers and
Explanations

PRACTICE TEST 1 ANSWER KEY

1.	B		29.	A
2.	D		30.	C
3.	A		31.	D
4.	A		32.	B
5.	C		33.	A
6.	D		34.	A
7.	C		35.	B
8.	B		36.	D
9.	A		37.	B
10.	B		38.	C
11.	D		39.	B
12.	A		40.	D
13.	C		41.	A
14.	A		42.	A
15.	A		43.	D
16.	D		44.	A
17.	C		45.	B
18.	A		46.	A
19.	D		47.	D
20.	B		48.	C
21.	A		49.	C
22.	D		50.	A
23.	B		51.	A
24.	A		52.	C
25.	C		53.	B
26.	D		54.	C
27.	B		55.	D
28.	B			

PRACTICE TEST 1 EXPLANATIONS

Multiple-Choice Questions

1. **B** One of the major effects of the development of cuneiform writing was that the civilizations that used it were able to organize effectively, develop written legal codes, keep transaction receipts, sign contracts, and so on, making (B) the best answer. Choice (A) goes too far, as published texts were not widely available until the printing press was invented in early modern Europe. Choices (C) and (D) describe things that the Sumerians did, but the tablet is a record of barley distribution, and thus wheel technology and the domestication of animals are too off-topic for this context.

2. **D** As ancient civilizations developed more sophisticated methods of farming, there was an increase in the number of cities as well as the populations of those cities. As food production increased due to advances in agriculture, societies became better organized and developed distinct cultural identities, making (D) the best answer. Choice (A) is backwards—as agriculture increased, hunter-gatherer lifestyles declined. Choice (B) is incorrect because the ancient Mesopotamians were polytheistic. Choice (C) is incorrect because women had very few economic (or other) opportunities during the time period in question.

3. **A** *Mesopotamia* means "between the rivers"—those rivers being the Tigris and Euphrates. One of the primary factors that enabled the success of the Mesopotamians (and other early civilizations) was access to plenty of water and good soil. Choice (B) refers to a mountain range in South Asia; (C) refers to the major river in Egypt; and (D) doesn't make sense because it is extremely difficult to grow crops in the desert. Therefore, the answer is (A).

4. **A** The text states that "class considerations not being allowed to interfere with merit; nor again does poverty bar the way, if a man is able to serve the state." In plain English, this means that a citizen's ability was more important than his wealth or status in classical Greek democracy, making (A) the best answer. Choice (B) is incorrect because the first sentence of the text contradicts the idea that the Greeks were imitating their neighbors. Choice (C) is incorrect because the last portion of the text describes people fearing, and thus obeying, the magistrates. Choice (D) is incorrect because the last portion of the text states that not all laws or codes are actually written down.

5. **C** During the classical period and the period of Athenian democracy, the only people allowed to participate in the democratic process were adult males who were citizens by birth, (C). Women were excluded, so (B) and (D) are incorrect. Slaves were also excluded, so (A) cannot be correct.

6. **D** One of the reasons Greek culture spread during the classical period was Greece's massive coastline. Because of the many natural harbors in the Greek mainland and islands, the Greeks were able to develop sophisticated methods of communication and commerce, making (D) the best answer. Choices (A), (B), and (C) do not correctly describe the geography of Greece.

7. **C** The map shows the extent of the Muslim conquest of the Middle East, North Africa, and southern Europe during and after the life of Muhammad, making (C) the best answer. Choice (A) is incorrect because the Roman Empire was at its largest in the second century C.E. Choice (B) is incorrect because the Crusades took place after the time period shown on the map. Choice (D) is incorrect because the Sassanid Empire did not reach as far west as the shaded parts of the map indicate.

8.   **B**   During the Arab conquests of the seventh century and beyond, people in conquered lands were encouraged to convert to Islam. Those who did not convert were forced to pay a tax, which is reflected in the first paragraph of the source text, making (B) the best answer.

9.   **A**   After the death of Muhammad, there was considerable debate among Muhammad's followers about the appropriate authority structure of the new religion. The Shia belief was that Muhammad's son-in-law, Ali, was the rightful heir to Muhammad's authority. The Sunni belief was that authority within Islam should not be hereditary but rather drawn from a broader segment of believers. Therefore, (A) is the best answer.

10.   **B**   Choices (A), (C), and (D) are beliefs shared by early Christians and early Muslims. While Jesus is viewed as an important prophet within Islam, Muslims do not believe that Jesus was divine, a foundational idea within Christianity. Therefore, (B) is the best answer.

11.   **D**   The account of Marco Polo's travels from Venice to China, which may or may not be completely factual, illustrates the European perspective of a man encountering a Mongol ruler and being well received at that ruler's court. The exchange of ideas and languages mentioned in the text makes (D) the best answer.

12.   **A**   One of the unique characteristics of the Mongols was that unlike other major civilizations of the ancient and medieval worlds, the Mongols conquered vast territories of diverse peoples without imposing their own cultural imprint upon the people whom they conquered. Generally, after the initial conquest had taken place, the Mongols left people alone to pursue their own cultural and religious practices as before. Choice (A) is therefore the best answer.

13.   **C**   There had always been antislavery sentiment among certain religious groups, particularly in England and the United States, but the date of the passage in question (1774) indicates that the author was probably associated with the growing evangelical movement in the late eighteenth century. In addition to their religious fervor, evangelical groups historically supported many social justice movements such as the fight against slavery. Therefore, (C) is the best answer. Choice (A) is too early chronologically. Choice (B) is a decent option, but the Freemasons were not generally known for their abolitionist views. Mormonism was not founded until the 1820s, so (D) is chronologically too late.

14.   **A**   The networks and movements of goods and people around three continents are often referred to as the "Triangular Trade." The classical understanding of this theory holds that slaves were brought from Africa to the Americas, where the use of African slaves was essential to growing cash crops, which were then shipped to Europe, where those goods or products made from those goods were used to purchase more slaves in Africa. Therefore, (A) is the best answer.

15.   **A**   The owners of slave ships involved in the transatlantic passage wanted to make their voyages as profitable as possible, which meant cramming as many slaves as possible into the ships. For the slaves, this meant a minimum of space in which to move and unbearable conditions that bred disease and death. Choice (A) is the best answer.

16.   **D**   The European colonization of Africa was decided by powerful individuals in Europe with very little concern for Africans' best interests. Even today, many of the national boundaries in Africa are reflective of decisions made in Europe during the late nineteenth century and do not necessarily reflect cultural, religious, tribal, or linguistic differences among African peoples. Choice (D) is the best answer.

17.   **C**   The attitude of the speaker in Source 2 clearly indicates that he views Europeans and European culture as inherently better than Africans and African culture. Unfortunately, this attitude was widespread in the nineteenth century. Choice (C) is the best answer.

18. **A** European colonists often forced African farmers to produce certain types of goods that were intended for export rather than local use. This policy led to numerous famines across Africa during the late nineteenth and early twentieth centuries. Choice (A) is correct.

19. **D** One of the hallmarks of scientific thinking during the time period mentioned in the question was a looking back to earlier Greek scholarship. That scholarship was preserved and expanded upon by various Byzantine and Islamic thinkers, who had a profound impact upon European scholarship, medicine, and science during the period of scholasticism. Choice (D) is the best answer.

20. **B** Well before the Enlightenment, Byzantine and Arab scholars began to move away from supernatural understandings of science and medicine in favor of more pragmatic, rational, and reason-based explanations of physical phenomena. These two passages do not contain supernatural explanations, (A); philosophical discussions, (C); or astrological discussions, (D). You're left with (B), which is the best answer.

21. **A** While scholars do not know how common human sacrifice was, there is solid archaeological evidence to support the reports from Spanish conquistadors that the Aztecs performed ritual sacrifices of human beings at temples such as the one at Tenochtitlan. Therefore, (A) is the best answer. (The Spanish viewed the Aztec practice as barbaric and "un-Christian.")

22. **D** It is true that the Spanish tried to convert the Aztecs to Christianity, (A), and established farms in the New World, (C). However, the primary motivation for the Spanish conquest was to obtain gold, spices, and other valuable goods, making (D) the best answer. The Aztecs lived in Central, not South America, so (B) is also incorrect.

23. **B** Cortés's description of the grandeur and architectural mastery of the temple at Tenochtitlan supports other accounts from the sixteenth century, as well as archaeological evidence that points to the Aztecs being highly advanced, with well-developed institutions and vast building programs. Therefore, (B) is the best answer.

24. **A** When Cortés refers to the "idols" in Tenochtitlan's temples, he is referring to the statues and other symbols representing the many Aztec deities worshipped in those temples. This polytheism on the part of the Aztecs was one of the principal sources of conflict between those in the New World and the Spanish conquistadors, who were predominantly Catholic (and thus monotheistic). Choice (A) is correct.

25. **C** The Meiji Restoration, which began in the late 1800s, was a period of reform in which the previously isolationist Japan began to welcome Western influence and initiate a rapid industrialization process. The charts show a concurrent rise in coal production and number of steamships, illustrating the period of technological and industrial growth that occurred under the Meiji Restoration. Thus, (C) is the best answer.

26. **D** By 1876, the Japanese warrior class had been abolished in favor of a policy of required military service for all adult males, making (D) the best answer. Choice (A) is not correct because many Japanese emigrated to the United States during the late nineteenth century. (Aggression toward Japanese in the U.S. occurred later, during World War II.) Choices (B) and (C) are both backward and thus incorrect.

27. **B** Because the process of industrialization started so much later in Japan than it did in Europe, Japan was able to use technologies that had been developed in Europe without reinventing the wheel. Japan was thus able to industrialize much more quickly than Europe, making (B) the best answer.

28. **B** By the 1890s, Japan's military had become quite strong. In a move of imperial-style expansion, Japanese forces defeated the Chinese and gained control over Korea. Choice (B) is correct.

29. **A** Japan's increased shipbuilding capability coincided with a rise of nationalism, and the country began a rapid process of militarization in the early twentieth century. Although it played a relatively small role in World War I, even by the 1910s Japan had proven to the world that it was an equal in terms of military power. (Of course, Japan's navy played a huge role in the Pacific Theater of World War II a few decades later.) Choice (A) is the best answer.

30. **C** The Russian Revolution and the abdication of Czar Nicholas II were precipitated by a number of factors. Chief among these were Russia's military losses to the Japanese, as well as the food shortages and other economic woes that followed, leading to the working classes' resentment of the aristocracy. Choice (C) is the best answer.

31. **D** Lenin was the leader of the Bolshevik party, which adhered to Marxist/Communist philosophical ideologies. Both before and after the Czar was forced from power, Lenin advocated an uprising among the working classes ("proletariat") and a radical change in Russia's system of government and economics. Choice (D) is the best answer.

32. **B** The sculpture in the photograph is a Roman copy of a Greek original. Greco-Roman art is characterized by heavy use of marble and naturalistic depictions of human beings. Therefore, (B) is correct.

33. **A** In both the classical and Hellenistic periods of Greek history, artisans made realistic sculptures of human beings. Common people, whether men, women, or children, were often the subjects of these sculptures, which were typically commissioned by wealthy individuals who used the sculptures and other artwork to decorate their homes and gardens. Choice (A) is the best answer.

34. **A** It was the Islamic traders who had the motivation and the desert skills to cross the treacherous Sahara Desert to reach the kingdoms of Songhai and Mali in the middle ages, making (A) the best answer. Europeans, (B), did travel to West Africa, but not through the desert.

35. **B** As Muslim traders came from the Middle East and southern Asia to the east coast of Africa, they brought with them the Arabic language. Swahili is, in fact, a hybrid of traditional African Bantu languages and Arabic, making (B) the best answer.

36. **D** Most of central Africa consists of jungle and mountains, so travel there was (and still is) quite difficult. It was not until the modern era that outsiders explored central Africa using the great river systems as a means of transportation. Choice (D) is the answer.

37. **B** When he refers to the "second wall," Luther is protesting the fact that in the sixteenth century, the Catholic Church held very conservative views about who had the authority to interpret the Bible. One of the impetuses for the Protestant Reformation was the development of the printing press, which led to the ability of more people to read the Bible for themselves in their own languages. Choice (B) is the best answer.

38. **C** When speaking of a "temporal power," Luther means a secular or state authority rather than a religious or spiritual one. One of the complaints of Luther and other Reformers was that the Catholic Church was not subject to any authority beyond the Pope. Choice (C) is correct.

39. **B** The author of this speech, Simón de Bolívar, was a famous military man and politician who led the fight for independence in large parts of South America. Therefore, the best answer is (B).

40. **D** In the last sentence of the passage, the author states that "proper morals, and not force, are the bases of law; and that to practice justice is to practice liberty." Choice (D) is correct.

41. **A** Simón de Bolívar successfully led a movement that resulted in the creation of several independent nations, including Venezuela and Colombia. His grand vision was to unify these separate nations politically, and he was president of this union, known as Gran Colombia, for more than a decade. Choice (A) is correct.

42. **A** This question is challenging, as all of the tactics named are drawn directly from the text. The task is to determine which one is the *most important*. Choice (C) is likely the easiest to eliminate, as this is characterized in the text as a precursor to an alliance with the Women's Liberation Movement rather than an end in itself. Choices (B) and (D) can also be eliminated, as they refer to ways to eliminate gender roles rather than the main goals of the movement that are discussed in the passage. According to the text, the only way to achieve the goals of the Gay Liberation movement is to eliminate social pressure to conform to gender roles, so (A) is the best answer.

43. **D** Source 1 states that there are "conditions that now prevent women from enjoying the equality of opportunity and freedom of which is their right," making (D) the best answer. Choice (A) is incorrect for the same reason, and (B) and (C) are both contradicted by the text.

44. **A** Source 2 states that the goal of Gay Liberation is "to rid society of the gender-role system which is at the root of our oppression," making (A) the best answer. Choice (B) is incorrect because the gay rights and women's rights movements were aligned. Choices (C) and (D) are not mentioned in the passage.

45. **B** In order to successfully answer this question, you need to choose the obstacle that is explicitly identified by BOTH sources. A lack of concrete action, (A), is mentioned as a problem only in Source 1, so eliminate it. The idea of forming new movements and alliances for equality appears in both sources, but as a positive measure to achieve their goals, not as an obstacle; eliminate (D). Choice (C) identifies an issue that, while plausible as an obstacle to the aims of both movements, is not mentioned in Source 1 and thus incorrect. Choice (B) is therefore the best answer.

46. **A** While this passage was actually written by a woman, the image it portrays of Chinese gender roles is very patriarchal. According to the passage, a woman's primary role should be within the domestic framework and in service to her husband, making (A) the best answer.

47. **D** This author emphasizes female purity, a theme common in ancient literature about gender roles. Most ancient societies (or at least the men in those societies) believed that a woman's virtue was closely related to her sexual purity and her body more generally. Choice (D) is correct.

48. **C** In the ancient world, after the Neolithic Revolution, humans began to live in more settled communities. As there was less need for women to participate in food gathering, cultural norms shifted such that women were expected to spend most of their time fulfilling domestic duties. There were exceptions to this, of course, but the general trend was such that women did less in public and more in the private, or domestic, sphere. Therefore, (C) is the best answer.

49. **C** Both of the source texts come from the period of the iconoclastic controversy in Byzantium at the end of the eighth century c.e. Source 1 mentions the value of visual images, while Source 2 mentions the value of pictorial representations. These two texts, therefore, were on the side of those who defended the use of iconography (religious images) within Christian worship. The best answer is (C).

50. **A** Historically, most Islamic groups (and in particular the Sunni) have opposed any type of religious iconography on the grounds that it constitutes idol worship. Islamic art, therefore, is typically composed of geometric shapes and calligraphy, as paintings of the prophet Muhammad would be considered offensive. Iconography can be found commonly in Buddhism, (B), Zoroastrianism, (C), and Jainism, (D). The best answer is (A).

51. **A** In the passage, Machiavelli states that "this is to be asserted in general of men, that they are ungrateful, fickle, false, cowardly, covetous." Because people are disloyal to their rulers, according to this line of thinking, it is better for rulers to be feared than to be loved (so as to ensure obedience). Thus, (A) is the best answer.

52. **C** At the time that this passage was written, Italy was governed by independent city-states that were often at war with each other, with the church, and with other nations such as France and Spain. Machiavelli's treatise is thus in some ways a reaction to the political uncertainty of his day, making (C) the best answer.

53. **B** In contrast to the scholars of the medieval period, who were much more religious-minded and concerned with morality, Machiavelli's worldview was more practical. Instead of relying upon abstract religious or philosophical arguments about what was right and wrong, Machiavelli focused on real-world situations (and some thought he was cruel and manipulative as a result). Choice (B) is the best answer.

54. **C** It was widely felt in Germany that the Treaty of Versailles had treated Germany poorly at the conclusion of World War I. While there are many causes behind the start of World War II, one of the principal ones was the Nazi Party's aggressive foreign policy, which, in part, was a reaction to a perception of national humiliation following World War I. Choice (C) is correct.

55. **D** In 1940, Britain was experiencing a grave threat from Nazi Germany. Hitler had already annexed large portions of Europe, and Britain was in a fight for its life. In particular, the Nazis conducted intense bombing campaigns of Britain's major cities. Churchill's speech is an example of the British leader's attempt not only to prepare his people for the possible trouble faced by the nation, but also to inspire them toward victory over the Axis Powers. Choice (D) is the best answer.

Short-Answer Questions

Question 1

a) The Watt Engine contributed in many ways to the Industrial Revolution, but two obvious and direct technological advances are

   • Robert Fulton's steamship

   • George Stephenson's locomotive

b) The long-term effects can include the following:

   • Bolstered by steamships and locomotives, global trade accelerated dramatically.

   • Employment spiked due to the creation of steam-powered factories and mills.

   • The rise of factories and mills, as well as the efficiency of travel, transformed Europe's population from rural to largely urban.

   • Due to the ample amount of coal in Great Britain, the empire industrialized quickly and went on to lead an imperial age.

   • Asian nations' share of global manufacturing declined (Indian and Egyptian textile, for example).

Question 2

The photograph shows the culmination of the Space Race, a competition of technology between the United States and the Soviet Union during the Cold War.

a) The Cold War brought about a game of one-upmanship between the two superpowers. In the arms race, each side wished to show the other its dominance in technology and military power, as well as its economic superiority. These same goals drove the space race. The Americans became especially alarmed when the Soviet satellite Sputnik was launched in 1957, demonstrating the possibility of delivering a long-range nuclear warhead.

b) The end of the Cold War in 1989 brought about opportunities for U.S.-Russian partnerships including:

   • the reduction of nuclear weapons (START I in 1991)

   • military alliances, such as standing against Iraq in the 1991 Gulf War

   • collaboration in space exploration

Question 3

a) Rome's emergence as a Mediterranean power can be attributed to any of the following:

- Rome was well protected geographically: The Alps to the north and its position as a peninsula made invasions unlikely.

- Rome's victories in the Punic Wars established Rome as the unquestionable power of the Mediterranean Sea.

- Rome was well organized with a representative system and a codified set of laws (Twelve Tables).

b) You might want to focus on any of the following ways that Greek culture influenced the Romans:

- The Roman gods were derived from Greek mythology.

- The social structure of landowners, other free men, and slaves paralleled the Greeks.

- Elements of Classical Greek architecture can be found in Roman buildings such as the Pantheon, Coliseum, and the Forum.

- While the Romans had a republic rather than an Athenian direct democracy, they still adopted the concept of a government by the people (those that owned land) when they created the Roman Republic.

- Roman sculptures bear more than a passing resemblance to the Hellenistic statues created in Ancient Greece.

Question 4

a) Adam Smith discusses division of labor, which is commonly understood as assembly line production (although Henry Ford's moving assembly line as we know it did not arise until 1913). The division of labor benefited unskilled laborers who could now find jobs in factories by performing a simple task. You can cite any of the following examples (among others):

- The Portsmith Block Mills aided the British Navy during the Napoleonic Wars by creating parts for the ships.

- Nasmyth, Gaskell, and Company mass-produced locomotives in England in the nineteenth century.

- Muhammad Ali's textile mills in Egypt

- development of railroads in Tsarist Russia

- Richard Garrett and Sons' Long Shop, which mass produced steam engines (1852)

- Henry Ford's automotive assembly line (1913)

b)   Possible critiques of Smith's laissez-faire economics could be found in the following:

- Karl Marx, a German economist and philosopher who spent a good part of his adult life living in poverty, pointed out that the factory workers had genuine opportunities but were being exploited as a consequence of capitalism.

- Other Utopian Socialists, such as Charles Fourier, are fair game on this question.

- A group of 19th century British workers known as Luddites destroyed equipment in factories in the middle of the night to protest working conditions and pitiful wages.

Document-Based Question (DBQ)

A strong essay for this prompt would acknowledge the common goal of human rights present in all seven documents, while distinguishing between the motivations behind each document. For instance, Documents 1 and 2 explicitly reference the horrors of the Second World War and express the necessity of human rights in avoiding such conflicts in the future. Another perspective is offered by Documents 6 and 7, which contend that human rights are bigger than individual nation states, and that the world community has a responsibility in ensuring human rights. Documents 3 and 5, on the other hand, express many of the same goals as the earlier documents, yet do so through the lens of post-colonialism. Accordingly, the documents from both India and Vietnam place an emphasis on the concepts of liberty and equality. A strong essay would show the commonalities between these documents, and highlight the key differences that informed their creation. The trickiest document might be Document 4. The creation of France's Fifth Republic is both a reaction to the Second World War and colonialism. The Fifth Republic established a strong presidency, which was not present when Hitler invaded France. But the Fifth Republic was more immediately a reaction to France's defeat in Indochina as well as the Algerian revolt—both of which showed the tenuousness of maintaining colonies in the post-World War II era. A strong essay would recognize that this document would fit into both aforementioned categories.

Long Essay

Question 2

For this essay, you should develop a thesis statement that claims Christianity had either a significant or minor impact on the Mediterranean region. To be considered a "pivotal point," the emergence of Christianity will have to have changed the region (i.e., the Roman Empire and later the Byzantine Empire) in ways that would not have occurred had the religion not emerged. To decide this, weigh your evidence:

What changed:

- The religious landscape of the Roman Empire changed quite drastically. While the empire had previously recognized polytheistic worship, Christianity brought about widespread monotheistic practice.

- The emergence of Christianity contributed to major changes in Judaism as the latter differentiated itself from Christianity in the form of Rabbinic Judaism.

- Christianity became an imperial power as Emperor Justinian adopted it as the official religion of the Roman Empire. Adherence to Christian faith not only influenced the rule of the later Byzantine emperors, but the presence of papal authority in Rome would provide a significant power dynamic in Western Europe throughout the Middle Ages and beyond.

- Christianity became a central theme in art following the Edict of Milan. The Christ figure, the Virgin Mary, and various saints were frequent subjects of painting and sculpture. Moreover, as Christianity spread, the construction of churches and basilicas led to innovations in architecture.

What stayed the same:

- The Roman imperial power that existed before Christianity maintained its power for centuries following the emergence of the new religion.

- Judaism, which contributed enormously to Christianity, continued to exist and evolve (albeit in the form of a Diaspora) despite the converts from the early years of Christianity.

- Women did not experience any more rights due to the emergence of Christianity. In fact, Christianity helped to maintain a patriarchal system of power in the Mediterranean region.

Question 3

In this essay, you should determine whether the changes of the Great Schism outweigh the status quo. Using the evidence enumerated in your outline, create a thesis that argues the Schism can be considered a pivotal point or that the Schism did not actually change the history of Christianity in a significant way. Either way, discuss both sides of the issue and let your analysis explain why the evidence shows your thesis to be correct. Here are some of the pieces of evidence you should consider.

What changed:

- While Christianity existed in distinct ways over the two different regions, there was still a sense that it was one religion and it is was not uncommon to see Roman churches in the East and Greek churches in the West. That changed in 1054 as the theological differences between the two groups culminated in the leaders from each church excommunicating one another, leading to the closure of Greek churches in Italy and Roman churches in Constantinople.

- The Schism led to increased calls for political reform. Marsiglio of Padua's *Defender of Peace* advocated the separation of church and state.

- Over the coming centuries, calls for spiritual reform (notably articulated by John Wycliffe) ultimately influenced the Protestant Reformation.

What stayed the same:

- The Great Schism may have gone unnoticed for all practical purposes since Eastern and Western Europe had long since been divided. Going back to the era of Diocletian, the East had firm differences from the West, including linguistic, political, economic, and artistic.

- Despite the Schism, Christianity continued to spread and thrive going into the Middle Ages. The Crusades (which further alienated the two groups from one another) reignited the Christian faith of Europeans and the emergence of philosophers such as Thomas Aquinas led to a more developed Christian theology.

Question 4

In this essay, you must juxtapose the similarities and differences between two movements. You can tackle this essay in a number of ways. You may introduce the two movements in your introductory paragraph, and then use one body paragraph to show similarities and one to show differences. Another approach would be to use one body paragraph to discuss one movement, your second body paragraph to discuss the other movement (while highlighting some similarities and differences), and a third body paragraph to demonstrate a general argument about whether these movements are mostly similar or different. Choose two movements that you feel most confident writing about. Here are some anti-colonial movements that fall within the time period and will fit this question well:

- Boxer Rebellion in China

- Mohandas Gandhi's independence movement in India

- South Africa's independence (won in 1931)

- Algerian independence from France

- Jomo Kenyatta's leadership in helping Kenya separate from Great Britain

- Vietnamese opposition to France

Part III
About the AP World History Exam

- The Structure of the AP World History Exam
- How the AP World History Exam Is Scored
- Overview of Content Topics
- How AP Exams Are Used
- Other Resources
- Designing Your Study Plan

THE STRUCTURE OF THE AP WORLD HISTORY EXAM

The AP World History Exam is 3 hours and 15 minutes long and broken up into two sections, each of which consists of two parts. Your performance on these four parts, outlined in the table below, is compiled and weighted to find your overall exam score.

Structure of the AP World History Exam				
Section	Description	Number of Questions	Time Allotted	Percentage of Total Exam Score
Section I	Part A: Multiple Choice	55	55 minutes	40%
	Part B: Short Answer	3	40 minutes	20%
Reading Period			15 minutes	
Section II	Part A: DBQ	1	45 minutes	25%
	Part B: Long Essay	1	40 minutes	15%

Here's what to expect in each of these sections.

- **Multiple Choice:** Questions will be grouped into sets of two to five and based on primary or secondary sources, including excerpts from historical documents or writings, images, graphs, maps, and so on. Each set of questions will be based on a different piece of source material. You'll have 55 minutes to answer 55 multiple-choice questions. This section will test your ability to analyze and engage with the source materials while recalling what you already know about world history.

- **Short Answer:** You will answer three of the four questions in this section. Questions 1 and 2 are required, and then for the third and final question, you will choose between Questions 3 and 4. These questions will require you to respond to a primary or secondary source, a historian's argument, or a general proposition about world history. Your response should be about a paragraph in length. The time allotted for this section is 40 minutes.

- **Document-Based Question (DBQ):** Here you'll be presented with a variety of historical documents that are intended to show the complexity of a particular historical issue. You will need to develop a thesis that responds to the question prompt, and support that thesis with evidence from both the documents and your knowledge of world history. To earn the best score, you should incorporate outside knowledge and be able to relate the issues discussed in the documents to a larger theme, issue, or time period. The 60-minute timeframe for this section includes a suggested 15-minute reading period so that you can familiarize yourself with the question and documents.

- **Long Essay:** You'll be given a choice of three essay options, and you must choose one to answer. The long essay is similar to the DBQ in that you must develop a thesis and use historical evidence to support an argument, but there will be not be any documents on which you must base your response. Instead, you will need to draw upon your own knowledge of topics you learned in your AP World History class. You'll have 40 minutes to write this essay.

HOW THE AP WORLD HISTORY EXAM IS SCORED

Each of the four parts of the exam is weighted differently to determine your overall score.

Test Section	Percentage of Overall Score
Multiple Choice	40%
Short Answer	20%
DBQ	25%
Long Essay	15%

Rubrics are provided for both the DBQ and long essay in later chapters.

Once the multiple-choice section of your test has been scanned and your essays have been scored by readers, ETS (your local testing giant) applies a mysterious formula and magically converts your results to the standard AP Exam 1 to 5 score you see when you rip open the test results that come in the mail. A score of 4 or 5 will most likely get you what you want from the college or university you'll attend—college credit for World History. A score of 3 is considered passing and might get you college credit; then again, it might not. Therefore, your goal is to get at least a 3, preferably a 4 or 5. If you receive below a 3, it is highly unlikely that you will get college credit for your high school AP course, but you still get a grade for that class. A good grade in an AP class always looks good on your transcript.

The tricky part about the 1 to 5 scoring system is that it is designed to compare you to everyone else who took the AP World History Exam during a given year. But if the test that year was particularly tough, the top 20 percent or so of scorers will still score 4s and 5s. In other words, if all the scaled scores are somewhat low, the top end will still earn high marks. Of course, the opposite is also true—if everyone does an excellent job, some people will still end up with 1s and 2s.

OVERVIEW OF CONTENT TOPICS

The AP World History Exam divides all history into six major periods from about 10,000 years ago to the present.

Period	Date Range
Period 1: Technological and Environmental Transformations	to c. 600 B.C.E.
Period 2: Organization and Reorganization of Human Societies	c. 600 B.C.E. to c. 600 C.E.
Period 3: Regional and Interregional Interactions	c. 600 C.E. to c. 1450
Period 4: Global Interactions	c. 1450 to c. 1750
Period 5: Industrialization and Global Integration	c. 1750 to c. 1900
Period 6: Accelerating Global Change and Realignments	c. 1900 to the present

Now, you may be wondering why the first period spans thousands of years while the last period spans a little more than 100 years. Well, when more and more societies came into being and became more complex, world history also became more complex. Also, we have more historical accounts and documents to study from recent history than we do from ancient history, so we simply know more about what happened in the last 100 years than we do about the earliest human societies. Even though there are roughly 8,000 years in the first period, 850 in the third period, and just over 100 in the last period, you can study each period for the same amount of time. The review of history included in this book divides world history into the periods covered on the exam in order to help guide your study.

The Free-Response Questions (a.k.a. the Essays)

There are three types of essays on the AP World History Exam. The first are the short-answer questions. You need to answer three of these, which require you to respond to a primary source, a historian's argument, sources such as data or maps, or general propositions about world history.

The second type of essay is the Document-Based Question (DBQ), a question based on approximately seven primary-source documents. You must formulate a thesis or claim in response to a prompt, and then support your thesis using evidence from the documents, as well as outside examples. You should incorporate as many documents as possible into your response.

The third type is the long essay, which is probably more like the type of question you might see on a classroom test. For this essay, you are given three options, and you must answer one. This essay requires you draw upon your knowledge of world history and what you learned in your AP World History course to respond to a historical issue.

What Do They Want From Me?

What is the AP World History Exam really testing? In a nutshell: Can you make connections between different societies over different periods of time? In other words, for any given period of history, can you explain who was doing what? How did what they were doing affect the rest of the world? What changed about the society during this period of time? To show what you know about world history, keep this big-picture perspective in mind as you study and answer multiple-choice questions or construct essays. To help you do this, keep an eye out for certain recurring themes throughout the different time periods. Specifically, be on the lookout for the following:

- How did people interact with their environment? Why did they live where they did? How did they get there? What tools, technology, and resources were available to them? How was the landscape changed by humans?
- What new ideas, thoughts, and styles came into existence? How did these cultural developments influence people and technology (for example: new religious beliefs or Renaissance thought)?
- How did different societies get along—or not get along—within a time period? Who took over whom? How did leaders justify their power? Who revolted or was likely to revolt? Were they successful?
- How did economic systems develop, and what did they depend on in terms of agriculture, trade, labor, industrialization, and the demands of consumers?
- Who had power and who did not within a given culture and why? What was the status of women? What racial and ethnic constructions were present?

For each time period covered in Part V of this book, you will find boxes that identify these major themes, plus a Big Picture overview and a Pulling It All Together summary for each period. The introduction to Part V will fill you in on how to use these tools as you study.

Furthermore, the College Board states that the AP World History Exam is designed to test specific skills, including

- analyzing historical evidence in both primary and secondary sources
- developing an argument, using specific historical evidence
- understanding and using the context of a historical event or development to explain its significance

The College Board says that the AP World History Course and Exam addresses five main themes of world history:
1. Interaction Between Humans and the Environment
2. Development and Interaction of Cultures
3. State Building, Expansion, and Conflict
4. Creation, Expansion, and Interaction of Economic Systems
5. Development and Transformation of Social Structures

- comparing historical developments and being able to identify their similarities and differences
- describing causes and effects of historical developments, as well as patterns of continuity and/or change over time

HOW AP EXAMS ARE USED

Different colleges use AP Exams in different ways, so it is important that you go to a particular college's website to determine how it uses AP Exams. The three items below represent the main ways in which AP Exam scores can be used:

- **College Credit.** Some colleges will give you college credit if you score well on an AP Exam. These credits count towards your graduation requirements, meaning that you can take fewer courses while in college. Given the cost of college, this could be quite a benefit, indeed.

- **Satisfy Requirements.** Some colleges will allow you to "place out" of certain requirements if you do well on an AP Exam, even if they do not give you actual college credits. For example, you might not need to take an introductory-level course, or perhaps you might not need to take a class in a certain discipline at all.

- **Admissions Plus.** Even if your AP Exam will not result in college credit or even allow you to place out of certain courses, most colleges will respect your decision to push yourself by taking an AP Course or even an AP Exam outside of a course. A high score on an AP Exam shows mastery of more difficult content than is taught in many high school courses, and colleges may take that into account during the admissions process.

Want to know which colleges are best for you? Check out The Princeton Review's College Advisor app to build your ideal college list and find your perfect college fit! Available for free in the iOS App Store and Google Play Store.

OTHER RESOURCES

There are many resources available to help you improve your score on the AP World History Exam, not the least of which are your teachers. If you are taking an AP class, you may be able to get extra attention from your teacher, such as obtaining feedback on your essays. If you are not in an AP course, reach out to a teacher who teaches World History, and ask whether the teacher will review your essays or otherwise help you with content.

Another wonderful resource is **AP Students**, the official site of the AP Exams. The scope of the information at this site is quite broad and includes

- a course description, which includes details on what content is covered and sample questions
- full-length practice tests from previous years
- essay prompts from previous years
- AP World History Exam tips

The AP Students home page address is: **https://apstudent.collegeboard.org.**

The AP World History home page for students is: **http://apstudent.collegeboard. org/apcourse/ap-world-history.**

Finally, The Princeton Review offers tutoring for the AP World History Exam. Our expert instructors can help you refine your strategic approach and add to your content knowledge. For more information, call 1-800-2REVIEW or visit **www. PrincetonReview.com.**

Go Online!
The College Board's AP Students home page for the AP World History Exam has a wealth of resources, including a course description, sample questions, and more!

DESIGNING YOUR STUDY PLAN

In Part I, you identified some areas of potential improvement. Let's now delve further into your performance on Practice Test 1, with the goal of developing a study plan appropriate to your needs and time commitment.

Read the answers and explanations associated with the multiple-choice questions (starting on page 49). After you have done so, respond to the following questions:

- Review the Overview of Content Topics on page 66 and, next to each one, indicate your rank of the topic as follows: "1" means "I need a lot of work on this," "2" means "I need to beef up my knowledge," and "3" means "I know this topic well."

- How many days/weeks/months away is your AP World History Exam?

- What time of day is your best, most focused study time?

- How much time per day/week/month will you devote to preparing for your AP World History Exam?

- When will you do this preparation? (Be as specific as possible: Mondays & Wednesdays from 3:00 to 4:00 P.M., for example)

- Based on the answers above, will you focus on strategy (Part IV), content (Part V), or both?

- What are your overall goals in using this book?

Part IV
Test-Taking Strategies for the AP World History Exam

PREVIEW

Review your responses to the first three questions on page 4 of Part I and then respond to the following questions:

- How many multiple-choice questions did you miss even though you knew the answer?

- On how many multiple-choice questions did you guess blindly?

- How many multiple-choice questions did you miss after eliminating some answers and guessing based on the remaining answers?

- Did you create an outline before you wrote each essay?

- Did you find any of the essays easier or harder than the others—and, if so, why?

HOW TO USE THE CHAPTERS IN THIS PART

For the following Strategy chapters, think about what you are doing now before you read the chapters. As you read and engage in the directed practice, be sure to appreciate the ways you can change your approach. At the end of Part IV, you will have the opportunity to reflect on how you will change your approach.

Study Aids Online!
We've created step-by-step study plans so you can use this book to your best advantage. Head over to your Student Tools (see the "Get More (Free) Content" page for instructions) to get started!

Chapter 1
How to Approach the Multiple-Choice Questions

THE BASICS

The multiple-choice part of the exam will consist of sets of two to five questions that are tied to primary sources, secondary sources, or historical issues. The directions will be pretty simple. They will likely be similar to the following:

> **Directions:** Each of the questions or incomplete statements below is followed by four suggested answers or completions. Select the one that is best in each case and then fill in the corresponding space on the answer sheet.

In short, you are being asked to evaluate a provided document or source and answer a series of questions. Once you select an answer, you will fill in the appropriate bubble on a separate answer sheet. You will *not* be given credit for answers you record in your test booklet (e.g., by circling them) but not on your answer sheet. Part A of Section I (the multiple-choice questions) consists of 55 questions, and Part B (the short-answer questions) contains four questions. You have 1 hour and 45 minutes to complete these two sections, so time management is key. The College Board breaks it down as follows: 55 minutes for the multiple-choice section, and 50 minutes for the short answers.

TYPES OF SOURCES

The AP World History Exam tests your ability to read, analyze, and draw conclusions about primary sources as well as their connection to historical events and ideas. The questions in the multiple-choice section will all be based in some way on a primary source, whether a chart of information, an excerpt from a historical document or text, a photograph, or a map—the list goes on!

Unlike many AP Exams, the multiple-choice questions on the AP World History Exam appear in sets associated with a primary source, secondary source, or historical issue. Primary sources are original materials, which provide a firsthand account or perspective. Many of the primary sources that you are likely to see on the exam will include direct excerpts from historical literary works, documents from ancient history, legislation, inscriptions, letters, and speeches. Secondary sources are pieces of information that relate to or are discussed in reference to information presented elsewhere (not firsthand information). Examples of secondary sources include historical perspectives on events, historical criticisms, artwork or cartoons, photographs, or retrospective analyses. Additional sources used on the exam may include charts or graphs that depict key historical relationships.

Here is an example of a primary source you may see on the AP World History Exam:

Questions 13–15 refer to the passage below.

1. If any one ensnare another, putting a ban upon him, but he can not prove it, then he that ensnared him shall be put to death.
2. If any one bring an accusation against a man, and the accused go to the river and leap into the river, if he sink in the river his accuser shall take possession of his house. But if the river prove that the accused is not guilty, and he escape unhurt, then he who had brought the accusation shall be put to death, while he who leaped into the river shall take possession of the house that had belonged to his accuser.
3. If any one bring an accusation of any crime before the elders, and does not prove what he has charged, he shall, if it be a capital offense charged, be put to death.
4. If he satisfy the elders to impose a fine of grain or money, he shall receive the fine that the action produces.
5. If a judge try a case, reach a decision, and present his judgment in writing; if later error shall appear in his decision, and it be through his own fault, then he shall pay twelve times the fine set by him in the case, and he shall be publicly removed from the judge's bench, and never again shall he sit there to render judgment.

Hammurabi's *Code of Laws* 1–5, circa 1780 B.C.E.

The series of legal prescriptions from Hammurabi's *Code of Laws*, excerpted above, outlines a few aspects of the Babylonian criminal justice system. On the AP World History Exam, you will be given primary sources like these that address key events or issues in world history. The accompanying questions will evaluate these sources from the perspective of the thematic learning objectives described in Part III of this book. Throughout this section, we have provided additional examples that represent the diversity of sources you may see on the exam. We will now discuss how to tackle the questions stemming from these sources.

TYPES OF QUESTIONS

The questions in the multiple-choice section will center on one or more key themes addressed by the source document provided for each set of questions. The majority of the questions will be pretty straightforward once the context of the source is understood. For instance, an example question stemming from the text quoted above may appear as follows:

13. The excerpt provided is best understood in the context of which of the following?

(A) The consolidation of power in the late Roman Mediterranean world

(B) The Arab conquest of North Africa

(C) The need for a universal set of regulations in ancient Mesopotamia

(D) The creation of the Athenian city-state

Often the test writers will throw in trickier, less straightforward questions, such as NOT/EXCEPT questions. For these types of questions, you are looking for the answer that is NOT true. Approach these as you would a simple "true or false" question. Take a look at the following EXCEPT multiple-choice question.

Questions 4–7 refer to the passage below.

Whereas, Most Christian, High, Excellent, and Powerful Princes, King and Queen of Spain and of the Islands of the Sea, our Sovereigns, this present year 1492, after your Highnesses had terminated the war with the Moors reigning in Europe, the same having been brought to an end in the great city of Granada, where on the second day of January, this present year, I saw the royal banners of your Highnesses planted by force of arms upon the towers of the Alhambra, which is the fortress of that city, and saw the Moorish king come out at the gate of the city and kiss the hands of your Highnesses, and of the Prince my Sovereign; and in the present month, in consequence of the information which I had given your Highnesses respecting the countries of India and of a Prince, called Great Can, which in our language signifies King of Kings, how, at many times he, and his predecessors had sent to Rome soliciting instructors who might teach him our holy faith, and the holy Father had never granted his request, whereby great numbers of people were lost, believing in idolatry and doctrines of perdition. Your Highnesses, as Catholic Christians, and princes who love and promote the holy Christian faith, and are enemies of the doctrine of Mahomet, and of all idolatry and heresy, determined to send me, Christopher Columbus, to the above-mentioned countries of India, to see the said princes, people, and territories, and to learn their disposition and the proper method of converting them to our holy faith; and furthermore directed that I should not proceed by land to the East, as is customary, but by a Westerly route, in which direction we have hitherto no certain evidence that any one has gone.

Christopher Columbus, personal journal, 1492

4. The effects of European exploration of the Americas included all of the following EXCEPT

   (A) The exchange of information about crops and other food items
   (B) The widespread conversion of Europeans to Native American religious belief systems
   (C) The introduction of new weapons to Native American tribes
   (D) The decimation of the Native American population due to diseases brought by the Europeans

A few times during the multiple-choice section, you will be asked to interpret an illustration source, often a map or other type of graphic. These questions are usually pretty easy. The key is not to try to read too much between the lines. To save time, read the question first, and then go to the graphic. This way you will know what you are looking for!

Here is an example of a map source and associated question.

Questions 33–35 refer to the map below.

33. Which of the following wars had a significant impact on the geographical region shown in the map above?

    (A)   The Hundred Years' War
    (B)   The Second Punic War
    (C)   The Vandal War
    (D)   The First Persian War

Finally, there will be a few questions on your test asking you to interpret a graph or chart. These are usually very straightforward, unless they are "EXCEPT" or "NOT" questions. Those tend to be time-consuming, and even strong students should probably do those at the end, if time permits. When you answer one of these chart or graph questions, realize that more than one answer might be valid, but only one will be supported by the information in the chart or graph.

The following is an example of a graph question.

Questions 40–44 refer to the table below.

World Population Growth, 1950–2050

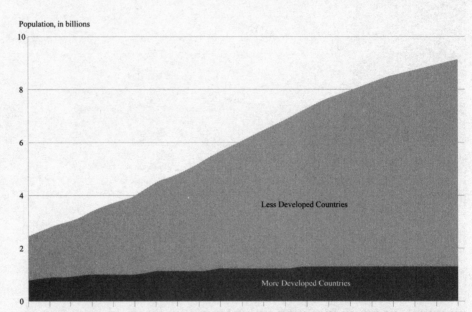

40. It can be inferred from the information in the table above that

(A)   the population of Africa is growing at a faster rate than that of Europe

(B)   the population of all countries is declining

(C)   the population of China is growing more quickly than that of any other nation

(D)   the population of more developed countries is greater than that of less developed countries

The Big Picture

One of the most important characteristics of the AP World History multiple-choice section is that the questions and answers are designed to illustrate basic principles of world history. These principles are evaluated through the five thematic learning objectives mentioned in Part III. Multiple-choice questions will NOT ask about exceptions to historical trends; the test ignores these because the test writers are trying to find out whether you have mastered the important generalizations that can be drawn from history. They do not want to know whether you have memorized your textbook (they already know that you haven't). Talk of historical exceptions is welcome in the essay section, though. Students who discuss exceptions in their essays often impress the readers. More on that later.

Overall, you should always keep the **big picture** in mind as you take this exam. As you approach questions, use the sources provided to help you focus on key points or themes that are being questioned. Even if you cannot remember the specific event or concept being tested, you should be able to answer the question by remembering the general social and political trends of the era and using the information that may be ascertained from the source. Let's look at a couple of illustrative examples.

Think Big
Remembering general concepts and major events of a given time and place in history can be the key to choosing the right answer the multiple-choice section. Even if you're not familiar with a specific source, being familiar with the general trends of the time period and place can help you BIG time.

Questions 51–54 refer to the passages below.

"Just as in the physical body of the embodied being is the process of childhood, youth, old age; similarly in the transmigration from one body to another the wise are never deluded."

—*Bhagavad Gita* 2.13, circa 500-200 B.C.E.

"But know that by whom the entire physical body is pervaded is indestructible. No one is able to cause the destruction of the imperishable soul."

—*Bhagavad Gita* 2.17, circa 500-200 B.C.E.

"The soul never takes birth and never dies at any time nor does it come into being again when the body is created. The soul is birthless, eternal, imperishable and timeless and is never terminated when the body is terminated."

—*Bhagavad Gita* 2.20, circa 500-200 B.C.E.

"As a person gives up old and worn out garments and accepts new apparel, similarly the embodied soul giving up old and worn out bodies verily accepts new bodies."

—*Bhagavad Gita* 2.22, circa 500-200 B.C.E.

51. Compared to the religious tradition exemplified in the excerpts above, Judaism in the ancient world differed in that Jews

    (A) were polytheistic
    (B) did not believe in reincarnation
    (C) believed in observing a set of moral laws
    (D) had a hierarchical caste system

Here's How to Crack It

At first glance, this question may appear to require you to remember a lot of details about this mysterious text known as the *Bhagavad Gita*. It's not really all that tricky, though. To answer this question correctly, you only need to remember the big picture about a few of the world's major religious traditions (and of course, you need to remember that the *Bhagavad Gita* is one of the primary sacred texts of Hinduism).

When you take a close look at the question stem, you can see that the point of the question is to figure out which answer choice correctly describes ancient Judaism but NOT Hinduism. Choice (A) is backwards, because it describes Hinduism but not Judaism. Eliminate it. Choice (C) describes nearly all major religious traditions, so you can eliminate that option as well. Choice (D) describes one of the most famous aspects of Hinduism, the caste system. Ancient Judaism had no such system, so eliminate (D). Choice (B) is the only remaining option, and is the correct answer. Hinduism (along with Buddhism, Jainism, and Sikhism) is characterized, in part, by a belief in reincarnation, but reincarnation is not a central belief of traditional Judaism.

The strategy used to answer this question is Process of Elimination, or POE for short. We'll go into this strategy in more detail in a few pages!

Let's look at another example.

Questions 13–14 refer to the passage below.

"And here it becomes evident that the bourgeoisie is unfit any longer to be the ruling class in society and to impose its conditions of existence upon society as an over-riding law. It is unfit to rule because it is incompetent to assure an existence to its slave within his slavery, because it cannot help letting him sink into such a state that it has to feed him instead of being fed by him. Society can no longer live under this bourgeoisie; in other words, its existence is no longer compatible with society.

The essential condition for the existence, and for the sway of the bourgeois class, is the formation and augmentation of capital; the condition for capital is wage-labor. Wage-labor rests exclusively on competition between the laborers. The advance of industry, whose involuntary promoter is the bourgeoisie, replaces the isolation of the laborers, due to competition, by their revolutionary combination, due to association. The development of modern industry, therefore, cuts from under its feet the very foundation on which the bourgeoisie produces and appropriates products. What the bourgeoisie therefore produces, above all, are its own grave diggers. Its fall and the victory of the proletariat are equally inevitable."

13. The quotation above appears in which of the following?

    (A) Plato's *Republic*
    (B) John Stuart Mill's *On Liberty*
    (C) Jean-Jacques Rousseau's *The Social Contract*
    (D) Karl Marx and Friedrich Engels' *The Communist Manifesto*

Here's How to Crack It

The first thing you may notice is that this question is pretty difficult; the quotation is one long sentence filled with archaic language and syntax. However, if you key in on the big picture, this question isn't all that hard, provided you've prepared for the exam. The central concept of the quotation, to oversimplify quite a bit, is that there is some sort of conflict between different classes in society and that the bourgeoisie (read: upper/middle classes who are the ones with capital, i.e., money) is bad.

Now let's take a look at the answer choices. Plato's *Republic*, (A), is an ancient Greek text written in dialogue form that contains the key themes of justice and what the ideal city-state should look like. The terminology of the quotation, such as "capital," "the advance of industry," and "bourgeoisie," should tell you that this text does not come from ancient Greece but is rather a product of Europe sometime in the early modern or modern period. Eliminate (A). John Stuart Mill's *On Liberty*, (B), is a philosophical work published in 1859 that emphasizes the importance of individuality and the liberty of individual citizens in opposition to tyrannical government. Choice (B) could match the correct time period, but the quote itself doesn't mention liberty or individualism, so eliminate it. Rousseau's *The Social Contract*, (C), is a treatise published in 1752 that discusses the conditions in which a society can form a legitimate political authority. Without knowing specifics, this might appear to be a possible answer, but (D) is better: *The Communist Manifesto*, published in 1848, theorizes that human history is characterized by class struggle and that the problems of the capitalist mode of production will lead to socialism and eventually communism. Even if you didn't recognize the quote right away, the fact that the author consistently repeats the term "bourgeoisie" and ends with a prediction about the "victory of the proletariat" (i.e., working class) should key you into the fact that you are dealing with a text about communism.

Process of Elimination (POE)

If it seems that we are focusing more on eliminating incorrect answers than on finding the correct answers, you're right. This is because eliminating wrong answers is the most efficient way to take a multiple-choice exam. We call this strategy **Process of Elimination (POE)**. You should use this technique to whittle down the answer choices to one, because incorrect answers are much easier to identify than correct ones. When you look for the correct answer among the answer choices, you have a tendency to try to justify how each answer *might* be correct. You'll adopt a forgiving attitude in a situation in which tough assertiveness is rewarded. Eliminate incorrect answers. Terminate them with extreme prejudice. Remember that "half wrong is all wrong," and mark up the test as you do this. You are probably used to teachers telling you not to write on the test. This test, however, is yours to mark up, and that will make it easier for you to decide what to guess. If you have done your job well, only the correct answer will be left standing at the end.

Remember POE
Process of Elimination, or POE, is an effective strategy when it comes to guessing on questions you're not completely sure about. If you can't eliminate any answer choices right off the bat, it's best to skip the question and come back to it later.

Common Sense Can Help

Sometimes an answer choice on the multiple-choice section contradicts common sense. Eliminate those answers. Evaluate the question below, which stems from a source on the development of human agriculture in the Neolithic period. Which of the answer choices to the question below lack common sense?

12. According to the passage, which of the following best explains the most important effect that developments in agricultural practices had on Neolithic societies?

    (A) The wide-scale domestication of plants and animals led to a transition from a transient hunter-gatherer lifestyle to more settled communities.

    (B) The immediate commercial success of wheat forced individuals in Mesopotamia to defend themselves against repeated attacks by the Chinese, who wanted to take control of the wheat trade.

    (C) The development of cotton cultivation led to its rise as the most important cash crop in the Near East.

    (D) Changes in agricultural practices led people to abandon their farms and return to a hunter-gatherer lifestyle.

Here's How to Crack It

Even if you didn't completely understand the passage (which would precede this question on the actual exam), common sense should allow you to eliminate (B) immediately. Even if you don't know much about the Neolithic period, hopefully you do know that the ancient Chinese never attacked Mesopotamia. Now let's consider the other answer choices. Was cotton the most important crop in the ancient Near East? No one knows exactly where cotton was first grown, but it was certainly not in the ancient Near East. (Evidence of early cotton production has been found in India, Pakistan, Mexico, and parts of South America, but not in Mesopotamia and not from the Neolithic period.) Eliminate (C). Choice (D) is completely backwards and violates common sense. The whole point of the agricultural revolution in the Neolithic period is that developments in agriculture enabled ancient societies to leave the hunter-gatherer lifestyle and establish permanent farming communities that thrived due to the domestication of plants and animals. Eliminate (D). The correct answer is (A).

Context Clues

Some questions contain context clues or vocabulary words that will either lead you to the correct answer or at least help you eliminate an incorrect answer. Look at the passage and question below.

Questions 38–41 refer to the passage below.

"When Tarik landed, soldiers from Cordova came to meet him; and seeing the small number of his companions they despised him on that account. They then fought. The battle with Tarik was severe. They were routed, and he did not cease from the slaughter of them till they reached the town of Cordova. When Roderic heard of this, he came to their rescue from Toledo. They then fought in a place of the name of Shedunia, in a valley which is called this day the valley of Umm-Hakim. They fought a severe battle; but God, mighty and great, killed Roderic and his companions. Mugheyth Errumi, a slave of Welid, was then the commander of Tarik's cavalry. Mugheyth Errumi went in the direction of Cordova, Tarik passing over to Toledo. He, then, entered it, and asked for the table, having nothing else to occupy himself. This, as the men of the Bible relate, was the table of Suleyman Ibn Dawid, may the blessing of God be upon him."

Ibn Abd-el-Hakem, *History of the Conquest of Spain*, circa 850 C.E.

38. The point of view expressed in the quotation above is most likely that of

   (A) a Spanish explorer preparing to embark upon a journey
   (B) a Dutch merchant considering trading options in southern Europe
   (C) a Muslim historian reflecting upon recent military victories
   (D) a Jewish religious authority lamenting the treatment of his people in exile

Here's How to Crack It

If you don't recognize all of the names of the people mentioned in this lengthy quotation, don't worry. There are a few big context clues in the bibliographical information that might give you enough of a framework to answer this question correctly. The title of this text is *History of the Conquest of Spain*. Do any of the answer choices have nothing to do with this topic? First, eliminate (B). Beyond the fact that there is no mention of anyone Dutch in the quotation, the date of the text (850 C.E.) should clue you in to the fact that this text has nothing to do with Dutch traders, who didn't make a big mark on the world until nearly 1,000 years after this passage was written. Choice (A) seems pretty unlikely, too. You might be tempted by this choice because of its connection to Spain, but there is nothing in the text about exploration. Furthermore, the Age of Exploration was much later than 850 C.E. Choice (D) might look plausible, especially if you remember that medieval Spain had a fairly large Jewish population, but think again about the title of this passage and ask yourself: Who conquered Spain in the Middle Ages? Furthermore, the author seems to be pretty happy about the defeat of the soldiers from Cordova (which is in Spain). Does the passage even mention anything about Jews? Eliminate (D). The correct answer, (C), makes the most sense because the (Muslim) Arabs conquered Spain in the eighth century, so it would be logical for a Muslim historian to reflect upon that in the following century.

Here are the answers to the questions in this chapter.

13.	C
4.	B
33.	D
40.	A
51.	B
13.	D
12.	A
38.	C

Summary

- The multiple-choice section consists of sets of two to five questions, which are tied to primary sources, secondary sources, or historical issues.

- Familiarize yourself with the different types of questions that will appear on the multiple-choice section. Be aware that you will see many questions about political, social, cultural, economic, and religious history. Tailor your studies accordingly.

- Look for "big picture" answers. Correct answers on the multiple-choice section confirm important trends in world history. This section will not ask you about weird exceptions that contradict those trends. It also will not ask you about military history featured on the History Channel. You will not be required to perform miraculous feats of memorization; however, you must be thoroughly familiar with all the basics of world history.

- Use Process of Elimination (POE) when working on a question you're not sure about. Once you have eliminated some choices and convinced yourself that you cannot eliminate any other incorrect answers, you should guess and move on to the next question.

- Use common sense, and look for context clues.

Chapter 2
Essay Basics and How to Approach the Short-Answer Questions

OVERVIEW

There are three types of essay questions on the AP World History Exam: the short-answer questions, the document-based question (DBQ), and the long essay question. In this chapter we will review some essay basics and discuss the short-answer section in more detail. In the chapters that follow, we will discuss the DBQ and the long essay question more in depth.

Reasons to Be Optimistic About the Free-Response Questions

AP graders know that you are given very little time to write the DBQ and the long essay question. They also know that you don't have enough time to cover the broad scope of the subject matter tested by the question. The fact is, many long books have been written about any one subject that you might be asked about on the DBQ and the long essay.

The College Board's AP World History Course Description (which can be downloaded from the College Board's AP Students website) advises students to write an essay that has a well-developed thesis, provides support for the thesis with specific examples, addresses all parts of the question, and is well organized. Therefore, expressing good ideas and presenting valid evidence in support of those ideas are hugely important. Making sure that you mention every single relevant piece of historical information is not so important.

Also, you should remember that graders are not given a lot of time to read your essays. When they gather to read the exams, the graders each go through more than one hundred essays per day. No one could possibly give detailed attention to all points in your essay when he or she is reading at such a fast clip. What he or she can see in such a brief reading is whether you have something intelligent to say and whether you have the ability to say it well. As many teachers and professors will tell you, when you read several bad essays, you tend to give those that are not completely awful more credit than they possibly deserve.

ESSAY BASICS: WHAT ARE THE AP ESSAY GRADERS LOOKING FOR?

In conversations with those who grade AP World History Exams, it is clear that what they want above all else is for you to address the question. In some of your classes, you may have gotten into the habit of throwing everything but the kitchen sink into an essay without truly addressing the question at hand. Do not try to fudge your way through the essay. The graders are all experts in history, and you will not be able to fool them into thinking you know more than you actually do.

It is also very important to focus on the phrasing of the question. Some students are so anxious to get going that they start writing as soon as they know the general subject of the question, and many of these students lose points because their essays do not answer the question. Take, for example, an essay question that asks you to discuss the effects of technological advances on the ability of European explorers to travel more widely around the globe in the fifteenth century. If you are an overanxious test taker, you might start rattling off everything you know about the Age of Exploration. No matter how well this essay is written, you will lose points for one simple reason—not answering the question!

Furthermore, a good essay does more than rattle off facts. Just as the multiple-choice questions seek to draw out certain general principles or the "big picture" of world history, the essay questions seek to do the same. The readers want to see that you understand some of the fundamental issues in world history and that you can successfully discuss this material in a coherent manner.

If all this sounds intimidating, read on! There are a few simple things you can do to improve your grade on the AP essays.

Things That Make Any Essay Better

There are two essential components to writing a successful timed essay. First, plan what you are going to write before you start writing! Second, use a number of tried-and-true writing techniques that will make your essay appear well organized, well thought out, and well written. This section is about those techniques.

Before You Start Writing

Read the question carefully. Underline key words and circle dates. Then brainstorm for one or two minutes. Write down everything that comes to mind in your test booklet. (There is room in the margins and at the top and bottom of the pages.) Look at your notes and consider the results of your brainstorming session as you decide what point you will argue in your essay; that argument is going to be your thesis. Tailor your argument to your information, but by no means choose an argument that you know is wrong or with which you disagree. If you do either of these things, your essay probably won't be a successful or effective one. Finally, sort the results of your brainstorm. Some of what you wrote down will be "big picture" conclusions, some will be historical facts that can be used as evidence to support your conclusions, and some will be irrelevant points that you can discard.

Next, make an outline. You should plan to write one paragraph for each of the short-answer questions and five paragraphs each for the DBQ and long essay. Plan to go into special detail in each of the paragraphs on the DBQ. (Remember, you will have the documents and your outside knowledge to discuss on the DBQ. Plus, you will have more time.) For the essays in Section II of the exam, your first paragraph should contain your thesis statement, in which you directly answer the question in just a few sentences. Your second, third, and fourth paragraphs should each contain one argument (for a total of three) that supports that statement, along with historical evidence to support those arguments. The fifth paragraph should contain your conclusion and reiterate your answer to the question.

Before you start to write your outline, you will have to decide what type of argument you are going to make. Here are some of the classics.

1. Make Three Good Points

This is the simplest strategy. Look at the results of your brainstorming session, and pick the three best points supporting your position. Make each of these points the subject of one paragraph. Make the weakest of the three points the subject of the second paragraph, and save the strongest point for the fourth paragraph. If your three points are interrelated and there is a natural sequence to arguing them, then by all means use that sequence; otherwise, try to save your strongest point for last. Begin each paragraph by stating one of your three points, and then spend the rest of the paragraph supporting it. Use specific, supporting examples whenever possible. Your first paragraph should state what you intend to argue. Your final paragraph should explain why you have proven what you set out to prove.

Circle Key Words
When you read a question, circle or underline key words and phrases that you can refer back to easily when you begin to create your outline and then write the essay.

2. Make a Chronological Argument

Many questions lend themselves to a chronological treatment. Questions about the development of a political, social, or economic trend can hardly be answered any other way. When you make a chronological argument, look for important transitions and use them to start new paragraphs. A five-paragraph essay about the events leading up to the French Revolution, for example, might start with an introductory discussion of France and the role of royal absolutism. This is also where you should state your thesis. The second paragraph might then discuss the economic crisis that led to the calling of the Estates-General. The third paragraph could deal with concern among members of the third estate that their interests might not be represented at Versailles, despite the vital economic role they played in eighteenth-century France. The fourth paragraph could be concerned with the events leading up to and including the King's agreement to meet the three estates as a National Assembly. Your conclusion in this type of essay should restate the essay question and answer it. For example, if the question asks whether the French Revolution was inevitable, you should answer "yes" or "no" in this paragraph.

3. Identify Similarities and Differences

Some questions, particularly on the long essay question, ask you to compare events, issues, and/or cultural practices. Very often, the way the question is phrased will suggest the best organization for your essay. Take, for example, a question that asks you to compare the impact of three events and issues on the decision to execute the English monarch Charles I in 1649. This question requires you to set the historical scene prior to the three events/issues you are about to discuss. Continue by devoting one paragraph to each of the three, and conclude by comparing and contrasting the relative importance of each. Again, be sure to answer the question in your final paragraph.

Other questions will provide options. If you are asked to compare Italian and Northern European humanism during the Renaissance, you might open with a thesis stating the essential similarity or difference between the two. Then, you could devote one paragraph each to a summary of certain trends and authors, while in the fourth paragraph you could point out the major similarities and differences between Italian and Northern European humanism. In the final paragraph, you could draw your conclusion (for example, "their similarities were more significant than their differences," or vice versa). Or, using another angle altogether, you might start with a thesis, then discuss in the body of your essay three pertinent philosophical, religious, or political issues, then discuss how Italian humanists dealt with such questions, then move on to the Northern European humanists, and wrap up with an overview of your argument for your conclusion.

4. Use the Straw Dog Argument

For this technique, choose a couple of arguments that someone taking the position opposite yours would take. State those opposing arguments, and then tear them down. Remember that proving your opposition wrong does not mean that you have proved that you yourself are correct; that is why you should choose only a few opposing arguments to refute. Summarize your opponent's arguments in paragraph two, dismiss them in paragraph three, and use paragraph four to make the argument for your side. Or, use one paragraph each to summarize and dismiss each of your opponent's arguments, and then make the case for your side in your concluding paragraph. Acknowledging both sides of an argument, even when you choose one over the other, is a good indicator that you understand that historical issues are complex and can be interpreted in more than one way, something teachers and graders like to see.

Conclusion

No matter which format you choose, remember to organize your essay so that the first paragraph addresses the question and states how you are going to answer it. (That is your thesis.) The second, third, and fourth paragraphs should each be organized around a single argument that supports your thesis, and each of these arguments must be supported by historical evidence. Your final paragraph ties the essay up into a nice, neat package. Your concluding paragraph should also answer the question. And remember, stay positive!

As you are writing, observe the following guidelines:

- **Keep sentences as simple as possible.** Long sentences get convoluted very quickly and will give your graders a headache, putting them in a bad mood.

- **Write clearly and neatly.** As long as we are discussing your graders' moods, here is an easy way to put them in good ones. Graders look at a lot of chicken scratch; it strains their eyes and makes them grumpy. Neatly written essays make them happy. When you cross out, do it neatly (better to erase). If you are making any major edits—if you want to insert a paragraph in the middle of your essay, for example— make sure you indicate these changes clearly.

- **Define your terms.** Most questions require you to use terms that mean different things to different people. One person's "liberal" is another person's "conservative" and yet another person's "extremist." What one person considers "expansionism," another might call "colonialism" or "imperialism." The folks who grade the test want to know what you think these terms mean. When you use them, define them. Take particular care to define any such terms that appear in the question. Almost all official College Board materials emphasize this point, so do not forget it. Be sure to define any term that you suspect can be defined in more than one way.

- **Use transition words to show where you are going.** When continuing an idea, use words such as *furthermore, also,* and *in addition.* When changing the flow of thought, use words such as however and yet. Transition words make your essay easier to understand by clarifying your intentions. Better yet, they indicate to the graders that you know how to make a coherent, persuasive argument.

Essay Essential
Don't underestimate the power of a neat essay. If your handwriting is questionable, try to print as clearly as possible.

- **Use structural indicators to organize your paragraphs.** Another way to clarify your intentions is to organize your essay around structural indicators. For example, if you are making a number of related points, number them ("First...Second...And last..."). If you are writing a compare/contrast essay, use the indicators *on the one hand* and *on the other hand*.

- **Stick to your outline.** Unless you get an absolutely brilliant idea while you are writing, do not deviate from your outline. If you do, you will risk winding up with an incoherent essay.

- **Try to prove one "big picture" idea per paragraph.** Keep it simple. Each paragraph should make one point and then substantiate that point with historical evidence and examples.

- **Back up your ideas with examples.** Yes, we have said it already, but it bears repeating: Do not just throw ideas out there and hope that you are right (unless you are absolutely desperate). You will score big points if you substantiate your claims with facts and specific examples.

- **Try to fill the essay form.** An overly short essay will hurt you more than one that is overly long.

- **Make sure your first and last paragraphs directly address the question.** Nothing will cost you points faster than if the graders decide you did not answer the question. It is always a safe move to start your final paragraph by answering the question. If you have written a good essay, that answer will serve as a legitimate conclusion.

- **Always place every essay into a historical context.** For example, if you are given an essay asking you to compare and contrast Newton's and Einstein's ideas on the universe, don't make it an essay on science. Instead, show how each of these men was a product of his respective time period, and show how their ideas influenced their contemporaries as well as future generations.

SHORT-ANSWER BASICS

The short-answer section of the exam (Part B of Section I) involves answering three short-answer questions in which you will respond to a primary source, historical argument, data or maps, or general propositions about world history. The questions may have multiple components, and you will be required to address all parts of a given question. Since these are short-answer prompts, you are not required to develop and support a thesis statement.

Remember, the short-answer section contains four questions, but you need to answer only three. Questions 1 and 2 are required, and then you choose EITHER Question 3 or Question 4.

Time Crunch

Perhaps the biggest challenge of the short-answer section is the time allotted. You have a total of 40 minutes to answer three questions. You'll be given up to a page to write each essay, but it is not necessary to fill all of the provided space. Quality matters more than quantity, though a longer essay will likely look more impressive to the reader. So there is no time to dawdle on the short essays! You must keep brainstorming to a minimum (no more than two or three minutes in total), and keep your pencil moving!

Strategy for Answering the Short-Answer Questions

The short-answer questions will consist of multiple parts, which center on a key learning objective. Some questions may give you the opportunity to choose from among several topics. For the questions that do not give you the opportunity to pick from a list of choice topics, read the question and each of the parts carefully. Many of these questions will resemble the following example.

3. **Use the image below to answer all parts of the question that follows.**

The image above shows the Greek Temple of Concordia in the Valley of the Temples, Sicily (Italy). The temple was constructed circa 440 B.C.E.

a)   Briefly explain how architectural monuments such as the one pictured above are evidence of Greek cultural influence across the Mediterranean world in the fifth century B.C.E.

b)   Briefly explain the role of temples such as the one pictured above in the religious beliefs and practices of classical Greek civilization.

Here's How to Crack It
1. Think.

You've probably seen photos of temples like this before. If you've been to Europe, the Middle East, or North Africa, you may have even seen such temples in person. The first step is to make sure to read the information provided under the photograph very carefully and glean whatever you can from that information. In the case of the photograph pictured above, note that we are dealing with a Greek temple in Italy, built in the middle of the fifth century B.C.E. Next, let's turn to the questions. Part (a) wants you to explain this photograph in terms of Greek cultural influence, while part (b) wants you to contextualize the photograph as it relates to ancient Greek religious beliefs and practices. Once you are sure that you understand the questions, brainstorm a little bit and jot down a few notes for yourself about key themes or concepts that relate to the questions asked.

For part (a), your brainstorming might look something like this:

- Ancient Greece: known for lots of temples, theaters, stadiums, etc.
- Greek architecture—marble
- Temples built to house statues?
- Greek culture spread throughout Mediterranean region and had a lot of influence on the Romans
- Greeks conquered parts of Italy
- Places conquered by Greece sometimes adopted Greek language and other stuff

For part (b), your brainstorming might look something like this:

- Temples built to house statues of the gods?
- Greek religion—polytheistic
- Sacrifices and rituals took place in/outside of temples
- Lots of myths and stories about the Greek gods
- Everyday life in ancient Greece dominated by religion

2. Write.
Here is a sample short-answer response using some of the ideas outlined above:

In ancient Greece, religion dominated most aspects of daily life. The Greeks were, for the most part, polytheistic, and had many myths and stories detailing the exploits and adventures of their gods and goddesses. Because religion was such an important aspect of classical Greece, the Greeks built temples in all of their major cities and towns in order to honor their deities. These temples often housed statues of the deities, and sacrifices and other religious rituals were performed outside of the temples. During the classical period, Greece expanded its influence around the Mediterranean region. Among other places, Greece conquered parts of Italy (including the island of Sicily). In places where the Greeks had conquered, Greek settlers had enormous cultural impact upon local populations. Some places adopted the Greek language, and many places were also influenced by Greek architecture, building temples, theaters, and other structures that were modeled on those found in Greece itself.

Summary

- Read questions carefully. Be sure you are answering the question that is asked. You must answer all parts of the question in order to get full credit.

- Do not start writing until you have brainstormed, chosen a thesis, and written an outline. The only exception to this is the short-answer section; the questions there do not require a thesis, and you will not have enough time to write an outline.

- Follow your outline. On the longer essays, stick to one important idea per paragraph. Support your ideas with historical evidence.

- Write clearly and neatly. Do not write in long, overly complex sentences. Toss in a couple of "big" words you know you will not misuse. When in doubt, stick to simple syntax and vocabulary.

- Use transition words to indicate continuity of thought and changes in the direction of your argument.

- Provide a strong historical context. You may be faced with questions focusing on science, economics, philosophy, literature and art, religion, and other disciplines. Always remember that this is a history exam, so everything you discuss needs to be situated within a broader context.

Chapter 3
How to Approach
the Document-
Based Question
(DBQ)

IT'S ALL IN THE DOCUMENTS

The first essay you'll see in Section II of the AP World History Exam is the Document-Based Question (DBQ). As the name implies, this question is based on approximately seven documents centered on a historical topic or issue within periods 3 to 6 (600 c.e. to present). Your job is to work through the documents to determine how they relate to each other, what changes can be seen over time, how the author's background may have influenced the contents of the document, and so on.

The DBQ measures your ability to develop a thesis, support your thesis with historical evidence and your outside knowledge of world history, and make historical connections. In other words, you're being asked to think like a historian by analyzing primary sources and building an argument (in response to a given prompt) around those sources. The question is intended to test a specific skill, such as the ability to recognize trends throughout history or cause-and-effect relationships between historical events.

Before the start of the essay portion of the exam, there will be a reading period for you to read the DBQ documents and question. It is suggested that you spend 15 minutes reading the documents and 45 minutes writing your response, but you may begin writing before the 15-minute reading period is over. To do well on this essay, you need to know exactly what to do with those 15 minutes. And to do that you need to know exactly what you are expected to write. Let's begin by looking at the scoring rubric for the DBQ.

How the DBQ Is Scored

The DBQ is graded on a 7-point scale. Here's how those points are earned.

Task	Points Possible	Description
Thesis/Claim	1 point	To earn this point, the thesis must make a claim that *responds* to the prompt rather than restating or rephrasing the prompt. The thesis must consist of one or more sentences located in one place, either in the introduction or the conclusion.
Contextualization	1 point	To earn this point, the response must relate the topic of the prompt to broader historical events, developments, or processes that occur before, during, or continue after the time frame of the question. This point is not awarded for merely a phrase or reference.
Evidence	3 points	*Evidence from the Documents* To earn 1 point, the response must accurately describe—rather than simply quote—the content from at least 3* of the documents to address the topic of the prompt. *Evidence Beyond the Documents* To earn 2 points, the response must accurately describe—rather than simply quote—the content from at least 6* documents. In addition, the response must use the content of the documents to support an argument in response to the prompt.
Analysis and Reasoning	2 points	To earn 1 point, a response must demonstrate a complex understanding of the historical development that is the focus of the prompt, using evidence. This can be accomplished in in a variety of ways, such as: • Explaining nuance of an issue by analyzing multiple variables • Explaining both similarity and difference, or explaining both continuity and change, or explaining multiple causes, or explaining both cause and effect • Explaining relevant and insightful connections within and across periods • Confirming the validity of an argument by corroborating multiple perspectives across themes • Qualifying or modifying an argument by considering diverse or alternative views or evidence This understanding must be part of the argument, not merely a phrase or reference.

*Rubric based on a DBQ with seven documents.

What the Rubric Actually Means

Here's what you need to do to get a good score on the DBQ:

- Formulate a relevant thesis or claim and support that thesis with the documents, as well as outside examples not covered in the documents. Did you answer the question that was asked? Make sure that your thesis directly addresses the prompt and accurately describes the contents of your essay. Be sure that the documents can be used to support your claim—students often make the mistake of coming up with an an interesting thesis only to find that the documents don't really support it.

- Analyze the documents. Your analysis must acknowledge the source of the documents and the author's point of view, purpose, and/or audience, which means that you must demonstrate that you understand the context of each source. You should also be able to explain the following:
  - What was the context (historical, political, or cultural environment) in which the document was authored? What else was going on around the author at the time this was written?
  - How does this author's perspective affect what he or she wrote and why? What is the author's position in society (gender, age, educational level, political or religious belief system)? How do these attributes inform what the author writes?
  - How does the content and tone of the document relate to that of the other documents? What does one document say that another doesn't? What accounts for these differences?
  - When was the document written? Who was the intended audience, and what was the author trying to express?

- Identify and explain additional examples and evidence that are not represented in the documents, and use them to support or expand your argument in some way. When brainstorming outside evidence and how to use it in your essay, consider the following questions:
  - What types of evidence offer information that is not already present?
  - What points of view are missing that would make your argument stronger? Consider groups typically not represented (women, the working class, peasants).
  - Why is this additional evidence important?

- Connect the topic of the prompt and the documents to broader historical themes, developments, or issues. You want to demonstrate your understanding of how the topic or issue at hand relates to other issues in world history.

So to write a decent DBQ essay, you need to write an essay that opens with a thesis, support that thesis with all of the documents, analyze the documents, include outside evidence and examples to bolster your argument, and make connections between the topic of the prompt and other historical issues and developments.

THE DOCUMENTS

Of course, before you can write anything, you need to work your way through the documents. *Working* the documents (not just reading them) is almost as important as writing the essay itself. Let's spend a few minutes learning exactly how to process, or work, the documents so that you can put together a high-scoring essay.

Work Those Documents

When the reading period begins, open up your test booklet to Part A of Section II (the DBQ). Study the DBQ directions in this book so that you do not have to spend a lot of time reading through them on test day. Still, you should do a quick scan of the directions to make sure they are the ones you are familiar with. Remember, the highest-scoring essays typically make use of all of the documents, so plan on using all of them in your essay. Also remember that not every document will be a passage of text. You may see images, charts, photographs, maps, and other visual sources as well.

Step 1: Process the Prompt

You cannot begin to think about the documents until you know what you are being asked to do. Read the question carefully. Underline the important details (such as time period, culture, location) and circle what you are supposed to analyze and the actions you need to take (for example, compare and contrast, change over time, and so on). You can also jot down any information about the question topic and time period that immediately springs to mind.

Give Me 15 Minutes and I'll Give You the World

Is 15 minutes really enough time to read through the documents? That depends on how well you know the topic. Most students will need the full 15 minutes to work through the documents and prepare to write the essay. But if those 15 minutes are up and you haven't finished planning your essay, keep working the documents. The actual writing of your essay will take less time if you are well prepared when you begin. Use the 15 minutes you are given plus any additional time you need (up to 10 more minutes) to plan your essay. Once you've gotten a handle on the documents and organized your thoughts, it will probably take you only about 20 to 30 minutes to actually write the essay.

The document-based question will most likely focus on a historical issue in periods 3–6 (that is, from about 600 C.E. to the present day). So while this example is a bit on the early side, it will still help you understand how you need to approach and work through the documents (while brushing up on your early world history).

Look at the following example of a DBQ:

Question 1: Using the documents and your knowledge of world history, compare and contrast the attitudes toward women found in early civilizations through about 600 C.E.

Based on the question, what do you know the documents are about?
Attitudes toward women in various cultures during various periods.

What are you being asked to do?
Compare and contrast the attitudes and look for any changes over time.

What could additional evidence do?
Clarify how existing attitudes affected women's daily lives.

But Where?

For the essay portion of the test, you will receive a booklet that contains the essay questions, space to plan your essays, and a sealed answer booklet. Use the spaces in the question booklet to do your prep work—outlining, summarizing documents, brainstorming. Don't be shy about what you write in the booklet—the graders won't see your notes. It's important to remember that you will only receive credit for what you wrote in the answer booklet. Even if your teachers in school sometimes give you credit for outlining, AP readers will not.

Step 2: Build a Framework

Once you've gotten a handle on the question, use it to create a framework for processing the documents you are about to read. For example, if a question asks you to compare and contrast two major religions, you would create a compare-and-contrast chart of the two religions in question. You can fill in the chart as you work through the documents. If the question focuses on change over time, create a space in which you can easily note any changes you come across. In the example above, the question asks you to both compare and contrast attitudes of different cultures and to look for any change over time. Your framework for this question might look like this:

Similarities in attitudes toward women	Differences in attitudes toward women

Changes in attitudes toward women?

_____

_____

_____

_____

These first two steps should take about two minutes. Then it's time to hit the documents.

Step 3: Work the Documents

Notice that we are not telling you to simply read the documents. *Read* is too passive a word for what you need to do. As you read each document, summarize and analyze it in light of your framework (what you need to use it for). Look at the following document that goes with our example.

Document 1

> Source: Hebrew Bible, Torah (Deuteronomy), primarily written in seventh century B.C.E. but based on ancient religious code.
>
> When a man takes a wife and marries her, if then she finds no favor in his eyes because he has found some indecency in her, and he writes her a bill of divorce and puts it in her hand and sends her out of his house, and she departs out of his house, and if she goes and becomes another man's wife, and the latter husband dislikes her and writes her a bill of divorce and puts it in her hand and sends her out of his house, or if the latter husband dies, who took her to be his wife, then her former husband, who sent her away, may not take her again to be his wife, after she had been defiled; for that is an abomination before the Lord, and you shall not bring guilt upon the land which the Lord your God gives you for an inheritance.

First, circle the source, making note of the kind of text this is and its date. This document is from a book of laws in the ancient Hebrew Bible, which would become the Old Testament to Christians in later centuries. What is the document's attitude about women? The emphasis here is on female purity. A woman who has remarried after divorce is "defiled," so she cannot be taken back by her first husband. Ancient Hebrew culture emphasized the importance of ritual purity, especially for women. Notice also that men controlled the terms of divorce and remarriage in this society.

You Read a Document. Now What?
Be sure to circle the source of the document, and note the type of text it is.

Let's see how this compares to the second document.

Document 2

Source: The Code of Hammurabi, 1792–1750 B.C.E.

If a man's wife, who lives in his house, wishes to leave it, plunges into debt, tries to ruin her house, neglects her husband, and is judicially convicted: if her husband offers her release, she may go on her way, and he gives her nothing as a gift of release. If her husband does not wish to release her, and if he takes another wife, she shall remain as servant in her husband's house.

If a woman quarrels with her husband, and says: "You are not congenial to me," the reasons for her prejudice must be presented. If she is guiltless, and there is no fault on her part, but he leaves and neglects her, then no guilt attaches to this woman, she shall take her dowry and go back to her father's house.

This document came from the Code of Hammurabi, written from 1800–1700 B.C.E. What was the attitude toward women under the Code of Hammurabi? While women are still subordinate to male authority, they have a few more rights. For example, if she tells him he is a jerk and is proven right, she gets to go home with her dowry, guilt-free. Notice, too, the increased level of judiciary involvement. The decisions seem to be less at the whim of the husband.

Try working the next three documents.

Document 3

Source: Plutarch, excerpt from "Women's Life in Greece and Rome," Moralia, 242 C.E.

27.   When music is played in two parts, it is the bass part which carries the melody. So in a good and wise household, while every activity is carried on by husband and wife in agreement with each other, it will still be evident that it is the husband who leads and makes the final choice.

Document 4

Source: Ban Zhou, leading female Confucian and imperial historian under Emperor Han Hedi, from *Lessons for a Woman*, an instruction manual in feminine behavior, circa 80 C.E.

If a husband be unworthy, then he possesses nothing by which to control his wife. If a wife be unworthy, then she possesses nothing with which to serve her husband. If a husband does not control his wife, then the rules of conduct manifesting his authority are abandoned and broken. If a wife does not serve her husband, then the proper relationship between men and women and the natural order of things are neglected and destroyed. As a matter of fact the purpose of these two [the controlling of women by men, and the serving of men by women] is the same.

Document 5

Source: Excerpt from "The Laws of Manu," the Rig Vedas, 100 B.C.E.–200 C.E.

[In the Rig Vedas (collection of hymns to the Aryan gods) of Classical India, Manu is the father of humanity.]

74. A man who has business (abroad) may depart after securing a maintenance for his wife; for a wife, even though virtuous, may be corrupted if she be distressed by want of subsistence.

75. If (the husband) went on a journey after providing (for her), the wife shall subject herself to restraints in her daily life; but if he departed without providing (for her), she may subsist by blameless manual work.

76. If the husband went abroad for some sacred duty, (she) must wait for him eight years, if (he went) to (acquire) learning or fame six (years), if (he went) for pleasure three years.

77. For one year let a husband bear with a wife who hates him; but after (the lapse of) a year let him deprive her of her property and cease to cohabit with her.

78. She who shows disrespect to (a husband) who is addicted to (some evil) passion, is a drunkard, or diseased, shall be deserted for three months (and be) deprived of her ornaments and furniture.

Visual Documents
Although the documents used for this example are all text-based sources, on the exam the documents may be a mix of text and visual sources, such as a map, political cartoon, graph, or other image.

What did you notice about these documents? Any differences or changes? Document 3, written in Greece and Rome in the third century C.E., shows clearly the attitudes of that time and culture—husband and wife are partners, but the husband is in command. Document 4 is the only document so far that was written by a woman. Notice how in Document 4 the woman is still subservient, but the discussion is about the responsibilities of both men and women. Document 5, which was written about the same time as Document 4, has far more detailed laws regarding the conduct of husbands and wives. Again, women are clearly subservient, yet men are charged with definite responsibilities to their wives.

Step 4: Frame the Documents

Once you've worked the documents (or as you go along), fill in your framework from what you've read. For example, using the four documents we just read, try filling in the compare-and-contrast chart.

Your chart should look something like this:

Similarities in attitudes toward women	Differences in attitudes toward women
All Documents—women subservient to men *All Documents—women far fewer legal rights*	*Doc 1—men in control, emphasis on female purity* *Doc 3—women subservient but more on equal footing* *Doc 2 and 5—more laws regarding male conduct* *Doc 4 and 5—analysis of both male and female roles/responsibilities; husbands culpable for wives* *Doc 4—written by woman; tone different. "If husband unworthy."*

What are the changes that have occurred over time in our example so far? Women went from being mere possessions with men free to make decisions (like to divorce their wives) without any judicial involvement, to more laws governing male conduct and more rights for women (though meager). Although the question doesn't specifically mention it, we should also be aware of the influence of culture when it came to the treatment of women. Some differences that appear in these documents may be a result of not only a change in thought process over time but also a differing attitude of a particular culture. If we were to read the rest of the documents that accompany this question, we would likely see even greater changes in the attitudes toward and treatment of women.

Step 5: Analyze and Add

In order to get as many points as possible, you must analyze as many documents as possible. According to the DBQ scoring rubric, an essay will earn the most points if at least six documents (for a seven-document DBQ) are sufficiently discussed in your essay. You must also pull in outside examples and evidence that support your line of argumentation in some way.

Point of View

Analyzing the documents' points of view is an extremely important part of earning a high score on the DBQ. For example, in our sample documents, Document 4 was written by Ban Zhou, the leading female Confucian during the Han age in China. Could the fact that she is a woman coupled with the fact that she was a Confucian have influenced what she chose to write? Absolutely. Look at Document 4 again.

Document 4

Source: Ban Zhou, leading female Confucian and imperial historian under Emperor Han Hedi, from *Lessons for a Woman*, an instruction manual in feminine behavior, 100 C.E.

If a husband be unworthy, then he possesses nothing by which to control his wife. If a wife be unworthy, then she possesses nothing with which to serve her husband. If a husband does not control his wife, then the rules of conduct manifesting his authority are abandoned and broken. If a wife does not serve her husband, then the proper relationship between men and women and the natural order of things are neglected and destroyed. As a matter of fact the purpose of these two [the controlling of women by men, and the serving of men by women] is the same.

As you can see, the author focuses on worthiness and the interaction between husbands and wives. She even put their responsibilities on equal footing, something that we did not see in any of the other documents. She did not live in an age in which women questioned their subservient role. Therefore, instead of challenging the roles, she tried to find a way to make sense of the subjugation of women. The period in which she lived clearly influenced her point of view. These are the types of issues you want to bring into your analysis of point of view.

As mentioned above, you should pay attention to who wrote the documents and when they were written, as both of these factors can help you determine the point of view. Choose another sample document to analyze for point of view. How about Document 3? It pertains to Greek and Roman societies and was written in the third century C.E. Take a look at it again.

Document 3

Source: Plutarch, excerpt from "Women's Life in Greece and Rome," Moralia, 242 C.E.

27.   When music is played in two parts, it is the bass part which carries the melody. So in a good and wise household, while every activity is carried on by husband and wife in agreement with each other, it will still be evident that it is the husband who leads and makes the final choice.

It reads almost as advice from one to another about how a marriage should be. Interestingly, the attitude of the Greeks and Romans toward women seems positive, yet clearly considered their role as secondary in a marriage. Could that be perhaps a result of the time and culture? Absolutely. The person (presumably a man) who wrote this was likely giving loving, caring advice to a friend, yet he does not acknowledge what a more modern reader would likely think about the subjugation of the woman in the marital relationship. This form of bias was imbedded in the culture of that time. This is therefore a good document to use to exemplify how context and culture can clearly influence a person's perspective.

Outside Evidence and Examples

So as not to forget this step, make a note of it now, and then plan to include it as part of your opening thesis.

In order to assess how the attitudes of a culture affected women's daily lives during a certain period, what types of additional evidence would be helpful? What about either other examples of texts written by women that reflected their thoughts or daily experiences, or examples that would illustrate the daily responsibilities of women in the given period? *Be sure to explain why you feel this evidence will add to your analysis;* just describing an example will not earn you the point.

Step 6: Organize the Documents

So far you've processed the question, built a framework, worked the documents to fill in that framework, analyzed the documents for purpose, audience, and point of view, and determined the type of additional evidence you need and why. Now it's time to organize your documents so that you know which ones you are using as support, which ones you are analyzing and exactly how you plan to use them in connection with one another. This last step will act as the outline for your essay.

Use the following chart to organize your essay.

Thesis	You will open your essay with a thesis. In your thesis, reference the strongest supporting documents. As part of your outline, decide which documents represent the core of your thesis and include them in your opening paragraph. Also, jot down a few brief notes about your thesis before moving on. (Be sure to make your notes on scratch paper—not in the essay booklet.)
Support	List the documents that you plan to use to support your thesis. Include all the documents you mention in your thesis (in the first paragraph). Also feel free to include any other document that will lend additional support.
Group 1	First, group the documents in the most obvious way. For example, if you are asked to compare and contrast a set of documents, break the documents into two groups so that each group contains documents with similar features but the two groups clearly contrast each other.
Group 2	Regroup the documents in a way that shows some sort of insight into how the documents relate to each other. For example, if you first created groups by putting together documents with obvious similarities, regroup them in a way that shows something different or less obvious about the documents. If the question asks about change over time, regroup the documents to show how things changed over some period.
Number of Documents	Use this as a checklist to be sure you include all of the documents in your essay. List the number of documents you've been given, then go through each category and check off the document number as you come to it. If you finish your check and realize that you omitted one (or more) documents, go back to that document to determine how and where you can use it.
Outside Examples/ Evidence	Once you've grouped your documents, consider what other kind or kinds of outside evidence would add something interesting to the analysis of the question posed. Be sure to include reasons why a particular piece of evidence would be useful.

Use our sample documents to fill your own organizational chart. It might resemble something like the following:

DBQ Essay Organizational Chart

Your Turn!
Consider creating a chart like this one on test day as a way to plan your essay and organize your thoughts before writing.

	Document Number(s)	Comments
Thesis	Doc 1—male control, ritual purity Doc 2—more laws Doc 5—still more laws and responsibilities	Attitudes toward women from 1800 B.C.E. up to approx. 200 C.E. definitely changed but men were still basically in control. Early times, female purity was emphasized and women were subordinate to men. Later, laws governing conduct of husbands that were slightly more fair to wives…
Support	Documents 1, 2, and 5 Document 3 softer yet holds women in same position Document 4 to show changes and difference in perspective	
Group 1	1 & 3 versus 2 & 5	Shows no law versus more laws and judicial involvement. Could include others.
Group 2	4 (and others) versus 1, 2, 3, & 5 (and others)	Written from the female perspective versus from the male perspective.
Group 3	1, 2, 3, 4, and 5 versus others	All define women only in terms of the role of wife. Other docs may not.
Number	1, 2, 3, 4, 5, __, __	Check off each as it is used in your outline so that you know that you have used them all.
Outside Examples/ Evidence		A text that portrays a woman who lived during one of the periods mentioned (in the provided docs) showing her defining herself as a citizen or individual rather than just as a wife. Examples of women questioning their position in society, wanting more.

Remember that the DBQ you see on test day may contain more documents, which will make your essay groupings more diverse. The way you group the documents should support your thesis and show changes or contrast as well.

FORMULATING YOUR DBQ THESIS

The number-one rule for writing an AP essay thesis statement is to make sure you answer the question. Here are some other basic rules for writing an effective essay thesis.

How Long Is 15 Minutes?
Right now this process may seem as if it will take two hours as opposed to 15 minutes. You need to practice doing it a few times to get a feel for how much time to spend on what. You may find that you can fill in your framework as you analyze the documents, or identify the documents' point of view as you go. The more you practice, the more efficient you will become. Remember, however, that analyzing the documents is as important as writing the essay. If you need to use the first five to ten minutes of your writing time to finish your analysis or outline, it will be time well spent.

- **Give Them What They Want**—Answer the question by restating key phrases from the question.

- **Show Them Where You Got It**—AP World History Exam essays are all about the evidence. Use your framework to support your assertions right from the beginning. Remember that evidence in your thesis is merely introductory—save the details for the body of the essay.

- **Help Them Get There**—Make a clear transition from your thesis to the body of your essay by using a phrase like, "To better understand the differences between these two societies…" or "To better understand the changes that occurred…" You might also want to suggest, describe, and justify the inclusion of the outside evidence or examples as part of this last sentence. That way you won't forget to include them, and they make for a good transition.

For our example, your thesis and introduction could be something like the following:

> *From a review of the five documents presented, it is clear that the role of women in various cultures from 1800 B.C.E. into the 200s C.E. was primarily one of servitude or worse in comparison to our contemporary ideas about the rights of women. However, there is also evidence that over time, women were seen less as subject only to the rule of law laid down by an individual (usually a husband) and more as people whose (albeit limited) rights were overseen by the rule of law. In earlier eras, women were seen more as property than as people, and that only men reserved the right to divorce with no lingering responsibility to care for their wives. However, some societies began to hold men more accountable for their treatment of women, a trend which eventually came to other societies as well, though at different times. With this added protection of the law, women are not only more protected, but are also held more accountable for their own conduct.*

Before moving on to the next chapter, practice writing your own thesis statement for the sample DBQ in this chapter. Try to come up with as many as possible, and then evaluate them using the scoring rubric on page 99.

When you write your thesis paragraph, imagine that a reader will only read your essay if he or she is convinced to do so by your first paragraph (no pressure). Then, use your framework to write the body of your essay. Your framework can act as both your outline and your checklist—once you've written the bulk of your essay, quickly scan through to make sure you didn't leave anything out. Finally, close with a recap of your points and get on to the next essay.

HOW LONG SHOULD THIS GO ON?

You have 60 minutes for the DBQ. It's suggested you use the first 15 minutes to read the question and documents, and then use the remaining 45 minutes to write the essay. Note that you are allowed to begin writing before the 15-minute reading period is up, but we encourage you to use the full time to plan your essay. And if you're still in the planning stages when the 15 minutes are up, we recommend you spend no more than 10 additional minutes working through the documents and planning your essay. In other words, you should begin writing by 10 minutes into the essay-writing part of the test. You can write a great DBQ essay in 20 to 30 minutes, but you don't want to cut into writing time for the long essay (which we'll cover in the next chapter).

AP essay graders tell us that spending too much time on the DBQ is an obvious problem for many students. Blowing off the Long Essay question will seriously endanger your score! Remember, the DBQ accounts for 25% of your score, and the long essay question accounts for 15% of your score, so be sure to leave yourself adequate time to get to both questions!

PUT IT ALL TOGETHER

Now it's time to try your hand at a practice DBQ. Remember to use all the steps and not to shortchange the prework on the documents. The more comfortable you are with the documents, the easier it will be for you to write this essay. Try keeping track of your time by noting your start time, and then noting how long it takes you to analyze the documents. When you are finished with the essay, note the time you finished. This will give you a rough idea of how much time you need to shave off in practice.

When you have finished, ask a classmate to score your essay using the scoring rubric at the beginning of this chapter.

Directions: Question 1 is based on the accompanying documents. The documents have been edited for the purpose of this exercise.

In your response you should do the following.

- **<u>Thesis/Claim:</u>** Respond to the prompt with a historically defensible claim that establishes a line of reasoning.

- **<u>Contextualization:</u>** Describe a historical context relevant to the prompt.

- **<u>Evidence:</u>** Support an argument in response to the prompt using at least **six** documents. Use at least one additional piece of specific historical evidence (beyond that found in the documents) relevant to an argument about the prompt.

- **<u>Analysis and Reasoning:</u>** For at least **three** documents, explain how or why the document's point of view, purpose, historical situation, and/or audience is relevant to an argument. Demonstrate an understanding of the historical development that is the focus of the prompt, using evidence to support or modify an argument that addresses the question.

Question 1: Using the documents and your knowledge of world history, analyze the rise of nationalism in Egypt and India in the early twentieth century. What additional evidence would help your analysis of causes for the nationalist feelings in these nations?

Document 1

Source: Sir Rabindranath Tagore, *Nationalism*, 1918.

Rabindranath Tagore, Bengali poet, playwright, and novelist, who was one of the earliest non-European recipients of the Nobel Prize for literature, wrote the following:

Has not this truth already come home to you now when this cruel war has driven its claws into the vitals of Europe? When her hoard of wealth is bursting into smoke and her humanity is shattered on her battlefields? You ask in amazement what she has done to deserve this? The answer is, that the West has been systematically petrifying her moral nature in order to lay a solid foundation for her gigantic abstractions of efficiency. She has been all along starving the life of the personal man into that of the professional.

Document 2

Source: Mahatma Gandhi, 1909.

We hold the civilization that you support to be the reverse of civilization. We consider our civilization to be far superior to yours. If you realize this truth, it will be to your advantage and, if you do not, according to your own proverb, you should only live in our country in the same manner as we do. You must not do anything that is contrary to our religions. It is your duty as rulers that for the sake of the Hindus you should eschew beef, and for the sake of Mahomedans you should avoid bacon and ham. We have hitherto said nothing because we have been cowed down, but you need not consider that you have not hurt our feelings by your conduct. We are not expressing our sentiments either through base selfishness or fear, but because it is our duty now to speak out boldly. We consider your schools and courts to be useless. We want our own ancient schools and courts to be restored. The common language of India is not English but Hindi. You should, therefore, learn it. We can hold communication with you only in our national language.

Document 3

Source: *Ganesh Janani* by Abanindranath Tagore, 1907.

Document 4

Source: Sarojini Naidu, *An Indian Nationalist Condemns the British Empire*, 1920.

I speak to you today as standing arraigned because of the blood-guiltiness of those who have committed murder in my country. I need not go into the details. But I am going to speak to you as a woman about the wrongs committed against my sisters. Englishmen, you who pride yourselves upon your chivalry, you who hold more precious than your imperial treasures the honor and chastity of your women, will you sit still and leave unavenged the dishonour, and the insult and agony inflicted upon the veiled women of the Punjab?

The minions of Lord Chelmsford, the Viceroy, and his martial authorities rent the veil from the faces of the women of the Punjab. Not only were men mown down as if they were grass that is born to wither; but they tore asunder the cherished Purdah, the innermost privacy of the chaste womanhood of India. My sisters were stripped naked, they were flogged, they were outraged. These policies left your British democracy betrayed, dishonored, for no dishonor clings to the martyrs who suffered, but to the tyrants who inflicted the tyranny and pain. Should they hold their Empire by dishonoring the women of another nation or lose it out of the chivalry for their honor and chastity? The Bible asked, "What shall it profit a man to gain the whole world and lose his own soul?" You deserve no Empire. You have lost your soul; you have the stain of blood-guiltiness upon you; no nation that rules by tyranny is free; it is the slave of its own despotism.

Document 5

Source: Taha Hussein, Muslim literary figure and Egyptian nationalist, *The Future of Culture in Egypt,* 1938.

Now that we have succeeded in restoring the honor and self-respect that come with independence, it is our plain duty to protect what we have won. We must rear a generation of Egyptian youth who will never know the humiliation and shame that was the lot of their fathers. Some Egyptians object to Europeanization on the grounds that it threatens our national personality and glorious heritage. I do not naturally advocate rejection of the past or loss of identity in the Europeans;… the only time that we might have been absorbed by Europe was when we were extremely weak, ignorant, and possessed of the notion that the hat was superior to the turban and the fez because it always covered a more distinguished head!... Although great powers imposed their will on us for many centuries, they were unable to destroy our personality. I am merely asking that the preservatives of defense, religion, language, art, and history be strengthened by the adoption of Western techniques and ideas.

Document 6

Source: Preamble to the Constitution of the Kingdom of Egypt, 1923.

We, the King of Egypt,

Having, since mounting the throne of our ancestors and vowing to keep safe the trust which God Almighty has entrusted to us, always done our utmost to pursue the good of our nation, and pursue the path which we know will lead to its welfare and advancement and to deriving the enjoyments of free and civilized nations;

And since such end cannot be properly attained unless in a constitutional system similar to the most advanced constitutional systems in the world, under which our nation can happily and satisfactorily live and pursue the path of an absolutely free life, and which ensures active participation in running state affairs and overseeing the drafting and enforcement of laws, and brings a sense of comfort and assurance about our nation's present and future, while maintaining the national qualities and distinctions which constitute the great historical heritage thereof;

And as the fulfillment of such end has constantly been our desire and one of the greatest endeavors we are determined to seek so as to help our People's rise to the highest of standards which the People is readily qualified and capable of meeting, which befit the ancient historical greatness of our People, and which enable our People to attain the appropriate status among peoples of civilized nations…

Document 7

Source: Female nationalist protesters in Cairo, Egypt, 1919.

Summary

- The DBQ is the first part of Section II of the exam. It is worth 25% of your total score.

- On the new AP World History Exam, you have a total of 60 minutes to write this essay: 15 minutes for reading and planning your essay, and 45 minutes for writing it. Remember to pace yourself and be mindful of the time.

- The 15-minute reading period is not mandatory, and you can begin writing your essay before the 15 minutes are up. However, we recommend you use the full time alloted. A well-planned essay is much easier to write.

- The DBQ directions will tell you exactly what your essay needs to do in order to get full credit. Be familiar with these directions before you sit down to take the test. This way, you won't need to waste any time reading the directions on exam day. Still, we recommend you give them a scan just to make sure that they align with the directions you've been practicing with.

- Make sure your essay has a clear thesis statement, which should be in the first paragraph. This thesis statement is the basis of your argument; the goal of the essay is to "prove" that argument using the documents and outside evidence.

- Use as many documents as possible. In a DBQ that contains seven documents, you should incorporate six into your response. And don't simply mention the document; you need to explain it and use it to support or qualify your argument in some way in order to get full credit.

- Don't forget about outside evidence! The AP essay graders want to see a firm grasp of the material and an ability to connect the documents to other historical events and topics you've learned about in class.

Chapter 4
How to Approach
the Long Essay

OVERVIEW OF THE LONG ESSAY

Part B of Section II contains the long essay question. You will be given three essay prompts, and you must choose ONE to answer. These prompts may take the form of a historical statement or stance, which you must then support, modify, or refute in a written essay. As with the DBQ, you are required to develop and defend a relevant thesis. Many of the outlining approaches for the DBQ described in the previous chapter are also applicable for this essay. However, unlike the DBQ, the long essay does not include documents; your essay will instead be based entirely on your knowledge of AP World History and the themes and concepts discussed in your class. You will have 40 minutes to write this essay, which constitutes 15% of your total score.

A simple, defendable thesis accompanied by an organized essay that effectively analyzes the given subject should result in a high score. Do not write an essay that is simply descriptive, in which you regurgitate everything you know about the topic of the essay prompt. Purely descriptive essays rarely get a top score, as they usually fail to analyze, assess, and evaluate the historical issue or topic. Here is an example of a set of long essay questions:

> **Question 2:** Using specific examples, compare and contrast the relationships the Roman Empire had with various religious groups between 100 B.C.E. and 400 C.E.

> **Question 3:** Using specific examples, analyze continuities and changes in the dynamics of trade between China and other nations from 600 C.E. to 1500 C.E.

> **Question 4:** Using specific examples, evaluate the relationships between the upper and lower classes in Europe from 1700 C.E. to the present.

As you can see, long essay questions are designed to prompt analysis and evaluation of subject matter that you have learned in class. The subjects should be familiar, and the questions are straightforward. The highest score you can earn on the long essay is 6 points. On the following page you'll find the scoring rubric, which you can also download from the College Board website.

Quick Note
On Section II of the exam, many students are tempted to ease up by the time they get to the long essay, or they invest all of their time in the DBQ because there's a lot of planning involved. Do not make this mistake. Reach down for the last bit of energy and finish strong!

Check for Exam Updates
While preparing for the AP World History Exam, it's important to check the College Board website regularly for test updates, including changes to the exam format and scoring.

How the Long Essay Is Scored

The long essay is graded on a 6-point scale. Here's how those points are earned.

Task	Points Possible	Description
Thesis/Claim	1 point	To earn this point, the thesis must make a claim that responds to the prompt (rather than restating or rephrasing the prompt) with a historically defensible thesis/claim that establishes a line of reasoning. The thesis must consist of one or more sentences located in one place, either in the introduction or the conclusion.
Contextualization	1 point	To earn this point, the response must relate the topic of the prompt to broader historical events, developments, or processes that occur before, during, or continue after the time frame of the question. This point is not awarded for merely a phrase or reference.
Evidence	2 points	To earn **1 point,** the response must identify specific historical examples of evidence relevant to the topic of the prompt. To earn **2 points,** the response must use specific and relevant examples of historical evidence to support an argument in response to the prompt.
Analysis and Reasoning	2 points	To earn the **first point,** the response must demonstrate the use of historical reasoning (e.g., comparison, causation, and change and/or continuity over time) to frame or structure and argument, although the reasoning might be uneven or imbalanced. To earn the **second point,** a response must demonstrate a complex understanding of the historical development that is the focus of the prompt, using evidence. This can be accomplished in in a variety of ways, such as: • Explaining nuance of an issue by analyzing multiple variables • Explaining both similarity and difference, or explaining both continuity and change, or explaining multiple causes, or explaining both cause and effect • Explaining relevant and insightful connections within and across periods • Confirming the validity of an argument by corroborating multiple perspectives across themes • Qualifying or modifying an argument by considering diverse or alternative views or evidence This understanding must be part of the argument, not merely a phrase or reference.

As you may have noticed, the long essay question is asking you to do many of the same tasks as the DBQ, just without the documents. AP graders want to see you make a thesis or claim, support that claim using historical evidence, and connect the historical issue with other developments in world history.

Choose to answer the question that you can write the most about. The more you know about the subject, the more you can say about it, and the better your essay score will be.

How to Write the Essays

We outlined a plan for writing longer essays in the previous chapter on the DBQ. These same directions apply here, though you will not need to worry about analyzing or incorporating specific documents into your response. As a refresher, here are the steps for structuring your essay:

1. Read the question and analyze it. Circle or underline important words and phrases in the question.

2. Create a grid or table in which to plan your essays and take notes.

3. Assess all of your notes and, based on that information, formulate a thesis statement.

4. Write a quick outline. Remember, you have only 40 minutes for the long essay question, so your outline should be brief. Write just enough so that you have a general idea of how your argument will be organized.

5. Write the essay.

Summary

- The long essay question is the last section of the test. You will be given three questions, and you must choose ONE to answer.

- Analyze the question you choose. Circle and/or underline important words and phrases. Once you understand the question, create a grid or columns in which to organize your notes on the essay.

- Formulate a thesis; then write an outline for your essay.

- Follow your outline (which should be brief, as you only have 40 minute for this essay). Stick to one important idea per paragraph. Support your ideas with historical evidence.

- Write clearly and neatly. Do not write in overly complex sentences. Toss in a couple of "big" words that you know you will not misuse. When in doubt, stick to simple syntax and vocabulary.

- Use transition words to indicate continuity of thought and changes in the direction of your argument.

Chapter 5
Using Time
Effectively to
Maximize Points

BECOMING A BETTER TEST TAKER

Very few students stop to think about how to improve their test-taking skills. Most assume that if they study hard, they will test well, and if they do not study, they will do poorly. Most students continue to believe this even after experience teaches them otherwise. Have you ever studied really hard for an exam, then blown it on test day? Have you ever aced an exam for which you thought you weren't well prepared? Most students have had one, if not both, of these experiences. The lesson should be clear: Factors other than your level of preparation influence your final test score. This chapter will provide you with some insights that will help you perform better on the AP World History Exam and on other exams as well.

PACING AND TIMING

A big part of scoring well on an exam is working at a consistent pace. The worst mistake made by inexperienced or unsavvy test takers is that they come to a question that stumps them, and, rather than just skip it, they panic and stall. Time stands still when you're working on a question you cannot answer, and it is not unusual for students to waste five minutes on a single question (especially a question involving a graph or the word EXCEPT) because they are too stubborn to cut their losses. It is important to be aware of how much time you have spent on a given question and on the section you are working. There are several ways to improve your pacing and timing for the test:

- **Know your average pace.** While you prepare for the multiple-choice section of the exam, try to gauge how long you take on 5, 10, or 20 questions. Knowing how long you spend on average per question will help you identify how many questions you can answer effectively and how best to pace yourself for the test.

- **Have a watch or clock nearby.** You are permitted to have a watch or clock nearby to help you keep track of time. It is important to remember however that constantly checking the clock is in itself a waste of time and can be distracting. Devise a plan. Try checking the clock after every 15 or 30 questions to see if you are keeping the correct pace or whether you need to speed up; this will ensure that your cognizant of the time but will not permit you to fall into the trap of dwelling on it.

- **Know when to move on.** Since all questions are scored equally, investing appreciable amounts of time on a single question is inefficient and can potentially deprive you of the chance to answer easier questions later on. If you are able to eliminate answer choices, do so, but don't worry about picking a random answer and moving on if you cannot find the correct answer. Remember, tests are like marathons; you do best when you work through them at a steady pace. You can always come back to a question you don't know. When you do, very often you will find that your previous mental block is gone, and you will wonder why the question perplexed you the first time around (as you gleefully move on to the next question). Even if you still don't know the answer, you will not have wasted valuable time you could have spent on easier questions.

- **Be selective.** You don't have to do any of the questions in a given section in order. If you are stumped by an essay or multiple-choice question, skip it or choose a different one. In the section below, you will see that you may not have to answer every question correctly to achieve your desired score. Select the questions or essays that you can answer and work on them first. This will make you more efficient and give you the greatest chance of getting the most questions correct.

- **Use Process of Elimination on multiple-choice questions.** Many times, one or more answer choices can be eliminated. Every answer choice that can be eliminated increases the odds that you will answer the question correctly. Review Chapter 1 and make sure you're completely familiar with all the strategies you can use to find these incorrect answer choices and increase your odds of getting the question correct.

Remember, when all the questions on a test are of equal value, no one question is that important, your overall goal for pacing is to get the most questions correct. Finally, you should set a realistic goal for your final score.

Keep Calm

Trying to relax and de-stress isn't important only on test day; it's also necessary for your test prep! As you work your way through this book, be sure to take intermittent study breaks to help yourself unwind and then refocus.

TEST ANXIETY

Everybody experiences anxiety before and during an exam. To a certain extent, test anxiety can be helpful. Some people find that they perform more quickly and efficiently under stress. If you have ever pulled an all-nighter to write a paper and ended up doing good work, you know the feeling.

However, too much stress is definitely a bad thing. Hyperventilating during the test, for example, almost always leads to a lower score. If you find that you stress out during exams, here are a few preemptive actions you can take.

- **Take a reality check.** Evaluate your situation before the test begins. If you have studied hard, remind yourself that you are well prepared. Remember that many others taking the test are not as well prepared, and (in your classes, at least) you are being graded against them, so you have an advantage. If you didn't study, accept the fact that you will probably not ace the test. Make sure you get to every question you know something about. Don't stress out or fixate on how much you don't know. Your job is to score as high as you can by maximizing the benefits of what you do know. In either scenario, it is best to think of a test as if it were a game. How can you get the most points in the time allotted to you? Always answer questions you can answer easily and quickly before you answer those that will take more time.

- **Try to relax.** Slow, deep breathing works for almost everyone. Close your eyes, take a few, slow, deep breaths, and concentrate on nothing but your inhalation and exhalation for a few seconds. This is a basic form of meditation, and it should help you to clear your mind of stress and, as a result, concentrate better on the test. If you have ever taken yoga classes, you probably know some other good relaxation techniques. Use them when you can (obviously, anything that requires leaving your seat and, say, assuming a handstand position won't be allowed by any but the most free-spirited proctors).

- **Eliminate as many surprises as you can.** Make sure you know where the test will be given, when it starts, what type of questions are going to be asked, and how long the test will take. You don't want to be worrying about any of these things on test day or, even worse, after the test has already begun.

The best way to avoid stress is to study both the test material and the test itself. Congratulations! By buying or reading this book, you are taking a major step toward a stress-free AP World History Exam.

REFLECT

Respond to the following questions:

- How long will you spend on multiple-choice questions?

- How will you change your approach to multiple-choice questions?

- What is your multiple-choice guessing strategy?

- How much time will you spend on the short-answer questions?

- How much time will you spend on the DBQ? The long essay question?

- What will you do before you begin writing an essay?

- How will you change your approach to the essays?

- Will you seek further help outside of this book (such as a teacher, tutor, or AP Students) on how to approach multiple-choice questions, the essays, or a pacing strategy?

Part V
Content Review for the AP World History Exam

HOW TO USE THIS BOOK TO TAKE ON THE WORLD

Now that you know the kinds of questions to expect on the AP World History Exam, you're ready to take on the world!—or at least the review of AP World History. Part V of this book is designed to maximize your AP World History review. Here's how it is organized:

As you read these content chapters, remember to underline key ideas or jot down notes in the margins. Remembering the key events and issues that took place during pivotal moments in history will help you when it comes to the source-based questions on the exam, which test your ability to tie a specific piece of evidence to a larger historical idea or theme.

- **Six Periods, Six Chapters.** The AP World History Exam divides world history into six distinct time periods, as we discussed in Part III. For ease of use, we have split our world history content review into these exact periods. Chapters 6 and 7 cover the first two Periods of AP World History as outlined by the College Board.

- **Get the Big Picture.** Each chapter begins with a "Stay Focused on the Big Picture" section so that you will—you guessed it—stay focused on the big picture while you review. To do well on this test, you're going to need to demonstrate that you not only have specific knowledge of people and events, but also that you understand how historical issues and events are connected. You'll also need to be able to think (and write) about concepts with a wide-angle lens, as well as use primary and secondary sources to investigate and analyze historical concepts and issues.

- **Make Those Connections.** Each chapter reviews the salient points of that period; the Compare Them, Contrast Them, Note the Change, and Focus On boxes help you make connections between different societies (that's the whole point of this test, remember?).

- **Pull It All Together.** Each chapter ends with a "Pulling It All Together" section to once again help you focus on the major points of the period.

KNOW WHERE YOU ARE IN THE WORLD

The AP World History Exam frequently refers to cultural regions of the world. So it is important to know where you are! The following map shows you the most commonly defined regions. Be aware that they don't always match up with physical boundaries. For example, parts of North Africa may be included when we're talking about the Middle East, and sub-Saharan Africa and Southeast Asia may be considered part of the Islamic world.

While You Read

Geographic Regions of the World

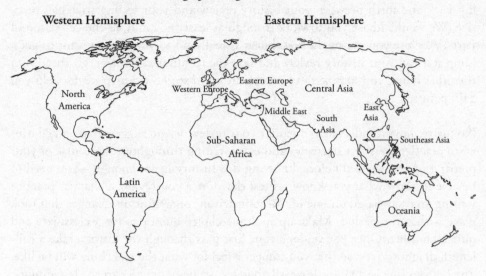

HOW TO GET THE MOST OUT OF YOUR REVIEW

Here's what we suggest. Read through each chapter once. You'll probably remember most of the people, places, events, and concepts from your AP class. The chapters will help you review and pull together the major points. This part won't be as detailed as the book from your AP class, or else this book would be as thick as your textbook, which would be kind of pointless. As you read through each chapter, consult your textbook if you've forgotten something entirely. After you finish going through a chapter once, spend some time in your AP textbook (or another world history source) going over the stuff you either didn't know or didn't remember. Then go back to the chapter to do mini-reviews of certain areas and to focus on the big-picture concepts and connections taking place in that period.

No, After You

It does not matter in which order you choose to review the material. If you love the Renaissance and hate the Middle Ages, review Chapter 9 first and Chapter 8 later. If you know that your knowledge of the Foundations era is lacking but you are pretty confident in what you know about recent history, dive into Chapter 6 first. This review is meant to be dynamic—we expect that you will return to it repeatedly as you prepare for your exam.

**Noticing Themes >
Memorizing Dates**
The chapters that follow are filled with tons of dates, people, place names, events, and more. It can seem overwhelming, but remember that you do not need to memorize every fact about World History in order to do well on the exam. Instead, try to think conceptually about each era: what changed and what stayed the same? Pay attention to trends as well as cause-and-effect relationships between historical events.

In addition, as we mentioned in the introduction to this book, you may wish to flip back and forth between your history review and your testing strategies practice. We would advise you to work through at least the multiple-choice section of Part IV before you get to the test, but it is really up to you. If you want to get a jump start on your history review and save the techniques for later, go ahead. On the other hand, you may wish to mix them up to see how our strategies help you gain points.

No matter how you decide to organize your review, we do suggest that you continue to practice your test strategies and essay writing throughout the course of your preparation. As we said before, knowing this history is not enough—you need to be able to show what you know on test day. Once you review a chapter, practice writing an essay based on one of the comparisons or significant changes that took place within the period. Make up multiple-choice questions for a classmate and quiz each other. Once you've done your first pass through the history, take a full-length diagnostic test so that you can get a feel for what the real thing will be like. The bottom line is: Do not leave all your test strategy practice to the last minute. Instead, use that practice to enhance your history review and zero in on the key concepts of each period.

Let the review begin...

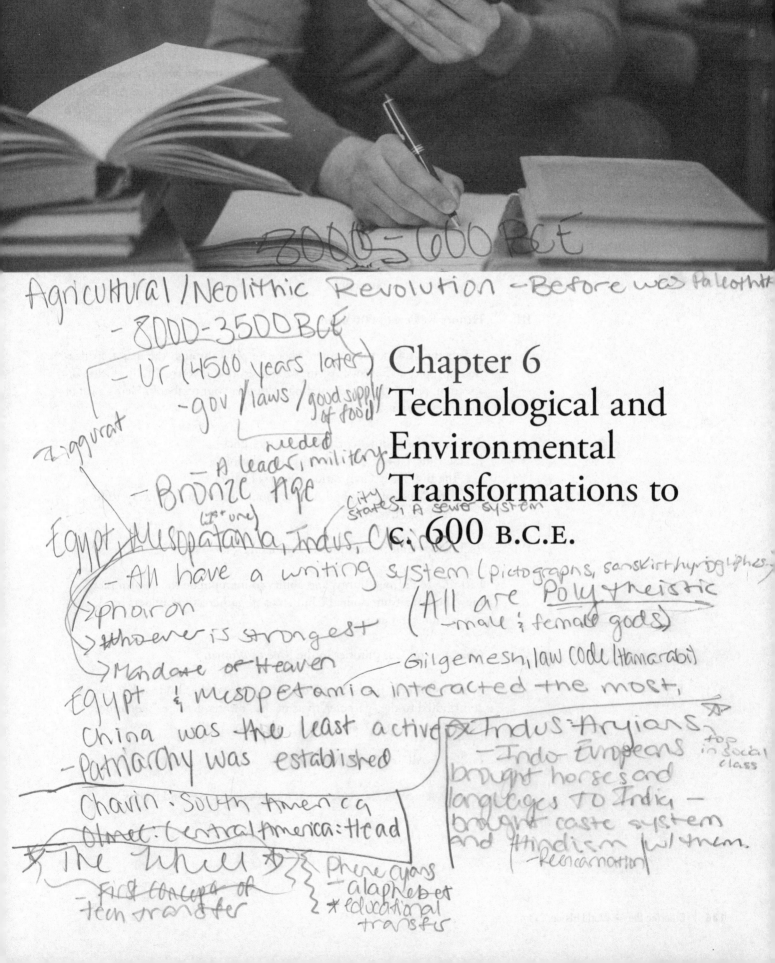

8000-600 BCE

Chapter 6
Technological and Environmental Transformations to c. 600 B.C.E.

Agricultural / Neolithic Revolution - Before was Paleolithic
- 8000-3500 BCE
  - Ur (4500 years later)
    - gov / laws / good supply of food
      - needed
    - A leader, military
  - Bronze Age
    - (1st one)
  - ziggurat

City states, A sewer system

Egypt, Mesopotamia, Indus, China
- All have a writing system (pictographs, sanskirt, hyrioglyphes
  - (All are Polytheistic
    - male & female gods)
→ pharoh
→ whoever is strongest
→ Mandate of Heaven   - Gilgemesh, law code (Hamarabi)
Egypt & Mesopetamia interacted the most,
china was the least active ☆ Indus=Aryians ☆
- Patriarchy was established   top in social class
                                      - Indo-Europeans
    Chavin: South America   brought horses and
    Olmec: Central America: Head   languages to India -
                                      brought caste system
☆ The Wheel ☆   Phenecians   and Hindism (w/ them.
  - First concept of - alaphabet   - Reincarnation
  tech transfer   ☆ educational
                        transfer

For more AP World History prep, check out *ASAP World History*, our visual, class-notes-style guide to the most important concepts you need to know for the exam. Use that book alongside this one to get the most out of your prep!

Handwritten margin notes:

PERSIA charts for all

- 8000 BCE – 6,000 BCE
  - River Civ – Indus, Egypt, Meso, China (shang, zhou), (Olmec, Chavin)
- 600 – 600
  - Classical civ: Persia, Roman, Greek, Gupta, China (Qin, Han), Mayan. — Important
- Agricultural Rev/Neolithic
  - 8000–3500
  - wheat, barley, Rex
  - Paleolithic (Before it)
  - Indo-European
- Aryan Invasions
  - Happened everywhere
  - Impacted India – Hinduism
  - Horses and Language
- Bantu Migration
  - Language, cattle, iron

I. CHAPTER OVERVIEW

There's a lot of stuff in this chapter, so before you begin, read through the outline below so you'll know where to find what you're looking for when you return to this chapter for a mini-review. (Remember, the key to doing well is to go through the chapter once, delve into the areas you are clueless or semi-clueless about, then return here for a mini-review.)

I.   Chapter Overview

     You're reading it!

II. Stay Focused on the Big Picture

     Organize the zillions of facts from the era covered in this chapter into some big-picture concepts.

III. History Review to 600 B.C.E.

     This is the bulk of the chapter, where we plow through the major civilizations, people, and events. Again, we suggest that if you're totally clueless on a section, review the corresponding section in your textbook. Here's a list of the major sections.

     A. Nomads: Following the Paleo(lithic) Diet
     B. Settling Down: The Neolithic Revolution
     C. The Big, Early Civilizations: Rivers Deliver
     D. Early Mesoamerica and Andean South America: For Every Rule There's an Exception

IV. Technology and Innovations to 600 B.C.E.

     Farming tools, metallurgy, and ability to manipulate the environment move humans from nomadic hunters and gatherers to builders of civilizations and empires

V.   Changes and Continuities in the Role of Women

     Women not only birthed, raised, and socialized the children but also contributed to the "gatherer" part of the "hunter-gatherer" equation, which was no small feat.

VI. Pulling It All Together

     A quick review of the review that focuses on themes and trends

II. STAY FOCUSED ON THE BIG PICTURE

As you review the details of the ancient civilizations in this chapter, stay focused on some big-picture concepts, including the following:

1. What are civilizations all about? Think about what makes a civilization a civilization in the first place. As you read through this chapter, we'll give you some ideas. Focus on things like the existence and development of cities, formal institutions (including political, economic, and religious), different social levels and occupations, the use of technology (we're not talking the Internet here, but basic and hugely important things such as wheels and weapons), the arts, and methods of communication and transportation.

2. How does change occur within a society? When change occurs, think about what caused it. Sometimes a society changed because it was exposed to a different way of doing things when it interacted with another culture (an effect that is sometimes called cultural diffusion). Other times a society changed because its members invented something new, or realized how to use something in a new way. Always pay attention to why things changed in a particular society or civilization.

3. How are people impacted by, and how do they impact, geography and climate? Focus on the interaction between people and nature. We'll draw your attention to this issue constantly in this chapter. Geography and climate help to explain where people live and build cities, why people suddenly move from one place to another, and how early civilizations chose to defend themselves against attack. They also greatly influenced which civilizations interacted with, or were isolated from, other civilizations. But people also use technology to impact their surroundings. Civilizations change the landscape by diverting water, moving natural resources, and building transportation networks. Nature impacts people; people impact nature. It's a great, big complicated cycle…that's why the AP people love to talk about it so much.

III. HISTORY REVIEW TO 600 B.C.E.

Historians (and the College Board) use periods of time to organize history. Be aware that not everything will fit neatly into a predetermined period, but we'll try to group events.

The first period we will look at is defined by the fact that everything that happened in these years sets the stage or provides the foundation for what happens later. This period is marked by some major changes: Nomadic movements and migration, figuring out farming and what happens when there actually is enough to eat, early settlers and civilizations, and the expansion and contraction of civilizations. Not bad for one chapter, huh?

R. 12 tables;
P Republic/ P Mandate of heaven
Empire
E Silk Road, E Silk Road
Med, India or tr
R Polytheistic R Confucianism
& Christian Doaism
S pottor S phalial piety
familias
I Olive I Silk
oil +
wine
A callicium A Great wall
Roads
n guidcups
cement

G. P Ashoka

E Silk Road, Indian Ocean
traded: Spices

R Hinduism, Poly

S Caste system

I Spices

A pillers of Ashoka

A. Nomads: Following the Paleo(lithic) Diet

Imagine early people. Really early people. They hadn't yet built cities. They didn't know how to farm. Their sole focus in life was to satisfy their most basic needs: shelter and food. Because they didn't have any advanced tools and hadn't yet developed anything as sophisticated as farming, the best way for them to get shelter was to find it, and the best way to get food was to follow it.

This was the Paleolithic Period, and it was marked mostly by the use of stone tools. You won't be asked a lot of questions about nomadic societies. However, you do need to understand why the development of more stable civilizations (which you will be asked a lot of questions about) was so significant, and the best way to do that is to learn what came before them. As you review world history before the Neolithic Revolution, focus only on the major developments. During this time period, those include the development of spoken language, the ability to control and use fire, and the ability to make simple tools out of stone.

Foraging Societies: Hunting and Gathering

Foraging societies (hunter-gatherer clans) were composed of small groups of people who traveled from point to point as the climate and availability of plants and animals dictated. Because they depended on nature for sustenance, they were also at the mercy of nature. Climate changes, disease, famine, and natural disasters could endanger or eliminate entire communities. Even when times were good, foraging societies were limited by the capacity of their surroundings, and by their inability to store food long-term. Members of these societies did not build permanent shelters and had only a few personal belongings. Think about how much you can carry in your backpack: That will give you an idea how many possessions they had.

Pastoral Societies: Taming the Animals

Pastoral societies were characterized by the domestication of animals. These societies were often found in mountainous regions and in areas with insufficient rainfall to support other forms of settlement. Many of these societies used small-scale agriculture to supplement the main food supply of animal products (usually milk or eggs, which were much easier to produce and store than meat). The extended family was a major institution. Women had very few rights; however, these societies were more egalitarian than those that came later. Stratification and social status, which were limited in foraging societies, were based on the size of one's herd in pastoral societies. But as in foraging societies, people in pastoral societies had few personal possessions. Even though they had domesticated animals (as opposed to having to hunt for animals), they didn't settle down in towns because they had to continually search for new grazing areas and water for the herds.

As pastoral societies increasingly domesticated more and more animals, they also began to experiment with securing a more dependable food supply through the cultivation of plants. This was a revolutionary development that led to…

B. Settling Down: The Neolithic Revolution

Agricultural Societies: This Is My Land

In a span of several thousand years from approximately 8000 B.C.E. to 3000 B.C.E., groups of people moved from nomadic lifestyles to agricultural lifestyles and town and city life. This transition period is often called the **Neolithic ("New Stone") Revolution** or the **Agricultural Revolution**. Keep in mind that we still aren't talking about full-blown civilizations. People still lived in relatively small, independent groups or communities. To be sure, the towns and cities that they built were bigger than anything else that came before them, but civilizations on a grand scale didn't get rolling until around 3000 B.C.E., give or take a few centuries, depending on the region of the world.

Here's how it worked: When people figured out how to cultivate plants, they could stay in the same place, as long as there was good soil and a stable source of water. Because they also knew how to domesticate animals and use simple tools, they could rely on a relatively varied and constant supply of food, and this encouraged them to stay in the same place for longer periods of time.

Staying in the same place changed things dramatically, because people in a community stayed within close proximity of each other, which added to their sense of unity and helped them build and sustain cultural traditions. What's more, unlike nomadic societies, agricultural communities were not just collections of people, but people tied to a particular piece of land. In other words, they began to think of property in terms of ownership.

Important Consequence of Agriculture: A Food Surplus

Imagine two people who only grow enough food for themselves. They both have to farm all day every day. There's little time left to do anything else. Now imagine that one person farms enough food for two people. The second person can do something else, say, make tools or dig an irrigation ditch or study to become a philosopher or religious leader. Now imagine that one person can farm enough food for five people, or ten people, or a hundred people. Now the other ninety-nine people can build towns, organize armies, develop a system of writing, create art, experiment, and discover new technologies. In other words, individual labor becomes specialized. Each person can get really good at doing a particular task because he or she no longer has to worry about where the next meal is coming from.

Contrast Them: Nomadic Versus Agricultural Societies

The difference between nomadic and agricultural societies is about more than just moving around versus staying put. It also involves emotional and psychological issues. Think about it this way: When you and everybody else are on the move a lot, the land more or less belongs to everybody. But when people stay in the same place for generations, they begin to think of the particular piece of land that they live on as home—*their* home. If someone else comes along and drinks from their river or builds a house on *their* hill, they might begin to think of the newcomers as intruders or invaders, not as neighbors. Once nomads started interacting with sedentary societies through trade or conflicts, things started to get complicated.

As agricultural societies became more complex, organized economies, governmental structures, and religious organizations began to emerge to keep things as predictable and orderly as possible. Suddenly, there was society, or the beginnings of what we'd call a civilization.

With the invention of irrigation techniques, lands that previously couldn't be farmed could be used for additional surpluses. This would lead to more growth and complexity, which would lead to more agricultural advancements, which would lead to more growth and complexity, and so on.

Focus On: What Contributes to the Development of a Civilization?

Specialization of labor is key. If everyone has to farm to have enough food, a great civilization won't develop. If a certain number of farmers can provide a surplus of food, then other people in the community are free to build, invent, and create tools, art, and institutions.

Impact of Agriculture on the Environment

There's no question that the Agricultural Revolution had an impact on the environment. Farming villages began to dramatically change the lay of the land by diverting water, clearing land for farming, and creating farmland where none previously existed. As villages grew into more permanent towns and cities, roads were built to link them, further altering the landscape. Stones were unearthed and cut to build increasingly large buildings and monuments. All of this activity led to a world in which land and resources were continually being reconfigured to fit the needs of growing, geographically stable populations.

What's more, the impact on the animal kingdom was equally momentous. With the development of large-scale agriculture, animals began to be used not only as a source of food and clothing, but also as a direct source of agricultural labor. For example, oxen were used to pull plows on ever-expanding farmland. This enabled farmers to increase the size of their fields dramatically because they no longer had to turn the soil by hand.

Technology: Metal Workers Deserve Medals

If there had been a stock market for new technologies in the Neolithic Era, it would have attracted many investors. During this period, hard stones such as granite were sharpened and formed into farming tools such as hoes and plows. Pottery was made to use for cooking. Weaving was invented to shape baskets and nets; more complex and comfortable clothing was designed. Eventually, wheels were invented for use on carts, and sails for use on boats. The list goes on and on.

But perhaps one of the most significant advances of the Neolithic Era was the knowledge of how to use metals. This greatly advanced the development of not only tools, but also weapons. When people figured out how to combine copper with tin to create an even harder metal, bronze, the building of civilizations was well on its way. This development was so significant that some people call the latter part of the Neolithic Era the **Bronze Age**. Bronze was superseded by the discovery of iron, but more on that later.

C. The Big, Early Civilizations: The Rivers Deliver

Most of the world's early great civilizations were located in **river valleys**. Think about it. Rivers provided a regular supply of water, which is, of course, necessary for survival. Also important is that the lowlands around rivers tend to be covered with soil that is loaded with nutrients, which are deposited when the river recedes after floods to nourish the soil. The river itself may be home to animals and plants that could also provide food for people. Rivers were also a vital means of transportation.

When we talk about civilizations, we're talking about large areas of land with large populations and distinct, organized cultures, as opposed to the smaller farming communities that characterized earlier time periods. Pay attention to the social, political, and economic developments of the civilizations in this section: These developments are what made them civilizations in the first place.

A piece of advice: Do not assume that all civilizations were headed by a central authority. Many early civilizations, in fact, were composed of loosely connected city-states, which were made up of an urban center and the agricultural land around it under its control. These city-states were sometimes combined into one because they shared common cultural characteristics; but they were also independent of each other in many ways and often competed with each other. This is true in modern times as well, of course. When we speak of Western civilization, for example, we mean a whole host of countries that have similar characteristics and cultures but that are distinct from one another and, often, compete with one another.

Major early civilizations developed and became dominant starting at around 3000 to 2000 B.C.E. They were located in Mesopotamia, Egypt, India, and China.

Mesopotamia: Lots of Water, Lots of History

Mesopotamia literally means "between the rivers"; the rivers were the **Tigris** and the **Euphrates**. A series of ancient civilizations—most notably Sumer, Babylon, and Persia—thrived along their banks. Mesopotamia is part of a larger area of relatively arable land known as the Fertile Crescent, which extends westward from Mesopotamia toward the Mediterranean.

Unfortunately, the flooding of the Tigris and Euphrates Rivers was very unpredictable, so some early settlements were frequently washed away. But soon people learned to build canals and dikes, and began to build their towns farther uphill, enabling large city-states to emerge. By 3000 B.C.E., Ur, Erech, and Kish were the major city-states of the first major civilization of Sumer.

Sumer: The First Major Mesopotamian Civilization

Sumerian civilization rose in the southern part of Mesopotamia. In addition to successful agriculture and river management, the Sumerians developed a form of writing known as **cuneiform**. Scribes used this form of writing to set down laws, treaties, and important social and religious customs; soon the use of cuneiform spread over the trade routes to many other parts of the region. Trade was also enhanced by the introduction of the wheel, a major development that greatly reduced the time it took to transport both goods and people between two points.

Sumerians also developed a twelve-month **calendar** and a mathematical system based on units of sixty (as in sixty seconds and three-hundred-sixty degrees). They also used geometry to survey the land and to develop architectural enhancements such as arches and columns.

Sumerians were **polytheistic**, meaning that they worshipped more than one god. The interesting thing about Sumerian polytheism was that each city-state had its own god that was worshipped only by its people. In addition, there were a bunch of gods that all the city-states worshipped collectively. Sumerians built temples, called **ziggurats**, which were terraced pyramids, to appease their gods. They believed that when disaster struck—such as a particularly devastating flood—it was because the gods were angry. Disaster often struck; no temple could stop the relentless flow of invasions of Sumeria. And by around 1700 B.C.E., the civilization had been completely overthrown; however, its conquerors adopted many Sumerian traditions and technologies.

From Sumer to Babylon to Nineveh to Babylon

As the Sumerian city-states declined, the city of Akkad, which was north of Sumer, rose to dominate the region. The Akkadians' major contribution was the first known code of laws, written in cuneiform, which they learned from the Sumerians. But by 1700 B.C.E., Akkad was overrun by a new powerhouse in Mesopotamia, **Babylon**. King Hammurabi of Babylon expanded on this idea of a code of laws by developing an extensive code that dealt with every part of daily life. **The Code of Hammurabi**, as it has come to be called, is often credited as a significant step toward our modern legal codes. It distinguished between major and minor offenses (a big deal at the time) and it established a sense of justice and fairness by applying the laws to nearly everyone (the beginnings of "rule of law").

But Babylon quickly fell due to the invasions of the Kassites and then the **Hittites**. By 1500 B.C.E., the Hittites dominated the region, especially because they learned how to use iron in their weapons. Because iron is a lot stronger than bronze, the Hittites quickly became a military superpower.

As you've no doubt figured out by now, news spread quickly even in ancient civilizations. As soon as one civilization figured out a new way to do something, the information was passed via the trade routes to other groups, who would quickly adopt and adapt the new technology to suit their cultures. In this way, within a hundred years, the **Assyrians** had learned to use iron, the very technology the Hittites had used to defeat them. This enabled the Assyrians to establish a capital at Nineveh and eventually build an empire that swept across the entire Fertile Crescent. Highly disciplined but cruel, the Assyrian army was hated by those it conquered. As a result, there were frequent uprisings against the Assyrian authorities, who, in response, sent large groups of people into exile. This action also played a part in enhancing cultural diffusion across the entire region and beyond.

In spite of their power, within a few hundred years the Assyrians were defeated by the Medes and the Chaldeans. The Chaldean king, **Nebuchadnezzar**, rebuilt Babylon as a showplace of architecture and culture. He extended his empire throughout the Fertile Crescent, as the Assyrians had done before him. But like all the civilizations before it, the new Babylon was doomed to fall. A new civilization, the **Persian Empire**, developed into a major world force.

Focus On: Continuity Through Change

Focus On: Continuity Through Change
You probably won't need to know specifics about the long list of civilizations that emerged one after the other in Mesopotamia in the centuries between the Sumerian and Persian Empires. However, the Code of Hammurabi and the growing use of iron are both pretty big developments. That said, we've given you a quick review because it is essential that you understand that as civilizations were conquered, their cultural heritage, religions, laws, customs, and technologies were rarely lost. Commonly, conquering civilizations adopted and adapted the customs and technologies of those they defeated. The series of civilizations that grew and then fell in Mesopotamia demonstrates this point well.

Ancient Egypt: Stay Awhile Along the Nile

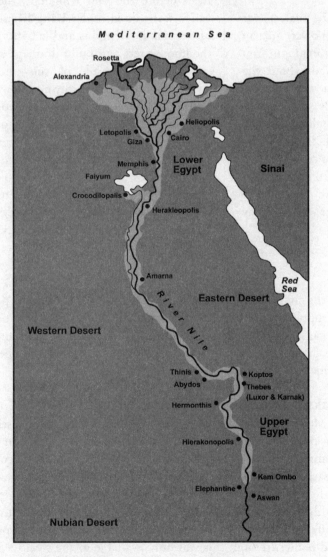

The Egyptian Empire (1450 B.C.E.)

The ancient **Egyptian civilization** developed along the Nile River, where the soil was rich and the agricultural opportunities were plentiful. The Nile cuts through an otherwise arid landscape, so the people clustered along the riverbanks, where, in addition to farms, they constructed towns and cities. Though we often think of ancient Egypt in terms of massive construction projects, such as the pyramids, most Egyptians lived in smaller towns. Unlike the Tigris and Euphrates Rivers, the Nile floods at a predictable time of the year and in relatively predictable stages. This made it possible for the ancient Egyptians to follow a very stable agricultural cycle and compile substantial food surpluses.

Three Kingdoms, One Civilization

You might remember from your studies that, as various dynasties rose to and fell from power, ancient Egypt was reorganized into different kingdoms. You don't need to remember all the details about the many kingdoms, but you should know that there were three major ones—Old, Middle, and New—and that it was during the New Kingdom that the ancient Egyptian civilization reached its height. By 1400 B.C.E., it stretched from the upper Nile River Valley (at least 800 miles upstream from Memphis) through the eastern Mediterranean regions of Palestine and parts of Asia Minor (present-day Turkey).

Egyptian Achievements

Even before the Old Kingdom, the entire river valley was united under **King Menes**, who built his capital at Memphis and led efforts to manage the floodwaters and build drainage and irrigation systems. As a result of the unification, the civilization became wealthy and powerful. Rulers, known as **pharaohs**, directed the construction of obelisks and the **pyramids**, enormous tombs for their afterlife. In addition, the Egyptians used a writing system to communicate. Known as **hieroglyphics**, this system consisted of a series of pictures (hieroglyphs) that represented letters and words. The Egyptians were also very interested in astronomy, which led to their creation of a fairly reliable calendar.

Over time, the civilization became dependent on trade because its people needed a constant supply of timber and stone for their many ambitious building projects and because Egyptian culture valued luxuries such as gold and spices. Besides giving the Egyptians access to the goods they wanted and needed, trading brought them into contact with other civilizations.

You *Can* Take It with You

Like most Mesopotamian societies, the Egyptians were polytheistic. The most significant aspect of their religious beliefs was the focus on life after death—the afterlife. Many societies shared this belief, but the Egyptians were convinced they could take earthly belongings with them to the afterlife, where they would be happy and well-fed and would continue doing many of the same things they did while in their earthly lives. They also believed that they would be able to use their bodies in the afterlife, and this led to the invention of **mummification**, a process of preserving dead bodies (though this was only available to the wealthier members of Egyptian society). The pharaohs, as you know, built huge pyramids to house their mummified bodies and earthly treasures.

Egyptian Women, Hear Them Roar

The longest reigning female pharaoh was **Queen Hatshepsut**, who ruled for 22 years during the New Kingdom and is considered one of Egypt's most successful rulers. She is credited with greatly expanding Egyptian trade expeditions. The relatively high status of women extended beyond royalty with most Egyptian women enjoying more rights and opportunities to express individuality than their counterparts in Mesopotamia. During the New Kingdom in particular, women could buy, sell, and inherit property and choose to will their property how they pleased. Women also had the right to dissolve their marriages (under certain circumstances).

That said, women were still expected to be subservient to men and were valued most when they bore children. Young girls were also not educated nearly as well as young boys.

Egyptian Social Structure: Another Pyramid

The tombs of the pharaohs weren't the only pyramids in Egypt. Egyptian social structure was in the form of a pyramid as well.

At the top of the pyramid was the pharaoh, of course, and below him were the priests. Below the priests were nobles, followed by merchants and skilled artisans, which included physicians; at the bottom of the pyramid was the largest group: peasants. The peasants worked the land and generated most of the wealth for the kingdom. Specifically, the pharaoh owned all the land in the kingdom, so the goods produced on the land were considered his property. Typically, the peasants were expected to give over half of what they produced to the kingdom. Also at the bottom level of the pyramid were the slaves, who were mostly either prisoners of war captured during the Egyptian conquest of surrounding regions or the descendants of those prisoners. It cannot be denied that most slaves lived a hard life, but in many cases they were not much worse off than many of the free peasants. Slaves worked on the land or on irrigation or building projects alongside the peasants, and on occasion were appointed to trusted positions within the government or within the palaces.

Ancient Egypt in Decline

By 1100 B.C.E. and for the next thousand years, ancient Egypt fell into decline, and both the Assyrian Empire and the Persian Empire conquered parts of this once-great civilization. Later, the Greeks occupied Egypt, and eventually the Romans completely absorbed Egypt into their empire. More on the Greeks and Romans later.

Pyramid Symbolism
The iconic pyramids of ancient Egypt, one of the wonders of the world, also serve as a symbol of the culture's social hierarchy, with the pharaoh at the top and slaves at the bottom, or base.

Indus Valley Civilization: Indus Industry Ruled

Like Mesopotamia and Egypt, the **Indus Valley** civilization was built along the banks of a river system. However, because of the huge mountains north and west of the Indus River, contact with outside civilizations was more limited there than in Mesopotamia, which was under continual threat by invaders. That is not to say that the Indus Valley was entirely cut off. The **Khyber Pass** through the Hindu Kush Mountains provided a connection to the outside world and was used by merchants on trade excursions. Later, as you might guess, it also gave invading forces a way into the land.

Compare Them: The Decline of Egypt and Mesopotamian Civilizations

Be sure to take note of the fact that whenever a civilization became powerful and prosperous, it attracted a lot of attention and envy from its neighbors, who wanted a piece of the action. Typically, this was the breeding ground for invasions. By the time it came under attack, the wealthy civilization was often so big it couldn't adequately protect all its borders, so over a period of time it began to weaken. This was true of the empires that arose in Mesopotamia and in ancient Egypt. As you continue to read, you'll learn that it was true of the Greeks and Romans as well.

From at least 2500 to around 1500 B.C.E., the ancient Indus Valley civilization stretched for more than 900 miles along the Indus River in what today is northwestern India. Its two major cities, **Harappa** and **Mohenjo-Daro**, were each home to perhaps more than 100,000 people—enormous cities by ancient standards. There is strong evidence that the cities were master-planned, uniformly constructed, and had sophisticated wastewater systems. This indicates that the Indus people had a strong central government, probably led by a priest-king. Like the major religions of Egypt and Sumer, those in the Indus Valley were polytheistic.

Like the architecture of its cities, Indus Valley industry was top-notch. In addition to using technologies such as potter's wheels, the Indus Valley farmers grew cotton and its artisans made cloth, which became an extremely important trade item among merchants traveling through the Khyber Pass to Mesopotamia.

Sometime around 1900 B.C.E., the cities of the Indus Valley were abandoned for reasons that remain unknown today. All that is known is that by 1500 B.C.E., the civilization crumbled with the arrival of the Aryans.

The Arrival of the Aryans

The **Aryans** were nomadic tribes from north of the Caucasus Mountains (near the Black and Caspian Seas). Using horses and advanced weaponry, they easily defeated the populations in the Indus Valley. Each of the Aryan tribes migrated to India independently; over a period of time, they began to settle in the Indus Valley, where they would give up their nomadic lifestyles.

The important thing to remember about the Aryan conquest of the Indus Valley is the establishment of their religious beliefs on the Indian subcontinent, in particular their belief in reincarnation. The Aryans, yet another polytheistic people, recorded their beliefs and traditions in the **Vedas** and the **Upanishads**. Over centuries, these early Aryan beliefs evolved to form the basis for what later became **Hinduism**.

The Aryan social structure also had a major impact on later developments in India. Combined with Hinduism, it formed the basis of what later became the caste system. Initially, the Aryan social structure divided its people into three classes, in this order from top to bottom: warriors, priests, and peasants. Later, a class of landowners and merchants would be added above the peasant class; the priest class (known as **Brahmans**) would be moved above the warrior class because its members were considered closer to the gods.

In the early days of this system, movement between classes was allowed. However, as the system became more complex and ingrained in society, it became more rigid. Eventually, subcastes were added to the four main castes, and social mobility among the castes was prohibited. Because members of different castes could not marry, children were born into the same castes as their parents and stayed there.

Early China: Shang on the Hwang

Shang China rose in the Hwang Ho River Valley (also known as the Yellow River Valley), and, like other river-basin communities, used its stable agricultural surplus to build a trade-centered civilization. At its height, the Shang controlled large parts of northern China and were militarily quite powerful. Thousands of Shang workers built walls around the towns and cities along the river; Shang warriors used chariots to defeat their enemies. The Shang Dynasty controlled the Yellow River Valley from around 1600 to around 1100 B.C.E.

However, Shang China had limited contact with the rest of the world, though it did trade with Mesopotamia (a very long journey!). The Shang were so isolated, in fact, that they believed themselves to be at the center of the world, which explains why they called their civilization "All Under Heaven." This belief contributed to the Shang's ethnocentric attitude, which means that they considered themselves superior to all others.

The Shang certainly had reasons to be proud. Not only were they accomplished bronze workers, but they also used horse-drawn chariots, developed the spoked wheel, and became experts in the production of pottery and silk. What's more, they devised a decimal system and a highly accurate calendar.

Focus on the Family

The extended family was an important institution in many ancient civilizations across the globe, but nowhere was it more important than in Shang China. There, multiple generations of the same family lived in the same household in a **patriarchal** structure (led by the eldest male). Shang religion held that gods controlled all aspects of peoples' lives; people also believed that they could call on the spirits of their dead ancestors to act as their advocates with the gods. This gave the extended family even greater significance.

Enter the Zhou

Around 1100 B.C.E., the Shang were ousted by Wu Wang, who established the **Zhou Dynasty** (also spelled Chou Dynasty), which maintained many of the traditions and customs developed under the Shang Dynasty (sound familiar?). The Zhou ruled China for nearly 900 years, longer than any other dynasty. Think of how long the United States has existed as an independent country, then multiply it by four. Now you have an idea of how long the Zhou Dynasty existed.

The Zhou Dynasty believed in what was called the **Mandate of Heaven**, meaning that heaven would grant the Zhou power only as long as its rulers governed justly and wisely. Put another way, the Zhou Dynasty would remain in power only as long as it had the blessing of heaven.

The Zhou developed a feudal system in China, similar to that of Europe during the Middle Ages (which we'll talk about more in the next chapter). The king was the ruler of the entire empire, but because it was too big for one person to manage, nobles were given power over smaller regions within the empire. This worked out well for a couple hundred years. The king gave each noble protection as long as the noble remained loyal to him. As time passed, however, a number of the nobles built up a lot of wealth and power within the regions under their control and eventually split off into independent kingdoms. Some of the most complex kingdoms developed **bureaucracies** within their governments, which was a way of organizing government tasks by department, or **bureau**, so that different parts of the government could specialize and stabilize. A bureaucratic form of government remained popular in China for thousands of years. Eventually, though, fighting and warfare among the feudal kingdoms brought an end to the Zhou Dynasty in 256 B.C.E.

West Africa: Bantu Migrations and the "Stateless Society"

Beginning around 1500 B.C.E., farmers in the Niger and Benue River valleys in West Africa began migrating south and east, bringing with them their languages (from the **Bantu** family of languages) and their knowledge of agriculture and metallurgy. These migrations, usually referred to as the **Bantu migrations**, continued over the course of the next 2,000 years. Bantu speakers gradually moved into areas formerly occupied by nomads. Some of the nomads simply moved on, and some of them adopted the more sedentary culture of the Bantu.

It is generally believed that the migration was spurred by climactic changes, which made the area now known as the Sahara Desert too dry to live in. People moved south out of the Sahara into the Bantu's homeland, which in turn caused them to move to the forests of Central Africa, then eventually beyond the forests to the east and south.

However, not all Bantu-speakers moved away. Further north in the upper Niger River Valley are the remains of Jenne-Jeno, which is believed to be the first city in sub-Saharan Africa. Beginning as a small fishing settlement around 250 B.C.E. and reaching urban size in 400 C.E., **Jenne-Jeno** is unusual because although it reached urban density, its architecture suggests that it was not a hierarchically organized society. Instead, archeologists believe that it was a unique form of urbanism comprising a collection of individual communities. It just goes to show, once again, that not all human societies have followed the same path toward sophistication, and that urbanization doesn't necessarily mean centralization.

Focus On: Migrations

Why do people migrate? People migrate for the same reason animals do: to find food and a hospitable environment in which to live. Nomadic peoples by definition are migratory, moving from place to place with the seasons to follow food sources. Agricultural peoples also migrated, following the seasons and therefore agricultural cycles. To maintain a stable home, people also migrated to avoid natural disasters or climatic changes that permanently change the environment, making it too hot and dry (the Sahara Desert's expansion), too cold (Ice Ages), or too wet (flooding cycles of major rivers such as the Yellow River in China).

Migration isn't always solely the result of random environmental change. Overpopulation of a particular area can exhaust the food supply, forcing people to move elsewhere, often displacing a smaller or weaker population in the process. Massive migrations of people from Ireland during the famines of the mid-nineteenth century were caused by a mix of politics, destructive farming methods, and an unpleasant fungus that wiped out the populace's main source of food. The Jewish diaspora, the slave trade, and the waves of immigrants coming from Europe to the Americas in the late nineteenth and early twentieth centuries are examples of more modern-day migrations caused by people rather than nature.

D. Early Mesoamerica and Andean South America: For Every Rule There's an Exception

In the Americas, two early civilizations existed: the **Olmec**, in what we know today as Mexico, from 1500 to 400 B.C.E., and the **Chavin** in the Andes from 900 to 200 B.C.E.

The Olmec were an urban society supported by surpluses of corn, beans, and squash. Like most early societies, they mastered irrigation techniques and constructed large-scale buildings; they were polytheistic and developed a system of writing and a calendar.

The Chavin were another urban civilization, and their people were also polytheistic. While mostly agricultural, they also had access to the coast, and therefore supplemented their diet with seafood. The Chavin developed ways to use metals in tools and weapons. Interestingly, the Chavin used llamas as their beasts of burden.

If much of this sounds familiar to you, it's because the Olmec and the Chavin developed similarly to other early civilizations discussed previously. So why bring them up separately? Two reasons. First, they demonstrate that the same patterns of development occurred in an entirely different part of the globe, a part that had no contact with the other civilizations discussed in this chapter. This suggests that developments within civilizations can occur independently—not necessarily as a result of exposure to other civilizations.

Second, neither the Olmec nor the Chavin civilization developed in a river valley. True, the Olmec and Chavin had access to water from streams and small rivers, but no major river system served as the generator of agricultural production or as the hub of culture and transportation. Their existence, therefore, disproves the hypothesis that river valleys are essential for the emergence of early civilizations. That's not to say, however, that rivers aren't extremely important—after all, the civilizations in the river valleys were among the most powerful and wealthy in all history.

Contrast Them: Olmec and Chavin Civilizations and Other Early Civilizations
Although you probably won't have to remember the details of the Olmec and Chavin civilizations, you should definitely remember this: they are unique in that they didn't develop in river valleys, as did all the other major early civilizations.

IV. TECHNOLOGY AND INNOVATIONS TO 600 B.C.E.

Farming tools, metallurgy, and the ability to manipulate the environment caused humans to transition from nomadic hunters and gatherers to builders of civilizations and empires in this 10,000-year period. In order to farm successfully, people need tools, a way to transport what they've grown, and a place to store their surplus. Thus, the most important technologies developed by early civilizations included farming tools: ploughs, hoes, rakes, the wheel (and therefore the cart), and finally, pottery in which to store surplus for the off-season. While effective tools can be made out of bone and stone, they last longer and work more efficiently if they're made of metal. Copper was the first metal used, and other metallurgical techniques developed from there.

From such primitive techniques developed more complex technologies that benefitted society in greater ways. The earliest public works projects focused on irrigation—often simple dikes and canals to capture flood water and precious fertile silt. As cities grew, populations needed steady water supplies and a fairly reliable plumbing and sewage system. The large cities of the Indus River Valley (around 2500 B.C.E) had elaborate public and private sewers, and similar systems were built much later in the Roman Empire. The most visible technological achievements are massive architectural monuments built by all civilizations—pyramids, ziggurats, walls, temples, aqueducts, coliseums, theaters, stadiums, and roads. These structures were used to assert the authority of leaders, facilitate the functioning of the state, and to keep the populace healthy, employed, and entertained.

A stable supply of food allowed people to develop specialized skills and crafts beyond the basic needs of their neighbors. Although a lot of the trade in early societies tended to be smaller luxury items—silk, cotton and wool, semi-precious gems, and jewelry; heavier goods including olive oil and spices were also traded.

V. CHANGES AND CONTINUITIES IN THE ROLE OF WOMEN

In hunter-gatherer Paleolithic cultures, the role of women tended to be more important than it was in Neolithic cultures. While a woman's first duty was always the nurturing of children, she was also responsible for the "gathering" part of the hunter-gatherer equation. Berries, nuts, seeds, edible plants—whatever could be scrounged up from the ground was her domain, and often, when the men were unsuccessful in killing an animal, these small efforts constituted the tribe's meals. The analysis of teeth and hair found in "Ice Man"—a perfectly preserved Paleolithic corpse discovered in the snows of the Alps in 1991—proves that most of his protein was in fact derived from vegetables and grains. Also, remember that such tribes had no method of refrigerating meat, so the importance of women's food-gathering efforts during this period makes sense.

Another role of Paleolithic women was the socialization of their children. Infants begin to learn how to speak primarily from their mothers, and since language forms the basis of community, it's through these verbal efforts that humanity ultimately began to learn to cooperate on bigger projects such as large-scale agriculture.

Other possible roles that women filled included lawgivers, counselors, storytellers, healers, shamans, and magicians.

VI. PULLING IT ALL TOGETHER

There are many ways to think about the big-picture themes that have emerged in this chapter, but we'll stay focused on the three presented in Section II of this chapter.

1. Civilizations

By now, you should have a good understanding of the types of developments common to most civilizations; for example, agriculture, written language, and the use of metals all contributed to the growth of early civilizations. You should also be able to explain how civilizations grow when people are less concerned with where their next meal is coming from than how they spread their influence (primarily through trade routes and conquest). Furthermore, you should be able to describe what happens when civilizations become so dominant that they have no rivals (a period of peace and prosperity or golden age emerges, making it possible to devote time and money to the arts and sciences). Finally, you should be able explain why those dominant civilizations begin to fall apart (they get too big, their own people get restless, foreign threats gain confidence and power, etc.).

By taking note of the patterns woven throughout the expansion and contraction of civilizations, you'll be well prepared to tackle the DBQ and long essay.

Invention and Innovation

You should be able to discuss some examples of changes brought about by invention and innovation. Two important ones are the use of the wheel and the use of iron.

2. Sources of Change

Regarding change occurring in civilizations through cultural diffusion, keep in mind that the two main methods are trade and conquest. Expansion of major belief systems also plays a major role, but don't forget that belief systems followed the trade routes and the military movements, too.

Notice that some civilizations were more innovative while others were more adaptive, but most cultures innovated and adapted simultaneously. Whatever they invent, they spread to others; whatever they borrow, they adapt for their own purposes. That said, certain civilizations adapted an incredible amount from others—the Romans and the Macedonians, for example, were hugely influenced by the Greeks.

3. Humans Versus Nature

You should be able to name many ways in which civilizations have changed their surroundings to suit their own purposes. The digging of canals and irrigation ditches, stone-cutting, plowing, and metal-working are just a few examples. Don't forget the more subtle examples, such as the development of calendars and sundials, which were very significant in the human quest to predict and control nature for its own purposes. To be sure, humans can't change the repetitive patterns that underlie the yearly calendar, but by understanding those patterns and keeping track of them, humans can predict and use them for their own purposes.

Notice that as civilizations developed, they were less subject to natural events causing their demise but more subject to other civilizations doing so. Notice also that as major belief systems developed, civilizations became less interested in appeasing the gods to protect them from the great unknowns and more interested in internal peace, oneness with a great human force, or salvation. This interest corresponds to humans' ability to figure out nature. Thus, people's focus shifted from the need for bodily protection to the desire for internal peace.

As you continue to review the major world events in the upcoming chapters, always keep in mind that if you can compare, contrast, and figure out how things are changing, you will be able to write very thoughtful essays.

CHAPTER 6 KEY TERMS

nomad
foraging societies
pastoral societies
cuneiform
polytheistic
ziggurat
Code of Hammurabi
pharaohs
hieroglyphics
mummification
pyramids
river valley
calendar
Hinduism
the Vedas
the Upanishads
Brahmans
patriarchy
Mandate of Heaven
bureaucracy, bureau
migration
Zhou Dynasty
Neolithic Revolution
   (Agricultural Revolution)
Bronze Age
Mesopotamia
Sumerian civilization
Tigris and Euphrates Rivers
Babylon
Hittites
Assyrians
Nebuchadnezzar
Persian Empire
Egyptian civilization
King Menes
Queen Hatshepsut
Indus Valley
Fertile Crescent
Khyber Pass
Harappa and Mohenjo-Daro
Aryans
Shang China
Bantu migrations
Olmec and Chavin

Chapter 6 Drill

See the end of the chapter for the answers and explanations.

Questions 1–4 refer to the image below.

1. This image most likely references developments in which historical period?

    (A) The Paleolithic Period
    (B) The Neolithic Period
    (C) The medieval period
    (D) The early modern period

2. The civilization depicted in this image was located around which of the following river systems?

    (A) The Nile River
    (B) The Yellow River
    (C) The Indus River
    (D) The Tigris and Euphrates Rivers

3. A historian would most likely be able to use this image as evidence for an argument on which of the following topics?

    (A) The kinds of crops produced by this civilization
    (B) Popular metalworking in this era
    (C) Prevailing legal codes at this time
    (D) Gender hierarchies during this period

4. Which of the following are marks of civilization that are shown in the image?

    (A) Division of labor, animal domestication, and writing
    (B) Animal domestication, writing, and art
    (C) Rudimentary tool use and evidence of hunting
    (D) Waterfowl and cows

TIMELINE OF MAJOR DEVELOPMENTS, 8000 B.C.E.–600 B.C.E.

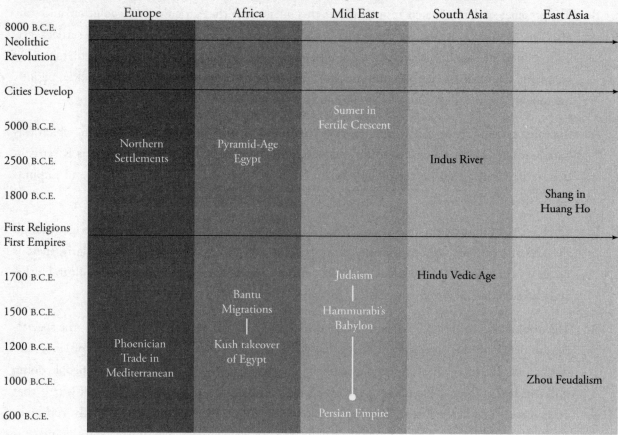

CHAPTER 6 DRILL EXPLANATIONS

1. **B**   The presence of domesticated animals places this image after the Agricultural Revolution, and thus after the Paleolithic Period, so (A) is incorrect. The evidence of division of labor and settled agriculture indicate that this image was created in or after the Neolithic Period, while the hieroglyphic script and depiction of clay pots and simple girdles indicate the medieval and early modern periods are much too late for this image. Therefore, (B) is the answer.

2. **A**   The hieroglyphic script and artistic style are characteristic of the Egyptian civilization, which was based around the Nile River, (A). The Yellow River is in what is now China, the Indus River is in present-day India, and the Mesopotamian civilizations sprung up around the Tigris and Euphrates. Choice (A) is correct.

3. **D**   Choice (A) is an unlikely answer, as there are no clearly identifiable crops in this image (though the presence of domesticated animals could speak to agriculture more broadly). Similarly, there is no clear evidence of metallic goods, (B). The depicted activities are domestic and agricultural tasks, and therefore not of a legal nature, (C). Therefore, (D) is the best answer.

4. **A**   The origins of civilization lie in agriculture, which created a food surplus and, in turn, the specialization of labor. The development of writing was one of the most important effects of labor specialization. The image provides evidence of the domestication of animals and shows people doing different tasks. The hieroglyphics next to the workers are evidence of writing. While it is true that art is represented in the image, art predates civilization by some 25,000 years. Similarly, rudimentary tools and hunting predate humans. Finally, the presence of particular animals in the image is not relevant to the question of markers of civilization. The correct answer is (A).

REFLECT

Respond to the following questions:

- For which content topics discussed in this chapter do you feel you have achieved sufficient mastery to answer multiple-choice questions correctly?

- For which content topics discussed in this chapter do you feel you have achieved sufficient mastery to discuss effectively in a short-answer response or essay?

- For which content topics discussed in this chapter do you feel you need more work before you can answer multiple-choice questions correctly?

- For which content topics discussed in this chapter do you feel you need more work before you can discuss effectively in a short-answer response or essay?

- What parts of this chapter are you going to re-review?

- Will you seek further help outside of this book (such as a teacher, tutor, or AP Students) on any of the content in this chapter—and, if so, on what content?

Chapter 7
Organization and Reorganization of Human Societies, c. 600 B.C.E. to c. 600 C.E.

I. CHAPTER OVERVIEW

This chapter picks up where the last one left off—kind of. Historical movements and trends often have ramifications for decades and even centuries beyond the initial impact, so history can't always be divided up into neat eras. To that end, you may read some material in this chapter that harkens back to topics covered in Chapter 6.

Remember: Read through this chapter once, then go back and focus on the things that you're not entirely clear about. Here's the chapter outline.

I.   Chapter Overview

       You're reading it.

II.   Stay Focused on the Big Picture

       Organize the many events that occurred during the 1,200 years covered in this chapter into some big-picture concepts.

III.   History Review: c. 600 B.C.E. to 600 C.E.

       This is the largest section of the chapter. In it, we'll delve into developments in each region or major civilization. If you're totally clueless on any part of this section, consider also reviewing the corresponding topic in your textbook. After all, we're talking about a large chunk of history, and this section is intended as a review, not as a primary source.

       Here's how we've organized the information.

       A. The Classical Civilizations: India and China
       B. The Classical Civilizations: Mediterranean
       C. The Classical Civilizations: Mesoamerica
       D. The Late Classical Period: Empires Collapse, People Move

IV.   Technology and Innovations from 600 B.C.E. to 600 C.E.

       From primitive farming tools to metallurgy to large-scale farming, man kept moving toward increasingly advanced technology in this era.

V.   Changes and Continuities in the Role of Women

       Women lose power as humans start to settle down. A comparative look at trends in the status of women across different regions of the world.

VI.   Major Belief Systems Through 600 C.E.

Although we'll make reference to the major belief systems within the history review, we've provided this separate section so that they're all grouped together in one place and you can refer to them easily. Major belief systems had a huge impact on the development of civilizations, so they're important to review in detail. Also keep in mind that you'll need to know the background of the major belief systems as you review the material in later chapters. Note that this section reviews the major belief systems covered in Chapters 6 and 7 (Periods 1 and 2 from the AP World History guidelines).

VII. Pulling It All Together

A quick review that focuses on themes and trends

II. STAY FOCUSED ON THE BIG PICTURE

As you review the details of the civilizations in this chapter, stay focused on the big-picture concepts and ask yourself some questions, including the following:

1.   Do cultural areas, as opposed to states or empires, better represent history? Cultural areas are those that share a common culture, and don't necessarily respect geographical limitations. States, like city-states and nation-states (countries), and empires, have political boundaries, even if those boundaries aren't entirely agreed upon.

2.   How does change occur within societies? As you review all the information in this chapter, you'll notice a lot of talk about trading, migrations, and invasions. Pay attention to why people move around so much in the first place and the impact of these moves. Furthermore, don't forget that sometimes change occurs within a society because of internal developments, not external influences. Pay attention to that too.

3.   How similar were the economic and trading practices that developed across cultures? Pay attention to monetary systems, trade routes, and trade practices. How did they link up?

4.   How does the environment impact human decision making? Pay attention to the way states respond to environmental changes. Do they move or send out raiding parties? Are they able to respond quickly and successfully to environmental changes?

III. HISTORY REVIEW

A. The Classical Civilizations: India and China

Your AP World History Exam will likely focus on four empires in India and China that existed from around 300 B.C.E. to around 550 C.E. These four empires are the Maurya and Gupta in India and the Qin and Han in China. Keep in mind that to fully understand these four empires, you will also need to review some of the major belief systems discussed in Section VI of this chapter.

1. The Mauryan Empire in India (321 to approximately 180 B.C.E.)

Around 330 B.C.E., Alexander the Great conquered the Persian Empire and continued into India (more on this in a few pages). During this time, the Aryan culture and belief systems continued to spread throughout India. Then, around 321 B.C.E., a new empire arose in India, one that would come to be the largest in that country to date. Spanning from the Indus River Valley eastward through the Ganges River Valley and southward through the Deccan Plateau, the **Mauryan Empire** was founded by **Chandragupta Maurya**, who unified the smaller Aryan kingdoms into a civilization. It was his grandson, **Ashoka Maurya**, who took the empire to its greatest heights.

A major reason that the Mauryan Empire became so powerful and wealthy was trade. Indian merchants traded silk, cotton, and elephants (among hundreds of other items) to Mesopotamia and the eastern Roman Empire. Another reason was its powerful military. Interestingly, it was Mauryan military strength that eventually caused a dramatic change in the empire. Stricken with disgust and filled with remorse for a very violent and bloody victory his forces claimed over the Kalinga in southeast India, Ashoka converted to **Buddhism**. For the rest of his reign, Ashoka preached nonviolence and moderation. (As you'll learn in Section IV of this chapter, during the previous century, Buddhism had recently taken root in this otherwise Hindu region.) Ashoka is also known for his **Rock and Pillar Edicts**, which were carved on—you guessed it—rocks and pillars throughout the empire. These edicts reminded Mauryans to live generous and righteous lives. Following Ashoka's conversion and commitment to Buddhism, the religion spread beyond India into many parts of Southeast Asia.

2. The Gupta Dynasty in India (320–550 C.E.)

After Ashoka's death in 232 B.C.E., the Mauryan Empire began to decline rapidly, primarily due to economic problems and pressure from attacks in the northeast. However, between 375 and 415 C.E., it experienced a revival under Chandra Gupta II, known as **Chandra Gupta the Great**. The **Gupta Empire** was more decentralized and smaller than its predecessor, but it is often referred to as a golden age because it enjoyed relative peace and saw significant advances in the arts and sciences. For example, Gupta mathematicians developed the concepts of pi and zero. They also devised a decimal system that used the numerals 1 through 9 (which were diffused to the Arabs and became known as **Arabic numerals**).

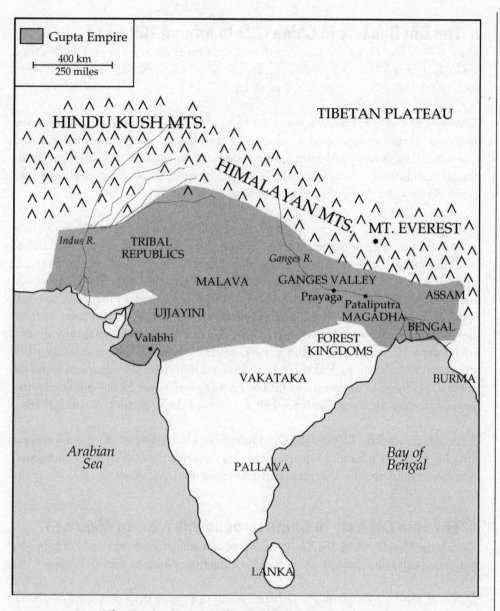

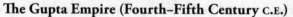

The Gupta Empire (Fourth–Fifth Century C.E.)

By the time of the Gupta Dynasty, Hinduism had again become the dominant religion in India. Hinduism reinforced the caste system, meaning that Indian social structures were very rigid. Though the empire as a whole was enjoying an era of peace, prosperity, and artistic endeavors, women were increasingly losing their rights. Totally under the control of men, Indian women lost the right to own or inherit property and could not participate in sacred rituals or study religion. Furthermore, stemming from an increasingly urban society that placed a growing importance on the inheritance of property, child marriage (involving girls as young as six or seven) also became the norm during this era. The Gupta Dynasty collapsed under pressure from the White Huns in 550 C.E.

3. The Qin Dynasty in China (221 to around 209 B.C.E.)

Unlike the Zhou Dynasty that preceded it, the **Qin Dynasty** was extremely short. Though it lasted little longer than a decade, it was significant enough to earn a spot in this AP review book 2,200 years later.

The story of the Qin Dynasty is similar to that of all the other civilizations we've reviewed in that it developed a strong economy based on agriculture, organized a powerful army equipped with iron weapons, conquered the surrounding territories, and unified the region under a single emperor. Same story, new time and place. So how did the Qin earn its spot here?

The Qin Dynasty is the empire that connected separate fortification walls that eventually became the **Great Wall of China**. That fact is more than just an interesting piece of trivia; it tells us that the empire was incredibly well organized, centralized, and territorial. Qin Shihuangdi, also known as **Qin Shi Huang**, was the dynasty's first emperor, and he recentralized various feudal kingdoms that had split apart at the end of the Zhou Dynasty; standardized all the laws, currencies, weights, measures, and systems of writing; and refused to tolerate any dissent whatsoever. If dissent occurred in a book, he had it burned; if dissent occurred in the mind of a scholar, he had the scholar killed. Given that introduction, it should come as no surprise to you that Qin China was patriarchal. What might surprise you, however, is that the dominant belief system of the Qin rulers was **Legalism**.

Although the emperor believed the Qin Dynasty would last forever, it fell only one year after his death at the hands of the peasants, who resented the Qin's heavy-handedness. The new dynasty that took its place lasted for more than 400 years.

4. The Han Dynasty in China (around 200 B.C.E. to 460s C.E.)

During the **Han Dynasty**, the **Xiongnu**, a large nomadic group from northern Asia who may have been Huns, invaded territories extending from China to Eastern Europe.

However, the Huns were much more successful in Europe than they were in China, largely due to the skills of **Wudi**, often called the Warrior Emperor, who greatly enlarged the Han Empire to central Asia. Trade thrived along the Silk Road to the Mediterranean; more significantly, along this same route, Buddhism spread. As usual, the trade routes carried far more than luxury items—they carried culture.

To reform his government, Wudi implemented Confucianism as the state religion of China. One of the most significant developments that took place during the Han Dynasty was the civil service system based on the teachings of Confucius. The Han believed that those involved in government should be highly educated and excellent communicators. To ensure strong candidates, Wudi developed a civil service examination, a very difficult test lasting for several days, along with Confucian Academies that would prepare students for civic life as well as the examinations. Though, ostensibly, the exam was open to everyone, generally only the wealthy could afford to prepare for it. The consequence was a government bureaucracy that was highly skilled and that contributed to stability in the system of government for centuries.

Also during this time, the Chinese invented paper, highly accurate sundials, and calendars, as well as making important strides in navigation such as the invention of the rudder and compass. Furthermore, like all the other major civilizations, they continued to broaden their use of metals.

B. The Classical Civilizations: Mediterranean

From approximately 2000 B.C.E. to around 500 C.E., two Mediterranean civilizations, Greece and Rome, dominated the region. Countless books have been written on these two empires. There is no doubt that your AP textbook dedicated a considerable chunk to the details of these two powerhouse civilizations. Why all the fuss? Simply put, Western civilization as we know it essentially began with these two empires. The Sumerians, the Babylonians, the Egyptians, the Hebrews, and the Phoenicians laid the groundwork, but the Greeks and the Romans left the most pervasive and obvious influence behind. Perhaps their most important contribution is the concept of representative government, but the Greeks, Romans, and Persians also made lasting contributions to art, architecture, literature, science, and philosophy.

1. Persian Immersion

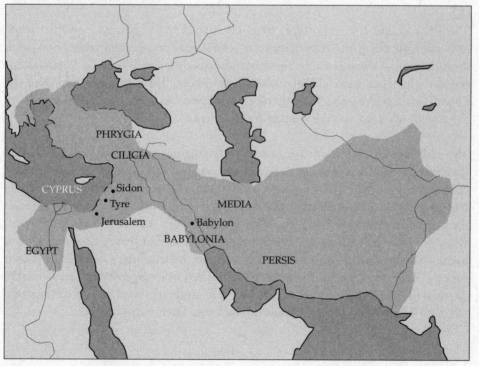

The Height of the Persian Empire (c. 500 B.C.E.)

The Persians established a big empire—a really big empire—that, by 500 B.C.E., stretched from beyond the Nile River Valley in Egypt around the eastern Mediterranean through present-day Turkey and parts of Greece, and then eastward through present-day Afghanistan. Huge! They did this by conquering all of those earlier ancient civilizations in Mesopotamia you just read about: the Babylonians, the Lydians, the Phoenicians, and the Egyptians. On account of the vast expanse of their empire, they delegated local administration of their provinces, or **Satrapies**, to important people in the provinces. As long as the governor, or **satrap**, paid his taxes and contributed soldiers to the Great King whenever they were requested, the satrapy was allowed a wide range of self government, which was vital to keeping such a far flung empire of so many different cultures together.

To improve transportation and communication across the vast empire, the Persians built a series of long roads. The longest was the **Great Royal Road**, which stretched some 1,600 miles from the Persian Gulf to the Aegean Sea.

Stay Tuned
We'll talk more about the Persian Empire later because the Persians butted heads with the other major world empires.

Lydians, Phoenicians, and Hebrews

Within and near the Persian Empire, many smaller societies existed and kept their own identities. Among these were the Lydians, Phoenicians, and Hebrews.

The **Lydians** are important because they came up with the concept of using coined money to conduct trade rather than using the barter system, in which goods are exchanged for other goods. This innovation led to a monetary system of consistent prices and allowed people to save money for future use. The idea of coined money, like everything else, spread over the trade routes and soon just about everybody was using it.

The **Phoenicians** are important, first, because they established powerful naval city-states all along the Mediterranean (you'll read more about this later), and, second, because they developed a simple alphabet that used only 22 letters as opposed to the much more complex cuneiform system. The Greeks later adopted the Phoenician alphabet, and from there it spread and changed, eventually leading to the system of letters you are reading on this page.

The **Hebrews** are significant because of their religious beliefs called Judaism. The Hebrews were the first Jews. In contrast to previous civilizations in the Fertile Crescent and beyond, the Hebrews were monotheistic, meaning that they believed in one god. By around 1000 B.C.E., the Hebrews had established Israel in Palestine on the eastern shores of the Mediterranean Sea. Although they were frequently invaded by neighboring empires (e.g., Nebuchadnezzar enslaved them), they managed to maintain their identity, in large part because they believed they were God's chosen people. Under the Persians, the Hebrews were freed from captivity and continued to develop a distinct culture that would later lead to the development of major world religions. Much more about Judaism can be found later in this chapter.

2. Greece

Ancient Greece was located on a peninsula between the waters of the Aegean and Mediterranean Seas. Because the land in Greece is mostly mountainous, there wasn't much possibility for agricultural development on the scale of the ancient river valley civilizations. But Greece did have natural harbors and mild weather, and its coastal position aided trade and cultural diffusion by boat, which is precisely how the Greeks conducted most of their commercial activity. The Greeks could easily sail to Palestine, Egypt, and Carthage, exchanging wine and olive products for grain. Eventually, they replaced the barter system with a money system (remember where this developed? Hint: Lydia, oh Lydia), and soon Athens became a wealthy city at the center of all this commercial activity.

Greek Geography

Greece's limited geographical area also contributed to its dominance. Land was tight, so Greece was always looking to establish colonies abroad to ease over-crowding and gain raw materials. This meant that the Greeks had to have a powerful military. It also meant that they had to develop sophisticated methods of communication, transportation, and governance.

Social Structure and Citizenship: It Takes a Polis

Like the other early civilizations, Greece wasn't a country then in the way that it is now. Instead, it was a collection of city-states, very much like those of early Mesopotamian civilizations in Sumer or Babylon. Each city-state, known as a **polis**, shared a common culture and identity. Although each polis was part of a broader civilization and shared a common language and many similar traditions, each was independent from, and often in conflict with, the others.

The two main city-states were **Athens** and **Sparta**. Athens was the political, commercial, and cultural center of Greek civilization. Sparta was an agricultural and highly militaristic region. Most citizens in Sparta lived a very austere, highly disciplined existence (which explains where modern-day terms such as "Spartan existence" come from). All the boys, and even some of the girls, received military training, which stressed equality but not individuality.

Each polis was composed of three groups.

- Citizens, composed of adult males, often engaged in business or commerce
- Free people with no political rights
- Noncitizens (slaves, who accounted for nearly one-third of the people in Athens, and who had no rights)

Among the citizens, civic decisions were made openly, after engaging in debates. All citizens were expected to participate. This practice led to Athens being regarded as the first democracy. But it's important to point out that only free adult males could participate, so it was not a democracy in the modern sense of the word. (Interestingly, it was in Sparta, not Athens, where women held a higher status and were granted greater equality than women of other city-states.)

Note: On the exam you may be asked about Draco and Solon. Just know that they were aristocrats who worked to create the democracy in Athens and to ensure fair, equal, and open participation.

It's also important to point out that democracy in Athens did not develop immediately. As Athens grew more and more powerful, the government changed from a monarchy to an aristocracy, and finally to a democracy.

Greek Mythology: Many Gods

The Greeks were polytheistic. The myths surrounding their gods, like those of Zeus and Aphrodite, are richly detailed and still hold our interest to this day. As you know by now, most early civilizations were polytheistic (the Hebrews being a notable exception), but Greek polytheism was unique in one major respect: The Greek gods were believed to possess human failings—they got angry, got drunk, took sides, and had petty arguments. Greek mythology remains part of Western heritage and language. Every time we refer to a task as "Herculean" or read our horoscopes, we're tipping our hats to the ancient Greeks.

War with Persia: Greece Holds On

Prior to the development of the democracy in Athens, Greece was involved in a series of wars that threatened its existence. **The Persian Wars** (499–449 B.C.E.) united all the Greek city-states against their mutual enemy, Persia. (Recall that the Persian Empire was the largest empire in the eastern Mediterranean and Mesopotamia to date.) Much of Athens was destroyed in these wars, but Greece held on and the wars ended in a stalemate. Two huge victories by the Greeks, one at Marathon and the other at Salamis, allowed the Greeks to maintain control of the Aegean Sea. With Persia held back, Greece was free to enter into an era of peace and prosperity, which is often called the **Golden Age of Pericles**.

The Golden Age of Pericles: Athens Wows the World

The Golden Age of Pericles (480–404 B.C.E.) saw Athens become a cultural powerhouse under the leadership of **Pericles**. Pericles established democracy for all adult males. It was also under Pericles that Athens was rebuilt after its destruction by the Persians (the Parthenon was built during this reconstruction). Furthermore, it was under Pericles that Athens established the **Delian League** with the other city-states, an alliance against aggression from its common enemies. Philosophy and the arts flourished, and continued to do so for the next two centuries.

Slavery and Democracy in Ancient Greece

Ironically, it was slavery that enabled the Greeks to develop their democracy. It was by slave labor that Greek citizens found themselves with free time to meet and vote and create great works of art and philosophy. Slaves, obtained by various means, were the private property of their owners. They worked as laborers, domestic servants, and cultivators. Educated or skilled slaves became craftsmen and business managers. Some owners helped slaves set up small businesses and then kept part of the profits; in a few cases, slaves who earned and saved enough money could eventually buy their freedom.

In philosophy, we find the names many would regard as the most famous of all the ancient Greeks: **Socrates**, **Plato**, and **Aristotle**. They believed that truth could be discerned through rational thought and deliberate and careful observation, and that virtue and the quest for goodness would lead to internal peace and happiness. Some of their observations proved false in time, especially with regard to the functioning of the universe on a cosmic scale, or microcosmic scale, but it was the process they established, rather than the actual conclusions they drew, that were so revolutionary. Although our modern understanding of the world differs in many ways from theirs, these three men are still revered today as the fathers of rational thinking.

During the Golden Age, Greek drama was dominated by the comedies and trage-dies of Aeschylus and Euripides, the sculptures of Phidias adorned the streets, and Greek architecture earned its place in history with its distinctive Doric, Ionic, and Corinthian columns. Math and science thrived under the capable instruction of Ar-chimedes, Hippocrates, Euclid, and Pythagoras (you probably remember the Py-thagorean theorem from geometry—guess which famous Greek that came from).

Of course, cultural achievement existed in Greece prior to the Golden Age. **Ho-mer**, for example, wrote the epic poems the *Illiad* and the *Odyssey* a few centuries earlier; they are widely regarded as Western civilization's first two masterworks of literature. But make no mistake about it, during the Golden Age, the arts and sciences became firmly cemented into the Western consciousness. The accomplish-ments of this period served as the inspiration for the European Renaissance and the Enlightenment nearly two millennia later—which is why we're making such a big deal out of them here.

Trouble Ahead for Athens

Although Athens dominated the Delian League with its powerful navy, other Greek city-states in the Aegean allied themselves with Sparta's great army to form the Peloponnesian League. Athens and Sparta, as leaders of their respective alli-ances, became increasingly fearful and envious of each other's power. After years of increasing tensions, a trade dispute involving the city of Corinth pushed Athens and Sparta into the **Peloponnesian War** (431–404 B.C.E.). Athens attempted a de-fensive strategy, hiding behind its great walls while allowing the Spartan army to ravage its farmlands. This worked well for the Athenians for a time until two trag-edies occurred. First, a great plague afflicted the city, killing vast numbers of the population, including Pericles. Then, Athens' navy suffered a devastating defeat at Syracuse on the island of Sicily. Athens was never the same again.

Although it could have, Sparta didn't destroy Athens out of respect for the defeat-ed city's former role in the Persian War. Sparta failed to dominate the region for long; despite its victory, it was so weakened by the war that it became vulnerable to outside aggression. The **Macedonians**, under the rule of Philip III of Macedon, who reigned from 359 to 336 B.C.E., invaded Athens from the north and con-quered the entire region. Fortunately, Philip respected Greek culture and, rather than destroy it, encouraged it to flourish.

Alexander Adds Greatness

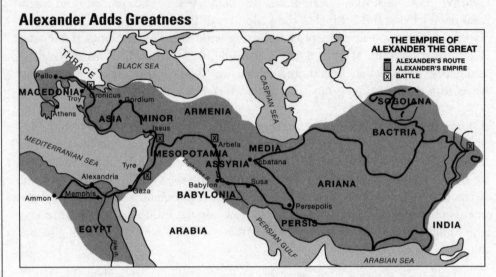

The Height of Alexander the Great's Empire, Fourth Century B.C.E.

The Macedonians didn't stop with Greece. Philip's son, **Alexander the Great**, who was taught by Aristotle, widely expanded Macedonian dominance. Under Alexander, the Macedonians conquered the mighty Persian Empire and moved eastward to the shores of the Indus River in what today is India, eventually creating the largest empire of the time. However, the strain of such conquests took its toll on the usually vigorous Alexander, and he died at the age of 33 in Babylon as he and his army were returning to Macedonia. Before his corpse got cold, however, his generals quickly fought over the spoils of his empire, dividing it amongst themselves.

Along with its size, the Macedonian Empire is notable for the fact that it adopted Greek customs and then spread them to much of the known world. Consequently, much of the world became connected under a uniform law and common trade practices. Therefore, **Hellenism**—the culture, ideals, and pattern of life of Classical Greece—didn't perish as a result of the victories over Athens and Sparta; instead, it came to be influential far beyond its original borders.

In the immediate aftermath of the expansion of Hellenism, the economies of Athens and Corinth revived through trade. Of the three Hellenistic empires, the Ptolemaic Empire became the wealthiest. Alexandria, its capital, was built at the mouth of the Nile. Wisely, the rulers of the Ptolemaic Dynasty in Egypt did not interfere in Egyptian society, and eventually Ptolemaic Egypt also became a cultural center, home of the Alexandria Museum and Alexandria Library, the latter of which contained the most scrolls of any location in the empire, perhaps the whole world.

When Alexander the Great died at age 33, his empire started to crumble. Because the Macedonians were focused on the East and on Egypt, the door was open in the West for a new power to rise to the world stage. That power was the Romans.

3. Rome (509 B.C.E.–476 C.E.)

Geographically, Rome was relatively well-situated. The Alps to the north provided protection from an invasion by land (although, ultimately, not enough). The sea surrounding the Italian peninsula limited the possibility of a naval attack unless a large armada floated across the sea. Yet, although it was somewhat isolated, Rome was also at a crossroads. It had easy access to northern Africa, Palestine, Greece, and the Iberian Peninsula (modern-day Spain and Portugal), which meant easy access to the rest of the world.

Social Structure in Rome: Organized and Patriarchal

The social and political structure in the Roman Republic consisted of **patricians** (landowning noblemen), **plebeians** (all other free men), and slaves. Does this sound familiar? It should. It's very similar to the social structure of ancient Greece. Roman government was organized as a representative republic. The main governing body was made up of two distinct groups: the Senate, which comprised patrician families, and the Assembly, which was initially made up of patricians, but later was opened to plebeians. Two consuls were elected annually by the Assembly. The consuls had veto power over decisions made by the Assembly.

This structure was much more stable than the direct democracies of the Greek *polis*, in which every male citizen was expected to participate on a regular basis. In a republic, the people have representatives, so they don't have to vote on every issue. This is similar to the constitutional democracy we have in the United States. Everyone in this country votes for representatives, so it's correct to call our system a democracy; however, our representatives in Congress vote on all the major issues, so our system of government is also very much a republic. Indeed, the structure of our government was modeled on the system used in the Roman Republic. Instead of two consuls, though, we have one, known as the president.

Early on, Rome developed civil laws to protect individual rights (in some ways similar to our Bill of Rights). The laws of Rome were codified (remember that the idea of a code was Hammurabi's, in Babylon) and became known as the **Twelve Tables of Rome** (the concept of "innocent until proven guilty" originated here). Later, these laws were extended to an international code that Rome applied to its conquered territories.

The social structure of the Roman family centered on the *pater familias*—eldest male in the family—though women did have considerable influence within their families, with some supervising a family business or family estate. Roman women could own property as well, but they were nevertheless considered inferior to men, just as in Greek society. Furthermore, as in Greece, slavery was an important element of the social structure of Rome—at one point, slaves comprised one-third of the population, most of whom came from conquered territories. Although life was difficult for all slaves, generally those living and working in the cities had better conditions than their country counterparts, and some had the possibility of freedom.

Roman Mythology: More Gods

Like the Greeks, the Romans were polytheistic. (Every time you see Cupid on a Valentine's Day card, you see the impact of Roman mythology on our world today.) Many of the Roman gods were of Greek origin, though appropriately renamed to suit the Roman culture and language.

Roman Military Domination: All Directions, All the Time

As Rome expanded, Carthage, a city-state in North Africa with powerful ambitions of its own, became its first enemy. It didn't take long for this conflict to escalate into full-fledged wars, which came to be called the **Punic Wars**. These lasted on and off from 264 through 146 B.C.E.

The First Punic War (264–241 B.C.E.) was fought to gain control of the island of Sicily; Rome won this one. The Second Punic War (218–201 B.C.E.) began with an attack by **Hannibal**, a Carthaginian general considered one of the greatest military geniuses of all time. In an amazing feat, Hannibal led his army all the way to northern Italy, crossed the Alps (on elephants no less!), and surprised the Romans, who were expecting an attack from the south. Hannibal's army destroyed many towns and villages to the north of Rome and were on the verge of destroying Rome. However, a Roman army had landed in North Africa, forcing Hannibal to return to Carthage to defend his city. Carthage eventually agreed to sue for peace, and this made Rome the undisputed power in the western Mediterranean. Fifty years later, the Third Punic War (149–146 B.C.E.) was instigated by Rome. Rome invaded Carthage and burned it to the ground. With Carthage out of the picture, Rome continued its expansion throughout the Mediterranean.

Part of that expansion was to obtain Greece by defeating the Macedonians. The Romans also fought the Gauls to the north and the Spaniards to the west. Warfare aided the spread of Roman culture (which, you'll recall, was linked to Greek culture) throughout much of Western Europe and the Mediterranean. To maintain their vast empire, the Romans built an extensive road network and aqueducts and greatly enlarged their navy.

Collapse of the Republic and the Rise of Imperialism

Following the Punic Wars, and even as Roman influence grew, the situation in and around Rome was becoming unsettled. Several events caused this restlessness. First, large landowners had begun using more slaves from the conquered territories. This displaced many small farmers, who moved into the cities, causing overcrowding among the plebeians and not enough jobs to support them. Second, the Roman currency was devalued, causing a high rate of inflation. This meant that the plebeians did not have enough money to buy the things they previously could afford. Third, political leaders began fighting amongst themselves. The result was that the power of the Senate weakened, ultimately to be transferred to three men, who came to be known as the **First Triumvirate**: Pompey, Crassus, and Julius Caesar.

Caesar was given power over southern Gaul (modern France) and other parts of Europe. He chose not to conquer the part of Europe we now call Germany, which would later prove significant. (Germany developed a different culture and ultimately served as a training ground for groups intent on conquering Rome.) Civil war between the Senate and Caesar's followers resulted in pushing Pompey and Crassus out of the picture, after which Caesar became "emperor for life." But his life didn't last long. His angry senators assassinated him in 44 B.C.E.

After the death of Julius Caesar, a **Second Triumvirate**, composed of Octavius, Marc Antony, and Lepidus, came to power. Things didn't improve the second time around. Power again shifted to one person, **Octavius**, who rose to power, assumed the name Augustus Caesar, and became emperor. The days of the Roman Republic were over once and for all. Rome was now an empire led by a single emperor.

Pax Romana: Peace and Prosperity

■	Conquered by Augustus, 30 B.C.E. – 14 C.E.
■	Roman Empire by the death of Augustus, C.E. 14
■	Roman Empire at the end of Trajan's reign, C.E. 117
■	Conquered and lost by Trajan, C.E. 114 - 117

The Height of the Roman Empire

Under Augustus, Rome became the capital of the Western world. Augustus established the rule of law, a common coinage, civil service, and secure travel for merchants. With all these elements in place throughout the empire, stability returned to its people, and for 200 years they enjoyed a period of peace and prosperity known as the *Pax Romana* (Roman Peace). Interestingly, however, though many of the laws were uniform throughout the empire during this period, a number of traditional customs of the people in the conquered territories survived. This, of course, meant that the distinct groups within the empire, such as the Hebrews or the Egyptians, maintained their individual cultural identities.

Under imperial power, the Roman Empire expanded to its largest geographical proportions through additional military conquests. But more important in the history of the Roman empire was the growth of the arts and sciences during this time. For centuries, Greece had been the arts center of the Western world. With the Roman peace, however, the arts in Rome flourished, especially literature (notably, Ovid's *Metamorphoses* and Virgil's *Aeneid*) and architecture (marked by the building of the Pantheon, Colosseum, and Forum). Science also reached new heights. Ptolemy looked to the heavens and greatly influenced achievements in astronomy, while Roman engineers went to work on roads and aqueducts.

Compare Them: *Pax Romana* with the Golden Ages of Greece, Gupta, and Others

In case you haven't noticed a pattern, we'll point it out for you. When a major empire greatly expands its territory, it becomes the center of artistic and scientific energy. This is because it has a tremendous amount of wealth flowing into its capital from its conquered regions, and because the people have the freedom and confidence to pursue goals other than military protection. This happened in Rome, Athens, Gupta India, Han China, and the other civilizations we've discussed so far.

Religious Diversity: New Chiefs of Beliefs

Throughout the days of the Roman Republic and during the early days of the Roman Empire, Roman citizens were required to make sacrifices to traditional Roman gods. However, shortly after the reign of Augustus, a new religion developed in the Mediterranean and Aegean regions. That religion was **Christianity**.

Christianity grew out of Judaism, which had been practiced by Hebrews in Palestine for thousands of years. Judaism was the first major monotheistic religion. (These two religions are described in detail in Section VI of this chapter.) Initially, both Judaism and Christianity were tolerated by the Romans. The Romans allowed the conquered territories to practice their own faiths as long as doing so didn't interfere with the functioning of the empire. Eventually, however, Jewish resistance to Roman control led to the suppression of Judaism. Furthermore, as the apostles of Jesus and missionaries extended the influence of Christianity throughout the empire, the Romans began to see the new religion and its leaders as threats to both traditional Roman religion and their power. Several Roman emperors, including Diocletian and Nero, persecuted and even killed Christians, but these persecutions were periodic and localized. These acts of violence failed to stop the spread of Christianity, but it took several hundred years after the death of Jesus for Christianity to become the dominant religion of the Roman world. Only when Emperor **Constantine** himself issued the **Edict of Milan** in 313 C.E. did the persecution end. By 391 C.E., Christianity had become the official religion of the Roman Empire.

C. The Classical Civilizations: Mesoamerica

Although the Maya are often grouped with later Mesoamerican empires, the Aztec and the Inca, they were actually contemporary with the Romans, the Han, and the Gupta and developed some of the same characteristics of these early empires.

Mayan Civilization: In Search of More Slaves

From about 300 B.C.E. to about 800 C.E., Mayan civilization dominated present-day southern Mexico and parts of Central America. The Mayan civilization was similar to many other civilizations at that time in that it was a collection of city-states; however, all the city-states were ruled by the same king. Interestingly, like the Egyptians, the Maya were pyramid-builders and also wrote using hieroglyphics. The golden age of the Mayan Civilization was from about 500 to about 850 C.E. During that time, the Maya produced many great works of scholarship and developed a complex calendar system, but we know the most about its architecture and city planning because many remains have been discovered. There is no question that the Maya built tremendous cities; Tikal, the most important Mayan political center, may have been populated by as many as 100,000 people.

The Maya divided their cosmos into three parts: the heavens above, the humans in the middle, and the underworld below. The Maya believed that the gods created humans out of maize (one of the main Mayan dietary staples) and water. They also believed that the gods maintained agricultural cycles in exchange for honors, sacrifices, and bloodletting rituals.

Mayan warfare was somewhat unique in that it was imbued with a tremendous amount of religious significance. Days of religious ritual would precede a battle, and the King and nobility would actively participate in combat. One unique characteristic of Mayan warfare was that it was generally conducted not to gain territory, but to acquire slaves, who were used in large-scale building projects and in agricultural production. The Maya had no large animals, as horses and oxen would not arrive until much later with the Europeans, so humans were their primary source of labor.

As was the case in most agricultural societies, the majority of the people were peasants or slaves. Kings, priests, and hereditary nobility were at the top of the social pyramid. Merchants also enjoyed a high status.

The Maya used advanced agricultural techniques, such as the ridged field system, to make the most of the rainfall and swamp conditions of the region. Cotton and maize were widely cultivated; the Maya are also known for their elaborate cotton textiles. Many well-preserved ruins of this civilization remain today, including the tiered temple at Chichen Itza, which is similar in design to the Egyptian pyramids and Mesopotamian ziggurats, and several ball courts, which were used for a ritual sport throughout ancient Mesoamerica. Significantly, the Mayan calendar, based on a number system that included zero, was among the most accurate for its time. Since you're reading this book now, it's safe to say that the Mayan calendar stopped at 2012 only because the Mayans got tired of counting days.

D. The Late Classical Period: Empires Collapse, People Move

During the late Classical Period (200–600 C.E.), all the greatest civilizations that the world had known collapsed or significantly declined. This included the fall of Han China, the Gupta Empire in India, the western part of the Roman Empire in the Mediterranean, and the mysterious decline of the Maya.

1. Collapse of the Maya

Nobody's sure exactly what happened to the Maya. Some say it was disease, drought, or the declining health of the large peasant population. Others say it was internal unrest and warfare. Chances are, like other collapses, an expanding population gradually exhausted the Mayan environment, and it could not respond to the needs of the Mayan population. But whatever the reasons, the Maya started to desert their cities in the ninth century C.E. and the great civilization fizzled out.

2. Collapse of Han China

The Han Dynasty was interrupted by the reign of **Wang Mang** (9–23 C.E.), who established the Xin Dynasty after seizing the throne from the ruling Liu family, successfully using the belief in the Mandate of Heaven to undermine them. Wang Mang had been a respected government official before he took power, but soon made some disastrous missteps that weakened the empire and his control over it. Attempted reforms of land ownership and the currency were unsuccessful and caused chaos in the local economy among both the rich and poor. Waging war on the edges of the empire led to conscription of a resentful population and heavy taxation of landowners, an action that forced landowners to pay farmers less money for more work. Persistent famines, devastating floods along the Yellow River, and increasing commodity prices added to the resentment and fueled peasant uprisings, all of which Wang Mang's enemies used to their advantage. The Xin Dynasty came to an end in 23 C.E. with the death of Wang Mang in battle.

The Han Dynasty was restored a couple of years later, but full recovery proved impossible and, in 220 C.E., the government collapsed. For the next 400 years, China was divided into several regional kingdoms.

3. Collapse of the Gupta Empire

The Gupta Empire fell for one simple reason: It was invaded by the Huns—not Attila's forces, which invaded Europe, but another group, the White Huns. The Gupta were able to hold off the Huns for the first half of the fifth century, but they did so at a tremendous cost, which weakened the state. By the end of the fifth century, there were Hun kingdoms in western and northern India. Though the underlying culture of India (including Hinduism and the caste system) survived the invasion, the empire did not.

4. Collapse of the Western Portion of the Roman Empire

The Division of the Roman Empire

One historical event that has been endlessly debated over time is the fall of the Roman Empire. Some of these theories are reasonable, while others are much less so. Many try to assign a single cause to this momentous occurrence, but the situation was much more complicated.

In short, however, it can be said that it was internal decay, in combination with external pressure (Attila's Huns, among others groups), that brought about the fall of the Roman Empire. The sheer size of the empire and the huge expense of maintaining it, coupled by a succession of weak—or just plain bad—leaders and a series of epidemics, are all factors that caused the empire to collapse.

In 284 C.E., **Diocletian** had become emperor. He attempted to deal with the increasing problems by dividing the empire into two regions run by co-emperors. He also brought the armies back under imperial control, and attempted to deal with the economic problems by strengthening the imperial currency, forcing a budget on the government, and capping prices to deal with inflation. Despite Diocletian's innovations and administrative talents, civil war erupted upon his retirement in 305 C.E.

After rising to power in 306 C.E. as a co-emperor, **Constantine** defeated his rivals and assumed sole control over the empire in 322 C.E. He ordered the building of **Constantinople** at the site of the Greek city of Byzantium, and in 340 C.E. this city became the capital of a united empire. Constantine, too, was an able emperor, but the problems of shrinking income and increased external pressures proved insurmountable. After Constantine's death, the empire was again divided into two pieces, east and west. The eastern half thrived from its center at Constantinople; the western half, centered in Rome, continued its spiral downward.

Rome faced external pressure from invaders on all of its frontiers, especially from the middle of the third century on. One such invader was the powerful and well-organized Sassanid Persian empire, which took over in Iran in 224 C.E. The Sassanids practiced the Iranian faith of **Zoroastrianism** and used that to consolidate their power. The Sassanids enjoyed a powerful military that was able to defeat the Romans in many engagements, though the two empires managed to fight each other to a standstill by the year 627 C.E.

In addition to the Persians, Germanic tribes happened to attack the Roman empire at the same time that the Romans were embroiled in costly civil wars or wars against the Persians. In defense, Roman authorities put Germanic peoples such as the Visigoths (who had adopted Roman law and Christianity) on the borders. However, in the early fifth century, Attila and his Huns began to press on the Germanic tribes; in response, the Germanic tribes began to press on the Roman Empire. Because the Germanic tribes had no other place to retreat from the Huns, they crossed the border into Roman territory. The Visigoths sacked Rome in 410 C.E., and by 476 C.E., the Roman emperor had been deposed. The fall of the western half of the Roman Empire was complete. The eastern half survived, but not as the Roman Empire. It was later renamed the Byzantine Empire.

Western Rome 476 C.E.	Gupta 550 C.E.	Han China 220 C.E.
Tax revolts by upper class and church exempt from taxes	Not enough taxes for military defense	Officials exempt from taxes; difficult to collect from peasant population
Decrease in trade upon which economy depended		Population increases lead to less land per family
25 of 26 emperors died violently in one 50-year span		Corruption of court officials
Division of empire weakened the western half	Land divisions increased power of provincial officials	Unable to control large estate owners
Unable to defend against migratory invasions of Goths and Huns	Unable to defend against invasions by the White Huns	Constant conflict with the nomadic Xiong-nu who invaded after collapse

5. Cultural Diffusion 200–600 C.E.

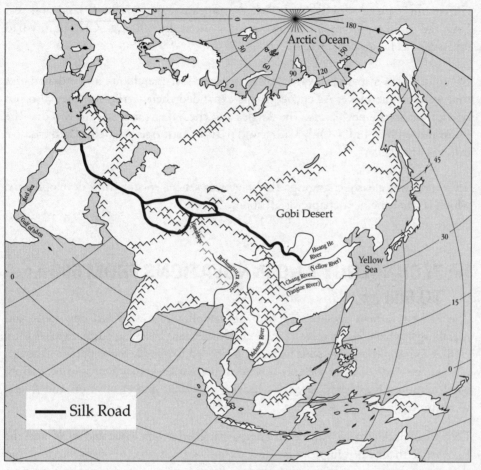

The Silk Road

Around the same time that major empires were collapsing, the known world was becoming an increasingly smaller place. Trade routes were flourishing, bringing cultures, religions, and invading tribes into constant contact with each other. Major trade routes over land, such as the **Silk Road** from China to the Roman Empire, took months to traverse. Pastoral communities along the way provided protection, shelter, and supplies for the merchants in exchange for payment. This meant that merchants not only interacted with people at their destination but also on the journey.

Unfortunately, disease traveled the same trade routes (and with invading armies). To give just a couple of examples, the Mongols carried the Black Death to China; Rome and China suffered from measles and smallpox epidemics, which quickly spread through the empires.

Contrast Them: The Fall of Han China, the Gupta Empire, and Rome

Two major causes of decline threaten any empire: internal (such as economic depression, natural catastrophes, and social unrest) and external (for example, invading armies). Unlike China, for example, which would later see a return to greatness, Rome would never again be at the center of such a great empire. The momentum had clearly changed to favor the invading German tribes and the powerful Byzantium Empire in the East.

Furthermore, as we mentioned earlier, religion also followed the roads of the merchants. Buddhism spread through East and Southeast Asia by way of trade routes. Christianity spread rapidly in the Mediterranean region via both land and sea. Even the invading Germanic tribes were converted. By 600 C.E., Christianity had taken root as far away as Britain.

By now, you're also well aware that it was not just merchants and missionaries that were on the move. As entire groups expanded their territories, they also put down roots in the new lands. The Angles and the Saxons moved into Britain. The Huns moved into India. Only China and parts of East Asia seemed spared massive influxes of outsiders.

The world was clearly changing. The stage was set for entirely new developments, which is what the next chapter is all about.

IV: TECHNOLOGY AND INNOVATIONS FROM 600 B.C.E TO 600 C.E.

The earliest human societies grew by developing primitive farming tools and metallurgy, which led to more complex technologies. These, in turn, enabled early civilizations to begin large-scale farming, which led to a stable food supply. Although a lot of the trade in early societies tended to be smaller luxury items—silk, cotton, wool, semi-precious gems, jewelry—heavier goods, including olive oil and spices, were also traded.

Of course, once a society had such goods, it needed a way to defend itself, and the knowledge that helped improve farming technology was used to create weapons and defense systems. It is not surprising that the first empires developed at the same time as iron technology and wheeled chariots, around 1500 B.C.E.! A major development in warfare, the stirrup, developed among the nomadic societies of the Eurasian steppe and spread to China as early as the third century B.C.E. The stirrup arrived late in Europe because the mountainous geography of the Mediterranean world limited the use of chariots and horses there. Additionally, the horses were initially too small to carry heavily armored soldiers. Because of this, the armies of Rome and Greece were mostly made up of foot soldiers armed with spears and bows and arrows.

To keep track of both increased trade and increased military, early societies developed means of communication and record keeping. Relatively accurate calendars were developed in all civilizations, but only the Maya had a 365-day solar calendar. Both the Maya and the Gupta separately invented the concept of zero. This was an especially inventive time for the Chinese; in addition to the building of the Great Wall and the massive terra cotta army of the Qin, the Daoist scholars of the Han Dynasty developed windmills and wheelbarrows, worked on some early forms of gunpowder, figured out how to distill alcohol, and produced paper from a variety of accessible materials, including tree bark.

V. CHANGES AND CONTINUITIES IN THE ROLE OF WOMEN

An unfortunate fact of sedentary societies is that women lost power as people settled, and women's roles in high-status food production became more limited. Nevertheless, women maintained power within the private sphere—by managing their households and taking responsibility for children's education, wives and mothers were often the unrecognized power behind the throne.

Although all of the early civilizations were decidedly patriarchal, women's freedoms differed depending on social status and class. Upper-class or elite women were more restricted in their public appearances, while lower-class women, peasants, and female slaves continued to work outside the home. Public veiling of upper-class women appeared as early as the Babylonian Empire and was widespread by Greek and Roman times.

Cultural and religious values also impacted the status of women. In both Buddhism and Christianity, women were considered equals in their ability to achieve salvation or nirvana. In both religions, women could choose to remove themselves from traditional roles to become nuns and live separate from society in convents. Hinduism and Confucianism were much more structured and restricted. A Hindu woman could not read the sacred Vedas or participate in the prayers and could not reach *moksha* in her lifetime. Daoism in China promoted male and female equality, but as Confucianism came to dominate, men were clearly considered superior to women. Under Confucian rule, some education was open to a large percentage of the female population, as it was believed they needed to be taught "proper" behavior and virtue.

Women's Status in Ancient Societies		
Rome/Greece	**India**	**China**
strict and patriarchal social divisions	strict patriarchal caste system	strict Confucian social order and guidelines for virtuous behavior
little land ownership	women not allowed to inherit property	only sons inherit property
high literacy among upper class	forbidden to read sacred texts	upper classes educated in arts and literature, and all educated in virtues
Spartan women given citizenship	no citizenship for women	no citizenship for women
women (especially widows) could own businesses	women needed large dowry; no remarriage for widows	arranged marriages, though widows were permitted to remarry
women could be priestesses or, later, nuns	women could not achieve *moksha*	Buddhist convents; Daoism promoted male and female equality

VI. MAJOR BELIEF SYSTEMS THROUGH 600 c.e.

As you review the major belief systems that were active during the era of the past two chapters (from the dawn of time up to 600 c.e.), keep a few things in mind.

1. Most of these belief systems have impacted world history from their inception through the present era. That said, the discussion here focuses on the impact of these systems during the ancient era. We'll talk more about the impact of these religions on later world events in subsequent chapters.
2. Most of the major religions have had schisms (divisions), resulting in a variety of subgroups and sects. The test writers will focus more on the overall religion than on particular sects (though there are a few exceptions that we'll get to in future chapters, such as the Protestant Reformation within Christianity and the rise of fundamentalism in Islam).
3. Don't focus only on the theological or philosophical basis of each belief system, but also on the impact those belief systems had on social, political, cultural, and even military developments.
4. Pay attention to where each belief system started and where it spread. As merchants and warriors moved, so did their religious beliefs. By looking at where religions branched out or came into conflict with one another, you'll get a good understanding of which cultures frequently interacted with each other.

For your convenience, here's a quick rundown of the belief systems covered in this section.

What About Islam?
Note that Islam is not included here. Why? Because Islam didn't come onto the scene until after 600 c.e. We'll talk a lot about Islam in the next chapter.

A. Polytheism
B. Confucianism
C. Daoism
D. Legalism
E. Hinduism
F. Buddhism
G. Zoroastrianism
H. Judaism
I. Christianity

A. Polytheism

Cultures that Practiced It

The vast majority of ancient civilizations were polytheistic. Through 600 c.e., the religions of all of the Mesopotamian and Mediterranean empires were polytheistic except for the Hebrews and the Christians. In the east, Aryan religions, Hinduism, and traditional Chinese systems were polytheistic. Some Buddhist sects were polytheistic, as were some Daoist sects.

Nuts and Bolts

Polytheists believe in multiple gods who impact daily life on earth to varying degrees, sometimes for good and sometimes not. For example, prior to the rise of Christianity, the ancient Greeks and Romans worshipped numerous gods who had very human qualities and who sometimes battled each other. In ancient Egypt, the gods were often considered benevolent and kind, while in ancient Sumer, the gods were to be feared and thus had to be appeased on a regular basis.

Broader Impact

Polytheism had a major impact on the development of civilization: It was absolutely at the center of art and architecture in most of the civilizations we have discussed so far. Many of the grand works of these civilizations were dedicated to the gods or made to appease them. More significantly, because the practice of polytheism in most early civilizations was very complicated and filled with rituals, it led to the rise of a priestly class whose members controlled most of the communication between the people and their gods. Thus, these civilizations became dependent on an elevated group of people who controlled their collective destinies, and rigid social structures with priests near the top quickly developed. Finally, because some polytheistic civilizations had separate gods for each city-state, as well as collective gods for the civilization as a whole, such as the systems practiced in Sumer and ancient Greece, the rise and fall of various city-states was seen as a drama played out not only on earth but also in the heavens. This belief added validity to a city-state's claim for predominance when it celebrated military success.

B. Confucianism

Cultures that Practiced It

Confucianism was developed specifically for the Chinese culture and was widely practiced throughout China from around 400 B.C.E. onward.

Nuts and Bolts

The son of an aristocratic family from northern China, Confucius spent most of his life trying to gain a high position in government. He was very strong-willed, and often his thinking was at odds with state policy. As a result, he never achieved his goal. Instead, he served as an educator and political advisor, and in this role he had a tremendous influence on China. He attracted many followers, some of whom helped share his teachings and others who collected his thoughts and sayings in the Analects, which would come to have a profound influence on Chinese thinking both politically and culturally. The most important distinction to make about Confucianism is that it is a political and social philosophy—not a religion. Though fundamentally moral and ethical in character, it is also thoroughly practical, dealing almost solely with the question of how to restore political and social order. Confucianism does not deal with large philosophical issues or with religious issues such as salvation or an afterlife.

Confucianism focuses on five fundamental relationships, which are considered the building blocks of society: ruler and subject, parent and child, husband and wife, older sibling and younger sibling, and friend and friend. When each person in these relationships lives up to his or her obligations in those relationships, society is orderly and predictable.

Confucianism concentrates on the formation of *junzi*, individuals considered superior because they are educated, conscientious, and able to put aside personal ambition for the good of the state.

There are also several values that Confucianism stresses:

> *Ren*—a sense of humanity, kindness, and benevolence
>
> *Li*—a sense of propriety, courtesy, respect, and deference to elders
>
> *Xiao*—filial piety, which means a respect for family obligation, including to the extended family

Confucius believed that individuals who possessed these traits would be not only good administrators but also influential in the larger society because they would lead by example. He also was convinced that to restore political and social order, morally strong individuals were required to exercise enlightened leadership. This belief is why Confucius did not support a particular political system but rather favored good people running whatever system was in place. Under Confucianism, women in China were considered of secondary status, although children were taught to honor their mothers as well as their fathers.

Broader Impact

Because Confucianism was an ethical, social, and political belief system, as opposed to a religion, it was compatible with other religions. In other words, a person could, for example, practice both Buddhism and Confucianism simultaneously.

This flexibility enabled Confucianism to flourish. Government leaders, too, embraced it, because it was intended to create an orderly society. Its widespread acceptance eventually led to a distinctive Chinese culture in which communities became extremely tight-knit; members had duties and responsibilities to many others in the community from birth to death.

Confucianism did not, however, have a similar impact on the rest of the world, because it evolved only within the context of the Chinese culture.

C. Daoism

Cultures that Practiced It

Some Chinese practiced Daoism, from around 500 B.C.E. onward.

Nuts and Bolts

The *Dao* (also spelled *Tao*) is defined as the way of nature, or the way of the cosmos. Founded by Lao-tzu, a legendary Chinese philosopher, this belief system is based on an elusive concept regarding an eternal principle governing all the workings of the world. The *Dao* is passive and yielding; it accomplishes everything yet does nothing. One image used to demonstrate this is of a pot on the potter's wheel: The opening in the pot is nothing, yet the pot would not be a pot without it. Daoists sometimes also use the image of water, soft and yielding, yet capable of wearing away stone. From this comes the idea that humans should tailor their behavior to the passive and yielding nature of the *Dao*. Thus, ambition and activism only bring chaos to the world. Within Daoism is the doctrine of *wuwei*, disengagement from worldly affairs, or a simple life in harmony with nature. Daoism isn't completely passive, however. Daoist priests often used magic that was intended to influence the spirits.

Broader Impact

Daoists advocated the formation of small, self-sufficient communities and served as a counter-balance to Confucian activism. As advocates of harmony with nature, Daoists promoted scientific discoveries, becoming great astronomers, chemists, and botanists. Daoism's impact, though, is greater than its philosophy. It's notable because it coexisted with Confucianism, Buddhism, and Legalism in China. One of the things to remember about Daoism, therefore, is that it added to the complexity of Chinese society, which in turn added to the uniqueness of China and other Eastern civilizations as separate and distinct from the Western world.

Contrast Them: Daoism and Confucianism

Though Daoism and Confucianism shared a core belief in the Dao, or "the Way," they diverged in how each understood the ways in which the Dao manifested itself in the world. While Confucianism is concerned with creating an orderly society, Daoism is concerned with helping people live in harmony with nature and find internal peace. Confucianism encourages active relationships and a very active government as a fundamentally good force in the world; Daoism encourages a simple, passive existence and little government interference with this pursuit. Despite these differences, many Chinese found them compatible and thus practiced both simultaneously. They used Confucianism to guide them in their relationships and Daoism to guide them in their private meditations.

D. Legalism

Cultures that Practiced It

The Chinese, specifically during the Qin Dynasty, are the most notable practitioners of Legalism.

Nuts and Bolts

Legalism developed at around the same time as Confucianism and Daoism. It maintained that peace and order were achievable only through a centralized, tightly governed state. Simply put, Legalists didn't trust human nature and therefore advocated the need for tough laws. They believed that people would be made to obey through harsh punishment, strong central government, and unquestioned authority. They focused only on things that were practical or that sustained the society. Not surprisingly, then, Legalists believed that two of the most worthy professions were farming and the military.

Broader Impact

By adopting Legalism, the Qin Dynasty was able to accomplish the unification of China swiftly, as well as the completion of massive projects like the building of the Great Wall. But because Legalism also caused widespread resentment among the common people who suffered under it, Legalism inadvertently led to wider acceptance of Confucianism and Daoism.

Contrast Them: Legalism and Confucianism

Although both Legalism and Confucianism are social belief systems, not religions, and both are intended to lead to an orderly society, their approaches are directly opposed. Confucianism relies on the fundamental goodness of human beings, whereas Legalism presupposes that people are fundamentally evil. Therefore, Confucianism casts everything in terms of corresponding responsibilities, whereas Legalism casts everything in terms of strict laws and harsh punishment. The Han successfully blended the best of both philosophies to organize their dynasty.

E. Hinduism

Cultures that Practiced It
The various cultures of the Indian subcontinent practiced Hinduism.

Nuts and Bolts
Hinduism began in India with the Aryan invaders. Review the history of India in Section III of this chapter if you need to.

Hindus believe in one supreme force called Brahma, the creator, who is in all things. Hindu gods are manifestations of Brahma—notably Vishnu, the preserver, and Shiva, the destroyer. The life goal of Hindus is to merge with Brahma. Because that task is considered impossible to accomplish in one lifetime, Hindus also believe that who you are in this life was determined by who you were in a past life, and that how you conduct yourself in your assigned role in this life will determine the role (caste) you are born into in a future life. If you behave well and follow the *dharma* (the rules and obligations of the caste you're born into), you'll keep moving up the ladder toward unification with Brahma. If not, you'll drop down the ladder. This cycle of life, death, and rebirth continues until you achieve **moksha**, the highest state of being, one of perfect internal peace and release of the soul.

There is no one central sacred text in Hinduism, though the Vedas and the Upanishads, sources of prayers, verses, and descriptions of the origins of the universe, guide Hindus.

Broader Impact
Hinduism is a religion as well as a social system—the caste system. In the caste system, you are born into your caste, and if you are dissatisfied with it, it's an indication you are not following the dharma; therefore, you will have an even worse lot in the next life. This explains why most faithful Hindus quietly accepted their stations in life. Though they knew that social mobility within one lifetime was out of the question, they were confident that they would accomplish it at death if they lived according to the tenets of Hinduism.

Hinduism's close identification with the caste system and the Indian social structure and customs have prevented its acceptance in other parts of the world. In recent years, modern Hindus are beginning to rebel against the strictures of the caste system. Nevertheless, Hinduism as a whole remains a powerful force—even regarding its adherents' relationship to the animal kingdom, because Hindus believe they can be reincarnated as animals.

Hinduism later spawned another religion—Buddhism.

F. Buddhism

Cultures that Practiced It

Eastern civilizations, most notably in India, China, Southeast Asia, and Japan practiced Buddhism.

Nuts and Bolts

Buddhism was founded by a young Hindu prince named Siddhartha Gautama, who was born and lived in Nepal from 563 through 483 B.C.E. He rejected his wealth to search for the meaning of human suffering. After meditating under a sacred bodhi tree, he became the Buddha, or Enlightened One.

There is no supreme being in Buddhism. Rather, Buddhists follow the **Four Noble Truths:**

1. All life is suffering.
2. Suffering is caused by desire.
3. One can be freed of this desire.
4. One is freed of desire by following what's called the Eightfold Path.

The Eightfold Path is made up of right views, right aspirations, right speech, right conduct, right livelihood, right endeavor, right mindfulness, and right meditation. Following this path enables you to move toward nirvana, the state of perfect peace and harmony. The goal in one's life is to reach nirvana, which may or may not take several lifetimes, meaning that Buddhists also believe in reincarnation. Buddhism holds that anyone can achieve nirvana; it is not dependent on an underlying social structure, such as the caste system.

After the death of Buddha in 483 B.C.E., Buddhism split into two large movements, **Theravada**, also known as **Hinayana**, Buddhism and **Mahayana** Buddhism.

Theravada (Hinayana) Buddhism emphasizes meditation, simplicity, and an interpretation of nirvana as the renunciation of human consciousness and of the self. In Theravada Buddhism, Buddha himself is not considered a god, and other gods and goddesses have very little significance. (Theravada means "the Way of the Elders"; Hinayana means "the Lesser Vehicle.")

Mahayana Buddhism ("The Greater Vehicle") is a more complicated form of Buddhism, involving greater ritual than Buddha specified. Mahayana Buddhism appealed to people who believed that the original teachings of Buddha did not offer enough spiritual comfort; therefore, they began to hypothesize that other forms of salvation were possible. In Mahayana Buddhism, the Buddha himself became a godlike deity. Moreover, other deities appear, including *bodhisattvas*, those who have achieved nirvana but choose to remain on Earth. Mahayana Buddhists also relied more on priests and scriptures. Detractors of this form of Buddhism view these additions as being too similar to the Hinduism that Buddha disapproved of.

Test Tip
You probably won't have to know the details of the two Buddhist movements for the AP World History Exam, but you should know that they exist.

Broader Impact

Because it rejected social hierarchies of castes, Buddhism appealed strongly to members of lower rank. And because Buddhism isn't attached to an underlying social structure, it can apply to almost anyone, anywhere. As a consequence, it spread rapidly to other cultures throughout Asia.

When Ashoka, the Mauryan Emperor who became appalled by one too many bloody battles, was moved to convert to Buddhism, the religion really took off as a major force in Asia. In India, however, Buddhism was eventually reabsorbed into Hinduism, which remained the dominant belief system there. In China, Japan, and Southeast Asia, Buddhism continued to thrive. Furthermore, as Buddhism spread via the trade routes, the cultures of Asia intertwined.

G. Zoroastrianism

Cultures that Practiced It

Iranians, especially under the Sassanid Empire, Central Asians, and some Indians practiced Zoroastrianism.

Nuts and Bolts

Zoroastrianism was created sometime in the second millenium B.C.E. in Central Asia and is typically attributed to the prophet Zoroaster. Zoroastrianism is a dualistic faith, which means that Zoroastrians believe in two gods representing good and evil. Ahura Mazda, the main god of good and truth, tries to lead his followers into overcoming the forces of evil and chaos, and humanity must play a role in ensuring that order survives. Thus, the individual actions of a person through his or her life determine the spiritual salvation of that soul, for Ahura Mazda will triumph over chaos at some point in the future. When chaos has been removed from the Universe, humans will transcend depending on their behaviors in their lifetimes. Its most important text is the Avesta, of which mostly fragmentary bits survive. We rely on quotations from later sources to make up for those that are lost to us.

Broader Impact

Zoroastrianism was an important religion to Iranian peoples, though its importance grew immensely when the Sassanid Persian dynasty was founded, as it became the state religion of the Sassanid Empire. Its dualistic tendencies clearly influenced Christian thinking before Christianity became the state religion of the Roman Empire, and led to another point of contact between cultures, this time in the realm of religion.

H. Judaism

Cultures that Practiced It

The Hebrews practiced Judaism.

Nuts and Bolts

Judaism holds that God selected a group of people, the Hebrews, and made himself known to them. If they followed his laws, worshipped him, and were faithful, he would preserve them for all time. This group became the Jews, and Judaism became the first of the great monotheistic faiths.

Judaism is not centered on many of the concepts typically associated with a religion, although a belief in an afterlife, a set of traditions and doctrines, and philosophy are part of its makeup. At the center of Judaism is the awareness of a unique relationship with God.

Jewish people believe that they were created by a personal, sovereign God, as was the world, for them to live in and enjoy and in which they could exercise free will. The destiny of the world is paradise, reached by human beings with divine help. Created in the image of God, human beings have an obligation to honor and serve God by following the texts of the Hebrew Bible, which include the Torah and other sacred texts that formed the basis of the Old Testament in Christianity. The Hebrew Bible contained accounts of miracles, laws, historical chronicles, sacred poetry, and prophecies and formed a central part of Jewish religious practice and social custom. Thus, Judaism is both a set of religious guidelines and a cultural system.

Broader Impact

Judaism was the first of the major monotheistic faiths; as such, it spawned the other two major monotheistic religions, Christianity and Islam.

Compare Them: Confucianism, Hinduism, and Judaism

At first glance, these three belief systems seem very different from one another. After all, Confucianism isn't a religion; Hinduism is polytheistic; and Judaism is monotheistic. However, they are similar in that they are all closely tied to the culture in which they are practiced, and therefore are not part of the sweeping, evangelical movements that seek to convert the rest of the world. Each not only arose out of a specific culture, but was also used to sustain that culture by providing guidelines and moral authority.

I. Christianity

Cultures that Practiced It
Originally a splinter group of Jews practiced the religion, but it quickly expanded into the non-Jewish community and throughout the Roman Empire.

Nuts and Bolts
Christianity came into existence with Jesus of Nazareth, a charismatic Jewish teacher who claimed to be the Messiah, a religious figure for whom Jews had long awaited. Many people were attracted to his teachings of devotion to God and love for human beings. The Roman and Jewish leaders were not among them, so in approximately 30 c.e., Jesus was crucified. His followers believed that he rose from the dead and ascended into heaven, and Christianity was born.

Christianity is based on both the Old and New Testaments of the Bible. Christians believe that Jesus Christ is the Son of God and that forgiveness of sins, and ultimately everlasting life, is achievable only through belief in the divinity, death, and resurrection of Christ. The Christian view is that the world was made by a personal and sovereign God, but that the world has fallen from harmony with God's will. As the Son of God, Christ was the link between God and human beings. Human beings are expected to seek to know God, to worship him, and to practice love and service to him and to other human beings. Many early Christians also believed that it was their duty to share this message with the unconverted (as do most Christian sects today).

Broader Impact
In the early days, Christianity was spread by the disciples of Jesus and by Paul of Tarsus. Paul was originally an extreme anti-Christian who was converted by a vision of Christ and became a principal figure in propagating the new religion. With its emphasis on compassion, grace through faith, and the promise of eternal life regardless of personal circumstances, Christianity appealed widely to the lower classes and women. By the third century c.e., Christianity had become the most influential religion in the Mediterranean basin. Following a period of sporadic and localized persecution, it became legal within, and then the official religion of, the Roman Empire; it continued to branch northward and westward into regions beyond the boundaries of the Roman Empire. In the ensuing centuries, this marriage of Christianity and empire would profoundly affect developments in a large segment of the world. More on that in future chapters.

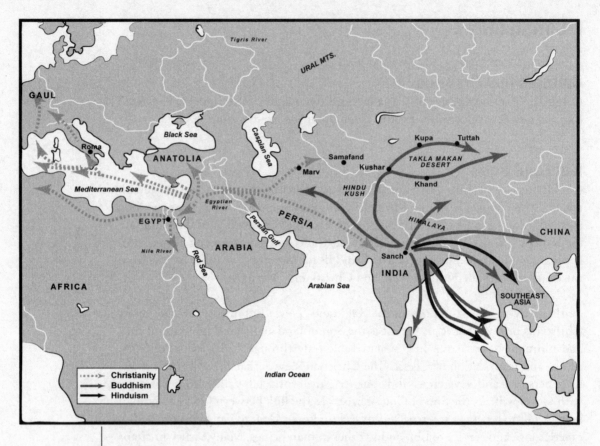

Map of World Religions, c. 600 C.E.

By 600 C.E., interaction through trade, warfare, and migration had spread Christianity, Hinduism, and Buddhism far beyond their areas of origin. Christianity became the dominant force in what was left of the Roman Empire, while the Silk Road and Indian Ocean trade routes brought Buddhism and Hinduism into east and Southeast Asia.

VII: PULLING IT ALL TOGETHER

1. Cultural Areas vs. States/Empires

When thinking about societies during this time period, it's more useful to think in terms of cultural areas than defined political borders; culture was more durable than political organization. Alexander's empire barely outlived him, but the Hellenic culture he spread across Eurasia lasted for centuries. Similarly, the Gupta and Han dynasties experienced political disruptions and fluctuating borders without affecting the extent of their respective cultures. Even the Romans went from republic to empire to collapse without their culture disappearing or even changing all that much (with some exceptions such as Christianity).

2. Change within Societies

Over this very long span, cultures and societies changed dramatically, which was driven by both internal and external factors. Internal factors include dramatic political changes such as the adoption of a new religion or religious practices, or domestic insurrection, perhaps caused by heavy tax burdens or widespread hunger, leading to peasant revolt. Or, aristocrats and generals might incite civil war or attempt to create their own state. External factors include foreign invasions, either by armies of another state or by migrating tribes and peoples, or the arrival of new ideas, practices, and religions via trade. These interactions could also bring plagues, weakening polities and affecting internal politics and culture.

3. Economic and Trading Practices

Empires developed their approach to trade and economics in broadly similar ways, as they responded to similar problems. As states grew and agriculture expanded, people needed reliable ways to figure out who owned what and how to trade goods beyond their local areas. Thus record keeping and currency developed as means of tracking, storing, and exchanging value. Larger-scale trade within and between regions led to a convergence in types of currency (thus the popularity of precious metals), while taxes and tribute boosted the importance of reading, writing, and records.

4. Environment and Decision-Making

One of the main obstacles faced by empires was the environment. When times were good, crops were abundant and the population grew. But if something went wrong—unseasonal storms, floods, a blight, or even just soil exhaustion—there were fewer crops to feed people, leading to famine, unrest, and even collapse. This dynamic was one of the contributing factors to the decline of the Gupta and Han Empires, and likely contributed to the fall of the Maya as well.

CHAPTER 7 KEY TERMS

Rock and Pillar Edicts

Arabic numerals

Han Dynasty

satrap

Delian League

Hellenism

patricians

plebeians

Twelve Tables of Rome

First Triumvirate

Second Triumvirate

Pax Romana

paganism

Christianity

Edict of Milan

Zoroastrianism

Confucianism

Daoism

polytheism

Legalism

Hinduism

Buddhism

Judaism

Theravada and Mahayana

Mauryan Empire

Chandragupta Maurya

Ashoka Maurya

Chandra Gupta the Great

Gupta Empire

Great Wall of China

Qin Shi Huang

Xiongnu

Wudi

Satrapies

Great Royal Road

Lydians

Phoenicians

Hebrews

Athens

Sparta

Persian Wars

Pericles

Socrates

Plato

Aristotle

Homer

Peloponnesian War

Macedonians

Alexander the Great

Punic Wars

Hannibal

Octavius

Constantine

Constantinople

Diocletian

Wang Mang

Chapter 7 Drill

See the end of the chapter for the answers and explanations.

Questions 1–4 refer to the passage below.

"After this, though not many years later, we at length come to what has been already related, the affairs of Corcyra and Potidaea, and the events that served as a pretext for the present war. All these actions of the Hellenes against each other and the barbarian occurred in the fifty years' interval between the retreat of Xerxes and the beginning of the present war. During this interval the Athenians succeeded in placing their empire on a firmer basis, and advanced their own home power to a very great height.

The Lacedaemonians, though fully aware of it, opposed it only for a little while, but remained inactive during most of the period, being of old slow to go to war except under the pressure of necessity, and in the present instance being hampered by wars at home; until the growth of the Athenian power could be no longer ignored, and their own confederacy became the object of its encroachments. They then felt that they could endure it no longer, but that the time had come for them to throw themselves heart and soul upon the hostile power, and break it, if they could, by commencing the present war.

And though the Lacedaemonians had made up their own minds on the fact of the breach of the treaty and the guilt of the Athenians, yet they sent to Delphi and inquired of the God whether it would be well with them if they went to war; and, as it is reported, received from him the answer that if they put their whole strength into the war, victory would be theirs, and the promise that he himself would be with them, whether invoked or uninvoked. Still they wished to summon their allies again, and to take their vote on the propriety of making war. After the ambassadors from the confederates had arrived and a congress had been convened, they all spoke their minds, most of them denouncing the Athenians and demanding that the war should begin."

Thucydides, *History of the Peloponnesian War*, circa 431 B.C.E.

1. What best characterizes the reasons the author gives for the Lacedaemonian declaration of war on Athens in this passage?

   (A) It was a religious war driven by the decree of their god to punish the Athenians for their sins.
   (B) It was an economic war, as the Lacedaemonians wanted to gain Athens' wealth for themselves.
   (C) It was a defensive war driven by Lacedaemonian concerns about Athenian power.
   (D) It was an alliance war driven by the concerns of Lacedaemonia's allies.

2. What form of religion does the text most clearly support as being practiced by the Lacedaemonians?

   (A) Pantheism, as the Athenians worshipped a pantheon of multiple gods
   (B) Worship of nature spirits and phenomena, such as lightning and the sea
   (C) Worship of a god or gods that actively intervene in mortal affairs
   (D) Monotheistic worship of a creator god that no longer intervenes in mortal affairs

3. What caused the retreat of Xerxes mentioned by the author?

   (A) Persian defeats at Marathon and Salamis
   (B) Spartan manhood and aggression
   (C) Internal problems within the Persian Empire
   (D) An alliance with Rome, which made Greece too strong to attack

4. Which of the following best characterizes Athens before and during the Peloponnesian War?

   (A) A culturally vibrant city-state emphasizing naval power and commercial pursuits
   (B) An austere city-state valorizing martial prowess
   (C) A center of industrial and agricultural production
   (D) The site of a Long Wall

TIMELINE OF MAJOR DEVELOPMENTS, 600 B.C.E TO 600 C.E.

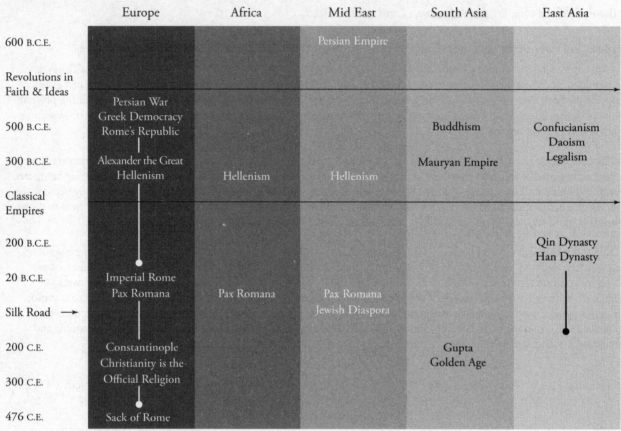

	Europe	Africa	Mid East	South Asia	East Asia
600 B.C.E.			Persian Empire		
Revolutions in Faith & Ideas					
500 B.C.E.	Persian War Greek Democracy Rome's Republic			Buddhism	Confucianism Daoism Legalism
300 B.C.E.	Alexander the Great Hellenism	Hellenism	Hellenism	Mauryan Empire	
Classical Empires					
200 B.C.E.					Qin Dynasty Han Dynasty
20 B.C.E.	Imperial Rome Pax Romana	Pax Romana	Pax Romana Jewish Diaspora		
Silk Road →					
200 C.E.	Constantinople Christianity is the Official Religion			Gupta Golden Age	
300 C.E.					
476 C.E.	Sack of Rome				

CHAPTER 7 DRILL EXPLANATIONS

1. **C**   Though the Lacedaemonians did appeal to their god, they were the ones to decide first that they would like to declare war; only after did they send to Delphi. Eliminate (A). Similarly, although the Athenians were wealthy and that wealth was resented, the text does not support this as the main cause of Lacedaemonian hostility toward Athens, so (B) is incorrect and can also be eliminated. Lacedaemonia's allies do not appear to be the main driver of hostility, though they are seen as agreeing with it; get rid of (D). However, it does appear to be true that the main cause was concern over growing Athenian power, which could no longer be ignored. Therefore, (C) is correct.

2. **C**   The passage does not discuss this issue in-depth, but it does indicate that the Lacedaemonians regarded a deity as "theirs" and believed the deity would help them in the war against Athens. Athenians were polytheistic, not pantheistic (which means the worship of *all* gods), so (A) is incorrect. Because the Lacedaemonians believed in at least one god that would help them, neither (B) nor (D) is correct. Therefore, (C) is the answer.

3. **A**   Contrary to pop culture, the Spartans were not particularly important in the defeat of the Persian invasions of Greece, so (B) can be eliminated. At the time of the Persian invasions, Rome was still a small fishing village in Italy, so it would hardly have been able to intimidate the Persian Empire; eliminate (D). Though internal problems are plausible, there is no evidence of that in the passage; get rid of (C). It was the defeats at Marathon and Salamis that ultimately forced Xerxes to abandon his campaign against Greece. Choice (A) is correct.

4. **A**   Choice (B) is a trap because it best describes Sparta, not Athens. Athenian power came from trade and sea power rather than industrial output. The term "industrial" is actually anachronistic for this period, which indicates that (C) is also a trap answer. While Athens did build several Long Walls, the question asks for the *best* characterization of the city-state, so the broader answer offered by (A) is the best choice.

REFLECT

Respond to the following questions:

- For which content topics discussed in this chapter do you feel you have achieved sufficient mastery to answer multiple-choice questions correctly?

- For which content topics discussed in this chapter do you feel you have achieved sufficient mastery to discuss effectively in a short-answer response or essay?

- For which content topics discussed in this chapter do you feel you need more work before you can answer multiple-choice questions correctly?

- For which content topics discussed in this chapter do you feel you need more work before you can discuss effectively in a short-answer response or essay?

- What parts of this chapter are you going to re-review?

- Will you seek further help outside of this book (such as a teacher, tutor, or AP Students) on any of the content in this chapter—and, if so, on what content?

Chapter 8
Regional and Interregional Interactions, c. 600 C.E. to c. 1450

I. CHAPTER OVERVIEW

This chapter picks up where the last one left off—kind of. You'll notice that a few things discussed in this chapter actually occurred before 600 C.E. We included them because they fit in better with the topics covered here.

Remember: Read through this chapter once, then go back and focus on the things that you're not entirely clear about. Here's the chapter outline.

I.   Chapter Overview

        You're reading it.

II.   Stay Focused on the Big Picture

        Organize the many events that occurred during the 800 or 900 years covered in this chapter into some big-picture concepts.

III.   Review of History Within Civilizations from 600 C.E.–1450

        This is the largest section of the chapter. In it, we'll delve into developments in each region or major civilization. If you're totally clueless on any part of this section, consider also reviewing the corresponding topic in your textbook. After all, we're talking about 850 years of history, and this section is intended as a review, not as a primary source. Here's how we've organized the information.

        A. The Rise of Islam
        B. Developments in Europe and the Byzantine Empire
        C. Developments in Asia
        D. The Rise and Fall of the Mongols
        E. Developments in Africa
        F. Developments in the Americas

IV.   Review of Interactions Among Cultures, 600 C.E.–1450

        To do well on the AP World History Exam, you need to understand more than just the events that occurred within each region or civilization. You need to understand how they interacted with and affected each other. This gets very complicated, so we've given the topic its own section. Make sure you review the material in Section III first. Once you have a firm understanding of the developments within each region of the world, this section will make a lot more sense. Here's how we've organized it:

        A. Trade Networks and Cultural Diffusion
        B. Expansion of Religion and Empire: Culture Clash
        C. Other Reasons People Were on the Move

V. Technology and Innovations, 600 C.E.–1450

Major advances in navigation, warfare, and ship building as trade expands and interaction increases

VI. Changes and Continuities in the Role of Women

The wealthier a society is, the less public presence and freedom women have

VII. Pulling It All Together

A review of the review

II. STAY FOCUSED ON THE BIG PICTURE

As you review the details of the civilizations in this chapter, stay focused on the big-picture concepts and ask yourself some questions, including the following:

1. Do cultural areas, as opposed to states or empires, better represent history? Cultural areas are those that share a common culture and don't necessarily respect geographical limitations. States, like city-states, nation-states (countries), and empires, have political boundaries, even if those boundaries aren't entirely agreed upon.

2. How does change occur within societies? As you review all the information in this chapter, you'll notice a lot of talk about trading, migrations, and invasions. Pay attention to why people move around so much in the first place and the impact of these moves. Furthermore, don't forget that sometimes change occurs within a society because of internal developments, not because of external influences. Pay attention to that too.

3. How similar were the economic and trading practices that developed across cultures? Pay attention to monetary systems, trade routes, and trade practices. How did they link up?

4. How does the environment impact human decision making? Pay attention to the way states respond to environmental changes. Do they move or send out raiding parties? Are they able to respond quickly and successfully to environmental changes?

III. REVIEW OF HISTORY WITHIN CIVILIZATIONS, 600 c.e.–1450

This period is defined by what rises out of the collapse of the classical civilizations and by the interactions—both positive and negative—that develop between these new states. This period is one of tremendous growth in long-distance trade: the caravans of the various Silk Routes, the multi-ethnic Indian Ocean sailors, the trips across the Sahara to West Africa, and continued trade in the Mediterranean all occur from 600 to 1450 c.e. These 850 years were also defined by a long period of decentralization in Western Europe and expansion on the trading empires of the Middle East and China. Remember interaction!

A. The Rise of Islam

In the seventh century, a new faith took hold in the Middle East. This faith, called Islam, was monotheistic, like Judaism and Christianity. The followers of Islam, called **Muslims**, believe that Allah (God) transmitted his words to the faithful through **Muhammad**, whose followers began to record those words in what came to be called the **Qu'ran**, or "recitation" (also spelled *Koran*). Muslims believe that salvation is won through submission to the will of God, and that this can be accomplished by following the **Five Pillars of Islam**. These five pillars are

- confession of faith
- prayer five times per day
- charity to the needy
- fasting during the holy month of Ramadan
- pilgrimage to Mecca at least once during one's lifetime (if finances permit)

Islam is also guided by the concept of *jihad*, which means "to struggle." This refers to both the struggle to be a better Muslim and the struggle against non-believers.

Islam shares a common history with Judaism and Christianity. It accepts Abraham, Moses, and Jesus as prophets (although it does not accept Jesus as the son of God), and holds that Muhammad was the last great prophet. Like Christians, Muslims believe that all people are equal before God and that everyone should be converted to the faith. Early on, Islam split into two groups: Shia and Sunni. The split occurred over a disagreement about who should succeed Muhammad as the leader of the faith.

Islam Takes Hold

Growing up in the city of **Mecca** in the Arabian desert (present-day Saudi Arabia), Muhammad was exposed to many different beliefs, in part because Mecca lay on the trade routes between the Mediterranean and the Indian Ocean. He was exposed to both Judaism and Christianity as a child, as well as the many polytheistic faiths that had traditionally influenced the region. Once he began preaching the monotheistic religion of Islam, which, as stated above, shares a foundation with Judaism and Christianity, he came into conflict with the leaders of Mecca, who had both a religious and economic interest in maintaining the status quo. In other words, the leadership in Mecca wanted to maintain the polytheistic shrines that attracted pilgrims and brought wealth to the community. Persecuted and threatened with death, Muhammad and his followers fled to **Medina** in 622 C.E. in what is known as the **hejira** (which also marks year 1 on the Muslim calendar). Muhammad and his followers found support in Medina and, in 630, he returned to Mecca and destroyed the pagan shrines—except for the Ka'aba, which became a focal point of Muslim pilgrimage to Mecca.

From Mecca, Islam spread throughout the Arabian Peninsula and beyond. The tenets of Islam came to be officially practiced in Arab culture, similar to the way the tenets of Christianity were practiced in the Roman and Byzantine Empires. Lands where Islam was practiced were known as "Dar al Islam," or House of Islam. As Islam spread rapidly through the Middle East and Africa and toward Europe, Christian leaders became increasingly alarmed. More on that later.

The Empire Grows as the Religion Splits

When Muhammad died unexpectedly in 632, **Abu Bakr**, one of his first followers in Mecca, became *caliph*, the head of state, military commander, chief judge, and religious leader. You can think of the caliph as a sort of emperor and religious leader wrapped up in one person. He ruled an empire, but he also made pronouncements on religious doctrine. In other words, the Islamic empire was what's known as a **theocracy**, a government ruled by immediate divine guidance or by officials who are regarded as being divinely guided. Because it was ruled by a caliph, the theocratic Islamic Empire was referred to as a **caliphate**. Islam would eventually branch out beyond the boundaries of the Islamic Empire and therefore exist independently as a religion, but in these early years, the growth of Islam was inextricably linked to the growth of this empire.

As time went on, the caliphs began to behave more like hereditary rulers, like those in a monarchy, except that there was no clear line of succession. The lack of clear succession caused a great deal of trouble down the road. The first four caliphs were Abu Bakr, Umar, Uthman, and Ali. The last of the four, Ali, was assassinated and was succeeded by his son, Hasan. But under pressure from a prominent family in Mecca, Hasan relinquished his title, making way for the establishment of the **Umayyad Dynasty**. This dynasty would enlarge the Islamic Empire dramatically, but it would also intensify conflict with the Byzantine and Persian Empires for almost a century.

Umayyad: by hasan

During the Umayyad Dynasty, the capital was moved to Damascus, in modern-day Syria, although Mecca remained the spiritual center of the Islamic world. Also during the Umayyad reign, Arabic became the official language of the government; gold and silver coins became the standard monetary unit; and conquered subjects were "encouraged" to convert to Islam in order to establish a common faith throughout the empire. Those who chose not to convert were forced to pay a tax.

As noted earlier, the Islamic Empire grew enormously under the Umayyads, expanding as far as northern Africa and Spain, where they ruled the southern Iberian peninsula (modern-day Spain and Portugal) from the city of Córdoba. Numerous times during the early eighth century, the Umayyads attacked the Byzantine capital of Constantinople but failed to capture the city. That didn't stop them from going elsewhere, and in 732 C.E., the Islamic Empire began to make a move on Europe by way of the Iberian Peninsula. At the time, Muslims held most of the Iberian peninsula and southern parts of Italy, while Christians dominated all the regions to the north. Charles Martel (686–741 C.E.), a Frankish leader, stopped the Muslim advance in its tracks as Muslim armies tried to advance toward Paris, so the Islamic Empire never flourished in Europe beyond parts of Spain and southern Italy. (More on the Franks and their activities a little later in the chapter.)

Despite the success of the Umayyad Dynasty (the **Dome of the Rock** was built on Temple Mount in Jerusalem during this time, and Córdoba was one of the richest and most sophisticated cities in Europe), problems with succession started to emerge. As was mentioned earlier in the chapter, after the death of Muhammad the Muslims split into two camps, Shiite and Sunni. **Shiite (Shia) Islam** holds that Muhammad's son-in-law, Ali, was the rightful heir to the empire based on Muhammad's comments to Ali. **Sunnis**, in contrast, though they hold Ali in high esteem, do not believe that he and his hereditary line are the chosen successors; rather, they contend that the leaders of the empire should be drawn from a broad base of the people. This split in Islam remains to this day.

As the Shia began to assert themselves more dramatically, the Umayyad Dynasty went into decline and ultimately demised. In a battle for control of the empire against the forces of Abu al-Abbas (a descendant of Muhammad's uncle who was supported by the descendants of Ali, the Shia, and the Mawali—non-Arab Muslims), the Umayyad Empire was defeated (punctuated by the slaughter of some members of the family). It was replaced by the Abbasid Dynasty around 750 in all areas except Spain.

The Abbasid Dynasty: Another Golden Age to Remember

The **Abbasid Dynasty** reigned from 750 to 1258, that is, until the Islamic Empire was defeated by the Mongols (more on them later). Throughout this time, like all major empires, the Abbasids had many ups and downs, but they oversaw a golden age beginning in the early- to mid-ninth century, during which the arts and sciences flourished. The Abbasids built a magnificent capital at **Baghdad** (modern-day Iraq), which became one of the great cultural centers of the world.

Like most of the other ancient civilizations we've discussed so far, the Islamic Empire was built around trade. The merchants introduced the unique idea of credit to the empire's trade mechanisms to free them of the burden—and the danger—of carrying coins. Necessarily, they also developed a system of itemized receipts and bills, innovations that were later used in Europe and elsewhere.

An Abbasid army had the good fortune to defeat a T'ang Chinese army (more on them in a few pages) during the Battle of the Talus River in 751 C.E. This fight for control of Silk Road trading posts in central Asia is relatively unimportant (the Muslims won) except for the fact that the Chinese POWs were carrying paper money. Once the Abbasids figured out how to make paper, they could continue one of their most important activities,

> ## Islamic Advancements
> In addition to the importance of trade, manufacturing played an important role in the expansion of the Islamic Empire. Steel, for example, was produced for use in swords. Islamic advancements were also seen in the medical and mathematics fields. **Muhammad al-Razi**, for example, published a massive medical encyclopedia that was unlike anything compiled before it. Islamic mathematicians expanded the knowledge they had learned from India; their contributions to algebra are especially noteworthy.

building libraries and universities and stocking them with scholarship from all over the known world. The location of the Muslims at the crossroads of Europe and Asia allowed them to monopolize trade routes. The cosmopolitan cities of the Islamic caliphs thrived on trade, international scholars, and expansion, both military and cultural.

Despite the hostility between the European and Islamic worlds, the Islamic Empire is credited with playing a significant role in preserving Western culture. (Recall that the Byzantines did this too.) In contrast to European civilizations during the Middle Ages, which were often decentralized and reluctant to embrace the teachings of "pagan" authors from antiquity, the Arabs kept the Western heritage of the region alive. For example, when the Muslims encountered the classic writings of ancient Athens and Rome, including those of Plato and Aristotle, they translated them into Arabic. Later, when Muslims and Christians battled for control of the Levant (present-day Israel, Jordan, Syria, Lebanon, and points north and south) during the European Crusades, Europe found its own history among the other treasures preserved in Arabic libraries and museums. This again demonstrates how the interaction between two peoples (even when violent) can lead to trade and cultural exchange.

The Muslims, like the Romans, were often tolerant of the local customs of the areas they conquered—although Christians and Jews were often persecuted in the Levant. That's not to say that the Islamic Empire didn't make every effort to convert the people it conquered (remember the tax we mentioned)? The point is that though it was a theocracy, the Islamic Empire's more flexible approach contributed to its rapid growth. The **Sufis**, Islamic mystics, were effective missionaries. They stressed a personal relationship with Allah, in contrast to other religions that emphasized a particular form of ritual. As you might guess, this made Islam highly adaptable to many different circumstances. By allowing, and even encouraging, followers to practice their own ways to revere Allah, and by tolerating others who placed Allah in the framework of other beliefs, the Sufis succeeded in converting large numbers of people to Islam.

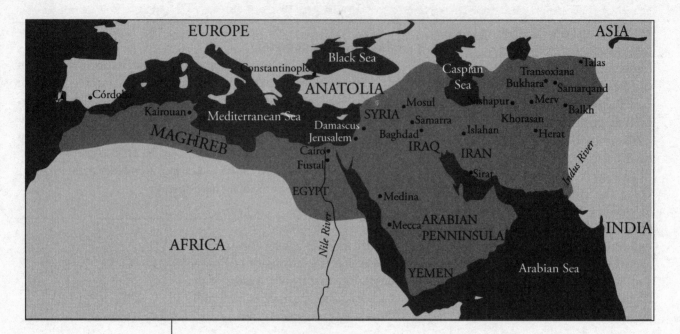

Map of the Abbasid Caliphate, ca. 850 C.E.

Women and Islam: For Better, for Worse

In Arabia, women traditionally did not have property rights or inheritance rights; rather, women were essentially viewed as property themselves—of men. If a man divorced a woman, for example, he would keep her dowry (the money and property from her father that she brought with her into the marriage). This widespread—really, institutionalized—low status for women eventually led to a culture in which baby girls were seen as less valuable than baby boys. Tragically this often translated into female infanticide, the killing of an unwanted baby girl. (This gender bias was, by the way, common in many patriarchal societies.)

The Qu'ran, the sacred book of Islam, established between 651 and 652 C.E., changed much of this. Although women remained subservient to men and under their direction and control, they began to be treated with more dignity, had some legal rights, and were considered equal before Allah. If a man divorced his wife, he would have to return her dowry to her. More important, infanticide was strictly forbidden. Women gained considerable influence within the home—and in early Islamic society, women sometimes had influence outside it. Khadija, Muhammad's first wife, had been a successful businesswoman, for example.

Islamic society was still a man's world, however. Men were permitted to have as many as four wives as long as they were able to support them and treated them equally. Women, on the other hand, had to be faithful to one man—in part because in this society land was passed through the males, and the identity of a boy's father couldn't be disputed. Legally, women were treated unequally; a woman's testimony in court, for example, was given only half the weight of a man's. Restrictions for women even included what they wore: Women sometimes had to be veiled in public—although this custom began in Mesopotamia and Persia, Islamic society adopted and adapted it.

[Handwritten margin note: Patriarchy, until Quran was revealed. (Although it was still mainly patriarchal)]

Over time, Islamic society became more structured and more patriarchal. A woman's primary duty was singular: to be loyal to and care for her husband and family. Within that structure, however, women were highly protected, and in some ways more respected, under the Qu'ran than they previously had been.

Decline of the Islamic Caliphates: Internal Rivalries and Mongol Invasions

The Islamic Empire regularly endured internal struggles and civil war, often arising from differences between the Sunni and Shia sects, and from ethnic differences between diverse groups in the rapidly expanding Muslim world. Numerous rival factions and powers developed, and although none of these threatened Islam, they did destabilize the central authority at Baghdad and cut tax revenues. The final blows came when Turkish warrior slaves revolted and established a new capital at Samarra in central Iraq, while other groups carved out pieces of the empire. There was a new Shia dynasty in northern Iran and constant threats from the Seljuk Turks, a nomadic Sunni group. Like the Romans before them, weakened by internal problems, the Abbasids also had external foes: the Persians, Europeans, and Byzantines.

However, it would be the Islamic Empire's most distant enemy, the Mongols, who would defeat it. During the crusades, in 1258, the **Mongols** overran the Islamic Empire and destroyed Baghdad, thereby signaling the end of the Abbasid Dynasty. Its people would flee to Egypt, where they remained intact but powerless. Eventually, the **Ottoman Turks** would reunite Egypt, Syria, and Arabia in a new Islamic state, which would last until 1918.

B. Developments in Europe and the Byzantine Empire

Developments in Europe and points east became quite complicated during the **Middle Ages**, which is the period after the fall of Rome and before the Renaissance. As you might recall from the last chapter, the Roman Empire, and eventually Christianity, was divided into two factions that split, reconnected, then split again. Ultimately, the eastern Roman Empire, centered in Constantinople, became the highly centralized government known as the Byzantine Empire; in the west, on the other hand, the empire collapsed entirely, although the Christian religion retained a strong foothold. The important point to remember about all of this is that even though both segments of the empire followed Christianity, they practiced different forms of the religion; moreover, their populations competed for supremacy.

Note the Change: As the Empire Turns

They meet. They flirt for a long time, and then marry and settle in Rome. Things get tough, so they take a short break from each other, but get back together in Constantinople where they build a new house. After a time they separate from each other geographically, but remain married by religion. Eventually, they get a divorce and follow their own religious paths. Will they ever be able to rekindle the romance?

The history of the Roman Empire reads a lot like a bad soap opera. Recall that the Roman Empire united the entire Mediterranean for centuries. However, it became too unwieldy to govern as a whole, so in 286 C.E., the empire was split into an eastern half and a western half, in what were hoped to be more manageable administrative regions. Then, in 313, Constantine converted to Christianity and made the religion legal in the empire. By the end of his reign, in the year 330, Constantine reunited the empire in Constantinople. It was still the Roman Empire, but it wasn't centered in Rome. The empire split again in 395, while the western half of the empire was sliced and diced by incoming barbarian tribes and disintegrated as a political unit in 476, at which time the eastern half became known as the Byzantine Empire. Almost 400 years later, in 800, the Pope attempted to revive the Western Empire by crowning Charlemagne "Emperor of the Romans." His empire continued to consider itself Roman throughout the Middle Ages. The Byzantines continued on as before in the east. So again there were two empires, but still one religion. That, however, was to change as well some two hundred years later when, in 1054, Christianity split, for both theological and political reasons, into two subgroups: Roman Catholicism and Christian Orthodoxy.

As you review the events in this region, the important points to remember are

- the Byzantine Empire was a lot more centralized and organized than the Western empire
- both practiced Christianity, though not in the same way

The Byzantine Empire: The Brief Details

The **Byzantine Empire** was distinct from the Roman Empire. It used the Greek language; its architecture had distinctive domes; its culture in general had more in common with Eastern cultures like those of Persia; and its brand of Christianity became a separate branch known as **Orthodox Christianity**.

Compared with what was going on at the height of the Roman Empire, much of Europe at the time was fragmented into small feudal kingdoms with limited power and fewer cultural and intellectual advancements. The Byzantine Empire, like the Islamic Empire to the south, was significantly different. The Byzantine emperors ruled by absolute authority, especially over the economy, whose industries, such as silk production (a trade learned from China), they monopolized. The Byzantines also used coined money, the value of which remained remarkably stable, making it a very desirable currency for business.

Under **Justinian**, who reigned from 527 to 565, the former glory and unity of the Roman Empire was somewhat restored in Constantinople. The region flourished in trade and the arts. Christian Constantinople and Islamic Baghdad rivaled each other for cultural supremacy. The Justinianic period is perhaps most remembered for three things: (1) the **Justinianic Code**, a codification of Roman law that kept ancient Roman legal principles alive (in the West these went unused for a time), and (2) the flourishing of the arts and sciences, evident in the construction of major buildings and churches, most notably **Hagia Sophia**, an enormous cathedral that still stands today (but now as a museum and former mosque). Finally, and most importantly, Justinian is known for his ambitious plan to reconquer the lost provinces of the western half of the Roman Empire. His plans went smoothly when his armies reconquered Africa from the Vandals, but intense siege warfare against the Ostrogoths in Italy that lasted 20 years halted Justinian's plans for further conquests. By the end of his reign, his empire was indeed larger, but at the cost of destroying what remained of Roman infrastructure in Italy, as well as bankrupting his coffers and exhausting the sources of his soldiers.

In contrast to the Roman Catholic emperors of the West, who regarded the Pope as the leader of the See of Rome, the Byzantine emperors nominated their own Patriarchs of the See of Constantinople. For centuries the two churches managed to tolerate each other while they butted heads for primacy over the whole of the Christian flock, but in time the differences, both political and religious, became too great. They disagreed over the sacrament of communion, whether priests should be allowed to marry, and the use of local languages in church. They were even at odds regarding the nature of God, specifically God as a trinity, and they disagreed over the placement of icons during worship. In 1054 C.E., unable to reconcile their differences, the Pope excommunicated the patriarch of Constantinople, who did the same to the Pope. From that point forward, the Church of Constantinople (otherwise known as Eastern Orthodoxy) influenced the East and Roman Catholicism influenced the West. Keep this schism in mind as you review the Crusades, Christian Europe's war with the Islamic world; the Byzantine Empire is right in the middle!

Byzantine Artistry
The Byzantines are also remembered and admired for their mastery of the mosaic art form they used to decorate churches.

Contrast Them: Religion and State in Roman Catholicism and Christian Orthodoxy

Remember that we said the secular empire was more centralized in the East (Byzantine Empire) than in the West (Roman Empire) during the Middle Ages? Interestingly, the reverse was true in terms of their religions. Christianity as practiced by Catholics was very centralized, with power stemming from Rome and services held in the Roman (Latin) form. In the East, Orthodox Christianity was more localized. Russian churches, for example, conducted services in their own language. In this sense local customs merged with Christian practices in the Orthodox Church.

A great deal of the evolution of these religious factions in these two empires centered on control. For stability, either the heads of the church or the heads of the state needed to be in control. During the Middle Ages, the West centralized power in the church, thereby decentralizing political power. Essentially this meant that the existing political leadership was blessed by the church, hence often under the control of the church as well, at least in the early centuries of the Middle Ages. In the East, the situation was the exact opposite: Political emperors were in control of both politics and the church, and while church practices were localized, political authority was not. The point to remember here is that in the early centuries of the Middle Ages, the East was more of a secular empire with an official church religion; the West was more of a religious empire with subservient political units.

Impact of Orthodoxy on Russia: Feast in the East

In the ninth century, the Slavic peoples of southeastern Europe and Russia were converted to Christianity by St. Cyril, an Orthodox Christian who used the Greek alphabet to create a Slavic alphabet known as the Cyrillic alphabet, which to this day is used in Russia and other parts of the region. Most of these areas were not part of the Byzantine Empire itself, but were influenced by it. When Vladimir, a Russian prince from Kiev, abandoned the traditional pagan religion and converted to Christianity, he also considered Islam, Judaism, and Roman Catholicism. Rumor has it that he chose Christian Orthodoxy because it had no restrictions about when or what he could and could not eat.

The dominance of Christian Orthodoxy in this region is significant because while Western Europe followed one cultural path, Eastern Europe followed another, and this had a tremendous impact on the development of Russia. The Russian Orthodox Church was aligned with Byzantine but not Roman traditions. So, when the Roman church reformed later (discussed in Chapter 7), the Russian and Greek churches did not. As a result of this and the Mongol invasion (coming up soon), Russia became culturally different from the other great powers of Europe, which grew out of the Catholic tradition.

Meanwhile Out West: The Franks Versus the Muslims

The best place to begin a discussion of political developments in Western Europe in the Middle Ages is with the Franks. After the classical Roman Empire fell apart, due in part to invasions from Germanic tribes, these tribes settled throughout Western Europe. Most of the tribes converted to Christianity relatively quickly, though politically they continued to run their own shows. That meant they came into regular conflict with each other, and they formed alliances and expanded, sometimes enough to be considered kingdoms. The most significant of these early kingdoms was the Franks.

The Franks were a Germanic tribe that united under the leadership of King Clovis in the late fifth century. He built a rather large empire that stretched from present-day Germany through Belgium and into France. He converted to Christianity and established his capital in Paris. After he died, his empire was divided among his sons, after which it declined in influence.

Nevertheless, the empire did help the various peoples of Western Europe solidify under a common culture, which made it easier for them to unify against Muslim invasions, which in the eighth century took over parts of Spain and Italy. Charles Martel (remember we mentioned him at the beginning of the chapter?) led the revolt against the advancing Muslim armies and in 732 defeated them at the Battle of Tours, not far from Paris. Again, interaction through conflict.

Martel then used his position as a political and military leader under the declining Frankish **Merovingian Dynasty** to put his sons forth as successors, thus founding the **Carolingian Dynasty** ("Carolus" is Latin for Charles). Martel had worked during his tenure to reunite the region under his control, and when his son **Pepin the Short** (there were several Pepins in Frankish history) ascended to the throne in 752 C.E., Charles chose to have his succession certified by the pope, a significant step that sent the clear signal that an empire's legitimacy rested on the Rome's approval.

Charlemagne: The Empire Strikes Back

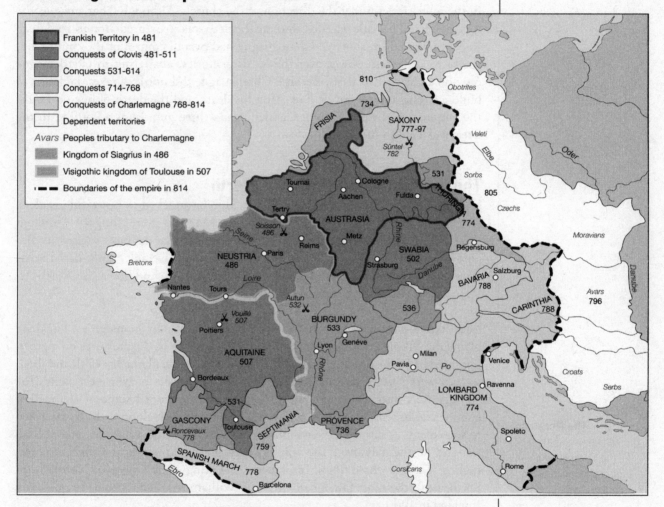

Central Europe around the Thirteenth Century

In the centuries following the breakup of the Roman Empire, no true empire existed in Western Europe. The Franks had built a large kingdom, but it could hardly be considered an empire by historical standards. It would be Pepin's son, Charles (747–814 C.E.), who would revitalize the concept of the empire in Western Europe. Like his father, Charles was crowned by the pope in 800 and became known as **Charlemagne** ("Charles the Great").

The empire Charlemagne built would come to be called the **Holy Roman Empire** upon the coronation of Otto the Great in 962. It's important to point out that this empire had little in common with the original Roman Empire, other than the fact that power was once again centralized and Rome began to think of itself as a world center again. The size of the Holy Roman Empire, in comparison to its namesake, was relatively small. It included northern Italy, Germany, Belgium, and France. Nevertheless, it marked the beginning of Western European ambition in terms of empire-building, especially among those in the church.

Under Charlemagne, a strong focus was placed on the arts and education, but not surprisingly with a much more religious bent—much of this effort centered in the monasteries under the direction of the church. Although Charlemagne was very powerful, his rule was not absolute. Society was structured around feudalism (more on feudalism shortly). Charlemagne had overall control of the empire, but the local lords held power over the local territories, answering to Charlemagne only on an as-needed basis. Because Charlemagne did not levy taxes, he failed to build a strong and united empire. After his death and the death of his son Louis, the empire was divided among Charlemagne's three grandsons according to the **Treaty of Verdun** in 843.

The Vikings: Raiders from the North

During this time, Western Europe continued to be attacked by powerful invaders, notably the Vikings from Scandinavia and the **Magyars** from Hungary. Although the **Vikings** were not the only raiders, they were perhaps the most successful. Beginning around 800 C.E., they used their highly maneuverable, multi-oared boats to raid well beyond their borders—on the open seas, up and down the North Atlantic coast, and along the inland rivers.

The Vikings got a bad reputation for raiding the Catholic monasteries, but don't blame the Vikings. Raiding was a normal consequence of the pressures on a growing society and the need for resources. The monasteries held much wealth and food, so they were natural targets. Raiding was just one aspect of Norse economy. The Vikings were also merchants and fishermen and developed some of the earliest commercial fisheries in northern Europe. These activities, along with the raids, led to settlements as diverse as Newfoundland, Canada around 1000 C.E., inland Russia, and northern France. The Vikings even got as far south as Constantinople, raiding it at least three times. In France, the Vikings were known as Normans (or north-men), the most famous of whom is William, who conquered Anglo-Saxon England in 1066.

The Normans
Vikings, in the form of the Normans, had an enormous influence on England, particularly on the English language.

Remarkably, however, in spite of their various victories, the Vikings, too, were converted to Christianity. This continued in a pattern of invading tribes assimilating to a common civilization in Western Europe because of religion, not political power. Catholicism became institutionalized at every level of life. By the middle of the Middle Ages, the Catholic Church had become the most powerful institution in Western Europe and one of the most powerful institutions in the world.

European Feudalism: Land Divided

Feudalism, the name of the European social, economic, and political system of the Middle Ages, had a strict hierarchy. At the top was a king, who had power over an entire territory called his kingdom. Beneath him were the **nobles**, who in exchange for military service and loyalty to the king were granted power over sections of the kingdom. The nobles, in turn, divided their lands into smaller sections under the control of lesser lords called **vassals**. The vassals could also split their lands into smaller pieces and give custody of them to subordinate vassals, who could divide their lands into even smaller pieces in the custody of even more subordinate vassals, and so on. Below the vassals were **peasants**, who worked the land. For this system to work, everyone had to fulfill obligations to others at different levels in the hierarchy: to serve in the military, produce food, or serve those who were at a higher level. If, say, you were a lesser-lord, you were obliged to your lord, and you were obliged to your vassals as well.

The estates that were granted to the vassals were called **fiefs**, and these later became known as **manors**. The lord and the peasants lived on the manor. The peasants worked the land on behalf of the lord, and in exchange the lord gave the peasants protection and a place to live. Many of the manors were remarkably self-sufficient. Everything that was needed to live was produced on them. Food was harvested, clothing and shoes were made, and so on. Advances made in the science of agriculture during this time helped the manors to succeed. One such advance, called the **three-field system**, centered on the rotation of three fields: one for the fall harvest, one for the spring harvest, and one not-seeded fallow harvest (the latter allowing the land to replenish its nutrients). In this way, manors were able to accumulate food surpluses and build on the success. Lords directed what was called the "Great Clearing," the clearing of huge areas of forest for the creation of more farmland.

Compare Them: Ancient Civilizations and the Middle Ages

You have no doubt noticed that European civilizations during the Middle Ages evolved in much the same way as the Mediterranean, Indus, and Shang civilizations a couple of thousand years earlier, and for the same reason: Agricultural surpluses enabled the early civilizations to build cities, which then made it possible to form complicated institutions and promote the arts and sciences.

In Western Europe after the fall of the Roman Empire, the practice of feudalism caused life to be centered on small, self-sustaining communities that didn't initially generate much of a surplus. But as they subsequently built up storehouses of food and supplies, and as people came into greater contact with each other, they were freed to pursue other endeavors (at the discretion of their overseer, of course). As a result, we begin to see the emergence of craftspeople, individuals skilled in highly specialized ways. Towns and cities grew, and eventually the Middle Ages came to an end.

The lord, as noted, owed his allegiance to the king but only had direct contact with him when the king called upon the lord to provide a service. Otherwise, the lord was in charge of his own manor—his own life. And though the various fiefs were, in theory, self-sustaining, and the lords all beholden to the same ruler, conflicts erupted between feudal lords on a regular basis (this is where the term feud comes from). The etiquette of these disputes and rules of engagement was highly refined and flowed from the **code of chivalry**, an honor system that strongly condemned betrayal and promoted mutual respect. Most of the lords (and knights, who were also considered part of the nobility) followed the code of chivalry.

The feudal system, like most of the civilizations we've discussed so far, was male-dominated. Land equaled power, and only males could inherit land, so women were pretty much powerless. Specifically, when a lord died under the feudal system his land and title passed down via **primogeniture, to his eldest son**. Even noblewomen had few rights, though they were socially elevated (and have come to be romanticized in literature). Women could inherit a fief, but they could not rule it. Furthermore, women's education was limited to domestic skills. As usual in most early societies, noblewomen were admired and valued primarily for their "feminine" traits—their beauty or compassion—but were regarded essentially as property to be protected or displayed.

Peasants (called **serfs**) in the feudal social system, whether male or female, had few rights. As manorial life evolved, an increasing number of peasants became tied to the land quite literally: They couldn't leave the manor without permission from their lord. Peasants were not quite slaves, but not free either. Ironically, however, it was this "imprisonment" on the land that led to the serfs becoming highly skilled workers. In short, they learned how to do whatever it took to make the manor self-sufficient.

Contrast Them: Feudal Europe and the Islamic Empire

Remember the Abbasid Dynasty? It flowered in the Islamic world at the same time that feudalism was taking root in Western Europe. Islamic merchants were trading with the world while European lords were governing their manors. Baghdad became a center of learning and art in the Islamic Empire, whereas small, secluded monasteries became centers of learning in the early Holy Roman Empire. In summary, it can be said that in the early Middle Ages, educated Europeans became very provincial, while educated Arabs became more worldly.

As many of the serfs became skilled in trades other than farming, and Europe slowly but surely started trading with the rest of the world, some of these skilled craftspeople began to earn extra income. Over time, this elevation in the status of craftspeople chipped away at the rigid social stratification of the manor system. When banking began in Europe, towns and cities started to gain momentum. The result was the emergence of a "middle class" made up of urban craftsmen and merchants. The success of this new middle class lured more people into towns in the hopes of making more money or learning new skills. By the eleventh century, Western Europe was re-engaging with the world.

Height of the Middle Ages: Trading and Crusading

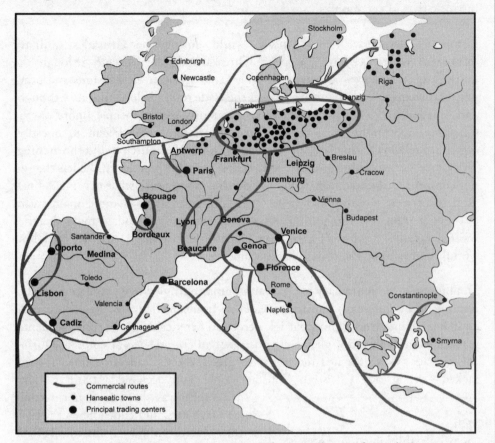

Trade Routes of the Hanseatic League (Thirteenth to Fifteenth Centuries)

Given the new importance of trade, towns with wealthy merchants arose near the once all-powerful manors. Towns were chartered on lands controlled by feudal lords (the charters gave the townspeople certain rights), and within the towns, the middle-class merchants, or **burghers**, became politically powerful. Like their manorial predecessors, the towns had a great deal of independence within the empire but were intrinsically more interdependent than the self-sufficient manors of the feudal system. Eventually, towns formed alliances, not unlike a city-state structure. One of the most significant alliances, the **Hanseatic League**, had an economic basis; established in 1358, it controlled trade throughout much of northern Europe. One effect of the interdependence of the towns was to initiate a drive toward nationhood; another was to increase social mobility and flexibility among the classes.

Among the greatest artistic achievements of the Middle Ages was its architecture, specifically its cathedrals. In the early Middle Ages, churches were built in the bulky Romanesque style; later architectural advancements led to what came to be called the Gothic style. Gothic cathedrals were designed to draw worshippers closer to God. To achieve this, architects of the day used "flying buttresses," which gave support for tall windows and vaulted ceilings. Over time, the cathedral became more than a place of worship; it became an art form and an arena for art. The church sponsored artists to adorn the inside of cathedrals with paintings and sculpture. Music, too, such as Gregorian chants, became an intrinsic part of ceremonies.

European contact with the Muslim world during the **Crusades** (military campaigns undertaken by European Christians of the eleventh through the fourteenth centuries to take over the Holy Land and convert Muslims and other non-Christians to Christianity) and over the trade routes helped spur new thought and broadened the perspective of these previously insular people (more on the Crusades in Section IV of this chapter). In time, people began to question organized religion (citing "reason"), which of course the church found threatening. This process of reasoning gave rise to **heresies**, religious practices or beliefs that do not conform to the traditional church doctrine. Sometimes what became defined as heresies were simply older beliefs that did not adapt to more mainstream changes in religious thought. In what may seem ironic today, many heretics wanted a return to the simpler ways of early Christianity; they rejected how worldly and wealthy the church had become.

Doubts about the supremacy of religious dogma continued to emerge until the beginning of the thirteenth century, when **Pope Innocent III** issued strict decrees on church doctrine. Under Innocent III, perceived heretics and Jews were frequently persecuted, and a fourth, ultimately unsuccessful crusade was attempted. During this crusade, which seemed motivated by greed, the Crusaders conquered—and sacked—the already Christian Constantinople, and declared a Latin Empire. (This empire was short-lived, lasting only some fifty years, and ended when the Byzantines overthrew the Latins in 1261). A few years later, Pope Gregory IX set into motion the now-notorious **Inquisition**, a formalized interrogation and persecution process of perceived heretics. Punishment for so-called nonbelievers ranged from excommunication and exile to torture and execution. Due to the pervasiveness of the church and its ultimate power at this time, it is sometimes referred to as the **Universal Church** or the **Church Militant**.

The Birth of Scholasticism

Another important effect of people thinking more openly was the founding of universities, where men (not women) could study philosophy, law, and medicine, and learn from the advances made in Muslim cultures. In science, the ideas of Aristotle, Ptolemy, and other Greeks were brought to Europe through contacts with Islamic and Byzantine Empires (again, via trading and crusading). This progression, called **scholasticism**, also sometimes came into conflict with the church because it relied on reason rather than faith.

Late in the thirteenth century, **Thomas Aquinas** (1225–1274 C.E.), a famous Christian theologian, made significant inroads in altering Christian thought. He wrote the *Summa Theologica*, which outlined his view that faith and reason are not in conflict, but that both are gifts from God and each can be used to enhance the other. His writings had a major impact on Christian thought, although the church remained a strict guardian of its own interpretations.

Focus On: The Bubonic Plague

Referred to as the Black Death, this epidemic originated in China, where it killed an estimated 35 million people. It spread rapidly through Europe in the mid-fourteenth century. Its transmission was facilitated by new forms of commerce and trade, including Mongol control of the central Asian Silk Routes, that increased the interaction between Europe and Asia. First occurring in the 1330s, the epidemic spread westward with traders and merchants and arrived in Italian port cities as early as 1347. Crowded conditions in Europe's cities and the lack of adequate sanitation and medical knowledge all contributed to its rapid spread. Within only two years, more than a third of Europe's population was dead, and traditional social structures nearly collapsed. The dramatic changes brought by the epidemic sped up social and economic movements that were already impacting Europe. These included a shift toward a commercial economy, more individual freedoms, and development of new industries.

The Emergence of Nation-States: Power Solidifies

Keep in mind that during the Middle Ages, Western Europe wasn't organized into countries (nation-states); rather, it was broken up into feudal kingdoms. However, by the close of the Middle Ages, Western Europe began to organize along cultural and linguistic lines. People who spoke French aligned themselves with France. Those who spoke English united under the banner of England. We'll be talking a lot more about this in the next chapter, but for now just keep this general concept in mind.

The various parts of Europe took different paths to achieve statehood during the thirteenth century. In Germany, for example, the reigning family died out without a suitable successor to the emperorship, so the region entered a period known as an **interregnum** (a time between kings). Germany and Italy became decentralized in a group of strong, independent townships and kingdoms, similar to city-states. In this environment, merchants and tradespeople became more powerful. In northern Germany, for example, the Hanseatic League (the influential association of merchants mentioned earlier) led the region's progress in international trade and commerce.

England, by contrast, unified much more quickly. Since the time of **William the Conqueror**, England had followed a tradition of a strong monarchy. However, during the rule of King John, powerful English nobles rebelled and forced him to sign the **Magna Carta** (1215 c.e.). This document reinstated the feudal rights of the nobles, but also extended the rule of law to other people in the country, namely the growing burgher class, laying the foundation for the Parliament. Initially, an assembly was established made up of nobles who were responsible for representing the views of different parts of England on law-making and taxation issues. After a trial period, the Parliament was established. Later, it was divided into two branches: the House of Lords (nobles and clergy) and the House of Commons (knights and wealthy burghers). The House of Lords presided over legal issues and advised the king; the House of Commons was concerned with issues of trade and taxation. The result was that England established its identity pretty early on.

The formation of France was bound up with England. In 987, **King Hugh Capet** ruled only a small area around Paris; for the next 200 years or so, subsequent French kings expanded the territory. Beginning in the twelfth century, England began to claim large parts of present-day France. The English occupation of the French-speaking territories led to revolts and, eventually, to French statehood. (The goal was to unite France under its own leadership.) This effort was spearheaded by an unlikely candidate.

Bourbon Beginnings
After the Hundred Years' War, royal power in France became more centralized. Under a series of monarchs known as **Bourbons**, France was unified and became a major power on the European continent.

As a teenager, farm girl **Joan of Arc** claimed to have heard voices that told her to liberate France from the hands of the English, who had by the early fifteenth century claimed the entire French territory. Remarkably, this uneducated youngster somehow managed to convince French authorities that she had been divinely inspired to lead men into battle, and they supplied her with military backing. With her army, she forced the British to retreat from Orleans, but was later captured by the French, tried by the English, and burned at the stake by the French. Nevertheless, she had a significant impact on the **Hundred Years' War** (1337–1453) between England and France, which eventually resulted in England's withdrawal from France.

At around the same time, Spain was united by **Queen Isabella**, the ruler of Castile (present-day central Spain). Power in the Spanish-speaking region of Europe had been divided for two reasons: first, Castile was one of three independent Spanish kingdoms, and therefore no single ruler controlled the region, and second, the peasants were split along religious lines (mostly Christian and Muslim), due to the lasting influences of the Muslim conquest of the Iberian Peninsula during the Middle Ages. To overcome these obstacles, Isabella married **Ferdinand**, heir to the Spanish Kingdom of Aragon, in 1469, thus uniting most of Spain in a single monarchy. Rather than compete with the church for authority, Isabella and Ferdinand, both Christians, enlisted the Catholic Church as a strong ally. Spanish statehood thrived under the new monarchy, and the alignment with the Catholic Church effectively ended religious toleration in the region. The result was that non-Christians (predominantly Muslim and Jewish people) were forced to convert to Christianity or leave the country. This policy marked the beginning of the **Spanish Inquisition**. The consequences for non-Christian Spaniards were tragic; the consequences for the Spanish monarchy were huge. Newly unified and energized, Spain embarked on an imperial quest that led to tremendous wealth and glory, eventually resulting in the spread of the Spanish language, Spanish customs, and Christianity to much of the New World (as you will see in the next chapter).

What About Russia?

Recall that Eastern Europe and Russia at this time were very different from the West. The Eastern Orthodox Christians of this area spent much time and effort defending themselves from the colonization of various western invaders. It wasn't until 1242 that Russia succumbed to the **Tatars** (a group of Mongols from the east) under Genghis Khan. The Tatars ruled a large chunk of Russia for two centuries, leading to a cultural rift that further split eastern and Western Europe.

By the fourteenth century, Mongol power started to decline and the Russian princes of Muscovy grew in power. By the late 1400s, Ivan III expanded Muscovy territory (the area surrounding Moscow) into much of modern-day Russia and declared himself **czar**, the Russian word for emperor or Caesar. As the center of the Eastern Orthodox Church, Moscow was declared the Third Rome, after the real Rome and Constantinople. By the mid-1500s, **Ivan the Terrible** had centralized power over the entire Russian sphere, ruling ruthlessly and using the secret police against his own nobles. The next chapter will go into more of the details about Russia. By this time, nationalism in Russia was well underway.

> ### Focus On: Urbanization
>
> If trade is the way you make your living, chances are you are spending lots of time in cities. Traders and merchants needed a place to meet and conduct business and this period saw the growth of urban culture throughout the world, mostly as a result of trade contacts and networks. Along with trade, cities showcased the wealth and power of the rulers who both controlled and benefited from the trade. Urban centers usually developed along trade routes or in locations necessary for strategic defense.
>
> In the early years, the most populous cities were in the Muslim world and China—cities that were part of the network of Silk Routes: Baghdad, Merv, and Chang'an. Prior to 1400, Constantinople was the only European city of any size and it was really considered part of the Eastern world. Along with their economic role, these cities became political and cultural centers for the new trade empires. After 1400, European cities begin to grow with Paris and the Italian city-states emerging as new trading powers.

C. Developments in Asia

1. China and Nearby Regions

The three powerful Chinese dynasties during this period, T'ang (618–907 C.E.), Song (960–1279 C.E.), and Ming (1368–1644 C.E.), developed Golden Ages with unique characteristics. T'ang and Song are grouped together (although they are very different) while the Ming came to power after a brief period of domination by Mongol invaders. You should understand from the outset that when we speak of China, we're actually talking about its influence throughout much of east and southeast Asia. We'll talk more specifically about Korea, Vietnam, and Cambodia in a minute. For now, you just need to understand that China had an enormous impact on cultural and political developments in those civilizations.

A Quick Review of the Rise and Fall and Rise and Fall and Rise

The **T'ang Dynasty** ruled China beginning in 618 C.E. Under **Emperor Xuanzong**, the T'ang expanded Chinese territory into parts of Manchuria, Mongolia, Tibet, and Korea. By 907, however, the empire had become so large that local warlords gained more and more power, and the T'ang Dynasty collapsed. In 960, after a brief era of restlessness, China was reunified under the **Song Dynasty** and Emperor Taizu. Despite a long period of peace and prosperity, the Song eventually fell to the Jurchen and then the Mongols until finally in 1279, the Mongols established the **Yuan Dynasty** in its place. That dynasty lasted less than a century. The Mongols were driven from China, and in 1368 the **Ming Dynasty** restored traditional Chinese rule to the empire.

From the seventh to the thirteenth centuries, the T'ang and then the Song Dynasties in China were accomplished in virtually every category of human endeavor—art, architecture, science, philosophy, porcelain-making, silk-weaving, construction of transportation systems, and more. Yet, it is probably poetry that made the T'ang Dynasty truly unique. Today, T'ang poetry tells us about daily life in China during that time. The Song built on the T'ang Dynasty's talent for poetry with more practical applications of words in the form of encyclopedias and histories. Under the Song Dynasty, China developed printing processes that facilitated the spread of its literary accomplishments throughout Asia and later influenced the development of literature in Korea and Japan.

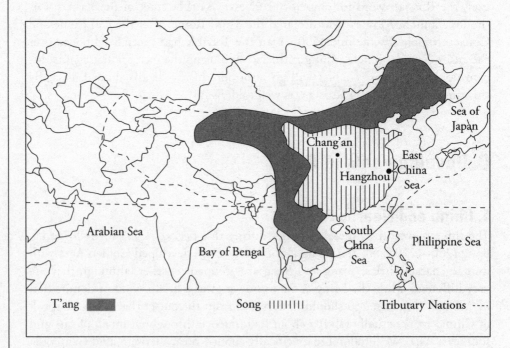

Extent of the T'ang (618–907 C.E.) and Song (960–1279 C.E.) Dynasties

At the height of both the T'ang and Song Dynasties, China was relatively stable. One of the many reasons for the stability was the bureaucratic system that was based on merit through the use of the civil service examinations (remember which dynasty created it? The Han Dynasty—see previous chapter for review). The T'ang and Song rulers continued to modify the civil service examination, but kept it focused on Confucian principles, which created a large core of educated, talented, and loyal government workers. The T'ang and Song also built an extensive transportation and communication network, including canals. They developed new business practices, including the introduction of paper money and letters of credit (hmmm…where have we seen these before?). All of this, of course, led to increased trade and cultural diffusion.

Because the power of the dynasties was based on trade and expansion, each developed an urban base to pursue its economic and political strategies. T'ang power was based on military garrisons along the central Asian trade routes and their capital at Chang'an (today Xi'an), the eastern terminus of the Silk Road and the largest city in the world at this time. This cosmopolitan city hosted a multinational and multireligious population. It was also the center of the T'ang **tribute system**, through which independent countries including Vietnam, Korea, Tibet, and various central Asian tribes acknowledged the supremacy of the Chinese emperor and sent ambassadors to the city with gifts. Indirect rule of these vassal states spread Chinese influence far and wide and brought religion, among other things, into China. A similar tribute system would be repeated during the early years of the Ming Dynasty.

Focus On: Civil Service in China

The bureaucracy contributed to China's stability in huge ways because it generally stayed in effect even as dynasties changed. Regardless of who was in charge, the leaders generally depended on the bureaucracy to carry out the functions of government. Remember, since appointment to a civil service position was earned by a strong performance on the civil service examination, the civil service was a meritocracy (earned) as opposed to an aristocracy (inherited). When power changed from ruling family to ruling family, it didn't impact the earned positions in the civil service.

Think about it in terms of the U.S. bureaucracy. No matter who gets elected president, most of the bureaucracy remains the same. Most CIA agents, Department of Agriculture employees, and IRS agents are going to keep their jobs regardless of who is president. Some of the higher-up positions get newly appointed leaders when a U.S. administration changes, but the underlying functions of the government remain remarkably stable.

Even when the Mongols ruled in China, the underlying bureaucracy remained. The Mongols brought in foreign government administrators, but the lower-level support and service jobs were kept by locals. Thus the system returned and stayed intact.

The Song Dynasty, under pressure from northern nomads, withdrew to the south and established a capital city at Hangzhou, the southern end of the Grand Canal. Here they concentrated on developing an industrial society, building on many of the ideas of the previous dynasty. An early form of **moveable type** resulted in an increase in literacy and bureaucrats among the lower classes. Printed books also spread agricultural and technological knowledge, leading to an increase in productivity and population growth. By the 1100s, the Song were an urban population with some of the largest cities in the world. Their wealth was based in part on their powerful navy and their participation in international trade throughout southeast Asia.

During the Song Dynasty, new technologies were applied to the military. Gunpowder started to be used in primitive weapons. The magnetic compass, watertight bulkheads, and sternpost rudders made the Chinese junks, as their ships were called, the best of their time. The junks were also used as merchant ships, of course.

Between 800 and 1100, iron production increased tenfold to about 120,000 tons per year, rivaling the British production of iron centuries later (in the 1700s). Song technology also included the production of steel using water-wheel-driven bellows to produce the needed temperatures.

The introduction of Champa, a fast-ripening rice from Vietnam, linked with new agricultural techniques, increased food supplies. This led to a rapid population rise from 600 to 1200 C.E. China's population more than doubled, increasing from 45 million to 115 million. The urban centers expanded greatly.

Chinese Women Under the T'ang and Song Dynasties

One of the more incredible events during the T'ang Dynasty was the rise of Wu Zhao, who became the first (and to date, only) Empress of China at the death of her husband, Emperor Gaozong. An able ruler, she was both ruthless toward her adversaries and compassionate toward peasants. The vast majority of women in China, however, never gained that kind of power. Highly patriarchal, Chinese men considered women inferior, and like European men of the Middle Ages, they considered a woman's beauty and femininity as virtues worth protecting. During the Song Dynasty, adherence to a new Confucianism justified the subordination of women, and **foot binding** became a widespread practice. A woman's feet would be bound shortly after birth in an effort to keep them small—if kept bound for a long enough time, they wouldn't grow even as the rest of the body did. Large feet were considered masculine and ugly. This practice, which lasted for centuries among elite families, was not only painful, but also often deforming and sometimes crippling.

Religion in China: Diverse Beliefs

Following the fall of the Han Dynasty, there were a number of different religious influences in China, such as Nestorianism, Manichaeism, Zoroastrianism, and Islam. The religion that had the greatest impact by far was Buddhism, especially in two of its forms: Mahayana and Chan. Mahayana Buddhism appealed to many because of its emphasis on a peaceful and quiet existence and a life apart from worldly values. With its emphasis on meditation and appreciation of beauty, Chan (or Zen) Buddhism won converts in the educated classes, who generally followed the tenets of Confucianism.

Both the Confucians and the Daoists reacted strongly to the spread of Buddhism. Many Confucians saw Buddhism as a drain on both the treasury and the labor pool, especially because Buddhism dismissed the pursuit of material accumulation. The Daoists saw Buddhism as a rival religion that was winning over many of its adherents. In the mid-800s under Emperor Wuzong, a wave of persecutions destroyed thousands of monasteries and reduced the influence of Buddhism in China.

2. Japan

Because Japan consists of four main islands off the coast of mainland Asia, it was relatively isolated for thousands of years. Ideas, religions, and material goods traveled between Japan and the rest of Asia, especially China, but the rate of exchange was relatively limited. Only in recent centuries has Japan allowed in Western influences.

Little is known of early cultures in Japan prior to 400 C.E., except that they were influenced by Korea and China. The first important ruling family was the **Yamato** clan, whose international connections helped them emerge as leaders in the fifth century. One of the unique things about Japan is that the Yamato clan was both the first and the only dynasty to rule it. The current emperor is a descendant of this same clan.

Neo-Confucianism in China

As China turned away from otherworldly ideas of the Buddhists during the late T'ang and early Song, new ideas about Confucian philosophy developed. Where older Confucianism had focused on practical politics and morality, the neo-Confucianists borrowed Buddhist ideas about the soul and the individual. This new tradition became the guiding doctrine of the Song Dynasty and the basis for civil service. At its core was a systematic approach to both the heavens and the role of individual. Filial piety, the maintenance of proper roles, and loyalty to one's superiors were again emphasized.

Early on, the **Shinto** religion took hold in Japan. Under Shinto, which means "the way of the gods," the Japanese worshipped the *kami*, which refers to nature and all of the forces of nature, both the seen and unseen. The goal under Shinto is to become part of the kami by following certain rituals and customs. The religion also encourages obedience and proper behavior. The Yamato clan claimed that the emperor was a direct descendant of the sun goddess, one of the main forces in the Shinto religion. This claim helped the Yamato stay in power—if you believe the emperor is divine, you're probably going to want to keep him around.

Can't Get Enough of China? Go to Japan.

In the sixth century, China's influence on Japan increased dramatically. In 522, Buddhist missionaries went to Japan and brought Chinese culture. In no time, Chinese things were all the rage. Buddhism spread quickly, but interestingly, it didn't replace Shinto. Instead, most Japanese adopted Buddhism while hanging on to their Shinto beliefs. In other words, they followed both religions simultaneously.

By the early seventh century, Chinese influence increased yet again. **Prince Shotoku** borrowed bureaucratic and legal reforms, which were modeled on the successes of the T'ang Dynasty in China. These reforms were enacted after his death as the **Taika Reforms** (645 C.E.). In the eighth century, when the Japanese built their new capital, they modeled it on the T'ang capital. At the risk of giving the impression that Japan became a "Little China," you should keep in mind one thing: the Japanese largely rejected Confucianism, as well as the idea of the civil service examination. Why? Both of these systems held the educated in high esteem. In Japan, education wasn't nearly as important as birth. The noble classes were hereditary, not earned.

Contrast Them: China and Japan

Even though China influenced Japan enormously, it didn't penetrate Japanese identity. Birth was more important than outside influence or education. The aristocracy remained strong. Despite the widespread influence of Confucianism and Chan (now Zen) Buddhism, the Japanese continued to observe the rites of their indigenous religion, Shintoism. Even at the height of T'ang influence, it can be said that Japan drew inspiration from China, but maintained its own distinctive traditions.

Here Come the Fujiwara: At Home in Heian

In 794, the capital was moved to Heian, and a new era of Japanese consciousness began. The Chinese influence abated, while the power of aristocratic families increased. One of the most powerful families, the **Fujiwara**, intermarried over several generations with the emperor's family and soon ran the affairs of the country. The emperor remained as a figurehead, but the real power had shifted to members of the Fujiwara family.

Under the Fujiwara, Japanese society experienced something like a golden age, especially in terms of literature. Japanese noblewomen were particularly prolific, especially when compared to women of other cultures. By the twelfth century, however, power in Japan had spread among a larger and larger pool of noble families, and soon they were fighting with each other for control over their small territories. In other words, Japan had devolved into a feudal system not unlike the one in Europe.

Feudal Japan

The interesting thing about feudalism in Japan is that it developed at around the same time as feudalism in Western Europe, but it developed independently.

In 1192, Yoritomo Minamoto was given the title of chief general, or shogun, by the emperor. As with the Fujiwara family, the emperor was the figurehead but didn't hold the real power, which was in the hands of the shogun.

Below the shogun in the pecking order were the **daimyo**, owners of large tracts of land (the counterparts of the lords of medieval Europe). The daimyo were powerful samurai, who were like knights. They were part warrior, part nobility. They, in turn, divided up their lands to lesser samurai (vassals), who in turn split their land up again. Peasants and artisans worked the fields and shops to support the samurai class. Just as in European feudalism, the hierarchy was bound together in a land-for-loyalty exchange.

The samurai followed a strict code of conduct known as the **Code of Bushido**, which was very similar to the code of chivalry in Europe. The code stressed loyalty, courage, and honor, so much so that if a samurai failed to meet his obligations under the code, he was expected to commit suicide.

Interestingly, unlike under European feudalism, women in Japan were not held in high esteem. Remember that in Europe, noblewomen were given few rights, but they were adored, at least to the extent that they were beautiful and possessed feminine traits. In contrast, Japanese women lost any freedom they had during the Fujiwara period and were forced to live harsher, more demeaning lives.

> ### Compare and Contrast Them: European and Japanese Feudalism
> They were similar in terms of political structure, social structure, and honor code. They were different in terms of treatment of women and legal arrangement. In Europe, the feudal contract was just that, a contract. It was an arrangement of obligations enforced in law. In Japan, on the other hand, the feudal arrangement was based solely on group identity and loyalty. In both cases, the feudal arrangement was based on culture, and so the feudal system stayed around for a very long time.

3. Vietnam and Korea

Because China's dynastic leaders were intent on expanding by means of trade and force, Chinese armies had been in Korea and Vietnam as early as the Han Dynasty. However, it was the large-scale military campaigns of the T'ang that resulted in cultural exchange in both regions.

Korea had its own independent and powerful dynasty, but in order to maintain the appearance of cordial relations with their powerful Chinese neighbors, it became a vassal-state of the T'ang. The gift-giving and exchanges resulted in Korean schools and the imperial court being organized like those of the Chinese, although the power of the royal houses and nobility in Korea prevented the development of a true bureaucracy based on merit. The tribute relationship was also responsible for the spread of both Confucianism and Chan Buddhism to Korea.

The Viet people of Southeast Asia were much less willing to accept even the appearance of a tribute relationship with their northern neighbors and actively resisted the T'ang armies. Although a tribute relationship was eventually established, Confucian education was accepted, and an active trade relationship existed between the two entities, the Vietnamese maintained local traditions and continued to actively revolt against T'ang authorities. After the fall of the T'ang, the Vietnamese maintained their independence in the face of later Chinese expansion.

4. India

As you should remember from the last chapter, India was the birthplace of two major religions: Hinduism and Buddhism. In the tenth century, another major religion made its way to the Indus valley: Islam.

The Delhi Sultanate

After defeating the disorganized Hindus, the Islamic invaders set up shop in Delhi under their leader, the sultan. Hence, this kingdom is referred to as the Delhi Sultanate. For over three hundred years beginning in about 1206, Islam spread throughout much of northern India. While many Hindus held on to their religious beliefs under this theoretically tolerant regime, individual sultans were highly offended by Hinduism's polytheistic ways and did their best to convert them. Like non-Muslims under the Umayyads in Arabia, non-Muslims under the sultans in India had to pay a tax. But more than that, the sultans were capable of religiously motivated destruction. Hindu temples were sometimes destroyed, and occasionally violence erupted in communities.

Despite the differences between the Islamic and Hindu cultures, an amazing amount of progress occurred in India under the sultans. Colleges were founded. Irrigation systems were vastly improved. Mosques were built, often with the help of Hindu architects and artists. Many Hindus in northern India converted to Islam. Sometimes the conversions were genuine; other times, they just made life easier. In any case, a considerable number of Hindus in northern India converted to Islam while the vast majority of Hindus in southern India held on to their traditions.

D. The Rise and Fall of the Mongols

The Mongols, the epitome of a nomadic culture, existed as a society for a long time before they became a force on the broader world scene. The Mongols were superb horsemen and archers and probably could have been a world power early on in the development of major civilizations. However, rivalries between tribes and clans kept them from unifying, so for centuries they fought with each other and remained fairly isolated from the rest of the world.

In the early 1200s, all that changed. Using his tremendous military and organizational skills, **Genghis Khan** (also spelled Chingiss Khan) unified the Mongol tribes and set them on a path of expansion that would lead to the largest empire the world had ever seen.

Genghis Khan unified several nomadic tribes of Mongolia and led the Mongol invasion of China in 1234, which was the beginning of the enormous Mongolian conquests. The **Mongol Empire** eventually spanned from the Pacific Ocean to Eastern Europe. Following the death of Ghenghis Khan, his followers splintered off into different groups they called hordes. The members of these hordes elected a new Great Khan after Ghenghis and his successor, but by the election of Kublai Khan these hordes, or Khanates, were largely independent of any sort of central leadership from the homeland in Mongolia proper. The **Golden Horde** conquered the region of modern-day Russia. In China, **Kublai Khan** ruled. Mongols destroyed cities and were ruthless warriors, but once their domain was established, the empire was relatively peaceful. (This peace is sometimes called the *Pax Mongolica*.) The continuous empire allowed for the exchange of goods, ideas, and culture from one distant region to another. Mongols, who were illiterate, nomadic people prior to their conquests and education reforms brought about by Genghis Khan, eventually became assimilated into the cultures of the people they defeated.

Warning! You Are Now Entering a Golden-Age-Free Zone

One of the most striking things about the Mongols is that their empire was one of territory, infrastructure, and conquest, but not one of "culture." Because the Mongol Empire was so enormous and conquered so many different kinds of civilizations, it did not attempt to force a unified religion or way of life on its people. That being said, although the Mongols did not make many advances in the arts and sciences themselves, their superior infrastructure allowed for the exchange and spread of ideas. Genghis Khan also established the first pony express and postal system and gave tax breaks to teachers and clerics within his empire. In other ways, however, the Mongol Empire had a profoundly negative impact on conquered cultures, stifling cultural growth rather than contributing to it by having been so brutal in their initial raids.

Contrast Them: The Mongol Empire and All Other Major Civilizations

We've seen the golden age of Gupta. The golden age of Shang. The golden ages of Greece, Rome, and Islam. The Mongol Empire was larger than any of the empires that produced those golden ages. Yet rather than imposing their own cultural developments on the areas it conquered, it generally accepted or ignored those of the people they conquered. Unlike the sultans who took over India, the Mongols allowed their subjects to practice their own religions without interference. It should be pointed out that because the Mongol empire was so expansive, it tied much of the world together and served as a conduit across which ideas and culture spread from the Pacific to the Mediterranean and vice versa. It's just that it wasn't the Mongols' own culture.

Timur Wasn't Timid

In addition to invading Russia, Persia, Central Asia, and China, the Mongols also found time on their itinerary for a layover in India. They swept in under their leader, the untamed Timur Lang, who destroyed just about everything in sight and massacred thousands, and then just as quickly swept out. The sultanate was destroyed, but after **Timur Lang** (sometimes referred to as **Tamerlane**) returned to his capital in Samarkand, the Mongols pulled out as well. Just a few years later, the sultanate was restored. Islam continued to grow in India for the next few centuries under the Mongol Empire, even as many Hindus hung on to their beliefs. Look for more on this later.

How the Mongols Did It: No Rest Until Conquest

Imagine that you live in a village that lies in the path of an advancing Mongol horde. You've heard the stories. If you put up a fight, they'll pummel you. If you retreat to your house, they'll burn it. If you organize a resistance in your place of worship or civic building, they'll level it. You've also heard that if you just give in, they might spare your city, but they also might not. They're not really interested in changing your culture. So your only real choice, if you want to stay alive, is to give in. If you do, you may or may not be able to keep your life and your culture, but if you don't, you'll suffer a certainly grotesque death. What would you do?

In the 1200s and 1300s, a lot of people gave in, and those who did not met their death. The Mongols weren't called ruthless warriors for nothing. They knew how to fight, but they were more than fierce fighters. They were also highly organized and highly mobile. Unlike the much-feared Roman army, which in its heyday could cover about 25 miles per day, the Mongol horsemen could cover about 90. Their bows, designed to be launched from horseback, had a range of up to 300 yards, way more than anybody else's. Their armies were divided into units, which were further separated into light and heavy cavalries and scouting units. They were extremely motivated—Genghis Khan punished traitors swiftly and rewarded the courageous generously. They were stealthy—they had an extensive network of spies who scouted their enemies before battle. Finally, their goals were made unmistakably clear—the consequences of putting up a fight against the Mongols meant certain destruction of the entire village, so most learned not to resist. In short, they were really, really good at what they did: conquering.

The Mongol Impact

The Mongols were great diffusers of culture. In some cases, Mongols assimilated into the cultures they conquered. For example, in Persia, most Mongols became Muslim. Elsewhere, Mongolian culture remained separate from the conquered people. In China, for example, Kublai Khan, the grandson of Genghis, thwarted Mongolization by prohibiting intermarriage as well as forbidding Chinese to learn the Mongol language. When the Chinese finally kicked out the Mongols in 1368, they established the Ming Dynasty rooted in traditional Chinese identity and practices.

There were two major consequences of Mongol rule. The first is that Russia, which was conquered by the Golden Horde and treated as a vassal state, didn't unify or culturally develop as quickly as its European neighbors to the west. The second is that world trade, cultural diffusion, and global awareness grew. Think about it: the Mongol empire touched Europe and very nearly touched Japan. It stretched southward to Persia and India, making possible not only trade but also the transmission of the Black Death (bubonic plague) in the fourteenth century. This single empire touched nearly all the major civilizations of the day. So, as strange as it sounds, the often brutal Mongols, in their own way, brought the world together. By 1450, as the Mongol Empire was well in decline, the world would never again be disconnected.

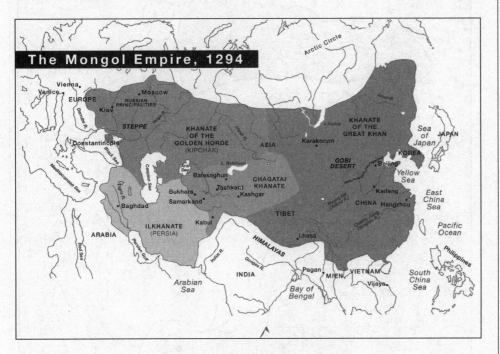

Map of the Mongol Khanates

E. Developments in Africa

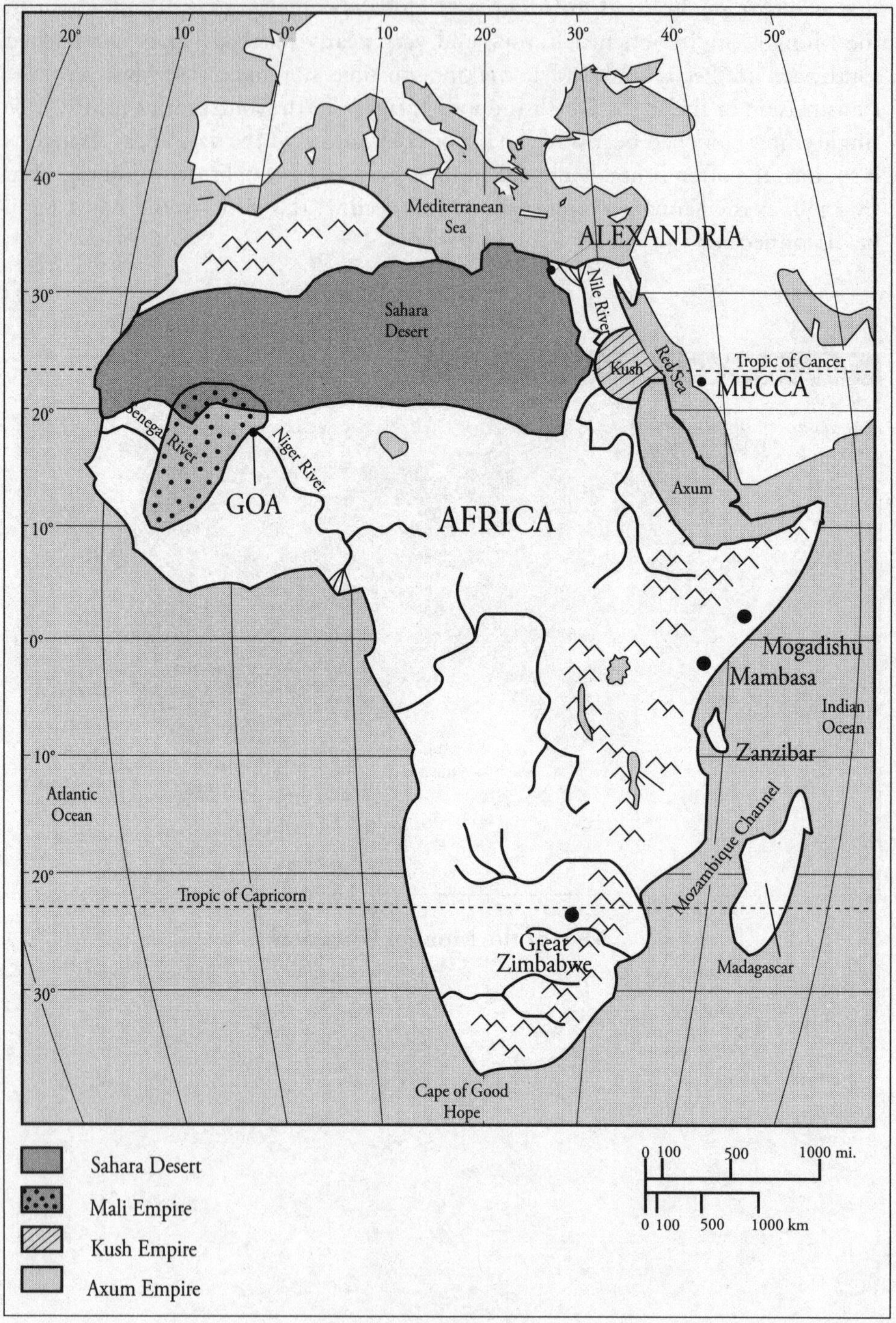

20°
10°
0°
10°
20°
30°
40°
50°
40°
30°
20°
10°
0°
10°
20°
30°
Mediterranean Sea
ALEXANDRIA
Sahara Desert
Nile River
Kush
Red Sea
Tropic of Cancer
MECCA
Senegal River
Niger River
GOA
Axum
AFRICA
Mogadishu
Mambasa
Indian Ocean
Zanzibar
Atlantic Ocean
Mozambique Channel
Tropic of Capricorn
Great Zimbabwe
Madagascar
Cape of Good Hope
Sahara Desert
Mali Empire
Kush Empire
Axum Empire
0 100 500 1000 mi.
0 100 500 1000 km

African Empires and Trade Cities

For the purposes of the AP World History Exam, the most significant early civilizations in Africa were Egypt and Carthage, both of which were discussed in the previous chapter. Both of these civilizations were located in North Africa along the Mediterranean, north of the Sahara Desert. But there were other civilizations in Africa too. Some of them existed long before 600 C.E., but we've included them in this section (rather than in the previous chapter) so that you can study them as a group.

Interaction Among Kush, Axum, and the Swahili Coast

The Kush and Axum civilizations developed to the south of Egypt in the upper reaches of the Nile River. **Kush** developed at about the same time as ancient Egypt, and at one point around 750 B.C.E. actually conquered part of it. Less than a hundred years later, however, Kush retreated southward back to its capital at Meroe, which became a center for ironworks and trade.

After the Kush decline around 200 C.E., another empire, **Axum**, rose to greatness to the south (in modern-day Ethiopia). Although Axum never conquered any other civilization, it traded with others frequently, especially in ivory and gold. In the fourth century, Axum converted to Christianity, and in the seventh century, many converted to Islam. These conversions illustrate that the people of Axum were in constant contact with the empires of the Mediterranean world. This contact has had a long-standing impact. Ethiopia's large Christian community in present times is a direct result of the Axum conversion.

Remember that this entire period is dominated by interactions. In addition to interaction with the Mediterranean world through the Red Sea, the eastern coast of Africa was linked to India and Southeast Asia through the shipping lanes of the Indian Ocean trade. The east coast of Africa was populated by Bantu-speaking peoples who settled into lives of farmers, merchants, and fishermen. This area is known as the Swahili Coast, from the Arabic word for "coasters" or traders, and indeed the Swahili language is a mix of the original Bantu language supplemented by Arabic. Trade with the Muslims began in the early tenth century as Swahili traders brought gold, slaves, ivory, and other exotic products to the coast.

The incredible wealth generated by this trade resulted in the growth of powerful kingdoms and trading cities along the coast in advantageous locations. Like wealthy trading cities throughout the world, they became cultural and political centers. By the fifteenth century, mud and wooden outposts became impressive coral and stone mosques, public buildings, and fortified cities with trade goods from all over the world.

To facilitate political and economic relationships, the ruling elites and merchant classes of the eastern African kingdoms converted to Islam but maintained many of their own cultural traditions. Eventually, Islam spread throughout most of East Africa.

Need More Review?
Are a ton of different names swirling around in your brain? To help with memorization, pick up our Essential AP World History Flashcards.

The Other Side of the Sand: Ghana, Mali, and Songhai

Kush and Axum were in eastern Africa, along the Nile River and near the Red Sea. Therefore, they had easy access to other cultures. The cultures of Ghana, Mali, and Songhai, however, were in west Africa, south of the Sahara.

When the Islamic Empire spread across North Africa in the seventh and eighth centuries, these African kingdoms began trading with the larger Mediterranean economy. Islamic traders penetrated the unforgiving Sahara desert and reached the fertile wealthy interior of Africa, called sub-Saharan (beneath the Sahara), while African traders pushed northward toward Carthage and Tripoli. Previously, the desert had acted as one gigantic "don't-want-to-deal-with-it" barrier, so people typically didn't. Increasingly, however, caravans of traders were willing to do what they had to do to get to the riches on the other side of the sand. At first, the west Africans were in search of salt, of which they had little but which existed in the Sahara. When they encountered the Islamic traders along the salt road, they started trading for a lot more than just salt. The consequence was an explosion of trade.

Why were the Islamic traders so interested in trading with west African kingdoms? Because in Ghana (about 800–1000 C.E.) and Mali (about 1200–1450 C.E.), there were tons, and we mean tons, of gold. A little sand in your eyes was probably worth some gold in your hand. So the Islamic traders kept coming. The constant trade brought more than just Islamic goods to Ghana and Mali; it brought Islam. For Ghana the result was devastating. The empire was subjected to a Holy War led by an Islamic group intent on converting (or else killing) them. While Ghana was able to defeat the Islamic forces, its empire fell into decline. By the time Mali came to power, the region had converted to Islam anyway, this time in a more peaceful transition.

One of the greatest Malian rulers, **Mansa Musa**, built a capital at Timbuktu and expanded the kingdom well beyond the bounds of Ghana. In 1324, Musa made a pilgrimage to Mecca (remember the Five Pillars of Islam?) complete with an entourage of hundreds of gold-carrying servants and camels. The journey was so extravagant, so long, and so impressive to everyone who saw it that Musa became an overnight international sensation. Had the Musa moment occurred in the social media age, you can bet it would have been all over social media.

The largest empire in west Africa was formed in the mid-fifteenth century, when Songhai ruler Sonni Ali conquered the entire region and established the Songhai Empire. The Songhai Empire lasted until around 1600 C.E., and during its reign, Timbuktu became a major cultural center, complete with a university that drew scholars from around the Islamic world.

The Arts in Africa

Oral literature was an important part of life in most African communities. History and stories were passed from one generation to the next, not through written texts, but through storytelling. The storytelling wasn't just Grandpa sitting next to the fire, but rather was a production akin to a dramatic performance. The stories were told the same way for so many generations that people knew the lines. Everyone was able to participate in the storytelling by reciting responses at the appropriate times. Think about what it's like to watch *Star Wars* with a room full of people—parents, grandparents, kids—who've already seen it; that will give you a good sense of what oral literature meant to those cultures.

Early sub-Saharan African cultures are also known for their sculptures, particularly out of pottery and bronze. The **Benin** culture (near present-day Nigeria) mastered a bronze sculpting technique. They made clay molds around a wax carving, melted the wax, filled the mold with melted bronze, and, after breaking the clay mold, revealed some of the most beautiful early bronze work created by any civilization.

F. Developments in the Americas

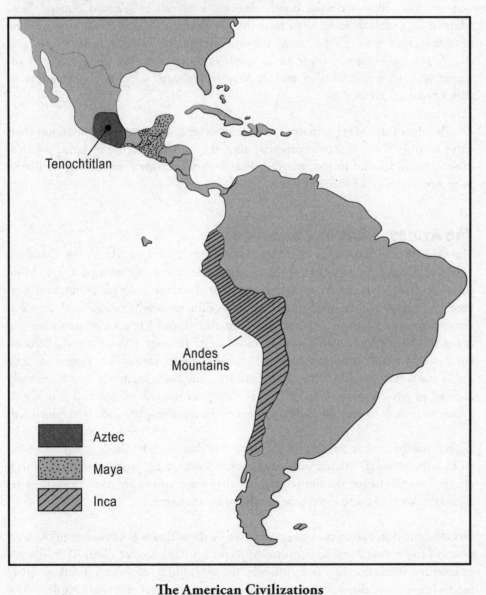

The American Civilizations

There were three great civilizations in what is now Central America and South America that developed before the arrival of the Europeans. One of the civilizations, the Maya, actually began around the time of the major classical civilizations and were discussed in the previous chapter. The other two civilizations, the Incas and Aztecs, were conquered by the Europeans after 1450. They will be discussed again in the next chapter. That said, we are including all three of them in this chapter so that you can review the cultural characteristics of these three civilizations in one place. We'll talk about their conquests in the next chapter.

Mayan Decline: Where Did They Go?

As a review, the Maya were organized in city-states ruled by a single king. Their largely agricultural peasant population was bound to nobility by ties of loyalty and religion. They occupied poorly drained lowlands in Central America and adapted by building terraces to trap the silt drained by numerous rivers. Some of these cities grew to be quite sizable—10,000 to 40,000 inhabitants, and engaged in long-distance trade as far north as central Mexico. The cities were often at odds with one another and in Mayan territory, war was about capturing slaves or sacrificial victims.

The decline of the Maya remains a source of debate. They began to abandon their cities around 800 c.e. Environmental degradation and overuse of land, political dissension and social unrest, natural disaster, and outside invaders have all been proposed as causes of their decline.

The Aztecs: Trade and Sacrifice

The Aztecs, also known as the Mexica, arrived in central Mexico in the mid-1200s and built their capital at **Tenochtitlan** (modern-day Mexico City). More than anything else, the Aztecs are known for their expansionist policy and professional army, which allowed them to dominate nearby states and demand heavy taxes and captives. Warriors were the elite in the Aztec social structure (the majority of the people were peasants and slaves). Through conquest and alliances, the Aztecs built an empire of some 12 million people. Despite the huge size, they didn't use a bureaucratic form of government. The conquered areas were generally allowed to govern themselves, as long as they paid the tribute demanded of them. Roads were built to link the far-flung areas of the huge empire, and trade flourished.

Aztec women had a subordinate public role but could inherit property. Like women in most all other traditional civilizations, Aztec women were primarily charged with running the household, but they were also involved in skilled crafts, especially weaving, and—to some extent—in commerce.

Notably, the Aztec religious system was tied to the military because one of the purposes of the military was to obtain victims for human sacrifice. Tens of thousands of men and women were killed annually; many would be sacrificed simultaneously for an important religious occasion, such as the dedication of a new temple.

The Inca: My Land Is Your Land

The Inca Empire, set in the Andes Mountains in Peru, was also expansionist in nature. At its zenith, it is thought to have controlled more than 2,000 miles of South American coastline. The Inca controlled this territory using a professional army, an established bureaucracy, a unified language, and a complex system of roads and tunnels.

Like the Maya (and the Aztecs), the Incas had no large animals, so the prime source of labor was human. A large proportion of the population was peasants, who worked the land or on construction projects. They were expected to give a proportion of their harvest to support the ruling classes and to provide famine relief. These surpluses eventually became large enough to support large cities. The capital at Cuzco may have had as many as 300,000 people in the late 1400s.

Incan women were expected to help work the fields, weave cloth, and care for the household. They could pass property on to their daughters and even played a role in religion. The Inca were polytheistic, but the sun god was the most important and was at the center of the state religion. Like the Aztecs, the Inca practiced human sacrifice, but in much smaller numbers, usually choosing instead to sacrifice material goods or animals. Incan religion also had a very strong moral quality, emphasizing rewards for good behavior and punishments for bad. Like the Egyptians, Incan rulers were mummified after death and became intermediaries between the gods and the people.

For the Inca, the concept of private property didn't exist. Rather, the ruler was viewed as having descended from the sun and, therefore, owning everything on Earth. The military was very important because each new ruler needed to ensure his place in eternity by securing new land, and that meant conquest. There was a state bureaucracy, manned by the nobility, which controlled the empire by traveling on a complex system of roads.

The Inca were excellent builders, stone cutters, and miners. Their skills are evident from the ruins of the **Temple of the Sun** in Cuzco and the temples of **Machu Picchu**. They never developed a system of writing. However, they were able to record census data and keep an accounting of harvests on *quipu*, a set of knotted strings.

IV. REVIEW OF INTERACTIONS AMONG CULTURES, 600 c.e.–1450

The purpose of this section is to help you pull together the history from this time period and view it from a global perspective. The examples below are by no means an exhaustive list of the ways that civilizations or groups of people interacted from 600 to 1450 c.e. To the contrary, they are examples that serve as a starting point in your studies. We strongly suggest that you add examples to the ones below as you work your way through this review and your materials from class.

A. Trade Networks and Cultural Diffusion

Trade has always been a big deal, historically speaking. Getting stuff and buying stuff is a huge incentive behind interactions. If you have everything you need and want, you can live in isolation. If you don't, and somebody else down the road has what you want, you've got two choices: take it or trade for it. If you're not into the whole conquest thing, then trading is probably your best option.

From 600 to 1450, trade exploded onto the world scene—so much so that the world after 1450 is inseparable from global interaction. Let's quickly review the global trade routes that you read about in this chapter.

- The Mediterranean Trade between Western Europe, the Byzantine Empire, and the Islamic Empire
- The Hanseatic League (more details in this chapter)
- The Silk Road (used heavily again from about 1200 c.e. until about 1600 c.e.—more on that later)
- The land routes of the Mongols
- Trade between China and Japan
- Trade between India and Persia
- The Trans-Saharan trade routes between west Africa and the Islamic Empire

Remember, too, that trade was not only aided by better boats and better roads, but also by monetary systems, lines of credit, and accounting methods that helped business boom. Record keeping and money management are key. If you're able to keep records or borrow money, you are by definition establishing a business relationship that extends into the future. Once you start thinking about a regular business-trade relationship extending into the future, you can get people to invest in that future, and pretty soon the wheels of international business are going 'round and 'round.

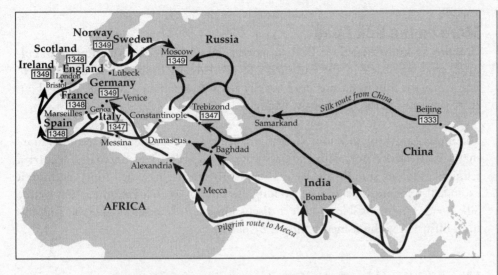

Spread of the Black Death (1333–1349 C.E.)

The trade routes are important, of course, not just because of their impact on business, but also because of their role in cultural diffusion. It is over the trade routes that religions and languages spread. It is over the trade routes that literature and art and ideas spread. And, unfortunately, it is over the trade routes that disease and plague sometimes spread. The **Bubonic Plague** (also called the Black Death) started in Asia in the fourteenth century and was carried by merchants along the trade routes all the way to Europe, where it destroyed entire communities and killed as many as one out of every three people in Western Europe. The plague quickened the decline of feudal society because many manors weren't able to function.

In addition to the trade routes mentioned above, there's one that we haven't discussed in detail yet—the Indian Ocean Trade. It's important, so we'll go into it in some detail.

Indian Ocean Trade

Throughout the period covered in this chapter, the Persians and the Arabs dominated the **Indian Ocean Trade**. Their trade routes connected ports in western India to ports in the Persian Gulf, which in turn were connected to ports in eastern Africa.

Unlike boats that were used on the Mediterranean Sea, boats that sailed the Indian Ocean were, necessarily, more resilient to the large waves common in those waters. The traders learned to understand the monsoon seasons and direction of the winds and scheduled their voyages accordingly. Despite these difficulties, the Indian Ocean trade routes were relatively safe, especially when compared to those on the Mediterranean, where constant warfare was a problem.

Since sailors often married the local women at the ends of their trade routes, cultures started to intermix rapidly. Many sailors took foreign wives home and created bilingual and bicultural families.

More on the Silk Road

You already know that the Silk Road connected China to the Mediterranean cultures even way back in the early days of the Roman Empire. You also need to know that the Silk Road was used heavily again from about 1200 C.E. until about 1600 C.E., during the reign of the Mongols.

The important thing to know about the Silk Road is that it carried so much more than silk. It carried porcelain and paper. It carried military technologies. It carried religions, such as Buddhism, Islam, and Christianity. It carried food. Because it extended so far and was used for so long, it's safe to say that East met West on the Silk Road. It's impossible to have a discussion about international trade and cultural diffusion without mentioning it by name.

More on the Hanseatic League

As you already know, the Hanseatic League was a collection of city-states in the Baltic and North Sea regions of Europe that banded together in 1241 to establish common trade practices, fight off pirates and foreign governments, and essentially establish a trade monopoly from the region to much of the rest of the world. It worked for a few hundred years. More than 100 cities joined the league. The result was enormous for two reasons. First, it resulted in a substantial middle class in northern Europe, a development that would drive changes in that region in later centuries (more on that in the next chapter). Second, it set a precedent for large, European trading operations that profoundly affected the Dutch and the English, which would also deeply affect the broader world in later centuries.

Was There a Global Trade Network?

If you think about it, after about 1200 C.E. or so, the world was very interconnected. Europe was trading with the Islamic world and Russia. The Islamic world was trading with Africa, India, and China. India was trading with China and eastern Africa. China was trading with Japan and southeast Europe. If you link up all the trade routes, goods could make their way from England to Persia to India to Japan. They could also travel to points north and south, from Muscovy to Mali.

The global network wasn't entirely controlled by one entity or laid out by one trading organization. It was more like a web of interconnected but highly independent parts. It required lots of managers at each site. It required people to be linked up through third and even fourth parties. No one person was managing it, yet almost all major civilizations (except those in the Americas) were a part of it. In short, it was like the Internet, only in geographic space instead of cyberspace.

B. Expansion of Religion and Empire: Culture Clash

One of the most significant influences on cultural interaction and diffusion has been the expansion of empires and the intentional diffusion of religion. Keep in mind that when we say intentional diffusion of religion, we mean methods like missionary work or religious warfare. This is opposed to the natural spread of religious ideas that occurs when people come into contact with each other, such as over trade routes.

Here's a quick list of some of the examples discussed in this chapter.

- The Mongol expansion into Russia, Persia, India, and China
- The Germanic tribes into southern Europe and England
- The Vikings' expansion from Scandinavia into England and Western Europe
- The Magyars' push from Eastern Europe into Western Europe
- The Islamic Empire's push into Spain, India, and Africa
- The Crusades
- Buddhist missionaries to Japan
- Orthodox Christian missionaries into Eastern Europe

When you think about it, the bulk of this chapter is about two things: the expansion of religion and empires leading to cultural contact, or the relative isolationism that resulted under the feudal systems in Europe and Japan. Another way to encapsulate this period: a time fueled by conquest and religious expansion. We've talked a lot about the efforts of expansionists that succeeded. We need to give you some more details about the efforts of some expansionists that didn't succeed, namely, the Crusaders.

Crusaders and Jihad

You'll recall that in the Middle Ages, the Islamic Empire expanded, and the Muslims conquered much of Spain. The Christians felt threatened by the expansion of the Muslims, especially as Islam became entrenched in areas that the Christians identified with historically. So, in 1096 C.E. Pope Urban initiated the **First Crusade** in response to the success of the Seljuk Turks, who took control of the Holy Land (present-day Israel and Palestine). The pope wanted Jerusalem, the most important city in Christianity, to be in the hands of Christians. He was also hoping that the efforts would help reunite the Catholic Church with the Eastern Orthodox Church in Constantinople, which had split apart 50 years before the start of the crusades. The Crusaders immediately set out to conquer the Holy Land, and initially captured several cities, including Antioch and, most important, Jerusalem. However, both cities quickly fell back into the hands of the Arabs.

Through the year 1204 c.e., a total of four crusades failed to produce results, and the Eastern Orthodox Church and the Catholic Church separated even further (five more crusades followed but were not successful in achieving major goals). As mentioned earlier, in the Fourth Crusade the Catholic Church sacked Constantinople and established a short-lived Latin Empire there (most of the Crusaders either died or returned to Europe). The impact on the Holy Land was violence and uncertainty. Most of the region remained in the hands of the Muslim Arabs, and the whole mess led to centuries of mistrust and intolerance between Christians and Muslims.

As you think about global interaction through conquest, there's much to point out about the Crusades. First, the Crusades were not only motivated by religious beliefs and purposes. There were economic and political incentives as well. No doubt there were some who fought for religious reasons, especially in the early crusades, but the lure of empire and wealth was certainly a major factor for many.

Second, even to the extent that it was a religious effort, the Crusades illustrate that religion, when combined with conquest and feelings of superiority, can be a very bloody enterprise. The death, rape, pillaging, and slavery perpetrated in the name of religion was startling. The same, of course, was true of Islamic conquests in India, Persia, and Africa. Because the religiously devout are sometimes willing to be martyred for their beliefs, intentional religious expansionism can be just as devastating and powerful as a politically driven military invasion.

Third, and perhaps most importantly for the AP World History Exam, the Crusades prove that even the efforts of conquest and expansion that fail to reach their goals still have a major impact on world history: They lead to interaction between cultures that might not otherwise interact. The Crusades put Europe back into the sphere of the Eastern Mediterranean for centuries. That interaction fueled trade and an exchange of ideas. It also led to Western Europe's rediscovery of new aspects of its ancient past, which was being preserved by the Byzantine and Islamic Empires. That rediscovery fueled huge changes in Europe, which we'll talk about in the next chapter.

C. Other Reasons People Were on the Move

Interaction among and within civilizations occurred during this period in history for many reasons other than trade or conquest. As populations grew, people needed more room to spread out. This not only led to huge movements of people, such as the Germanic tribes into southern Europe, but also to more crowded conditions on the manor or in small towns. The result was the burgeoning of ever-larger cities; once the cities became larger, more opportunities were created there, which pulled more and more people in from the countryside.

Some cities grew not just because of a general population increase, but because they were intentionally established as centers of civilization. Think about the empires in this chapter. The eastern Roman Empire, which of course became the Byzantine Empire, was headquartered at Constantinople, which was specifically built as a center to draw people. In fact, capitals were moved all the time to create an aura of a rising empire. The Islamic Empire moved to Baghdad under the Abbasid Dynasty. The Fujiwara moved the capital of Japan to Heian. The Mongols built a city at Samarkand, as did the Malians at Timbuktu, and the Maya at Tikal. The list goes on and on. Every time an empire built a new city to flaunt itself, it drew thousands of people. This is true especially to the degree that these civilizations built universities, which by their nature drew people from around the empire. That meant people who weren't living in the same city in the past were now living together. The result? More cultural diffusion.

Pilgrimages were a third reason that people during this time period were constantly on the move. Rome and Constantinople certainly attracted thousands to their grand cathedrals, but the Islamic duty to travel to Mecca was no doubt the most significant destination of religious pilgrimages. Imagine the thousands upon thousands who traveled from the vast reaches of the Islamic world. Imagine the amount of cultural diffusion that occurred as a result. Just think of Mansa Musa and you'll be convinced.

V. TECHNOLOGY AND INNOVATIONS, 600 C.E.–1450

Once again, it is interaction that leads to innovation. This period is marked by expanding trade, expanding empires, and expanding interactions. All lead to increased wealth, frequent cultural borrowing, and the development of new ideas. Many of these new innovations came from the eastern societies—China and India, filtered through the Islamic world. By 1450, most of these new ideas had made their way back to Europe, following the Crusaders, merchants, and missionaries.

Islamic World	China
paper mills (from China)	gunpowder cannons
universities	moveable type
astrolabe and sextant	paper currency
algebra (from Greece)	porcelain
chess (from India)	terrace farming
modern soap formula	water-powered mills
guns and cannons (from China)	cotton sails
mechanical pendulum clock	water clock
distilled alcohol	magnetic compass
surgical instruments (syringe etc.)	state-run factories

Trade Networks and Agriculture
In addition to ideas that began to move around the world, trade networks moved agricultural products. Some of these would result in great environmental changes, influence trade networks, and motivate exploration and conquest.

VI. CHANGES AND CONTINUITIES IN THE ROLE OF WOMEN

The spread of Islam, the openness of Christianity and Buddhism, the development of new empires based on wealth and acquisition of property, and the revitalization of neo-Confucianism impacted the status of women around the world. Continuing from the previous time period, restrictions on women's freedoms depended on which caste or class they belonged to. At the uppermost levels, a woman could overcome the status of her gender and assume leadership roles if there was no male heir or if the male heir was very young. Generally, however, as societies became more urban and wealthy, women, especially those of the elite or upper classes, had their freedoms further restricted even as their status in society rose. This can be seen in the increased veiling of women in the Islamic world and among Christians in the Mediterranean world (especially Italy and Spain), the custom of foot binding in neo-Confucian China, and the young age of marriage in South Asia.

Trade and the arrival of new religions did not significantly change the role of women in African societies—as pastoral nomads, many of the African societies were relatively egalitarian. Even when sedentary lifestyles developed, women had a great deal of freedom and societies were sometimes matrilineal and matriarchal. Women commanded a bride-price rather than having to give a dowry, and were considered a valuable source of wealth. "Mother of the King" was a political office in many African societies, and women participated in specific religious rituals controlled solely by women. Although both Islam and Christianity found converts in Africa, women were less eager to convert than men and the practice of veiling was met with mixed reactions.

Changes in the status and role of women included access to more education as societies continued to prosper and interact. This is true of the Confucian cultures of China and Japan, where women were highly literate and expected to understand proper virtue and their role in the household. Overall, however, even when they were educated and wealthy, most women had far less power than their male counterparts and were subject to any number of cultural and legal restrictions.

Women's Status in Ancient Societies			
Europe	**Islam**	**India**	**China**
strict and patriarchal social divisions	equality in religion, but separate in mosque	strict patriarchal caste system	strict Confucian social order and guidelines for virtuous behavior
could inherit land and take oaths of vassalage, but property belonged to husband	received half inheritance of male children	child marriages	access to dowries and owned businesses
could bring a court case, but not participate in decision	testimony had less weight than male	practice of *sati* for widows (See Chapter 9.)	widow to remain with son; no property if remarried
division of labor; women in textiles		family textile labor	silk weaving as female occupation
Christian monogamy	concubines and seclusion in harems	marriage limited to caste members	concubines and seclusion in harems
education limited to upper class males	literate society	education limited	literate society, but state education limited to men
did not recognize illegitimate children	all children are seen as legitimate		
veiling of upper class	veiling in public	*purdah*: veiling or seclusion	foot binding

VII. PULLING IT ALL TOGETHER

There's no question that the spread and growth of religion had enormous consequences during this time period. There's also no question that the issue of centralization verses noncentralization seems to have an impact on a civilization. Look at what it meant for Europe, Japan, China, and India. Beyond the issues of interaction, centralization, and the growth of religion, there's something else you should be thinking about: how to organize the world in your head.

Today, we have clear boundaries between countries, but in addition to using those political boundaries, we talk of cultural regions all the time. We'll say things like "the West" or "the East." That's fine, but where's the dividing line? Is modern-day Russia part of the East or the West? What about Saudi Arabia? What about Japan?

Moreover, we often split even our own country into manageable pieces that don't have specific, exact geographic boundaries. In the United States, for example, when one refers to "the South," it's usually in reference to a culture rather than a specific geographical place. Is Florida part of "the South?" Northern Florida probably is, but the rest of Florida has a very different feel.

This kind of stuff is a big deal for the AP test writers. Sometimes it's easier to think about and write about history in terms of cultural areas rather than political boundaries. "The Islamic World," for example, is used to refer not only to countries that are predominately Muslim, but also communities and individuals within non-Muslim countries who participate in the culture of Islam. Or think about the "Jewish community." In the time period covered by this chapter, Jews were scattered throughout Europe, Africa, and Asia. There was no Jewish state, only a Jewish culture. Nevertheless, the Jewish culture maintained its identity.

You might want to think of the world in terms of major cultural divisions. Religions help. You can think of developments in the Christian sphere, the Islamic sphere, the Hindu sphere, and the Buddhist sphere. Don't forget, though, that some of these spheres overlap, and some of them coexist with other religions or belief systems like Confucianism and Buddhism. You can also think of developments in terms of expanding empires and feudal systems. Even more generally, think of the world in terms of cultures that interacted and those that did not.

However you choose to think about the world, whether in terms of cultural areas or structural similarities, the important thing is that you try to analyze the history. Doing so will force you to make comparisons between cultures, which is exactly the kind of critical thinking you need to do on the AP World History Exam. The more you think about how these cultures can be organized, the more familiar you'll be with world history.

CHAPTER 8 KEY TERMS

Islam (Shiites and Sunnis)

Five Pillars of Islam

Qu'ran

hejira

theocracy

caliphate

Umayyad Dynasty

Dome of the Rock

Abbasid Dynasty

Middle Ages

Orthodox Christianity

Justinianic Code

Merovingian Dynasty

Carolingian Dynasty

feudalism

nobles

vassals

serfs (peasants)

fiefs

manors

three-field system

code of chivalry

primogeniture

burghers

Hanseatic League

heresy

scholasticism

bubonic plague

interregnum

Magna Carta

T'ang, Song, Yuan, and Ming
   dynasties

tribute system

bureaucracy

civil service

foot binding

shogun

Code of Bushido

Delhi Sultanate

oral literature

Indian Ocean trade

Silk Road

Muhammad

Mecca

Medina

Baghdad

Mohammad al-Razi

Levant

Sufis

Mongols

Ottoman Turks

Justinian

Hagia Sophia

St. Cyril

Vladimir

the Franks

King Clovis

Charles Martel

Battle of Tours

Pepin the Short

Charlemagne

Holy Roman Empire

Treaty of Verdun

Magyars

Vikings

Crusades

Pope Innocent III

the Inquisition

William the Conqueror

the Spanish Inquisition

Hundred Years' War

Tatars

Ivan the Terrible

Genghis Khan

Mongol Empire

Kublai Khan

Tamerlane

Axum

Mansa Musa

Benin

Tenochtitlan

First Crusade

Chapter 8 Drill

See the end of the chapter for the answers and explanations.

Questions 1–4 refer to the passage below.

"In the name of God, the Merciful and Compassionate. This is a letter to the servant of God Umar [ibn al-Khattab], Commander of the Faithful, from the Christians of such-and-such a city. When you came against us, we asked you for safe-conduct for ourselves, our descendants, our property, and the people of our community, and we undertook the following obligations toward you:

We shall not build, in our cities or in their neighborhood, new monasteries, Churches, convents, or monks' cells…

We shall not teach the Qur'an to our children.

We shall not manifest our religion publicly nor convert anyone to it. We shall not prevent any of our kin from entering Islam if they wish it.

We shall show respect toward the Muslims, and we shall rise from our seats when they wish to sit.

We shall not seek to resemble the Muslims by imitating any of their garments, the qalansuwa, the turban, footwear, or the parting of the hair….

We shall not mount on saddles, nor shall we gird swords nor bear any kind of arms nor carry them on our persons….

We shall not sell fermented drinks….

We shall always dress in the same way wherever we may be….

We shall not display our crosses or our books in the roads or markets of the Muslims…. We shall not bury our dead near the Muslims."

Pact of Umar, treaty between Muslims and Christians of modern-day Syria, seventh century C.E.

1. The text of this passage is best viewed as evidence of which of the following in Arabic conquests of non-Muslim territories?

    (A) Relatively mild treatment received by non-Muslims following Arabic conquests
    (B) Extremely harsh treatment received by non-Muslims following Arabic conquests
    (C) Uncompromising suppression of Christianity in favor of Islam
    (D) Heartfelt respect for Islam on the part of those conquered

2. Which of the following best describes the expansion of the Islamic Caliphate, which existed from 632 C.E. to 1258 C.E.?

    (A) A rapid expansion across Arabia, northern Africa, and western Asia followed by defeat and collapse at the hands of the Second Crusade
    (B) A rapid initial expansion followed by a long period of overall border stability before defeat and collapse at the hands of the Mongols
    (C) A slow and steady expansion across the Middle East, northern Africa, and large parts of Asia until it reached its greatest extent under Ottoman emperors
    (D) A slow and steady expansion across the Middle East and southern Europe until defeat by Charles Martel

3. The arrangements indicated in this text best support which aspect of life in Islamic society during the Caliphate?

    (A) Christian opposition to fermented drinks and wearing turbans
    (B) The necessity of safe conducts for the populations of every Arabic city
    (C) A sharp distinction between Shia and Sunni branches of Islam
    (D) The centrality of religion to cultural and social rights held by individuals

4. When compared to the previous state of affairs, which of the following best illustrates the change in the status of women brought about by the Caliphate?

    (A) The spread of Islam brought with it some improvement in the legal rights of women, including an independent legal existence and the right to testify in court.
    (B) The spread of Islam substantially worsened the legal position of women, removing previously existing rights and subordinating them to men.
    (C) Under the Caliphate, women achieved parity with men in almost every aspect of life.
    (D) The Caliphate did not substantially change the role of women in the areas it grew to control.

TIMELINE OF MAJOR DEVELOPMENTS, 600 C.E.–1450

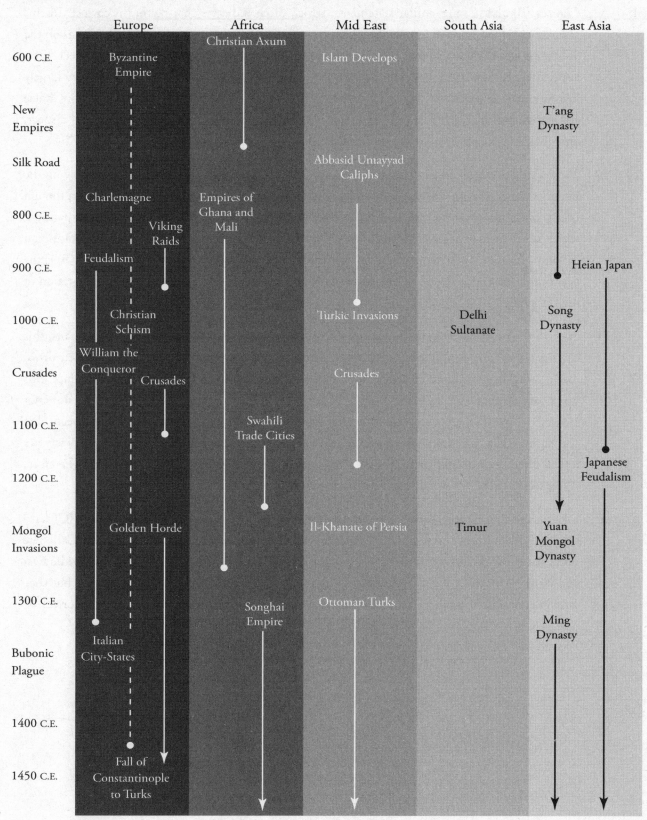

	Europe	Africa	Mid East	South Asia	East Asia

600 C.E.

New Empires

Silk Road

800 C.E.

900 C.E.

1000 C.E.

Crusades

1100 C.E.

1200 C.E.

Mongol Invasions

1300 C.E.

Bubonic Plague

1400 C.E.

1450 C.E.

Europe: Byzantine Empire, Charlemagne, Viking Raids, Feudalism, Christian Schism, William the Conqueror, Crusades, Golden Horde, Italian City-States, Fall of Constantinople to Turks

Africa: Christian Axum, Empires of Ghana and Mali, Swahili Trade Cities, Songhai Empire

Mid East: Islam Develops, Abbasid Umayyad Caliphs, Turkic Invasions, Crusades, Il-Khanate of Persia, Ottoman Turks

South Asia: Delhi Sultanate, Timur

East Asia: T'ang Dynasty, Heian Japan, Song Dynasty, Japanese Feudalism, Yuan Mongol Dynasty, Ming Dynasty

CHAPTER 8 DRILL EXPLANATIONS

1. **A** Choices (B) and (C) are similar statements, which often indicates that neither is correct. In this case, though the Christian population of the city described in the passage accept restrictions on the public display of their religion, they are not prohibited from practicing, so (C) is incorrect. Similarly, though there are a series of restrictions imposed on the conquered population, they largely involve public displays and thus cannot be characterized as extremely harsh; eliminate (B). Choice (D) mischaracterizes the relationship; there is no evidence that the conquered people feel respect, only that they are required to *display* respect. Therefore, (A) is the best answer.

2. **B** The Caliphate expanded very rapidly across the Middle East and North Africa, but following the initial era of expansion, the areas under its political control remained generally stable even though Islam continued to spread across central and southern Asia. Choice (D) indicates a slow expansion, which is incorrect. Choice (C) also characterizes the expansion as slow and conflates the Ottoman Empire with the Caliphate, which is also incorrect. The main difference between (A) and (B) is the agent of defeat and collapse. As the Mongols were responsible for the defeat and disintegration of the Caliphate, (B) is correct.

3. **D** Though the treaty banned Christians from consuming fermented drinks and wearing turbans, this is a sign of Islamic opposition to fermented drinks and subordinate peoples adopting their dress, so (A) is incorrect. Choice (B) goes too far; though this particular furnished a safe conduct, this was a consequence of conquest and not Islamic society. Choice (C) is a true statement but does not answer the question; the text does not give any information about the distinction between Shia and Sunni Islam. Choice (D) is supported by the text, as the rights of individuals in the society are linked directly and explicitly to religion: Muslims enjoyed more rights than Christians. Therefore, (D) is the answer.

4. **A** Like European societies, Islamic societies were fundamentally patriarchal in orientation, so (C) is incorrect. Still, both the theological and practical innovations introduced under the Islamic Caliphate improved the legal and social status of women when compared with earlier societies of Middle East and North Africa. Therefore, eliminate (B) and (D). Women did not enjoy equal rights, but they were not considered property, and they even gained some rights of their own. Thus (A) is correct.

REFLECT

Respond to the following questions:

- For which content topics discussed in this chapter do you feel you have achieved sufficient mastery to answer multiple-choice questions correctly?

- For which content topics discussed in this chapter do you feel you have achieved sufficient mastery to discuss effectively in a short-answer response or essay?

- For which content topics discussed in this chapter do you feel you need more work before you can answer multiple-choice questions correctly?

- For which content topics discussed in this chapter do you feel you need more work before you can discuss effectively in a short-answer response or essay?

- What parts of this chapter are you going to re-review?

- Will you seek further help outside of this book (such as a teacher, tutor, or AP Students) on any of the content in this chapter—and, if so, on what content?

Chapter 9
Global Interactions,
c. 1450 to c. 1750

I. CHAPTER OVERVIEW

By 1450 C.E., global interaction really got cranking. That's why this chapter only covers about 300 years, whereas the previous chapter covered nearly 800 years, and Chapter 6 covered an astonishing 8,000 years. Since the time period covered in this chapter is narrower, the amount of detail provided is greater. The rise of Europe as a major player on the world scene was very important during this time period, and because the AP focuses so much on the interaction among cultures, most of the regions of the world in this chapter are discussed in terms of their relation to Europe.

As with previous chapters, we suggest that you read through this chapter once, and then go back and focus on the things that you're not entirely clear about. To help you do that, here's the chapter outline.

I. Chapter Overview

    You're reading it now.

II. Stay Focused on the Big Picture

    Organize the huge social, political, and economic changes that occurred during this time period into some big-picture concepts.

III. Major European Developments, 1450–1750

    This section focuses on developments that influenced all of Europe, as opposed to more localized developments that affected particular countries or empires. Of course, the developments discussed in this section had an impact beyond the borders of Europe, which is why they're so important to the study of world history. We've organized the major developments into two main groups.

    A. Revolutions in European Thought and Expression
    B. European Exploration and Expansion: Empires of the Wind

IV. Developments in Specific Countries and Empires, 1450–1750

    After you've studied the major social, religious, economic, and political developments that swept through Europe and beyond, you should be able to put developments in individual countries and empires in the proper context. In addition to reviewing developments that occurred within the individual European powers, we'll help you review the unique civilizations that existed elsewhere on the globe, particularly the Ottoman Empire, India, China, and Japan. In the next chapter, we'll review the impact of European expansion on Africa and Asia in the nineteenth century. Here's how we've organized this section.

Read Russia

II. STAY FOCUSED ON THE BIG PICTURE

As you review the details of the developments in this chapter, stay focused on some big-picture concepts. As you read, keep in mind the following questions:

1. Why did Europe become a dominant power during this time period? Was it because European nations vied for world dominance while other civilizations didn't, or because of technological superiority? Was it for some other reason? Why did some of the European nation-states develop vast empires while others did not? What motivated Europeans to explore, conquer, and colonize? There are lots of legitimate answers to these questions, and the content of this chapter will help you think about some of them.

2. What were some of the differences among the ways in which non-European cultures interacted with Europe? What influences contributed to these differences? What were the consequences? You'll notice that European powers penetrated different parts of the globe to different degrees. Pay attention to why this was true—it will not only tell you a lot about Europe, but also about those individual non-European cultures as well.

3. How did the global economy change during this time period? What was the impact on the world's civilizations? As you read, notice how economic considerations drove much of the world's interactions. Pay attention to how the larger global economy impacted the various regions of the globe.

4. What were the impacts of global interaction on the environment? Conversely, what were the impacts of the environment on human societies? What ideas, diseases, plants, and animals traveled the globe along with human settlement? The need for new resources brought massive changes, but at the same time, the environment acted on human societies, sometimes with disastrous consequences. Pay attention to the effects of the 500-year period of global cooling that began around 1500 and resulted in shortages of crops, famines, and susceptibility to diseases.

III. MAJOR EUROPEAN DEVELOPMENTS, 1450–1750

[handwritten margin note: Lots of changes in Europe for the citizens, gov., religious view points, and with the rest of the world]

During the three centuries covered in this chapter, profound changes occurred on the European continent. These changes affected life on all levels: the way people viewed themselves (their past, their present, and their future potential), the way governments viewed their authority, the way religion intersected with politics and individuality, and the way Europeans thought about and interacted with the rest of the world.

By the end of these 300 years, the European countries will have used their new technologies, new ideas of governing, and new forms of economic organization to become the dominant world powers. Much of their success was based on competition and rivalry as they raced to secure faster trade routes, new colonial possessions, and attempted to gain control of key resources. However, much of their success came at the expense of the land-based empires of Asia and the declining empires in the Americas. *[handwritten: success bc of Asia + declining America]*

While the previous chapter was all about interactions, this one covers the period of European maritime empire-building that resulted from those initial interactions across Asia and the Indian Ocean. As you review the enormous developments in Parts A and B below, think about how they were linked together and impacted each other.

A. Revolutions in European Thought and Expression

[handwritten margin note: Society structured around relationship]

[handwritten: A first]

By the 1300s, much of Europe had been Christian for a thousand years. The feudal system had dominated the political and social structures for several hundred years, and the ancient classical civilizations of Greece and Rome had faded into the ancient past.

The history of the Middle Ages was dominated by local issues, a concern with salvation, territorial disputes, disease and famine, limited access to education, and small-scale trade. As you read in the last chapter, near the end of the Middle Ages, countries began to unify under centralized rule. The Crusades exposed Christians to the advanced Islamic civilizations, increased trade fueled contact with other parts of the world, and universities became great centers of learning. This increased contact with foreign powers, along with scholasticism, exposed Europeans not only to developments in the rest of the world but also to history. Recall that the Byzantine and Islamic Empires had preserved much of the heritage of ancient Greece and Rome, even as they built unique civilizations of their own and made huge contributions to ancient texts, especially in the areas of mathematics and science. As Europe expanded its worldview and interacted more frequently with these two empires, it placed a greater emphasis on its own classical past.

following the past successful empire)

The combination of a rediscovered past and a productive present led to major changes in the way Europeans viewed the world and themselves. These new perspectives led to four massive cultural movements: the Renaissance, the Protestant Reformation, the Scientific Revolution, and the Enlightenment. These revolutions in expression and thought changed the world. In a span of just a few hundred years, Europe went from being a backward outpost on the perimeter of the major civilizations to the east to the home of some of the most dominant civilizations in the world.

Major transformation for Europe

We'll talk about the details of European global exploration and expansion later in this chapter. In the meantime, you should understand that this exploration and expansion were partly causing—and partly caused by—the major developments in thought and expression that are listed below.

1. The Renaissance: Classical Civilization Part II

After the Black Death abated and the population of Europe once again began to swell, the demand for goods and services began to increase rapidly. Individuals moved to the cities. A middle class made up of bankers, merchants, and traders emerged due to increased global trade. In short, Europe experienced an influx of money to go along with its newfound sense of history. It shouldn't be too surprising that a sizeable chunk of this money was spent on recapturing and studying the past.

Humanism: A Bit More Focus on the Here and Now

In medieval Europe, thoughts of salvation and the afterlife so dominated personal priorities that life on Earth was, for many, something to be suffered through on the way to heaven rather than lived through as a pursuit of its own. As Europeans rediscovered ancient texts, they were struck with the degree that humanity—personal accomplishment and personal happiness—formed the central core of so much of the literature and philosophy of the ancient writers. The emphasis began to shift from fulfillment in the afterlife to participating in the here-and-now.

This is not to say that medieval Europeans had no concerns in the present or that early modern Europeans suddenly became hedonistic, focused on worldly pleasures. To the contrary, the Catholic Church and a focus on the afterlife remained dominant. However, Europeans were fascinated with the ancient Greek and Roman concepts of beauty and citizenship, and as a consequence they began to shift their focus to life on Earth and to celebrating human achievements in the scholarly, artistic, and political realms. This focus on human endeavors became known as **humanism**. Its impact was far-reaching because a focus on present-day life leads to a focus on individuals, and a focus on individuality inevitably leads to a reduction in the authority of institutions.

Renaissance: basically the rebirth of Europe, more intrest in human life

THE ITALIAN STATE SYSTEM DURING THE RENAISSANCE

ALPS

OTTOMAN EMPIRE

DUCHY OF SAVOY

DUCHY OF MILAN

VENETIAN REPUBLIC

M. OF MONTFERRAT

M. OF MANTUA

DUCHY OF MODENA

DUCHY OF FERRARA

REPUBLIC OF GENOA

REPUBLIC OF FLORENCE

REP. OF SIENA

PAPAL STATES

CORSICA (to Genoa)

ISTRIA

DALMATIA

ADRIATIC SEA

KINGDOM OF NAPLES

SARDINIA (to Spain)

TYRRHENIAN SEA

KINGDOM OF SICILY

MEDITERRANEAN SEA

The Arts Stage a Comeback

The Renaissance literally means "rebirth," and this was nowhere more apparent than in the arts. In Italy, where powerful families in city-states such as Florence, Venice, and Milan became rich on trade, art was financed on a scale not seen since the classical civilizations of Greece and Rome. The **Medici** family in Florence, for example, not only ruled the great city and beyond (several family members not coincidentally became popes!), but turned it into a showcase of architecture and beauty by acting as patron for some of the greatest artists of the time, including **Michelangelo** and **Brunelleschi**.

Unlike medieval paintings, which often depicted humans as flat, stiff, and out of proportion with their surroundings, paintings of the Renaissance demonstrated the application of humanistic ideals learned from the ancients. Painters and sculptors such as **Leonardo da Vinci** and **Donatello** depicted the human figure as realistically as possible. Careful use of light and shadow made figures appear full and real. Many artists were so committed to this realism that they viewed and participated in autopsies to fully understand the structure of the human body.

Artists also employed a technique known as linear perspective, developed by Tommaso Masaccio and Fillipo Brunelleschi, in which nearby objects were drawn bigger while far objects were drawn smaller; the lines of perspective merged into a distant focal point, giving the painting a three-dimensional quality. This use of perspective was a huge development toward realism.

The Catholic Church noticed the developments in artistic techniques, and soon the greatest artists were hard at work adorning the great palaces and cathedrals of Italy. For four years, 1508 to 1512 C.E., Michelangelo painted the now-famous ceiling of the Sistine Chapel while lying on his back on scaffolding. Meanwhile, Renaissance architects borrowed heavily from the Greek and Roman traditions to build huge domes on cathedrals in Florence and Rome.

The artistic movement that engulfed the Italian city-states also spread northward and westward through much of Western Europe, although it was generally more subdued and often more religious there than it was on the Italian peninsula. Still, even in northern Europe, especially in artistic centers such as Flanders, the influences of the resurgent Western heritage could be felt. For example, the Dutch **Van Eyck** brothers and the German painter **Albrecht Dürer** adopted the naturalism of the Italian painters and gained fame as portraitists. While highly realistic in style, most northern paintings were religiously motivated, and thus even secular paintings or portraits were filled with religiously symbolic objects and color choices that resonated with the Christian faithful.

Still, while the northern painters and sculptors were quite talented, they were outnumbered and in many cases outdone by their Italian counterparts. The more significant contribution of the northern Renaissance came not from the visual arts, but from literature.

Western Writers Finally Get Readers

Although printing was developed in China centuries earlier (remember which dynasty? The Song), moveable type wasn't invented in Europe until the mid-1400s, when **Johannes Gutenberg** invented the printing press. Prior to Gutenberg's invention, the creation of books was such a long and laborious task that few were made. Those that were made were usually printed in Latin, the language of scholars and the Catholic Church. Because of this and the lack of public education, the typical person couldn't own books or even read.

Contrast Them: Art in the Middle Ages and the Renaissance

Medieval art was almost entirely religious; Renaissance art was religious and secular, combining both Christian and humanist elements. Medieval art existed mostly in cathedrals; Renaissance art was commissioned by both religious and secular leaders, and adorned public plazas and homes. Medieval art was flat and stiff; Renaissance art was realistic, softer, and more human. In short, medieval art didn't try to be worldly; Renaissance art tried very much to be of this world. Medieval artists rarely signed their own names on their works, whereas Renaissance artists proudly signed their works and competed in a competitive marketplace of patronage and art sales.

With the invention of the **printing press**, all that changed. Books became easy to produce and thus were far more affordable. The growing middle class fueled demand for books on a variety of subjects that were written in their own **vernacular**, or native language, such as German or French. The book industry flourished, as did related industries such as papermaking, a craft that was learned from the Arabs, who learned it from the Chinese. More books led to more literate and educated people. The newly literate people desired more books, which continued to make them more educated, which again increased their desire for books, and so on. The most commonly circulated books and pamphlets were religious in nature. New translations of the Bible into vernacular languages encouraged public debate and personal interpretation of the Bible and helped usher in the Reformation.

Many of the first books and pamphlets that were published were practical or political in nature. In 1517 C.E., **Machiavelli**, for example, published *The Prince*, a how-to book for monarchs who wanted to maintain their power. The work had a profound impact because it suggested that monarchy should be distinct from the church and that a leader should act purely in self-interest of the state rather than on the basis of vague moral tenets (since then, the term *Machiavellian* often has a negative connotation, implying a ruler who is ruthlessly selfish, scheming, and manipulative). The printed word, however, extended well beyond the courts of nobles. It changed life for the developing middle class because reading became a casual endeavor. Books were printed for no purpose other than entertainment or diversion, and this led to literature that increasingly focused on the daily lives of regular people, and humanized traditional institutions such as the military or the nobility.

Literature blossomed in the Renaissance of northern Europe, especially in the Low Countries (today known as the Netherlands, Luxembourg, and Belgium) and in England. In the early sixteenth century, **Erasmus**, one of the most well-known learned men of the time, counseled kings and popes. He wrote *In Praise of Folly*, which satirized what he thought were the most foolish political moves to date. At around the same time, **Sir Thomas More** of England wrote *Utopia*, which described an ideal society, in which everyone shared the wealth, and in which everyone's needs were met. More and Erasmus were Christian humanists, meaning that they expressed moral guidelines in the Christian tradition, which they believed people should follow as they pursued their personal goals. The Renaissance also produced **William Shakespeare**, arguably the most famous European writer from this time. Shakespeare's works reflected the period well because they not only exemplified humanism in its extreme—focusing on character strengths and flaws, comedy and tragedy—but also illustrated the era's obsession with the politics and mythology of classical civilization. Shakespeare's plays *Julius Caesar* and *Antony and Cleopatra* are among his many works that explored the classical world.

2. The Protestant Reformation: Streamlining Salvation

You might recall from the previous chapter that during the Middle Ages (600–1450), the Catholic Church was an extremely powerful force in Europe. While political power was diffused under the feudal system, and while the various European princes and political powers frequently clashed with the pope, emperors and princes knew that their power increased if the church blessed their reign. As a consequence, the pope wielded considerable political power.

The church was one of the most important institutions that unified ordinary people in Western Europe. It was a unifying force, an institution believed to be sanctioned by God. With such widely accepted credentials, the church held itself out as not only the undisputed authority on all things otherworldly, but also the ultimate endorsement on all things worldly. With one foot on Earth and the other in heaven, the pope—and with him the hierarchy of the Catholic Church—acted as the intermediary between man and God. Nearly everyone in Europe understood this clearly: To get to heaven, you had to proceed by way of the Catholic Church.

The church understood the power it had over the faithful. When it needed to finance its immense building projects plus pay for the huge number of Renaissance artists it kept in its employ, it began to sell **indulgences**. An indulgence was a piece of paper that the faithful could purchase to reduce time in purgatory (the place Catholics believed they would go after death). There, they would atone for their sins and then be allowed to enter heaven. Because purgatory was not thought of as a happy place to go, people greatly valued the concept of reducing their time there. Selling indulgences was not only a means of generating income, but also a way for the church to maintain power over its members.

During this time, landowning nobles grew increasingly resentful of the church, which had amassed an enormous amount of power and wealth and exploited a huge number of resources at the expense of the nobles. This resentment and mistrust fueled anti-church sentiments. The selling of indulgences propelled the frustration into the ranks of the peasant class and helped set the stage for confrontation. The selling of indulgences also confirmed to many the corrupt nature of the church.

Martin Luther: Monk on a Mission

In 1517, a German monk named **Martin Luther** supposedly nailed a list of 95 theses on a church door—a list that was distributed quickly and widely by aid of the newfangled printing press. His list outlined his frustrations with current church practices, including the church's practice of selling indulgences, which he said amounted to selling salvation for profit. Luther's frustrations had been building for some time. He had traveled to Rome, and was unnerved by the worldly nature of the city and the Vatican (the seat of the Catholic Church), which was in the midst of getting a Renaissance makeover—upgrades that were clearly paid for with money from churchgoers in far-away places.

Among Luther's many complaints was his insistence that church services should be conducted in the local languages of the people, not in Latin, a language that the German people didn't understand. To help in this effort, he translated the Bible into German so that it could be read and interpreted by everyone, as opposed to making people dependent on the church for biblical understanding. Luther's most significant claim was that salvation was given directly by God through grace, not through indulgences, and not through the authorization of the church. In other words, Luther suggested that the Bible teaches that people could appeal directly to God for forgiveness for sins and salvation. This revolutionary concept significantly reduced the role of the church as the exclusive middleman between God and man. In essence, the church was marginalized to an aid for salvation as opposed to the grantor of salvation.

Luther's followers: Lutherans

Pope Leo X was outraged, and ordered Luther to recant, or formally retract, his theses. Meanwhile, Luther's ideas were spreading through much of northern Europe as the printing presses continued to roll. When Luther refused to recant, he was excommunicated. When he was allowed to address church leaders and princes at an assembly in Worms (1521), he refused to abandon his convictions. The pope called for his arrest, but a nobleman from Luther's hometown protected him, and Luther continued to write and spread his ideas.

Christianity Splits Again

The consequences of Luther's actions were enormous. Luther's followers began to refer to themselves as **Lutherans**, and began to separate themselves from the Catholic Church. What's more, other theologians began to assert their own biblical interpretations, some of which were consistent with Luther's; others were wildly different. Once the floodgates were opened, Luther had no control over the consequences.

John Calvin from France led a powerful Protestant group by preaching an ideology of predestination. Calvinist doctrine stated that God had predetermined an ultimate destiny for all people, most of whom God had already damned. Only a few, he preached, would be saved, and those people were known as the Elect. In the 1530s, the city of Geneva in Switzerland invited Calvin to construct a Protestant theocracy in their city, which was centrally located and near France. From there, Calvinist teachings spread and were as influential to successive Protestant Reformations as were the doctrines of Luther. **Calvinism**, for example, greatly influenced religious development in Scotland under John Knox, and in France with the growth of the Huguenots.

In time, the Reformation spread to England, motivated by political as well as religious reasons. **King Henry VIII** did not have a son as heir to his throne and sought to end his marriage to Catherine of Aragon because of it. When the pope denied an annulment of the marriage, Henry VIII renounced Rome and declared himself the head of religious affairs in England. This sat well with those in England who already were becoming Protestants, but much of England remained Catholic. Nevertheless, Henry pushed forward and presided over what was called the **Church of England**, also known as the Anglican Church.

Focus On: Independent Thinking

The **Protestant Reformation** was a huge deal in world history. Its significance went well beyond the religious arena. While previous skirmishes between the pope and the nobles had been about papal political authority, Luther's challenges were theologically based and directed at the pope's religious role. Luther asserted that the people did not need the Catholic Church, or its priests, in order to interact with God; they only needed their Bibles. If the religious authority of the pope could be so openly and brazenly challenged, and commonly accepted understandings of God's relationship to man could be reevaluated and rearticulated, then people's understanding of other concepts might need to be reevaluated as well. Put simply, by challenging the pope, Luther made it acceptable to question the conventional wisdom of the church. With newly printed Bibles available in their own languages, laypeople could learn how to read and form their own relationships with God. As the common people became literate and better educated, more and more Europeans began to question both the world around them and the authority of the church. Europeans desired to search for their own answers to the questions of the universe. In short, the Protestant Reformation paved the way for revolutions in education, politics, and science.

The Counter-Reformation: The Pope Reasserts His Authority

During the **Catholic Reformation** (also known as the **Counter-Reformation**) of the sixteenth century, the Catholic Church itself reformed, while also succeeding in winning back some of the souls it had lost to the fledgling Protestant denominations.

At first, the Catholic Church responded ineffectively to the new religious trends. However, when Luther refused to recant and German princes started to convert to Lutheranism, the Catholic Church began to institute reforms, which were led by Spain, a dedicated Catholic country. By banning the sale of indulgences, consulting more frequently with bishops and parishes, and training its priests to adhere to Catholic teaching more strictly, the Catholic Church regained some of its lost credibility. However, make no mistake, the Counter-Reformation was as much about reaffirming as it was about reforming, and the church made it clear that it was not bowing to Protestant demands but rather clarifying its position. Weekly mass became obligatory, and the supreme authority of the pope was re-established. During this time, a former Spanish soldier and intellectual, **Ignatius Loyola**, founded the society of Jesuits, which was influential in restoring faith in the teachings of Jesus as interpreted by the Catholic Church. The **Jesuits** practiced self-control and moderation, believing that prayer and good works led to salvation. The pious example of the Jesuits led to a stricter training system and higher expectations of morality for the clergy. Because of their oratorical and political skills, many Jesuits were appointed by kings to high palace positions.

A group of church officials held a series of meetings known as the **Council of Trent** to direct the Counter-Reformation period from 1545 to 1563, dictating and defining the Catholic interpretation of religious doctrine and clarifying the Catholic Church's position on important religious questions such as the nature of salvation. During this period, "heretics" were once again tried and punished, and the Catholic Church re-established Latin as the language to be used in worship.

The result? The Catholic Church staged an amazing comeback. The Counter-Reformation proved successful in containing the southward spread of Protestantism. By 1600, southern Europe (especially Italy, Spain, and Portugal), France, and southern Germany were heavily Catholic. Northern Germany and Scandinavia were mostly Lutheran. Scotland was Calvinist, as were pockets within central Europe and France. England, as mentioned previously, was Anglican.

The result of the result? Wars, of course. But more on that when we discuss developments in individual countries.

Henry VIII: An Epilogue
Henry VIII went on to marry five more wives and to father a son, who died young. His daughter Elizabeth, also a Protestant, rose to the throne, but more on that later when we discuss political developments in England.

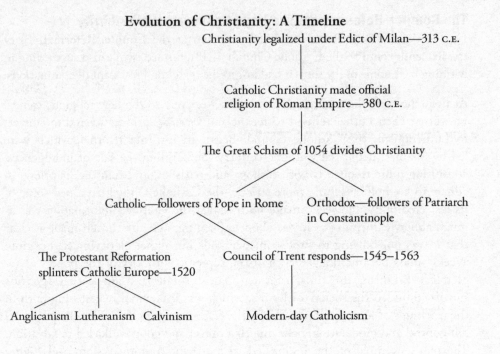

Evolution of Christianity: A Timeline

Christianity legalized under Edict of Milan—313 c.e.

Catholic Christianity made official
religion of Roman Empire—380 c.e.

The Great Schism of 1054 divides Christianity

Catholic—followers of Pope in Rome   Orthodox—followers of Patriarch
                                       in Constantinople

The Protestant Reformation   Council of Trent responds—1545–1563
splinters Catholic Europe—1520

Anglicanism Lutheranism Calvinism   Modern-day Catholicism

3. The Scientific Revolution: Prove It or Lose It

Prior to the Scientific Revolution, Europe and most of the world believed, as Aristotle asserted, that Earth was the center of the universe and that the sun, stars, and planets revolved around the earth. There certainly were numerous inconsistencies observed by scientists with regard to this theory, but most scientists continued to attempt to explain the inconsistency rather than investigate the theory itself. As Europe changed dramatically due to the Renaissance and the Protestant Reformation, and as the growth of universities gave structure to burgeoning questions about the world, educated Europeans began to examine the world around them with new vigor. The results were revolutionary.

The Copernican Revolution: A Revolution About Revolutions

Just as the Counter-Reformation was gaining momentum, **Nicolaus Copernicus** developed a mathematical theory that asserted that the earth and the other celestial bodies revolved around the sun and that the earth also rotated on its axis daily. This was pretty shocking stuff to many in the "establishment." Although most educated people had accepted the world was a sphere for centuries, even well before Columbus's voyage in 1492, the earth's position at the center of the universe was widely accepted. Copernicus's heliocentric theory of the solar system brought about much debate and much skepticism. In 1543, Copernicus published *On the Revolutions of the Heavenly Spheres* to prove his points, but it wasn't until Galileo—who discovered the moons of Jupiter with his telescope—that the Copernican model really took off.

In 1632, **Galileo** published his *Dialogue Concerning the Two Chief Systems of the World*. He wrote the work in Italian in order to reach a wide audience and defeat the defenders of Ptolemy (the scientist who promoted the earth as the center of the universe). He showed how the rotation of the earth on its axis produced the apparent rotation of the heavens, as well as how the stars' great distance from the earth prevented humans from being able to see their changed position as the earth

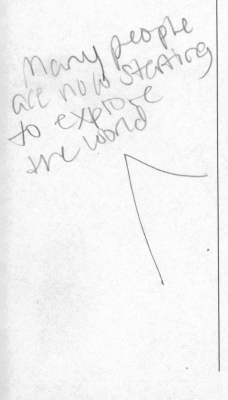

Many people are now starting to explore the world

moved around the sun. Galileo's proofs made it difficult for scholars to continue to accept the Ptolemaic model, which just so happened to be the model sanctioned by the Catholic Church. The church put Galileo on trial before the Inquisition in Rome for heresy and he was forced to recant. His book was placed on **The Index**, a list of banned heretical works. Nevertheless, while under house arrest, Galileo continued to research and document his findings.

The Scientific Method: In Search of Truth

Recall that during the High Middle Ages and the early Renaissance, the scholastic method of reasoning was deemed the most reliable means of determining scientific meaning. Scholasticism was based on Aristotelianism and therefore used reason as the chief method of determining truth. Sometimes reason led to heresies, while other times reason was used to explain and complement faith, as was the case with Thomas Aquinas.

The scientific method was born out of the scholastic tradition, but it took that tradition to considerable new levels. Reason alone wasn't good enough. Under the scientific method, one had to prove what the mind concluded, document it, repeat it for others, and open it up to experimentation. At its highest stage, the scientific method required that any underlying principles be proven with mathematical precision.

Copernicus and Galileo, of course, were two fathers of the scientific method, but it took more than a century for the method to be widely used. There were many contributors. **Tycho Brahe** (1546–1601) built an observatory and recorded his observations, and **Francis Bacon** (1561–1626) published works on inductive logic. Both asserted that scientists should amass all the data possible through experimentation and observation and that the proper conclusions would come from these data. Then, **Johannes Kepler** (1571–1630) developed laws of planetary motion based on observation and mathematics. **Sir Isaac Newton** took it one step further. In *The Mathematical Principles of Natural Philosophy* (1697), he invented calculus to help prove the theories of Copernicus, Galileo, Bacon, and others. He also developed the law of gravity.

Together, these men and others developed a widely used system of observation, reason, experiment, and mathematical proof that could be applied to every conceivable scientific inquiry. With precise scientific instruments, such as the microscope and the telescope, a scientist could retest what another scientist had originally tested. Many scientific inquires were conducted with practical goals in mind, such as the creation of labor-saving machines or the development of power sources from water and wind. Francis Bacon, for example, argued that science was pursued not for science's sake but as a way to improve the human condition.

All of this eventually led to the Industrial Revolution, which will be discussed in the next chapter. In the meantime, however, you need to understand that the Scientific Revolution led to a major rift in society. While many highly educated Christians were able to hold on to their beliefs even as they studied science, many also began to reject the church's rigid pronouncements that conflicted with scientific findings. Many of these people either became **atheists** (who believe that no god exists) or **deists** (who believe that God exists but plays a passive role in life).

Fun Fact
Astonishingly, Galileo's book remained on The Index until 1822!

Deism: God as a Watchmaker

The Scientific Revolution contributed to a belief system known as deism, which became popular in the 1700s. The deists believed in a powerful god who created and presided over an orderly realm but who did not interfere in its workings. The deists viewed God as a watchmaker, one who set up the world, gave it natural laws by which to operate, and then let it run by itself (under natural laws that could be proved mathematically). Such a theory had little place in organized religion.

Focus On: The Church Defends Itself on Two Fronts

Both the Protestant Reformation and the Scientific Revolution challenged the absolute authority of the pope. The Reformation challenged the pope's authority on theological grounds; the Scientific Revolution challenged his authority on scientific and mathematical grounds. Don't presume that the Protestant Revolution was the main instigator of religious change during this time period. The religious implications of the Scientific Revolution were just as huge.

4. The Enlightenment: Out of Darkness, Into the Light

While the scientists put forth revolutionary ideas, the philosophers and social critics had a revolution of their own. The Enlightenment of the seventeenth and eighteenth centuries focused on the role of humankind in relation to government, ideas that greatly influenced the framers of the U.S. Constitution. Because the U.S. Constitution has since been a model for so many others across the globe, it's safe to say that the writers of the Enlightenment period changed the world.

Who were these Enlightenment writers? Here's an overview:

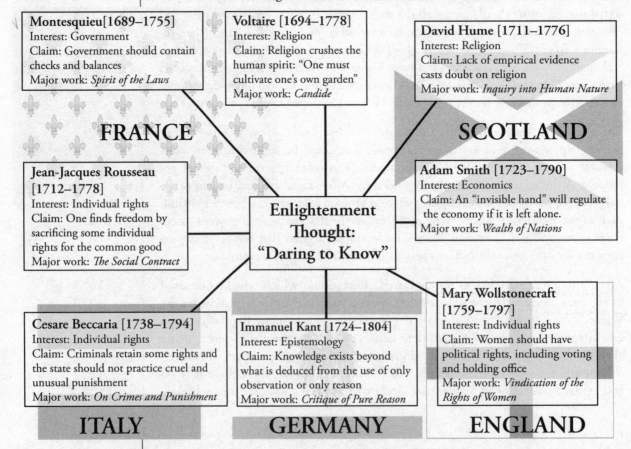

Montesquieu [1689–1755]
Interest: Government
Claim: Government should contain checks and balances
Major work: *Spirit of the Laws*

Voltaire [1694–1778]
Interest: Religion
Claim: Religion crushes the human spirit: "One must cultivate one's own garden"
Major work: *Candide*

David Hume [1711–1776]
Interest: Religion
Claim: Lack of empirical evidence casts doubt on religion
Major work: *Inquiry into Human Nature*

FRANCE

SCOTLAND

Jean-Jacques Rousseau [1712–1778]
Interest: Individual rights
Claim: One finds freedom by sacrificing some individual rights for the common good
Major work: *The Social Contract*

Enlightenment Thought: "Daring to Know"

Adam Smith [1723–1790]
Interest: Economics
Claim: An "invisible hand" will regulate the economy if it is left alone.
Major work: *Wealth of Nations*

Cesare Beccaria [1738–1794]
Interest: Individual rights
Claim: Criminals retain some rights and the state should not practice cruel and unusual punishment
Major work: *On Crimes and Punishment*

Immanuel Kant [1724–1804]
Interest: Epistemology
Claim: Knowledge exists beyond what is deduced from the use of only observation or only reason
Major work: *Critique of Pure Reason*

Mary Wollstonecraft [1759–1797]
Interest: Individual rights
Claim: Women should have political rights, including voting and holding office
Major work: *Vindication of the Rights of Women*

ITALY

GERMANY

ENGLAND

First a Little Background: Divine Right

During the High Middle Ages and through the Renaissance and counter-reformation, the church allied itself with strong monarchs. These monarchs came to power by centralizing authority, uniting people under a common banner of nationalism, forming empires by promoting exploration and colonization (much more on this later), and ruling with absolute authority. Because the vast majority of their populations were Christian, the best way to rule was to align oneself with God. Monarchs became convinced that God had ordained their right to govern, and that meant that people had a moral and religious obligation to obey them. This concept was known as the **divine right** of monarchs. James I of England, who ruled from 1603 to 1625, summed it up this way: "The king is from God and the law is from the King." His statement made it pretty clear that an illegal act was an ungodly act.

Because the pope also claimed to be ordained by God, the question of ultimate authority became very confusing indeed. During the Reformation, monarchs who resented the power of the church supported the reformists (Luther, Calvin, and others). Other monarchs, particularly in Spain and France, allied themselves with the church during the Counter-Reformation. In both cases, monarchs claimed to have divine right. Divine right could be used to support either position because the bottom line was that God supported whatever the monarchs chose.

Contrast Them: Divine Right and Mandate of Heaven

Recall that under the Zhou Dynasty in China, the emperor ruled under what became known as a **Mandate of Heaven**, which sounds a whole lot like Divine Right, and it was except for an important difference. Under the Mandate of Heaven, the emperors believed they were divinely chosen, but would only be given authority to rule so long as they pleased heaven. If they didn't rule justly and live up to their responsibility, heaven would ensure their fall. Divine Right, on the other hand, was used to justify absolute rule without any corresponding responsibilities. Monarchs who ruled under a strict theory of Divine Right saw themselves as God's personal representatives, chosen specifically for the task of ruling. In other words, Divine Right was a privilege without any qualification, whereas the Mandate of Heaven was upheld only so long as rulers acted justly.

The Social Contract: Power to the People

During the seventeenth century, philosophers and intellectuals began to grapple with the nature of social and political structures, and the idea of the social contract emerged. The social contract held that governments were formed not by divine decree, but to meet the social and economic needs of the people being governed. Philosophers who supported the social contract theory reasoned that because individuals existed before governments did, governments arose to meet the needs of the people, not the other way around. Still, because different philosophers looked at human nature differently, they disagreed about the role of government in the social contract.

Russia
- Golden Horde was ruling
- Katherine after Peter
- 130 mil pop
- One of the last countries to get rid of forced labor.

Thomas Hobbes (1588–1679), who wrote *Leviathan*, thought that people by nature were greedy and prone to violent warfare. Accordingly, he believed the role of the government under the social contract should be to preserve peace and stability at all costs. Hobbes therefore advocated an all-powerful ruler, or Leviathan, who would rule in such a heavy-handed way as to suppress the natural war-like tendencies of the people.

John Locke (1632–1704), who wrote *Two Treatises on Government*, had a more optimistic view of human nature, believing that mankind, for the most part, was good. Locke also believed that all men were born equal to one another and had natural and unalienable rights to life, liberty, and property. Since mankind was good and rational, and thus capable of self-rule, Locke believed the primary responsibility of the government under the social contract was to secure and guarantee these natural rights. If, however, the government ever violated this trust, thus breaking the social contract, the people were justified in revolting and replacing the government.

Rousseau's Legacy
Needless to say, Rousseau's beliefs not only had a tremendous effect on revolutionary movements in the colonies of the European empires, but also inspired the anti-slavery movement.

Jean-Jacques Rousseau (1712–1778) took the social contract theory to its furthest extreme, arguing that all men were equal and that society should be organized according to the general will, or majority rule, of the people, an idea he outlined in his famous work *The Social Contract* (1762). In a rational society, he argued, each individual should subject himself to this general will, which serves as the sovereign or ruling lawmaker. Under this philosophy, the individual is protected by the community, but is also free (or as free as one can be in organized society). He argues the essence of freedom is to obey laws that people prescribe for themselves.

Among the other Enlightenment thinkers and writers were Voltaire and Montesquieu. **Voltaire** espoused the idea of religious toleration. **Montesquieu** argued for separation of powers among branches of government. In all cases, Enlightenment writers didn't presume that government had divine authority, but instead worked backward from the individual and proposed governmental systems that would best serve the interest of the people by protecting individual rights and liberties.

While the real fruits of the Enlightenment were the revolutionary movements in the colonies and later in Europe, the new political ideas also affected the leadership of some eighteenth-century European monarchs. The ideals of tolerance, justice, and improving quality of life became guidelines for rulers known as **enlightened monarchs**, such as Joseph II of Austria and Frederick II of Prussia. To be sure, they still ruled absolutely, but they internalized the Enlightenment philosophy and made attempts to tolerate diversity, increase opportunities for serfs, and take on the responsibilities that their rule required.

the Enlightenment
- a time of great intellectual and logical advancement
- A time of declining interest in new forms of art
- led to more tech

Ironically, though the Enlightenment was a time of great intellectual and logical advancement, it was also a time of declining interest in new forms of art. The **Neoclassical Period**, which began in the middle of the eighteenth century, imitated the balanced, symmetrical style of ancient Greek and Roman architecture. This is the reason that many American federal buildings in Washington, D.C. are designed to look like Greek temples—that was the style when our country was founded.

- they started to question the church
- the second renaissance

B. European Exploration and Expansion: Empires of the Wind

Exploration before the late fifteenth century was largely limited to land travel. To be sure, ships were used on the Mediterranean and Indian Ocean trade routes for centuries, but they were linked up to land routes through Persia, Arabia, northern Africa, or central Asia on the Silk Road.

Eager to eliminate Muslim middlemen and discover more efficient trade routes to Asia, the Portuguese and their Iberian rivals, the Spanish, set out to sea. Advances in navigation, shipbuilding, and the development of gunpowder weapons allowed for increased sea travel. These "floating empires of the wind" soon controlled major shipping routes in the Indian Ocean, Indonesia, and the Atlantic Ocean.

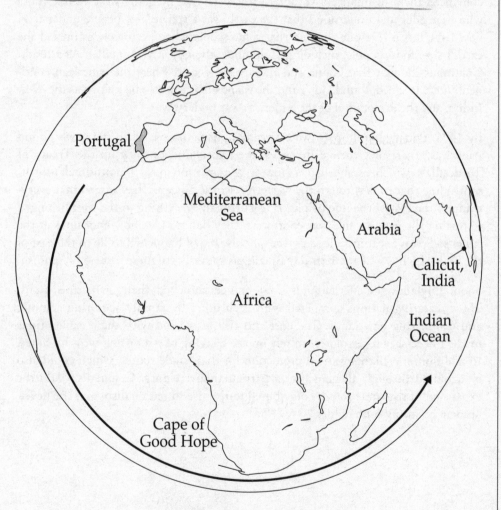

Portuguese Exploration in the 1500s

Handwritten margin notes:

-Two most powerful trading companies were the dutch (first) and the British

Peninsilaras
Creols
mestidos
Indigonous

The increase in European trade encouraged by the formation of the Hanseatic League and the Crusades spawned a search for new, efficient trade routes on the seas. Portugal led the way because it was strategically situated near the coast of Africa, had long-standing trade relations with Muslim nations, and, most importantly, was led by a royal family that supported exploration (King John I of Portugal's most famous son was **Prince Henry the Navigator**). In 1488, Portugal financed a voyage by Bartholomew Dias, who rounded the tip of Africa (which became known as the Cape of Good Hope). In 1497, **Vasco da Gama** rounded the Cape of Good Hope, explored the east African kingdoms, and then went all the way to India, where he established trade relations.

Shortly thereafter, Spain, which had recently been unified under Isabella and Ferdinand, wanted in on the action. As you well know, in 1492 **Christopher Columbus** convinced them to finance a voyage to reach the east by going west. While those who were educated understood that the earth was a sphere, few people understood how large it was. Despite the fact that some scholars had accurately estimated the earth's size, most people, including Columbus, thought it was smaller. As a result, Columbus thought that China and India were located where the American continents are. He sailed, found Cuba and the islands that came to be known as the West Indies, and the exploration of the Americas was underway.

By 1494, Portugal and Spain were already fighting over land in the newly found Americas. To resolve their differences, the two countries drew up the **Treaty of Tordesillas**, which established a line of demarcation on a longitudinal (north-south) line that runs through the western Atlantic Ocean. They agreed that everything to the east of the line belonged to Portugal; everything to the west belonged to Spain. The western side was enormous (they had no idea how enormous at the time) so Spain became a mega-power quickly. Brazil happened to lie to the east of the line, which is why modern-day Brazilians speak Portuguese instead of Spanish.

Soon, England, the Netherlands, and France launched their own expeditions. These seafaring nations competed with each other by rapidly acquiring colonies and conquering new lands. The cost and risk associated with these explorations made it necessary for explorers to rely on the backing of strong and wealthy states. In addition, merchants wanted protection for their trade routes, which could also be acquired through allegiance to a particular sovereignty. Colonialism and the expansion of the trade routes contributed to the rise in nationalism and the development of strong monarchies.

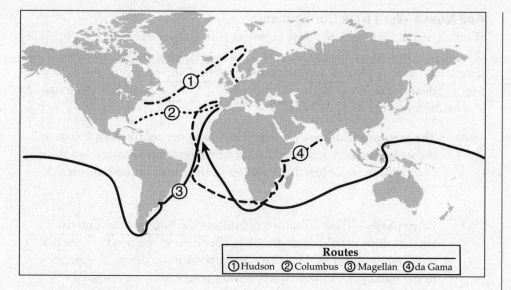

European Exploration in the Early Sixteenth Century

Here's a quick list of other explorers.

- **Amerigo Vespucci**—He explored South America on several trips around 1500; realized that the continent was huge and not part of Asia; America was named for him.

- **Ponce de Leon**—In 1513, he explored Florida for Spain in search of the fountain of youth.

- **Vasco de Balboa**—In 1513, he explored much of Central America for Spain; laid sight on the Pacific Ocean.

- **Ferdinand Magellan**—In 1519, he sailed around the tip of South America to the Pacific Ocean for Portugal. He made it as far as the Philippines, where he died; his crew continued, however, and became the first to circumnavigate the globe.

- **Giovanni da Verrazzano**—In 1524, he explored the North American coast for France.

- **Sir Francis Drake**—In 1578, he became the first Englishman to circumnavigate the globe.

- **John Cabot**—In 1497, he explored the coast of North America for England.

- **Henry Hudson**—Beginning in 1609, he sailed for the Dutch, looking for a **Northwest Passage** to Asia. He explored the Hudson River and made claims to the area for the Dutch.

And Now a Word from Our Sponsors

Why, all of a sudden, were so many explorers sailing around the globe? Why didn't this happen sooner? In the late fifteenth century, innovation was combined with determination to apply new technologies to political and economic goals. In addition to advanced mapmaking techniques, the Age of Exploration was brought to you by the following fine products:

- **The Sternpost Rudder**—Invented in China during the Han Dynasty, the sternpost rudder allowed for better navigation and control of ships of increasing size. How did it end up in the hands of the Europeans? Trade, of course.

- **Lateen Sails**—These sails, invented during the early Roman Empire, allowed ships to sail in any direction, regardless of the wind. This was a huge improvement to ships that were dependent on the wind, especially in the Indian Ocean waters, where monsoons kept ships docked for long periods of time. Once these sails were used regularly on the Indian Ocean routes, they quickly became standard on transatlantic voyages.

- **The Astrolabe**—Sailors used this portable navigation device, developed in the Hellenic world around 150 B.C.E., to help them find their way. By measuring the distance of the sun and the stars above the horizon, the astrolabe helped determine latitude.

- **The Magnetic Compass**—Borrowed from the Chinese, who developed it during the Han Dynasty, the magnetic compass traveled west through trade with Arabs and allowed sailors to determine direction without staying in sight of land.

- **Three-Masted Caravels**—These large ships employed significantly larger lateen sails and could hold provisions for longer journeys in their large cargo rooms.

To be sure, many of these inventions existed prior to the fifteenth century, but so much of history is about timing. In the late fifteenth century, these inventions had converged on one continent, a continent that was fiercely competitive about trade routes, newly wealthy, increasingly organized under strong leaders, and racing with the innovation and imagination of the Renaissance. We've said it before and we'll say it again: The events of this time period are so interrelated that you can't separate them. The era needs to be understood as one giant glob of inseparable, indistinguishable forces.

The New World: Accidental Empire

Although Columbus failed to locate gold or spices in the Americas, the next generation of Spanish explorers found great wealth in the Aztec and Inca Empires. In 1519, **Hernan Cortes** landed on the coast of Mexico with a small force of 600 men. He found himself at the heart of the Aztec Empire, which you read about in the previous chapter. As you might recall, the Aztecs used the conquest of neighboring communities to secure humans for religious sacrifices. Many of these neighboring states loathed the Aztecs and were more than willing to cooperate with the Spaniards. Cortes alternatively subjugated or slaughtered those that were not.

Cortes, aided and guided by the resentful neighbors, first approached the magnificent Aztec capital of Tenochtitlan on horseback. Horses were as yet completely unknown in America (and in fact were introduced to the continent by Spanish conquistadores). Montezuma, the Aztec ruler, sent a gift of gold to appease this newcomer to his lands, but unfortunately for the Aztecs, this offering only fueled the appetite of the new conquerors. Because the Spaniards' sole motivation for exploring the New World was to acquire gold and spices, the Spanish didn't hesitate to seize Montezuma and begin a siege of Tenochtitlan.

Disease: The Ultimate Weapon of Mass Destruction

Although the Aztecs resisted the occupation and fought to rid their capital of the invaders, the Spanish had incredibly powerful weapons on their side, including diseases such as smallpox. These infections were completely new to the Americas, thanks to their geographic isolation prior to Europeans' arrival, and quickly decimated the Aztecs, who had no natural resistance to them. The combination of disease, superior weapons, and assistance from Aztec enemies reduced the native population of the region from well over 20 million in 1520 to fewer than 2 million by 1580. Because so many of the deaths occurred in the first few years, the Spaniards were able to seize control of the empire by around 1525.

A similar fate met the Inca Empire. In 1531, **Francisco Pizarro** set out in search of the Incas with a tiny force of 200 men. Disease, superior weapons, and help from enemies quickly destroyed what little resistance the Incas could mount. In addition, Pizarro happened to land shortly after a very destructive civil war that had left the current emperor of the Incas in a shaky political position. By 1535, Pizarro was in control of the region.

Contrast Them: Expansion in the Americas Versus Empire-Building Elsewhere

We've talked about a lot of empires that expanded into far-reaching territories: the Romans, the Mongols, the Muslims, and the Macedonians, for example. In each of these cases, the empires either allowed existing cultural traditions to remain intact, or converted the existing population to their way of doing things, forcibly or not. By contrast, in the case of the Americas, the existing populations were largely wiped out. In addition, huge numbers of people moved in, far outnumbering the natives who had survived. Even the Mongols, who didn't hesitate to wipe out communities in their paths, didn't totally supplant the native populations the way the Europeans did in the Americas. Never before had an empire moved into such a vast territory that was so unpopulated (or, more accurately, depopulated). All of the other empires had to merge with, convert, or be converted by the existing populations. In the Americas, the Europeans created two new continents strictly in their own image.

The *Encomienda* System

Once Spain established a foothold in the New World, thousands of Spaniards arrived to build a new colonial empire. The colonial society was a hierarchical organization. At the top were the **peninsulares**, the select group of Spanish officials sent to govern the colonies. Below them, the *crillos* or **creoles**, were people born in the colonies to Spanish parents. Because they weren't born in Spain, they were looked down upon by the Spanish monarchy and were consequently barred from high positions. Yet, because they were the children of Spaniards, the creoles were educated and wealthy, and after many generations, they were able to organize and demand recognition. They later became the leaders of the independence movements (more on that in the next chapter). Below the crillos were **mestizos**, those with European and Native American ancestry, followed by the **mulattos**, those with European and African ancestry. Finally, there were the native Americans, who had little or no freedom and worked on estates or in mines.

To run the empire, the **viceroys**, who were appointed governors of each of the five regions of New Spain, established the *encomienda* system, which was a system of forced labor. The system provided the peninsulares with land and a specified number of native laborers. In return, the peninsulares were expected to protect the natives and convert them to Christianity. Shocked at the treatment of some of the natives, Christian missionaries appealed to the viceroys, emperor, and the Catholic Church to improve the natives' lot. Some in the empire agreed that reform was needed, but disastrously, the reform that was viewed as most important was the need for more workers. The reformers agreed to reduce the strain on the natives by bringing in new workers for the hardest jobs. Those new workers were African slaves. Not only was this a cruel and ironic way to solve the problem (relieve the burden on one group of victims by creating a second group), but it also ended up not improving the lot of the natives. Within a few decades, both slaves and natives were at the bottom of the social structure, and neither had significant rights.

The African Slave Trade: The Love of Money at the Root of Evil

Even before transatlantic voyages began, Europeans had begun exploiting a system of slavery that already existed in Africa. While many African tribes and nations practiced a form of slavery by requiring prisoners taken in battle to serve their captors for a period of time before being eventually released (when their captors judged that prisoners' honor, lost in battle, had been restored by their service), Europeans traded guns and other goods to African leaders in exchange for their surplus slaves but did not understand (or chose to ignore) the custom of eventual release. By the mid-fifteenth century, the Portuguese were also capturing slaves while exploring the coasts of Africa. When the plantations (and mines) of the New World demanded more labor, the money-hungry empire builders knew where to go. So began a forced migration of people that would forever change the fate of millions of lives and the history of the New World.

Some African rulers cooperated with the slave trade, while others protested, but they were in a difficult position—as demand for the transatlantic slave trade increased, Europeans became increasingly ruthless in their methods, kidnapping Africans in their own raids or pitting groups against one another through control of the weapons trade. Kings and other leaders faced the choice of cooperating with the Europeans or seeing their people seized or slaughtered, so the slave trade expanded.

Africans were rounded up, forced onto ships, chained together, taken below deck, and forced to endure the brutal **Middle Passage** to the Americas. By historians' best estimates, at least 13 million Africans were taken from the continent and carried to the New World; approximately 60 percent went to South America, around 35 percent to the Caribbean, and about 5 percent to North America. Along the way, some suffocated from the hot, unventilated conditions below deck, others starved or died from outbreaks of disease, and yet others were killed attempting revolt or jumped overboard to their deaths, preferring suicide to the dishonor of slavery. Based on slave traders' existing records, historians believe average mortality rates were around 20 percent, though some voyages lost a much larger portion of their human cargo. Those who survived the journey were taken to the auction blocks, sold into slavery, and forced to work in plantation fields or in mines until their deaths, as were their children and their children's children.

Slavery and Gender

Since men were seen as more capable of the arduous agricultural labor demands required of slaves, they were disproportionately sold in the early years of the Atlantic slave trade. However, as men were given more specialized labor tasks (e.g., blacksmiths, carpenters), women were increasingly added to the plantations, eventually outnumbering men in agricultural settings.

Focus On: Demographic Shifts

The demographic changes of the sixteenth and seventeenth centuries were, in a word, huge. The Aztecs and Incas were wiped out. Huge cities were depopulated. Europeans moved by the hundreds of thousands. Africans were forced to migrate by the millions. Cities in Europe swelled as the feudal system evaporated and urban, middle class merchants lined their pockets with the fruits of trade and empire. By 1750, the continents of Europe, Africa, North America, and South America were unrecognizable from their 1450 portraits.

The Columbian Exchange: Continental Shift

One consequence of the Spanish and Portuguese empires in the New World was what became known as the Columbian Exchange—the transatlantic transfer of animals, plants, diseases, people, technology, and ideas among Europe, the Americas, and Africa. As Europeans and Africans crisscrossed the Atlantic, they brought the Old World to the New and back again. From the European and African side of the Atlantic, horses, pigs, goats, chili peppers, and sugarcane (and more) flowed to the Americas. From the American side, squash, beans, corn, potatoes, and cacao (and more) made their way back east. Settlers from the Old World carried bubonic plague, smallpox, typhoid, influenza, and the common cold into the New, then carried Chagas and syphilis back to the Old. Guns, Catholicism, and slaves also crossed the Atlantic. Never before had so much been moved across the oceans, as ship after ship carried the contents of one continent to another.

The American food crops (cassava, corn, peanuts, and potatoes) that traveled east made population increases possible throughout Europe, Asia, and Africa. Urban populations and commercial interests grew throughout Europe and led to increased cultivation and enclosure of land. With increased cultivation came increased use of previously rural areas. Despite some threat of famine, shortages due to a long cooling period or "little ice age," and out-migration, overall the trend throughout much of northern Europe was that of a growing population.

Two key products of the Columbian Exchange were **sugar** and **silver**. Sugarcane roots had arrived in the Caribbean from India with Columbus, who saw an opportunity to monopolize a profitable crop in a new environment. Sugarcane production resulted in the development of plantations throughout the Spanish colonies and an increased need for enslaved or forced labor once the native populations of the islands declined. The results of the plantation system were brutal, dangerous labor and a transformation of the natural landscape.

The Spanish also monopolized the world's silver market from the mines they controlled in Mexico and in the Andes Mountain of Peru. This industry also resulted in a harsh system of forced labor: the previously mentioned *encomienda*. Like the sugar plantations, early silver mining depended on native labor until that grew too scarce to make a profit, when labor shifted to African slaves provided by Portuguese traders.

More importantly, Spanish control of Latin American silver opened doors in Ming China. Spanish access to the Philippines, China, and the Pacific Ocean trade routes made the world a much smaller place.

The Commercial Revolution: The New Economy

The trading, empire building, and conquest of the **Age of Exploration** was made possible by new financing schemes that now form the basis of our modern economies. Though many elements had to come together at once for the new economy to work, timing was on the side of the Europeans, and everything fell into place.

First, the church gave in to state interests by revising its strict ban on what are now standard business practices, such as lending money and charging interest on loans. Once banking became respectable, a new business structure emerged: the **joint-stock company**, an organization created to pool the resources of many merchants, thereby distributing the costs and risks of colonization and reducing the danger for individual investors. Investors bought shares, or stock, in the company. If the company made money, each investor would receive a profit proportional to his or her initial investment. Because huge new ships were able to carry unprecedented cargoes, and because the goods were often outright stolen from their native countries, successful voyages reaped huge profits. A substantial middle class of merchants continued to develop, which in turn attracted more investors, and the modern-day concept of a stock market was well under way.

These corporations later secured royal charters for colonies, such as the Jamestown colony in Virginia, and funded them for business purposes. Even when they didn't establish colonies, monarchies granted monopolies to trade routes. The **Muscovy Company** of England monopolized trade routes to Russia, for example. The **Dutch East India Company** controlled routes to the Spice Islands (modern-day Indonesia).

Increased trade led to an early theory of macroeconomics for the nations of Europe. Under the theory of **mercantilism**, a country actively sought to trade, but tried not to import more than it exported; that is, it attempted to create a favorable balance of trade. Trade deficits forced dependencies on other countries, and therefore implied weakness. Of course, one country's surplus had to be met with another country's deficit. To resolve this dilemma, European countries were feverish to colonize. Colonies gave the mother country raw resources (not considered imports because the mother country "owned" them), while creating new markets for processed exports.

To further aid the effort, monarchies promoted domestic industry and placed tariffs on imports from competing empires. As you'll see in the next chapter, once the Industrial Revolution was under way, mercantilism really took off.

It shouldn't be surprising that mercantilism fostered resentment in colonies. The colonial resources were shipped back to Europe while the colonists were forced to pay for products from Europe. Add taxes, and you've got major resentment. You already know that the American Revolution was in part due to colonial fury over this arrangement. One by one, beginning with America, European colonies revolted against the abuses by the unforgiving mercantilist economies of the European powers.

Oh Yeah…Remember Asia?

Recall that the original Portuguese explorers were trying to figure out a shortcut to India and China. Once they stumbled upon a couple of continents along the way and began wiping out native civilizations, building empires, and forcibly transporting millions of Africans to do hard labor, they forgot the original purpose of their exploration. In time, European explorers, armed with bottomless resources of energy and greed, remembered and pursued the East.

Asian colonization didn't really get rolling until the nineteenth century, so that will be covered in the next chapter. From the sixteenth through the eighteenth centuries, however, the Europeans managed to establish trade with the Asian empires, although it was more limited than they would have liked due to Asian protectionist policies and the difficulty of travel.

After making their way around the Cape of Good Hope, the Portuguese set up a trading post in Goa on the west coast of India. They also gained control over the Spice Islands by establishing naval superiority in the Straits of Malacca. In less than a century, however, other European powers coveted Asian riches. The Dutch, under the backing of the newly formed Dutch East India Company, conducted deliberate raids on Portuguese ships and trading posts. In the seventeenth century, the Dutch became the biggest power in the spice trades. Meanwhile, England and France set up trading posts in India.

As for China and Japan, both empires severely limited trade with the Europeans. Throughout this time period, the two Asian empires couldn't have been more unlike their European counterparts. They were highly isolationist. Not only did they not go out and try to find the rest of the world, they also pushed the rest of the world away when it came to find them. You'll read more about China and Japan in the next section.

IV. DEVELOPMENTS IN SPECIFIC COUNTRIES AND EMPIRES, 1450–1750

It's dangerous to presume that because the Renaissance, the Protestant Reformation, the Scientific Revolution, the Enlightenment, and the Age of Exploration eventually had enormous consequences that they did so quickly, broadly, or in equal proportions. In reality, the major movements impacted different parts of Europe at different times and took a long time to penetrate all circles of society. Most people with power guarded it jealously, regardless of the intellectual or religious movements that brought their power into question. What's more, most of the peasant class didn't participate in the intellectual, scientific, or commercial developments because they weren't educated or in a position to be immediately impacted by the consequences.

Outside of Europe, the major developments of the time period also had widely varying consequences. In the previous section, we discussed the consequences on the Americas and on much of Africa. Lest you think the rest of the world remained passive in the face of European growth, it is important to note that powerful and centralized states were established (or reestablished) in the Middle East, India, China and Japan. The empires of Asia, too, had unique experiences, which are discussed in detail later in the chapter. As you review the developments in the European empires, keep in mind that most nations were led by monarchs, or sovereigns, who felt that the right to govern was ordained by God. Under this idea of divine right, it was essential for royal families to retain pure bloodlines to God, so intermarriage among royal families of different nations was common. Thus, the monarchies of one country also gained international influence as the ties of marriage and inheritance led to alliances.

Monarchies also contributed to the development of strong national loyalties, which led to many conflicts, internally and externally. The European wars of this time fall into three categories: religious fights between Protestants and Catholics, internal civil wars between a monarch and disgruntled nobles, and battles stemming from the trade disputes between rival nations. In the beginning of this era, Spain became the world's strongest nation with a powerful naval fleet and an extensive empire. As the balance of power in Europe shifted, the rival nations of England and France emerged as great powers.

A. The European Rivals

1. Spain and Portugal

As you read in the previous chapter, in 1469, **King Ferdinand**, from the Christian Kingdoms in northern Spain, and **Queen Isabella**, from the more Muslim regions of southern Spain, initiated the consolidation of Spanish authority under one house, and thereby created a nation-state that would become one of the world's most powerful forces over the next century. By aggressively supporting exploration (initially by underwriting Columbus's exploration and then later by establishing empires in the New World), Ferdinand and Isabella had a long-term impact on cultural world developments—they ensured the survival and expansion of the Spanish language and culture, including Catholicism, by extending them across the Atlantic. Ferdinand and Isabella also built a formidable naval fleet, allowing Spain to rule the seas for the next century.

Portugal: The Middleman of an Empire

As Spain focused on western exploration and its empire in the New World, the Portuguese continued their domination of coastal Africa, the Indian Ocean, and the Spice Islands. A small country with limited manpower, Portugal had to be content as the middleman of a "floating empire." It was an early player in the transatlantic slave trade, and it controlled sea routes and garrisoned trading posts; still, it was unable to exert control over large sections of the interior of Africa and India. Inevitably, Portugal could not maintain control of its far-flung colonies and lost control of them to the Dutch and British who had faster ships with heavier guns.

The international importance of Spain grew under **Charles V**, who inherited a large empire. Charles was from the Hapsburg family, which originated in Austria and, through a series of carefully arranged marriages (recall that divine right promoted intermarriage among royalty), created a huge empire stretching from Austria and Germany to Spain. While one set of Charles's grandparents were Hapsburgs, his other grandparents were Ferdinand and Isabella, who themselves had married to solidify the Spanish empire. Talk about family connections.

In 1519, Charles was elected Holy Roman Emperor by German princes, which meant that he then held lands in parts of France, the Netherlands, Austria, and Germany in addition to Spain. These possessions, plus the new colonies in the Americas, brought wars as well as riches. Spain fought France for control of Italy and the Ottoman Turks for control of Eastern Europe, which led to an expansion of Ottoman rule into much of Hungary (more on that later). In Germany, Charles defended Catholicism from the encroachment of Protestantism (recall that Spain was allied with the Catholic Church during the Counter-Reformation). Frustrated over trying to manage such an enormous empire at a time of expansion in the New World and revolution in Europe (the Protestant Reformation and Scientific Revolution, for example), he decided in 1556 to retire to a monastery and thereby abdicate the throne. He gave control over Austria and the Holy Roman throne of Germany to his brother, **Ferdinand I**. To his son, **Philip II**, he conferred the throne of Spain and jurisdiction over Burgundy (in France), Sicily, and the Netherlands as well as Spain's claim in the New World. Phillip II also gained control over Portugal.

For More on Ferdinand...
We'll talk more about Ferdinand's half of the empire later in this chapter.

Under Philip II, the Spanish Empire in the west saw some of its greatest expansion in the New World and a rebirth of culture under the Spanish Renaissance, but it also started showing signs of decay. A devoutly religious man, Philip oversaw the continuation of the **Spanish Inquisition** to oust heretics, led the Catholic Reformation against Protestants, and supported an increase in missionary work in the ever-expanding empire in the New World. Increasingly eager to develop their own empire, Dutch Protestants (of the Netherlands) revolted. By 1581, the mostly Protestant northern provinces of the Netherlands gained their independence from Spain and became known as the Dutch Netherlands. The mostly Catholic southern provinces remained loyal to Spain (this region would later become Belgium).

Exhibiting further signs of weakness, Spanish forces fighting for Catholicism in France fared poorly, and to the shock of many Spaniards, the English defeated and devastated the once mighty Spanish Armada as it tried to attack the British Isles. The defeat invigorated the English, who by the late sixteenth century were expanding their own empire, and signaled containment of Spanish forces.

Although Spain amassed enormous sums of gold from the New World, it spent its wealth quickly on wars, missionary activities, and maintenance of its huge fleets. By the mid-seventeenth century, Spain still had substantial holdings, but its glory days had passed. England and France were well poised to replace it as the dominant European powers.

2. England

As you read earlier in the discussion of the Protestant Reformation, **King Henry VIII**, who ruled from 1509 to 1547, nullified the pope's authority in England, thereby establishing (under the 1534 **Act of Supremacy**) the Church of England and placed himself as head of that church. Henry took this action so that he could divorce his wife and marry Anne Boleyn in an effort to father a male heir. He didn't succeed in getting a male heir. Instead, he got another daughter, **Elizabeth I**, who oversaw a golden age in the arts known as the Elizabethan Age.

The **Elizabethan Age** (1558–1603) boasted commercial expansion and exploration and colonization in the New World, especially after the English fleet destroyed the Spanish Armada in 1588. During this time, the **Muscovy Company** was founded as the first joint-stock company, and the **British East India Company** quickly followed suit. Drake circumnavigated the globe. The first English colonists settled in the Roanoke colony in present-day Virginia. To top it all off, Shakespeare wrote his masterpieces. Simply put, England experienced a golden age under Elizabeth.

The religious battles that were unleashed by the Protestant Reformation still unsettled the region. Anglicans (Church of England) were battling Catholics, while other Protestant groups such as the Puritans were regularly persecuted. When **James I** came to power in 1607 after the death of Elizabeth, whose reign brought together the crowns of England and Scotland, he attempted to institute reforms to accommodate the Catholics and the Puritans, but widespread problems persisted. The Puritans (who were Calvinists) didn't want to recognize the power of the king over religious matters, and James reacted defensively, claiming divine right. It was at this point that many Puritans decided to cross the Atlantic. The Pilgrims' establishment of the Plymouth colony (1620) occurred during James's reign. Jamestown colony, as you might have guessed, was also founded during the reign of James I. The English aren't known for their innovative naming.

Charles I, son of James, rose to power in 1625. Three years later, desperate for money from Parliament, he agreed to sign the **Petition of Right**, which was a document limiting taxes and forbidding unlawful imprisonment. Charles ignored the petition after he secured the funds he needed and, claiming divine right, ruled without calling another meeting of Parliament for eleven years.

In 1640, when Scotland's resentment toward Charles resulted in a Scottish invasion of England, Charles was forced to call Parliament into session. Led by Puritans, this Parliament was known as the **Long Parliament** because it sat for twenty years from 1640 through 1660. The Long Parliament limited the absolute powers of the monarchy. In 1641, the parliament denied Charles's request for money to fight the Irish rebellion, and in response he led troops into the House of Commons to arrest some of the members. This sparked a civil war. Parliament raised an army, called the Roundheads, to fight the king. The Roundheads, under the leadership of **Oliver Cromwell**, defeated the armies of Charles I, who were called Cavaliers. The king was tried and executed. Oliver Cromwell rose to power, not as a monarch, but first as leader of what was called the **English Commonwealth**, then after reorganizing the government, as **Lord Protector**.

When Cromwell ruled as Protector, he ruled with religious intolerance and violence against Catholics and the Irish. He encouraged Protestants to settle in Northern Ireland (this would cause many problems in future centuries). All of this caused much resentment, and after Cromwell died, Parliament invited Charles II, the exiled son of the now-beheaded Charles I, to take the throne and restore a limited monarchy. This is called the **Stuart Restoration** (1660–1688). A closet Catholic, Charles II acknowledged the rights of the people, especially with regard to religion. In 1679, he agreed to the **Habeas Corpus Act** (which protects people from arrests without due process). Following Charles II's death, his brother James II took over.

James II was openly Catholic, and he was unpopular. Like so many before him, he believed in the divine right of kings. In a bloodless change of leadership known as the **Glorious Revolution**, he was driven from power by Parliament, which feared he'd make England a Catholic country, and he fled to France. He was replaced in 1688 by his son-in-law and daughter, William and Mary, the Protestant rulers of the Netherlands, who promptly signed the **English Bill of Rights** in 1689. The Glorious Revolution ensured that England's future monarchs would be Anglican and that their powers would be limited.

Focus On: The Enlightenment Writers

Keep in mind that the Enlightenment writers were busy at work by this time. Hobbes published *Leviathan* in 1651 in response to the English Civil War, a time during which the monarch, Charles I, was beheaded. Hobbes's violent view of human nature and desire for an all-powerful ruler to maintain peace are completely understandable within the context of the English Civil War. While Hobbes missed the peaceful resolution of the war in the Glorious Revolution and the English Bill of Rights (1688–1689), John Locke did not. Locke's more optimistic view of human nature can be viewed in the context of the bloodless transition of power between James II and William and Mary. In addition, Locke's writings in *Two Treatises on Government* justified this change of leadership by suggesting that James II had violated the social contract. Political events in England during this time, and such events in general, cannot be separated from the development of social and political philosophy and vice versa.

3. France

After the Hundred Years' War (1337–1453) drove the English from France, the French began to unify and centralize authority in a strong monarchy. As elsewhere, however, religious differences stood in the way. France was largely Catholic, but during the Protestant Reformation, a group of French Protestants, known as **Huguenots**, developed into a sizeable and influential minority. Throughout the mid- to late-sixteenth century, Catholics and Huguenots bitterly fought each other, sometimes brutally, until, in 1598, **Henry IV** issued the **Edict of Nantes**, which created an environment of toleration. Henry IV was the first of the Bourbon kings, who ruled France for nearly two centuries until 1792.

Cardinal Richelieu, a Catholic, played an important role as the chief advisor to the Bourbons. His primary political role was to strengthen the French crown. While clashes erupted among Catholics and Huguenots (Protestants) in France, Richelieu did not seek to destroy the Protestants; he compromised with them and even helped them to attack the Catholic Hapsburgs of the Holy Roman Empire, an empire that he wanted to end in order to make France a stronger power in Europe. A new bureaucratic class, the *noblesse de la robe*, was established under Richelieu. The bureaucracy established by Richelieu and his successor, **Cardinal Mazarin**, prepared France to hold the strong position it would achieve in Europe under Louis XIV.

Louis XIV was four years old when he inherited the crown of France. His mother and Cardinal Mazarin ruled in his name until he reached adulthood, at which time he became one of the most legendary monarchs of European history. Louis XIV's long reign (1643–1715) exemplified the grandiose whims of an absolute monarchy. Calling himself the "Sun King" and "The Most Christian King," he patronized the arts as long as they contributed to the glorification of France and its culture, which became much admired and emulated. Ruling under divine right, he reportedly declared, "I am the State," and he built the lavish palace of Versailles to prove it. He never summoned the Estates-General, the lawmaking body, to meet. He revoked the Edict of Nantes, forcing many Huguenots to leave France. Perhaps most importantly, he appointed **Jean Baptiste Colbert** to manage the royal funds.

A strict mercantilist, Colbert wanted to increase the size of the French empire, thereby increasing the opportunity for business transactions and taxes. To accomplish this, France was almost constantly at war. For a while, warfare and mercantilist policies allowed France to increase its overseas holdings and gain the revenue needed for the

Contrast Them: England and France in the 17th Century

Unlike England, France was ruled by a series of strong and able monarchs under the Bourbon Dynasty. After the death of Elizabeth, England went from monarchy to Commonwealth to Restoration to Glorious Revolution. Hardly stable. On the other hand, France's Estates-General (a governing body representing clergy, nobles, merchants, and peasants) was not nearly as powerful as the English Parliament. It didn't even meet for the bulk of the seventeenth century because the French kings ruled successfully under the justification of divine right.

extravagances of a king named for the sun. However, the **War of Spanish Succession** (1701–1714) proved to be a disaster for the grand plans of France.

Recall that European royalty was intermarrying and reproducing. It turned out that the twisted branches of the royal family trees led to a situation in which, in 1701, one of Louis XIV's grandsons inherited the Spanish throne. This alarmed the rest of Europe, which feared that Spain, although substantially weaker than it had been in the previous century, and France, already quite powerful, would form an unstoppable combo-power, especially given their American holdings at the time (France owned a huge chunk of North America, Spain the bulk of Central and South America). It's a complicated story, but England, the Holy Roman Empire, and German princes all united under the perceived common threat, and thirteen years later, the question of Spanish succession was settled. **Philip V**, the grandson, was able to rule Spain, but Spain couldn't combine with France, and France had to give up much of its territory to England, a country that then became even more powerful.

The bottom line is that Colbert and Louis XIV's many territorial invasions and wars proved costly and ineffective. France remained powerful, but by the eighteenth century, its position as a military power was weakening. Nevertheless, by 1750, its position as a center for arts was firmly established.

4. German Areas (The Holy Roman Empire, Sort of)

The situation in German and Slavic areas of central Europe during this time period was complicated. The Holy Roman Empire wasn't really in Rome but rather in present-day Austria and parts of Germany and surrounding regions because Italy was controlled by ruling families in the Italian city-states. The Holy Roman Empire geographically dominated the region, but was also still very feudal with lots of local lords running their own shows. Therefore, the Holy Roman Emperor was pretty weak. This is further complicated by the rise of the powerful Hapsburg family of Austria, which, as we already stated, kept intermarrying so that it dominated not only substantial territory within the Holy Roman Empire but also Spain and parts of Italy. It was complicated further by the fact that northern Germany was essentially a collection of city-states, such as Brandenburg, Saxony, and Prussia. Finally, remember that northern Germany went Lutheran during the Protestant Reformation, while southern areas of the Holy Roman Empire stayed Catholic, along with Spain and France. Got it? It's nutty, so we're only going to hit the highlights, or else your head will be spinning.

Contrast Them: "Germany" with Spain, England, and France

Germany unified under a central government much later than Spain, England, and France did. You'll read about German unification in the next chapter. You won't read about a huge German empire in the New World or a strong German monarchy, because for centuries Germany remained caught in a complicated web of rulers of the Holy Roman Empire, the Hapsburgs of Austria, and the princes of city-states. It was also a tangle of religious movements, because it was at the heart of the Protestant Reformation.

You need to grasp the following three things from this time period:

- The Holy Roman Empire lost parts of Hungary to the Ottoman Turks in the early sixteenth century (this is discussed in the section on the Ottoman Empire).

- The Thirty Years' War (1618–1648) devastated the region and significantly weakened the role of the Holy Roman emperors, leading to the rise of hundreds of nation-states in the region in the nineteenth century.

- By the eighteenth century, the northern German city-states, especially Prussia, were gaining momentum and power.

Now for a few of the details.

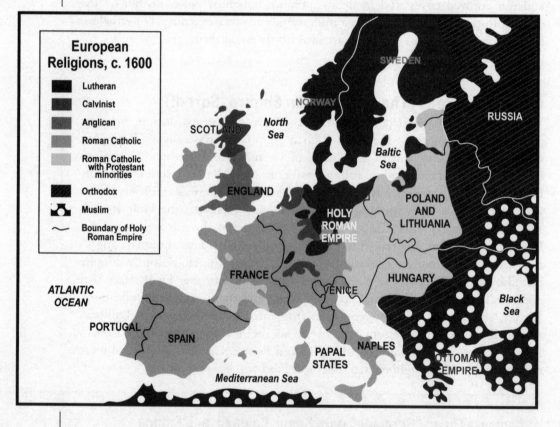

Religious Divisions Around 1600

In 1555, the **Peace of Augsburg** was intended to bring an end to the constant conflicts between Catholics and Protestants that engulfed the region during the Reformation and Counter-Reformation. The peace didn't last. The **Thirty Years' War** began in 1618 when the Protestant territories in Bohemia (which was under the rule of the Catholic Hapsburg clan) challenged the authority of the Holy Roman Catholic emperor, a situation that frequently arose prior to the Peace of Augsburg. This time, though, the conflict grew bigger than anything before it and developed into a huge religious and political war. Everyone seemed to want a piece of the action, including other countries such as France (under Richelieu), Denmark, and Sweden. Although this grew into a war between major European powers, the actual fighting stayed within the German empire, meaning that after thirty years of fighting, many parts of Germany were left depopulated and devastated. Some estimates suggest that the Holy Roman Empire lost one-third of its population during these thirty years, some 7 million people.

When the **Peace of Westphalia** was negotiated in 1648, the independence of small German states was affirmed, and Prussia became the strongest of them. The Holy Roman Empire was left barely limping along. Its territories had been reduced and its emperor, along with the Hapsburg family, was much less powerful. Somehow the Holy Roman Empire survived in name until 1806, but it hardly had any power after Westphalia.

The biggest beneficiary of the war was France. It became the most powerful country in Europe during the seventeenth century under Louis XIV, although, as you already read, it was weakened by the eighteenth century after the country overspent and overplayed its hand, particularly during the War of Spanish Succession. The other war beneficiary was Prussia, the German city-state centered in Berlin, which also controlled parts of Poland. Prussia eventually rose to dominate the German territories, unifying them into the powerful country of Germany, but you'll read about that in the next chapter.

B. Russia Out of Isolation

When the Turks conquered Constantinople and the Byzantine Empire fell, the center of Orthodox Christianity moved northward to Moscow, which was called the "Third Rome" (after Rome itself and then Constantinople). At around the same time, Russian leaders were overthrowing the Mongols. In 1480, **Ivan III** of Moscow refused to pay tribute to the Mongols and declared Russia free of Mongol rule. He, and later his grandson **Ivan IV**, established absolute rule in Russia, uniting it and expanding it ever eastward. They recruited peasants and offered them freedom from their feudal lords if they agreed to settle in new lands to the east. The catch was that these peasants had to conquer the land themselves! Known as **Cossacks**, these peasant-soldiers expanded Russian territories in the sixteenth through the eighteenth centuries well into Siberia and southward to the Caspian Sea.

Ivan IV was such a strong leader and held such absolute power that he became known as **Ivan the Terrible** (not necessarily meaning bad, but instead formidable or impressive). Taking on the title of czar (Russian for "Caesar"), Ivan the Terrible expanded Russia's holding, but not without cost to the Russian people. By the 1560s, he ruled under a reign of terror, regularly executing anyone whom he perceived as a threat to his power, including his own son (executed in 1580).

Contrast Them: Russia and Western Europe

Despite the centralization of authority under the Ivans, Russia remained very much a feudal arrangement, with local lords exercising considerable power. While Western Europe basked in the glow of the Renaissance, explored and expanded its influence across oceans, and debated about religion, science, and government in a series of movements, Russia remained isolated from the west and pushed eastward instead. Its growth was territorial, but not intellectual or artistic. During the fifteenth, sixteenth, and most of the seventeenth centuries, it had nothing that could be labeled a Renaissance or Enlightenment. It wasn't part of the Renaissance because it was under the control of the Mongols at the time. It wasn't part of the Reformation because it wasn't part of the Catholic Church in the first place. So even though today we often see Russia as a European power, its history progressed along a very different path. It wasn't until the late seventeenth century that Russia turned its eyes westward.

After the death of Ivan IV in 1584, and with no strong heir to take the throne, Russia's feudal lords continually battled over who should rule the empire. The situation grew especially messy from 1604 to 1613, a period that historians refer to as the **Time of Troubles**, because one pretender to the throne would be killed by another pretender and yet another. In 1613, the madness subsided when **Michael Romanov** was elected czar by the feudal lords. The Romanov Dynasty added stability to the empire. It ruled until 1917.

Like the Ivans, the Romanovs consolidated power and often ruled ruthlessly. The peasants, now serfs, were practically slaves. By the late 1600s, the Romanovs had expanded the empire, with the help of the Cossacks, eastward through Siberia. By 1689, Russian territory spread from the Ukraine (west of Moscow) to the Pacific Ocean, north of Manchuria.

Compare Them: Forced Labor Systems

Although slavery was not a new system, the demands of the newly global economy resulted in an expansion of systems of forced labor in the empires. At the same time, Russia's attempts to control their large land mass relied on the forced labor of the peasants or serfs. All three systems took advantage of the laborers and were frequently managed by harsh and brutal overseers. In the Spanish part of the New World, *haciendas* were established in which natives owed labor to their landlords—not unlike the feudalism of Europe. This system fell apart as the native populations diminished due to disease, and as natives converted to the Catholic faith. The Portuguese took advantage of the already thriving intra-African slave trade and transformed it into a trans-oceanic one. The majority of transported Africans wound up on plantations in Brazil and the Caribbean where life expectancy was just three to five years. Russian serfdom differed in that the Russian economy was domestic and both the laborers and the landowners were Russian.

At around this same time, **Peter the Great**, who ruled from 1682 through 1725, came to power. He was convinced he needed to Westernize Russia. He built Russia's first navy and founded St. Petersburg on the Baltic Sea as his new capital. The "window to the west," St. Petersburg became the home to hundreds of Western European engineers, scientists, architects, and artists who were recruited specifically to Westernize Russia. Women of the nobility were forced to dress in Western fashions. Men were forced to shave their beards. Most of the hard labor of building the great new city was accomplished, of course, by serfs turned slaves.

Under **Catherine the Great**, who ruled from 1762 until 1796, more enlightened policies of education and Western culture were implemented. Still, Russia suffered because Catherine fiercely enforced repressive serfdom and limited the growth of the merchant class. Catherine continued the aggressive westward territorial expansion, gaining ground in Poland and, most significantly, territory on the Black Sea. This advance ensured Russia's access to the Mediterranean to its south and west.

C. Islamic Gunpowder Empires: Ottoman, Safavid, and Mughal

The history of the **Ottoman Empire** actually precedes 1450. You might recall from the previous chapter that the territories of the former Islamic Empire were overrun by the ubiquitous Mongols in the thirteenth century. Recall also that the Byzantine Empire, centered in Constantinople, controlled most of Turkey and influenced southeastern Europe and Russia. As the Mongol Empire fell, the Muslim Ottoman Empire, founded by **Osman Bey**, rose in Anatolia (eastern parts of Turkey) to unify the region and challenge the Byzantine Empire. As it grew in the fourteenth century, the Turks (as the Ottomans were called) came to dominate most of modern-day Turkey and eventually, in 1453, invaded Constantinople, thereby ending the Byzantine Empire. Perhaps 1450 isn't such an artificial boundary after all.

> **Focus On: Westernization of Russia**
> Both Peter and Catherine are important because they positioned Russia for engagement with the rest of the world, particularly the Western world. By the late eighteenth century, Russia was in a significantly different position than it had been at the beginning of that century. It gained physical access to the West by both the Baltic and the Black Seas, and it gained cultural access to the West by actively seeking interaction. Unlike China and Japan, which repelled the West from their shores in the same time period, the Russians wanted to engage with and emulate the West.

The Ottomans made Constantinople their capital city, renamed it Istanbul, and converted the great cathedrals such as the Hagia Sophia into mosques. In the expanding empire, Christians and Jews were allowed to practice their religions, making the empire more tolerant than both the previous Islamic Empire and the other major regimes of the era. Within a hundred years, the Ottomans conquered the expanse of the old Byzantine Empire, except for Italy westward. In other words, the Ottoman Empire extended from Greece eastward to Persia, and then all the way around the Mediterranean into Egypt and northern Africa.

As the empire grew, so too did religious persecution. To conquer large territories, the Ottomans enslaved children of their Christian subjects and turned them into fighting warriors, known as Janissaries. Much of this expansion occurred during the reign of **Selim I**, who came to power in 1512. Significantly, Selim claimed that he was the rightful heir to Islamic tradition under the Arab caliphs. With that claim, and with such a huge empire, Istanbul became the center of Islamic civilization.

Just eight years later, **Suleiman I** (a.k.a. Suleiman the Magnificent) rose to power. He not only built up the Ottoman military, but also actively encouraged the development of the arts. For this reason, the Ottoman Empire experienced a golden age under his reign, which lasted from 1520 until 1566. During this time, the Ottomans tried to push into Europe through Hungary. You already read that the Holy Roman Empire was weakening during the Protestant Reformation. The Ottomans took advantage of this weakness; after taking parts of Hungary, the Turks tried to move into Austria. In 1529, the empire laid siege to Vienna, a significant European cultural center. Had the Turks successfully taken Vienna, who knows what the history of Western Europe would have been. From Vienna, the Turks could have easily poured into the unstable lands of the Holy Roman Empire, but it wasn't meant to be. Vienna was as far as the Turks ever got. Although Austrian princes and the Ottomans battled continually for the next century, the Ottomans were never able to expand much beyond the European territories of Byzantine influence.

The Safavids

It is worth mentioning the chief rivals of the Ottoman were their eastern neighbors, the Safavids. This centralized state was based on military conquest and dominated by Shia Islam. Its location between the Ottomans and the Mughals, in what is modern-day Iran, resulted in often contentious relationships between the Muslim states, alliances with European nations against the Ottomans, and a continuation of the long-standing rift between the Sunni and Shia sects.

Still, the Ottoman Empire lasted until 1922, making it one of the world's most significant empires. In that time, it greatly expanded the reach of Islam, while also keeping Eastern Europe in a constant state of flux. This allowed the powers of Western Europe to dominate, and once they started exploring the oceans, they were able to circumvent their eastern neighbors and trade directly with India, China, and their American colonies.

Remember the Mongols? After several false starts, in 1526, **Babur**, a leader who claimed to be descended from Genghis Khan but was very much Muslim, invaded northern India and swiftly defeated the Delhi Sultanate (also Muslim). Babur quickly established a new empire, known as the **Mughal Empire**, which dominated the Indian subcontinent for the next 300 years.

The Mughal Empire was distinctive for several reasons. First, within about 150 years, it had united almost the entire subcontinent, something that hadn't previously been done to the same extent. Recall that northern India experienced a series of invasions and empires, many of which you reviewed in previous chapters. The same was not true of southern India. The Deccan Plateau in southern India had remained mostly isolated. It was there that Hinduism became very firmly established.

Babur's grandson, **Akbar**, who ruled from 1556 to 1605, was able to unify much of India by governing under a policy of religious toleration. He allowed Hinduism and Islam to be practiced openly. He eliminated the jizya, the head tax on Hindus that had been a source of great anger to the people, and tried to improve the position of women by attempting to eliminate sati, the practice in which high-caste Hindu women would throw themselves onto their husbands' funeral pyres. He even married a Hindu woman and welcomed Hindus into government positions.

For nearly 100 years, Hindus and Muslims increasingly lived side-by-side and, consequently, became more geographically mixed. The result was a golden age of art, architecture, and thought. Under **Shah Jahan**, Akbar's grandson, the **Taj Mahal** was built. However, after Akbar, two developments forever changed India.

The first was that religious toleration ended. When a new emperor, Aurangzeb, who was a very pious Muslim, came to the throne, he enacted pro-Muslim policies and waged wars of expansion to try to conquer the remaining portions of India still not under Mughal control. The Muslim government reinstated the jizya; Hindu temples were destroyed. The consequences of this development were significant for later centuries, but for the moment, understand that by 1700, Muslims began to persecute Hindus who were beginning to organize against their Muslim rulers and neighbors.

The second development was the arrival of the Europeans. In the early seventeenth century, the Portuguese and British were fighting each other for Indian Ocean trade routes. In the beginning, Portugal had established trade with the city of Goa, where it also sent Christian missionaries. By 1661, the British East India Company had substantial control of trade in Bombay. By 1691, the British dominated trade in the region and founded the city of Calcutta as a trading outpost. While the Mughal emperors were annoyed with the Europeans, they generally permitted the trade and regarded the Europeans as relatively harmless. Of course, the Industrial Revolution would turn Britain into an imperial superpower. But before 1750—the calm before the storm—India didn't feel particularly vulnerable to the Europeans, except in its port cities. It was a huge country with tons of resources united under strong Muslim rulers. It couldn't be conquered, right? At the time, Indians probably couldn't imagine that a century later, a British woman named Victoria would be crowned Empress of India.

D. Africa

Beginning in the tenth century, strong centralized states developed in southern and western Africa based on the wealth accumulated from trade. The trend of increased power continued with the trans-Atlantic slave trade and the establishment of powerful kingdoms by the **Songhai**, and in the kingdoms of **Kongo and Angola**, among others. While you are not expected to know each of these kingdoms in detail, you should recognize the pattern of state-building and the relationship of Africa to both the Islamic world and the Europeans.

The sub-Saharan empire of Songhai was mentioned briefly in the previous chapter. Like its predecessors, Ghana and Mali, this was an Islamic state with economic ties to the broader Muslim world through the trans-Saharan trade of salt and gold. Like other empires, this was built on conquests and military force. Sunni Ali (ruled 1464–1493) consolidated his empire in the valley of the Niger River using an imperial navy, established a central administration, and financed the city of Timbuktu as a major Islamic center. Like all great empires, Songhai fell to a superior military force: Moroccans with muskets.

Adjacent to the Songhai Kingdom, the **Asanti** (Ashanti) Empire arose in 1670. Deriving its wealth from the gold trade, the Asanti were more prepared to face invasions due to its highly organized military. Accordingly, the Asanti greatly expanded its territory.

On the west coast of Africa, the centralized kingdom of **Kongo** was bolstered by its trade with Portuguese merchants as early as the 1480s. The Europeans established close economic and political relationships with the king, a situation that initially worked to everyone's advantage. The kings of the Kongo converted to Catholicism, and **King Alfonso I** was particularly successful at converting his people. Over the long term, Portuguese tactics and the desire for slaves from the interior undermined the authority of the kings of Kongo and the state gradually declined. Eventually, there were outright hostilities and war between the two former allies and the kingdom was mostly destroyed.

South of Kongo, the Portuguese established a small trading post in Ndongo, or **Angola**, as early as 1575 for the sole purpose of expanding their trade in slaves from the interior. As a result, Angola grew into a powerful state and when the Portuguese attempted to further exert their authority and control, **Queen Nzinga** fiercely resisted. For 40 years, the warrior queen led her troops in battle, studied European military tactics, and made alliances with Portugal's Dutch rivals. Despite her efforts, in the end, she could not unify her rivals nor overcome the superior weaponry of the Portuguese.

E. Isolated Asia

1. China

By 1368, the Ming Dynasty booted out the last of the Mongol rulers in China and restored power over the empire to the native Chinese. The Ming Dynasty ruled until 1644. During this time, the Ming built a strong centralized government based on traditional Confucian principles, reinstated the civil service examination, and removed the Mongol influence by reinvigorating Chinese culture.

In the early fifteenth century, the Chinese also did something quite extraordinary: They built huge fleets. **Zheng He**, a Chinese navigator, led fleets throughout southeast Asia and the Indian Ocean all the way to East Africa a century before the Europeans did the same. Had the Chinese continued to explore and trade, they may have become the dominant colonial power. Instead, within a few decades, the Chinese abruptly stopped their naval voyages. Increasingly, Chinese society turned inward.

The Ming government attempted to prop up its failing economy by changing easily counterfeited paper money to a "single-whip" system based on silver currency. Initially, Japan supplied the silver (much to the benefit of the shoguns in Japan), but with the discovery of American silver sources, China established trade relations with the Spanish through the Philippines. Although this exchange fueled a period of commercial expansion, inevitably the silver flooded the Chinese market, and the government was unable to control the resulting inflation.

By the sixteenth century, the Ming Dynasty was already in its decline, just as the Europeans were beginning to sail toward China. Pirates increasingly raided port cities, and the Portuguese set up shop in Macao. Still, the Chinese were able to keep the Europeans at a safe distance. However, internal problems persisted. By the seventeenth century, famines crippled the Chinese economy, and peasant revolts erupted against the increasingly powerless Ming rulers. In 1644, the Ming emperor invited a group of **Qing** warriors from nearby Manchuria to help him quell a peasant uprising, but instead, the Qing ousted the emperor. With that act, the Ming Dynasty ended and the Qing (or Manchu) Dynasty began. The **Manchus** ruled China until 1911.

Focus On: Environmental Change and Collapse

The new food crops that arrived in Europe, Africa, and Asia from the Americas (cassava, corn, peanuts, and potatoes) were high in calories, easy to grow in previously uncultivated areas, and, as a result, allowed for massive population increases. These crops, along with new agricultural technologies and political stability, were initially a boon to China's economy and productivity. However, the new population levels could not be sustained over the long term, and a period of global cooling in the late seventeenth century put pressure on agricultural lands and hastened the collapse of the Ming Dynasty. In Europe, the arrival of potatoes finally stabilized a food supply and a population that had been devastated by centuries of cold weather, poor farming, and epidemic disease.

Because the Qing were from Manchuria, they were not ethnically Chinese. They attempted to remain an ethnic elite, forbidding the Chinese to learn the Manchu language or to marry Manchus. However, because the Manchus comprised a mere three percent of the population, they needed the help of ethnic Chinese to run the country. Therefore, the civil service examination gained new status. Even members of the lower classes were able to rise to positions of responsibility as the Manchus opened up the floodgates to find the best talent.

Manchu emperors were well steeped in Chinese traditions. Both **Kangxi**, who ruled from 1661 to 1722, and his chief successor, **Qianlong**, who ruled from 1735 to 1796, were Confucian scholars. Both emperors not only supported the arts, but also expanded the empire. Kangxi conquered Taiwan and extended the empire into Mongolia, central Asia, and Tibet. Qianlong added Vietnam, Burma, and Nepal to the vassal states of China.

In all of this expansion, the Chinese did not aspire to conquer the rest of the world, or even interact with it very much. They stayed focused on China and its surrounding neighbors. The Manchus did trade with the Europeans and granted rights to the Portuguese, Dutch, and British, but they were vigilant about and successful at controlling trade relations through the mid-eighteenth century. The Manchu were fierce protectors of their culture. When they felt threatened by European advances, they expelled the Europeans. In 1724, for example, Christianity was banned. In 1757, trade was restricted to just one city, Canton. Still, trade with Europeans was substantial. The Europeans bought large quantities of tea, silk, and porcelain. In exchange, the merchants received huge sums of silver, which created a new rising class of merchants in Chinese coastal cities.

2. Japan

In the sixteenth century, a series of shoguns continued to rule Japan while the emperor remained merely as a figurehead. As the century went on, Japanese feudalism began to wane and centralized power began to emerge. The shogun still ruled (as opposed to the emperor), but the power of the feudal lords was reduced. This centralization of power coincided with Japanese exposure to the West. In 1542, the Portuguese established trade with the empire (they also introduced guns to the Japanese). Within a decade, Christian missionaries streamed in. By the end of the century, not only had a few hundred thousand Japanese converted to Christianity, but the Jesuits took control of the port city of Nagasaki and trade flourished. Japan was well on its way to westernization.

In 1600, the trend changed dramatically. That year, **Tokugawa Ieyasu** established the Tokugawa Shogunate, a strict and rigid government that ruled Japan until 1868. The shogun further consolidated power away from the emperor and at the expense of the daimyo (feudal lords). Ieyasu claimed personal ownership to all lands within Japan and instituted a rigid social class model, inspired somewhat by Confucianism but in practice was more like the caste system. Four classes (warrior, farmer, artisan, and merchant) were established and movement among the classes was forbidden.

The Tokugawa period—also known as the **Edo period** because Tokugawa moved the capital to Edo (modern-day Tokyo)—was marked by a reversal in attitudes toward Western influences. Within two decades, Christians were persecuted. By 1635, a **National Seclusion Policy** prohibited Japanese from traveling abroad, and prohibited most foreigners from visiting Japan (limited relations were kept with China, Korea, and the Netherlands). In other words, Japan became increasingly secluded. The policy remained in place for nearly 200 years.

Tokugawa was very serious about this policy. He was worried that Japan would be overrun by foreign influences. Keep in mind that Spain had claimed the nearby Philippines and that the English and Portuguese kept trying to make their way into China. So, in 1640, when a group of Portuguese diplomats and traders sailed to Japan to try to negotiate with the emperor and convince him to open up a dialogue, the shogun had every member of the Portuguese delegation executed on the spot. The message was clear. Japan was off limits.

Contrast Them: India, China, and Japan on European Aggression

No doubt about it, under the Tokugawa Shogunate, the Japanese reacted most decisively against European colonialism. China and India both allowed trade and European occupation of port cities, although in China it was increasingly limited under the Manchus. India was least suspecting of the Europeans and paid dearly for it. In the next chapter you'll see the consequences of these three attitudes toward the Europeans: India was overrun, China was partially overrun, and Japan, after briefly falling prey to outside influence, turned the tables and became a colonizing empire itself.

The absence of foreign influences allowed Japanese culture to thrive. During this time period, Buddhism and Shintoism remained at the center of culture, and unique Japanese art forms also prospered. **Kabuki** theatre and a new form of poetry, **haiku**, became very popular. Artists dedicated themselves to the creation of richly detailed scrolls, wood-block prints, and paintings. In other words, under a strong central authority, Japanese culture underwent its own renaissance. Unlike the European Renaissance, however, it was strictly intended for domestic consumption.

V. TECHNOLOGY AND INNOVATIONS, 1450–1750

Europe became a powerful force during this time period because of its willingness to adapt and use three key innovations that existed in other parts of the world: gunpowder weapons, navigation and ship-building technology, and finally the printing press (which developed independently in Germany). At a time when competition among the Europeans resulted in big risks and innovations, the Chinese and Japanese returned to more traditional lifestyles in order to maintain stability, and the Muslims, while retaining powerful land-based empires, allowed innovations in shipping and weaponry to pass them by.

The biggest impact of these new technologies was the expanded knowledge of the world that resulted from exploration by the European nations. Using their superior weapons and larger trading ships, the Europeans established new overseas trading empires, moved lots of plants and animals, enslaved and transported people across oceans, and generally transformed the interactions of the entire world. They fought wars with one another in Europe and—when they were unable to establish suitable trading relationships—went to war in the places they wished to conquer.

Increased contact meant the spread of new ideas and technology (such as the printing press), and the exposure to new cultures transformed both education and religion. The establishment of new Protestant churches in northern Europe increased the power of the kings and nation-states at the expense of the Catholic Church. Conversely, religious conflicts led to increased migrations from northern Europe and the resettlement of large numbers of colonists in the New World.

VI. CHANGES AND CONTINUITIES
IN THE ROLE OF WOMEN

A number of powerful women took charge of the most dominant empires of this time. These included Elizabeth I of England, Isabella of Spain, and Nur Jahan of Mughal, India. With the exception of Elizabeth, who chose never to marry, most of these women shared power with their husbands. In spite of the great power and visibility of these few elite women, for the most part the status and freedoms of women changed little from the previous period—legally they were often considered property of their husbands, inherited less than sons or brothers, and had few rights in legal or political spheres.

The biggest change in the lives of women came from the mixing of previously unknown cultures. The result of global exploration and colonization, these new relationships produced offspring considered mixed, or mestizo. Racial categories began to be more widely used in determining status or class hierarchy, and restrictions developed regarding marriages and legal relationships between classes. Changes in trade and production also placed a greater premium on male labor and jobs that women had traditionally held, such as textile weaving, were increasingly dominated by men.

Some regions of the world served as exceptions to these general patterns but were still impacted by the global interactions. The forced migration of males in African societies resulted in a disproportionate number of females left behind in what were already matrilineal societies. These numbers reinforced polygyny, or multiple marriages. Although large numbers of men also migrated from Europe, the predominately Christian societies did not allow multiple marriages, and as the number of unmarried women increased, this created a problem in societies that regarded marriage as the goal of all women.

The non-European areas of the world tended to regard older or widowed women with both respect and superstition. In both Africa and many Native American societies, councils of older women were part of the political decision-making process. However, older women were also feared, as they couldn't necessarily be controlled. It was this need for control that led to a continuation of Neo-Confucianism values in eastern Asia. This social philosophy designated proper roles and virtues for women within the home with the understanding that if the home were stable so was the state.

In Europe, the revolutionary new ideas of the Renaissance and the Enlightenment included women, at least nominally. Education was more widely available to all classes, but opportunities for girls lagged far behind those for boys, and the highest levels of education were only open to males. Even the less hierarchical new Protestant religions limited the roles of women to wife and mother and did not have convents or monastic systems as alternatives to traditional roles. Eventually, the Protestant countries grew even more puritanical in their regulation of sex, marriage, and illegitimacy.

VII. PULLING IT ALL TOGETHER

In the context of the Age of Exploration, "exploration" has lots of connotations. Of course, the most obvious is that it involved European exploration of the Americas and the beginnings of direct contact with Asia. But more than that, its exploration was also internal. In the Renaissance, Europe explored its own lost history. During the Protestant Reformation, it explored its relationship with God. During the Scientific Revolution, Europe explored the universe and the laws by which the universe functioned. During the Enlightenment, it explored the rights of man and the appropriate role of government, even as its empire depended on slavery. Finally, during the Commercial Revolution, Europe explored its potential.

Combined, these explorations were going in all directions—outward, upward, inward, backward to the past, forward to the future—and it was all going on simultaneously. If you're confused by the developments, you should be. It's hard to figure out which movements in which combination impacted which events. Historians haven't sorted it out either. It's open to debate.

What we can say is this: During the time period discussed in the chapter, Europe was where the energy was. There was so much change for so many reasons, that the boundaries of the continent couldn't contain it. Unlike China and Japan, which largely looked inward, and unlike the Islamic world, which didn't take to the seas or radically shake up religious and social orders, Europeans were dynamic at this particular time in history. They analyzed everything and were full of inconsistencies. At various points in history, other civilizations had at least as much energy and unrest, but because the Europeans had the technology, the political motivation, and the financial structure, they were able to quickly explode onto the world scene. Add in the evangelical nature of Christianity (an explicit desire to convert the world), and it's clear that the desire for expansion ran deep.

Some would say that European monarchs ruled absolutely during this time period and adopted a controlling, ethnocentric attitude with regard to the cultures they dominated. Perhaps this was precisely because Europe was in such cultural chaos itself. Who knows? We'll leave that to your further studies. In any case, it's hard to deny that even as Europeans explored their own history, culture, and structures to unprecedented degrees, they had little trouble marginalizing the complexities of others.

What About Non-European Cultures?
Why Was Their Interaction with the West So Varied?

There are lots of ways to answer these questions, but we'll get you started. China and Japan were both highly organized, confident civilizations. The contingencies of Europeans on their shores were modest. Because the Japanese and Chinese wanted desperately to preserve their own cultures, and because they had the power and sophistication to keep the Europeans, for the moment, at bay, that's precisely what they did. Why didn't the others?

In Africa, societies were fragmented. No centralized power existed, so the Europeans were harder to fend off. What's more, the Europeans weren't initially obsessed with penetrating the entire continent. Because they didn't have to overtake entire civilizations to achieve their goals, they were able to trade goods and abduct individuals one by one, with little concern for long-term impact on the continent.

In the Americas, of course, civilizations were quickly overwhelmed by European technology and disease. In the Ottoman Empire and Arabia, the interaction was somewhat limited because the Europeans weren't as dependent on the overland routes in their efforts to trade with India and China. This diminished the importance of the Middle East to the Europeans. What's more, because the Crusades ended unsuccessfully for the Europeans, trade with the Muslims was important, but conquest of the region was off the radar.

Finally, What About the Global Economy? How Did It Change?

Sailing, mercantilism, and private investment changed the global economy. Improvements in sailing diminished the need for the Asian land routes and connected the world like never before. Mercantilism and its dependence on the establishment of imperialism married economic and political developments. The establishment of joint-stock companies took major economic motivation out of the hands of governments and put it into the hands of the private sector. This meant that now thousands, tens of thousands, or even hundreds of thousands of people had a direct stake in trade routes and conquest. Because the benefits of economic prosperity were diffused among a larger group of individuals than ever before, governments began to lose their grip on controlling their own economies.

CHAPTER 9 KEY TERMS

humanism
printing press
indulgences
atheists
Enlightenment
divine right
Mandate of Heaven
enlightened monarchs
Neoclassical period
Treaty of Tordesillas
peninsulares
viceroys
encomienda system
hacienda system
Middle Passage
Age of Exploration
joint-stock company
Dutch East India Company
Muscovy Company
British East India Company
mercantilism
Spanish Inquisition
Act of Supremacy
Elizabethan Age
Petition of Right
Long Parliament
English Commonwealth
Habeas Corpus Act
English Bill of Rights
Huguenots
Edict of Nantes
National Seclusion Policy
haiku
Tokugawa (Edo) period
Michelangelo
Leonardo da Vinci
Donatello
Johannes Gutenberg
Machiavelli
Erasmus
Sir Thomas More
William Shakespeare
Martin Luther
Pope Leo X
John Calvin
King Henry VIII
Protestant Reformation

Catholic Reformation
    (Counter-Reformation)
Ignatius Loyola
Council of Trent
Galileo
Sir Isaac Newton
Thomas Hobbes
John Locke
Jean-Jacques Rousseau
Voltaire
Montesquieu
Prince Henry the Navigator
Vasco de Gama
Christopher Columbus
Hernan Cortes
Francisco Pizarro
Elizabeth I
James I
Charles I
Oliver Cromwell
Stuart Restoration
Glorious Revolution
Cardinal Richelieu
Cardinal Mazarin
Louis XIV
War of Spanish Succession
Peace of Augsburg
Thirty Years' War
Ivan III, Ivan IV, Ivan the Terrible
Time of Troubles
Peter the Great
Catherine the Great
Osman Bey
Mughal Empire
Akbar
Kongo and Angola
Zheng He

Chapter 9 Drill

See the end of the chapter for the answers and explanations.

Questions 1–5 refer to the image below.

1. This image most likely depicts which of the following?

    (A) A Portuguese caravel
    (B) A Viking longship
    (C) A Chinese junk
    (D) An Arabic dhow

2. Ships such as the one in the image were primarily salient to world history in that they

    (A) enabled Arabic control over the Indian Ocean
    (B) enabled diplomatic ties and cooperation across oceans
    (C) carried relatively large numbers of armed men, goods, and guns over long distances
    (D) facilitated Chinese colonialism

3. Which of the following were the most valuable goods by weight in international trade during the period in which the ship depicted would have been used?

    (A) Spices
    (B) Ivory and other animal products
    (C) Fraud and violence
    (D) Slaves

4. Ships such as the one in the image were most likely to be financed by

    (A) wealthy individual investors, such as aristocrats and factory owners
    (B) piracy and theft
    (C) letters of marque
    (D) royal beneficence or joint-stock companies

5. Which of the following most accurately characterizes the responses of the Chinese and Japanese Empires to the Age of Exploration?

    (A) Active participation in colonialism and trade
    (B) Passive participation in trade with European powers
    (C) Isolation and rejection of large-scale interaction with other states
    (D) Helpless victims of European colonial expansion

TIMELINE OF MAJOR DEVELOPMENTS, 1450–1750

	Americas	Europe	Africa	Mid East	South Asia	East Asia
1450		Fall of Constantinople Renaissance		Ottoman Turks		Ming Dynasty
1475			Kingdom of Songhai			Japanese Feudalism
	Discovery of Americas *African Slave Trade*	*Reconquista* Spanish Inquisition				
1500	Fall of Inca and Aztec Empires	Protestant Reformation	Portuguese Slave Trade	Suleiman the Magnificent	Mughal Empire	Magellan claims Philippines
1525	Spanish/ Portuguese Viceroyalities		Russian Czars			Portuguese at Nagasaki
1550	*Encomienda* system		British Slave Trade			Portuguese Macao
1575	Inquisition	Spanish Armada	Serf Labor			
1600	Jamestown Colony	Commercial Revolution			English trade concessions	
1625		Romanov Dynasty				Dutch East Indies
1650	English and French Colonies	Louis XIV	Dutch Cape Town			Portugal expelled Qing or Manchu Dynasty
1675		Glorious Revolution			Sikh States	
1700		Peter the Great				
1725						
1750		Enlightenment				

CHAPTER 9 DRILL EXPLANATIONS

1. **A** The prominent crosses on the ship's sails indicate that this is likely a European vessel, and the rows of gun ports for cannon cement that impression. In this era (the Age of Exploration), only European vessels routinely carried large numbers of gunpowder cannon, so eliminate (C) and (D). Viking longships, (B), were not sailing vessels, and in any case, were largely obsolete by the Age of Exploration. The answer is (A).

2. **C** Large sailing ships armed with broadside cannon made the Age of Exploration possible. Neither Islamic states nor China built or operated such vessels, so eliminate (A) and (D). The Age of Exploration was a period of fostered interaction between formerly separate peoples and states, but it was an age more of violent expansion than diplomatic cooperation, so (B) is incorrect. Choice (C) is the answer.

3. **A** This is more of a recall question, which might pop up on the AP World History Exam. This question is made more challenging by the fact that all of the listed "goods" were indeed very valuable. You can eliminate (C) first, since it's a practice rather than a trade good. Of the remaining choices, (A), spices, is the best answer. During this age, spices were worth many times their weight in gold in European markets. Ivory and slaves became substantially more valuable in trade after 1700.

4. **D** Large sailing ships armed with cannon were the single-most expensive good during this period. (This would remain true until the advent of ships driven by steam.) Therefore, ships were generally beyond the reach of even very wealthy individuals. Piracy, though certainly popular and at times lucrative, generated wealth on the individual, not state, scale. For a long time, only states had the fiscal resources to build and equip such vessels. By the end of the period, however, joint-stock companies had come into their own and, by aggregating individual wealth in return for shares, allowed the private raising of sufficient capital for these ships. Choice (D) is therefore correct.

5. **C** Though they had their share of internal problems, the Ming and Qing dynasties ruled a powerful centralized state that was perfectly capable of resisting initial European advances. Therefore, (D) is incorrect. Neither power was much interested in expansion beyond their own borders, so (A) is incorrect. Although China engaged in some small-scale trade with European powers, Japan under the Tokugawa Shogunate sealed its borders to foreign powers. Therefore, (C) is correct.

REFLECT

Respond to the following questions:

- For which content topics discussed in this chapter do you feel you have achieved sufficient mastery to answer multiple-choice questions correctly?

- For which content topics discussed in this chapter do you feel you have achieved sufficient mastery to discuss effectively in a short-answer response or essay?

- For which content topics discussed in this chapter do you feel you need more work before you can answer multiple-choice questions correctly?

- For which content topics discussed in this chapter do you feel you need more work before you can discuss effectively in a short-answer response or essay?

- What parts of this chapter are you going to re-review?

- Will you seek further help outside of this book (such as a teacher, tutor, or AP Students) on any of the content in this chapter—and, if so, on what content?

- France helped America
- John Locke hated divine right
- King Loui 16th beheaded
- Slaves had a successful revolution in Haiti
- Steel replaced iron
- Bolivar's dream: Grand Columbia
- didn't work bc of nationilism
- Marx supports the proletariats
- Goal of Meijeing empire: industrialize
- Napolean is responsible for the rise of nationilism
- America and Russia still had forced labor
- Cheaper things (why industrialization was good)
- x Steamships, locomotive, and machine guns; made countries globalized
  wrong!
- Nationibm caused countries to not want to work together
- Liberia + Ethiopia - not claimed in Africa
- Thailand not claimed in east Asia
- Steam = power of industrialization
- Coal made steam
- Marx - critic of capitilism
- Adam Smith - critic of mercentilism
- Europeans did Spheres of Influence to China
- Creoles took over South America
- Roles Pies - leader of lead of tuner

-Meijing treaty ended the Opium War
-"sick man of Europe"- Ottoman nickname

Chapter 10
Industrialization and Global Integration,
c. 1750 to c. 1900

I. CHAPTER OVERVIEW

Although this chapter covers only about 150 years, the world changed dramatically during that time. Europe's influence in the West waned even as it rose in the East. Napoleon tried to conquer Europe. Italy and Germany unified into modern nation-states. Japan became an imperial power. India was entirely overrun by the British. The United States rose to become a world power. The Industrial Revolution—the single biggest event of the time period—seemed to impact everything it touched, from political and economic developments, to the drive for colonial holdings in Africa and Asia, to daily life.

Here's the chapter outline.

I.   Chapter Overview

        You're in it.

II.   Stay Focused on the Big Picture

        Organize the major social, political, and economic changes that occurred during this time period into some big-picture concepts.

III.   Enlightenment Revolutions in the Americas and Europe

        A. Two Revolutions: American and French
        B. Lots of Independence Movements: Latin America

IV.   Industry and Imperialism

        This section focuses on the Industrial Revolution and its consequences, especially as it impacted social and economic developments in Europe and European imperialism in Africa and Asia. Here's how we've organized this section.

        A. The Industrial Revolution
        B. European Imperialism in India
        C. European Imperialism in China
        D. Japanese Imperialism
        E. European Imperialism in Africa

V.   Nationalist Movements and Other Developments

        While Africa and Asia were increasingly dominated by Europe in the eighteenth and nineteenth centuries, the Europeans lost most of their holdings in the Americas due to successful revolutionary movements. In the meantime, Europe underwent continuous political restructuring, and strong centralized nation-states were formed.

Here's how we've organized this section:

Big machines, assembly lines, and new products.

More education and more work!

Refocus on the big-picture concepts now that you've reviewed the historical details.

II. STAY FOCUSED ON THE BIG PICTURE

As you review the details of the developments in this chapter, stay focused on some big-picture concepts and ask yourself some questions, including the following:

1.   How are the events of this time period interconnected? The Industrial Revolution and imperialism are not only interconnected but are connected to other developments in this time period as well. Stay focused on how developments in one region of the world had an impact on developments in another. Also, stay focused on how regional developments had a global impact through improvements in communication and transportation, as well as through colonialism.

2.   Why did nationalism grow during this time period? How did the impact of nationalism vary among different countries? Whether in the Americas, Europe, or Asia, nationalism was a huge force. It sparked rebellions, independence movements, and unification movements. It also sparked domination and colonialism.

3.   How and why does change occur? Stay focused on the complexity of social, political, and economic developments, as opposed to presuming that the dominant economic or political philosophies were shared universally among people in a certain country or region. Think about change as an evolving process in which certain ideas gain momentum, while other ideas lose steam but don't entirely die out.

4. How did the environment impact industrial and economic development? In Europe, the earliest phases of the Industrial Revolution were fueled by the resources available in England, so the resulting imperialism on a global scale was driven by the need for additional resources. Keep in mind the political and economic decisions that resulted in environmental change. At the same time, the environment impacted people. The general global cooling that began around 1500 C.E. put pressure on the populations of Europe and contributed to great poverty and peasant revolts, especially in the northern countries.

III. ENLIGHTENMENT REVOLUTIONS IN THE AMERICAS AND EUROPE

A. Two Revolutions: American and French

1. The American Revolution

For the most part, you won't need to know much about American history for the AP World History Exam. However, you will need to know about events in the United States that impacted developments in the rest of the world. The American Revolution is one of those events.

Calling All History Buffs!
Taking the AP U.S. History Exam as well? You're in luck! Check out our *Cracking the AP U.S. History Exam* for a comprehensive content review, strategy tips, and tons of practice.

Britain began colonizing the east coast of North America during the seventeenth century. By the mid-eighteenth century, British colonists in America felt threatened by France's colonial settlements on the continent. France and Britain were long-time rivals (archenemies in the Hundred Years' War and since), and they carried this rivalry with them into fights in America. The French enlisted the Algonquin and Iroquois tribes to fight alongside them against the encroaching colonists, but in 1763, England prevailed over the French in a war that was known in the colonies as the **French and Indian War** but known in Europe as the **Seven Years' War.** The British victory changed the boundaries of the two empires' American possessions, pushing French territory to the north while English territories expanded westward into the Ohio River Valley.

While the colonists were thrilled with the results of the war, the British felt the colonists had not adequately shared the burden. Of course, the colonists resented this, claiming that it was their efforts that made colonial expansion possible in the first place. At the same time, Britain's **George Grenville** and later **Charles Townshend** passed very unpopular laws on behalf of the British crown. These laws, including the **Revenue Act** (1764), the **Stamp Act** (1765), and the **Tea Act** (1773), were intended to raise additional funds for the British government. These laws created great unrest among the colonists, who not only felt the taxes were economically unfair, but also politically unjust: they had not been represented in Parliament when the laws had been passed. Thus arose the revolutionary cry, "No taxation without representation."

After the colonists dumped tea in Boston Harbor to protest the Tea Act, relations between crown and colonies deteriorated rapidly. On April 19, 1775, British troops battled with rebellious colonists in Lexington and Concord, and by the end of that bloody day, nearly 400 Britons and Americans were dead. The War of Independence had begun.

Independence Can't Happen Without a Little Paine

The overwhelming majority of American colonists had either been born in England or were children of those born in England, and therefore many colonists felt ambivalent about—if not completely opposed to—the movement for independence. Even those who sought independence were worried that Britain was too powerful to defeat. One student of the Enlightenment, Thomas Paine, urged colonists to support the movement. In his widely distributed pamphlet, *Common Sense*, he assailed the monarchy as an encroachment on Americans' natural rights and appealed to the colonists to form a better government. A mere six months later, Americans signed the **Declaration of Independence**. The printing press, the powerful tool of the Protestant Reformation, quickly became a powerful tool for the American Revolution as well.

France: More than Happy to Oblige

By 1776, as the war moved to the middle colonies and finally to the South, the Americans endured defeat after defeat. But in 1777, the French committed ships, soldiers, weapons, and money to the cause. France and England, of course, had been bickering for centuries, and so the French leapt at the opportunity to punish England. In 1781, French and American troops and ships cornered the core of the British army, which was under the command of General George Cornwallis. Finding himself outnumbered, he surrendered, and the war was over. Within a decade, the Constitution and Bill of Rights were written, ratified, and put into effect. A fledgling democracy was on display.

2. The French Revolution

After the reign of Louis XIV, the Bourbon kings continued to reside in the lavish Versailles palace, a lifestyle that was quite expensive. More costly, however, were France's war debts. The War of Spanish Succession, the Seven Years' War, the American Revolution, you name it—France seemed to be involved in every major war both in Europe and abroad. With droughts damaging the French harvests and the nobility scoffing at spending restrictions, Louis XVI needed to raise taxes, but to do that he needed to get everyone on board. So, in 1789, he called a meeting of the **Estates-General**, a "governing body" that hadn't met in some 175 years. Bourbon monarchs, you'll recall, ruled under divine right, so no other input was generally seen as necessary.

> **Focus On: Causes and Consequences of the American Revolution**
> Don't worry too much about knowing the details of the American Revolution. You certainly don't need to know battles or even the personalities. Instead, understand that the Enlightenment had a huge impact because it not only helped to inspire the revolution itself, but also the type of government that was created after it succeeded. Also remember that mercantilist policies drove the American colonists nuts, as was the case in European colonies everywhere. These same forces—the Enlightenment and frustration over economic exploitation—are common themes in the world's revolutionary cries against colonialism throughout the 1800s.

However, the king's poor financial situation made it necessary to call on this all-but-forgotten group.

The Estates-General: Generally a Mess

French society was divided into three estates (something like social classes). The First Estate comprised the clergy. Some were high ranking and wealthy; others were parish priests and quite poor. The Second Estate was made up of the noble families. Finally, the Third Estate comprised everyone else—peasant farmers and the small but influential middle class, or bourgeoisie, including merchants. The overwhelming majority (more than 95 percent) of the population were members of the Third Estate, but they had very little political power.

When Louis XVI summoned the Estates-General, he was in essence summoning representatives from each of these three estates. The representative nobles of the Second Estate came to the meeting of the Estates-General hoping to gain favors from the king in the form of political power and greater freedoms in the form of a new constitution. The representatives of the Third Estate (representing by far the greatest proportion of France's population), always suspicious of the nobility, wanted even greater freedoms similar to what they saw the former British colonies had in America. They went as far as suggesting to the king that the Estates-General meet as a unified body—all Estates under one roof. However, the top court in Paris, the parlement, ruled in favor of the nobility and ordered that the estates meet separately.

Frustrated at the strong possibility of being shut out of the new constitution by the other two estates, the Third Estate did something drastic on June 17, 1789—they declared themselves the **National Assembly**. The king got nervous, and forced the other two estates to join them in an effort to write a new constitution. But it was too little, too late. By then, peasants throughout the land were growing restless and were concerned that the king wasn't going to follow through on the major reforms they wanted. They stormed the Bastille, a huge prison in Paris, on July 14, 1789. From there, anarchy swept through the countryside and soon peasants attacked the nobility and feudal institutions.

By August, the National Assembly adopted the **Declaration of the Rights of Man**, a document recognizing natural rights and based on the ideas of the Enlightenment, the American Declaration of Independence, and particularly the writings of Jean-Jacques Rousseau. This declaration was widely copied and distributed across Europe, furthering the ideas of freedom, equality, and rule of law. The Assembly also abolished the feudal system and altered the monopoly of the Catholic Church by declaring freedom of worship. Meanwhile, the king and his family were taken to Paris, where the Third Estate revolutionaries could ensure that they wouldn't interfere with the work of the National Assembly. Perhaps most importantly, the French Revolution established the nation-state, not the king or the people (as in the United States), as the source of all sovereignty or political authority. In this sense, France became the first "modern" nation-state in 1789.

A New Constitution Causes Consternation

In 1791, the National Assembly ratified a new constitution, which was somewhat similar to the U.S. Constitution ratified just two years before, except that instead of a president, the king held on to the executive power. In other words, it was a constitutional monarchy, rather than a constitutional democracy. Those who wanted to abolish the monarchy felt cheated; those who wanted to retain the feudal structure felt betrayed.

Remember how most of the royalty in Europe intermarried? Well, it just so happened that Marie Antoinette, who was the wife of the increasingly nervous Louis XVI, was also the sister of the Emperor of Austria. The Austrians and the Prussians invaded France to restore the monarchy, but the French revolutionaries were able to hold them back. Continuing unrest led French leaders to call for a meeting to draw up a new constitution. Under the new constitution, the **Convention** became the new ruling body, and it quickly abolished the monarchy and proclaimed France a republic. Led by radicals known as the **Jacobins**, the Convention imprisoned the royal family and, in 1793, beheaded the king for treason.

Contrast Them: American and French Revolutions

The American Revolution involved a colonial uprising against an imperial power. In other words, it was an independence movement. The French Revolution involved citizens rising up against their own country's leadership and against their own political and economic system, and in that sense was more of a revolution. In other words, at the end of the American Revolution, the imperial power of England was still intact, and indeed the new United States was in many ways designed in the image of England itself. In contrast, at the end of the French Revolution, France itself was a very different place. It didn't simply lose some of its holdings. Instead, the king was beheaded and the socio-political structure changed.

That said, the word revolution aptly describes the American independence movement because the United States was the first major colony to break away from a European colonial power since the dawn of the Age of Exploration. What's more, the ideas adopted in the Declaration of Independence, the U.S. Constitution, and in the French Revolution inspired colonists, citizens, and slaves across the globe. Quite revolutionary indeed!

The Reign of Terror: The Hard-Fought Constitution Gets Tossed Aside

While Prussia and Austria regrouped and enlisted the support of Great Britain and Spain, the Convention started to worry that foreign threats and internal chaos would quickly lead to its demise, so it threw out the constitution and created the **Committee of Public Safety**, an all-powerful enforcer of the revolution and murderer of anyone suspected of anti-revolutionary tendencies. Led by **Maximilien Robespierre** and the Jacobins, the Committee of Public Safety certainly wasn't a committee of personal safety, since it was responsible for the beheading of tens of thousands of French citizens. Even though the Committee was successful at controlling the anarchy and at building a strong national military to defend France against an increasing number of invading countries, after two years the French had enough of Robespierre's witch hunt and put his head on the guillotine. France quickly reorganized itself again, wrote a new constitution in 1795, and established a new five-man government called the **Directory**.

Napoleon: Big Things Come in Small Packages

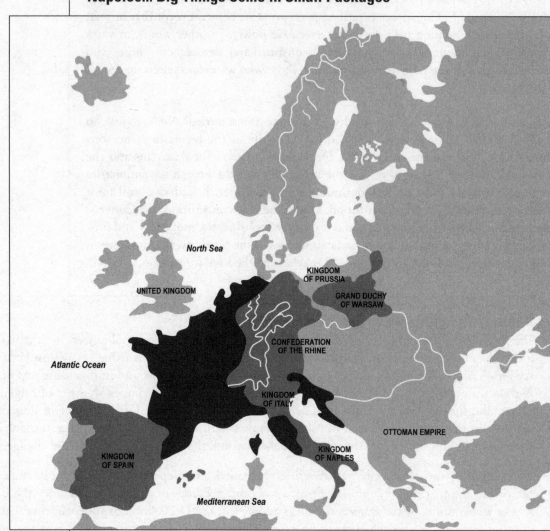

North Sea

KINGDOM OF PRUSSIA

GRAND DUCHY OF WARSAW

UNITED KINGDOM

CONFEDERATION OF THE RHINE

Atlantic Ocean

KINGDOM OF ITALY

OTTOMAN EMPIRE

KINGDOM OF SPAIN

KINGDOM OF NAPLES

Mediterranean Sea

The Height of Napoleon's Empire

While the Directory was not so great at implementing a strong domestic policy, the five-man combo was good at building up the military. One of its star military leaders was a teenager named **Napoleon Bonaparte**, who was a general by age 24. After military successes on behalf of the Directory, Napoleon returned to France and used his reputation and immense popularity to overthrow the Directory in 1799. He legitimized his actions by putting them before a popular vote, and once affirmed, he declared himself the First Consul under the new constitution (if you're counting, that makes four constitutions since the Revolution began).

Domestically, Napoleon initiated many reforms in agriculture, infrastructure, and public education. He also normalized relations with the church and restored a degree of tolerance and stability. Most importantly, his **Napoleonic Codes** (1804) recognized the equality of French citizens (meaning men) and institutionalized some of the Enlightenment ideas that had served as the original inspiration for many of the revolutionaries. At the same time, the code was also extremely paternalistic, based in part on ancient Roman law. The rights of women and children were severely limited under the code. Still, the code was a huge step forward in the recognition of some basic rights and in the establishment of rules of law. The code has since been significantly modified to reflect more modern sensibilities, but it is still in effect today, and has served as the model for many other national codes, especially in Europe.

Napoleon's biggest impact was external, not internal. In a stunning effort to spread France's glory throughout Europe and the Americas, Napoleon not only fended off foreign aggressors, but also made France an aggressor itself. Napoleon's troops conquered Austria, Prussia, Spain, Portugal, and the kingdoms within Italy. He dissolved the Holy Roman Empire, which was on its last legs anyway, and reorganized it into a confederacy of German states. In 1804, he crowned himself emperor of this huge new empire, fancying himself the new Charlemagne. By 1810, the empire was at its peak, but it didn't stay there for long. France lacked the resources to control a far-flung empire, and conflicts including an attempted blockade of powerful Britain cost it dearly. Nationalistic uprisings, such as unrest in Italy and fierce guerilla warfare in Spain and Portugal, undermined Napoleon's power.

In 1812, Napoleon's greed got the better of him. He attacked the vast lands of Russia, but was baited into going all the way to Moscow, which the Russians then set aflame, preventing Napoleon from adequately housing his troops there. As winter set in and with no place to go, the troops had to trudge back to France and were attacked all along the way. Short on supplies, the retreat turned into a disaster. The army was decimated and the once-great emperor was forced into exile.

The leaders of the countries that had overthrown Napoleon met in Vienna to decide how to restore order (and their own power) in Europe. The principal members of the coalition against Napoleon were **Prince von Metternich** of Austria, **Alexander I of Russia**, and the **Duke of Wellington** of Britain. At first, disagreements among them prevented much progress. Hearing this, Napoleon returned from exile and attempted to regain power. His enemies, of course, rallied. At **Waterloo** in 1813, the allies united against their common threat. Defeating Napoleon decisively, they sent him to permanent exile on the island of St. Helena, where he later died. The allies eventually came to an agreement, in a meeting known as the **Congress of Vienna**, over what to do with France and its inflated territories.

The Congress of Vienna: Pencils and Erasers at Work

In 1815, the Congress decreed that a **balance of power** should be maintained among the existing powers of Europe in order to avoid the rise of another Napoleon. France was dealt with fairly: Its borders were cut back to their pre-Napoleonic dimensions, but it was not punished militarily or economically. And although it rearranged some of the European boundaries and created new kingdoms in Poland and the Netherlands, the Congress also reaffirmed absolute rule, reseating the monarchs of France, Spain, Holland, and the many Italian states. While remarkably fair-minded, the Congress of Vienna ignored many of the ideals put forth by French revolutionaries and the rights established under France's short-lived republic. In other words, it essentially tried to erase the whole French Revolution and Napoleon from the European consciousness and restore the royal order.

B. Lots of Independence Movements: Latin America

The European colonies in Latin America were inspired by the success of the American Revolution and the ideas of the French Revolution. To be sure, there had been unsuccessful revolts and uprisings in the Latin American colonies for two or three centuries prior to those revolutions. In the early nineteenth century, however, the world order was different. Europe was in chaos because of the rise and fall of Napoleon, and this distracted the European powers from their American holdings, a development that gave rebellious leaders an opportunity to assert themselves more than they previously could have.

Haiti: Slave Revolt Sends France a Jolt

The first successful Latin American revolt took place in Haiti, a French island colony in the Caribbean. The French, true to their mercantilist policies, exported coffee, sugar, cocoa, and indigo from Haiti to Europe. French colonists owned large plantations and hundreds of thousands of slaves, who grew and harvested these crops under horrible conditions. By 1800, 90 percent of the population was enslaved and working on large plantations.

In 1801, as Napoleon was gaining momentum in Europe, **Pierre Toussaint L'Ouverture**, a former slave, led a violent, lengthy, but ultimately successful slave revolt. Enraged, Napoleon sent 20,000 troops to put down the revolt, but the Haitians were capable fighters. They also had another weapon on their side—yellow fever—that claimed many French lives. The French did succeed, however, in capturing L'Ouverture and imprisoning him in France, but by then they couldn't turn back the revolutionary tide. L'Ouverture's lieutenant **Jacques Dessalines**, also a former slave, proclaimed Haiti a free republic in 1804 and named himself governor-general for life. Thus, Haiti became the first independent nation in Latin America.

South America: Visions of Grandeur

In 1808, when Napoleon invaded Spain, he appointed his brother, Joseph Bonaparte, to the Spanish throne. This sent the Spanish authorities in the colonies into a tizzy. Who should they be loyal to? The colonists decided to remain loyal to their Spanish king and not recognize the French regime under Bonaparte. In Venezuela, they ejected Bonaparte's governor and, instead, appointed their own leader, **Simón Bolívar**. Tutored on the republican ideals of Rousseau during his travels to Europe and the United States, Bolívar found himself in the midst of a great opportunity to use what he learned. In 1811, Bolívar helped establish a national congress, which declared independence from Spain. Royalists, supporters of the Spanish crown, declared civil war. Bolívar proved to be a wily and effective military leader, and during the next decade, he won freedom for the area called Gran Colombia (which included modern-day Colombia, Ecuador, and Venezuela). Bolívar envisioned a huge South American country spanning across the continent, similar to the growing United States in North America, but it wasn't meant to be. In the following decades, the individual nation-states of northwestern South America formed their own governments.

Meanwhile, farther south in Argentina, the conflict between the French governor and those who still wanted to support the Spanish crown created another opportunity for liberation. **José de San Martin** was an American-born Spaniard (or Creole) who served as an officer in the Spanish army. In 1814 he began to put his extensive military experience to use—but for the rebels—taking command of the Argentinian armies. San Martin joined up with Bernardo O'Higgins of Chile and took the revolutionary movement not only through Argentina and Chile, but also to Peru, where he joined forces with Bolívar. The Spanish forces withered away. By the 1820s, a huge chunk of South America had successfully declared its independence from Spain.

Brazil: Power to the Pedros

Brazil, of course, was a Portuguese colony, and so when Portugal was invaded by Napoleon's armies in 1807, **John VI**, the Portuguese king, fled to Brazil and set up his royal court in exile. By 1821, Napoleon had been defeated and it was safe for John VI to return to Portugal, but he left behind his son, Pedro, who was 23 years old at the time, and charged him with running the huge colony. Pedro, who had spent most of his childhood and teenage years in Brazil and considered it home, declared Brazilian independence and crowned himself emperor the next year. Within a few more years, Brazil had a constitution.

In 1831, Pedro abdicated power to his son, **Pedro II**, who ruled the country through much of the nineteenth century. While he reformed Brazilian society in many ways and turned it into a major exporter of coffee, his greatest single accomplishment was the abolition of slavery in 1888 (which actually occurred under the direction of his daughter, Isabel, who was running the country while Pedro II was away). This action so incensed the landowning class that they revolted against the monarchy and established a republic in 1889.

Mexico: A Tale of Two Priests

As in other parts of Latin America, a revolutionary fervor rose in Mexico after the French Revolution, especially after Napoleon invaded Spain and Portugal. In 1810, **Miguel Hidalgo**, a Creole priest who sympathized with those who had been abused under Spanish colonialism, led a revolt against Spanish rule. Unlike in South America, however, the Spanish armies resisted effectively, and they put down the revolt at Calderon Bridge, where Hidalgo was executed.

Hidalgo's efforts were not in vain, however, because they put the revolution in motion. **José Morelos** picked up where Hidalgo left off and led the revolutionaries to further successes against the loyalists. Similar to what later happened in Brazil, the landowning class turned against him when he made clear his intentions to redistribute land to the poor. In 1815, he was executed.

It wasn't until 1821, after the landowning class bought into the idea of separation from Spain, that independence was finally achieved. In the **Treaty of Cordoba**, Spain was forced to recognize that its 300-year-old domination of Latin America was coming to an end. Mexico was granted its independence and Central America soon followed.

Neocolonialism

Independent countries in Latin America that were still largely controlled by outside economic and political interests found themselves in a condition known as **neocolonialism**. Following independence movements in the 19th century, many Latin American nations saw significant increases in trade. However, the riches accumulated in these counties largely stayed within the confines of the wealthy, landowning class, inspiring working class movements to challenge these economic conditions.

One such movement occurred in Mexico. The **Mexican Revolution** began as a rejection of the 30-year dictatorship of **Porfirio Díaz**, who was seen as a pawn for landowners. He was defeated in an election by revolutionary aristocrat Francisco Madero. Madero was eventually overthrown in 1913 following a two-year presidency once he too was rejected by the revolutionary masses. The Mexican Revolution culminated in 1917 with the creation of Mexico's current constitution.

The Effects of the Independence Movements: More Independence Than Freedom

While Europe was effectively booted out of many parts of the American continents during a 50-year time span beginning in about 1780, in some Latin American countries the independence from colonial power wasn't accompanied by widespread freedom among the vast majority of citizens. As in the United States, slavery still existed for decades. Peasants still worked on huge plantations owned by a few landowners. Unlike in the United States, however, a significant middle class of merchants and small farmers didn't emerge, and many of the Enlightenment ideas had only influenced the educated elite.

There were several reasons for this. The Catholic Church remained very powerful in Latin America, and while many of the priests advocated on behalf of the peasants and of the slaves (some martyred themselves for that cause), the church hierarchy as a whole protected the status quo. The church, after all, was one of the largest landowners in Latin America.

What's more, the economies of Latin America, while free from Europe politically, were still dependent on Europe economically. Latin American countries still participated in European mercantilism, often to their own detriment. They specialized in a few cash crops, exported almost exclusively to Europe, and then bought the finished products. In other words, most Latin American economies didn't diversify, nor did they broaden opportunities to a larger class of people, so innovation and creativity rarely took root.

There are notable exceptions. Chile diversified its economy fairly successfully, and Brazil and Argentina instituted social reform and broadened their economies to include a growing middle class. Ultimately, the hugely successful independence movements in Latin America didn't result in noticeable changes for a majority of the population for more than a century.

Comparison Chart of Independence Movements

	American Colonies 1764–1787	France 1789–1799	Haiti 1799–1804	Latin America 1810–1820s
Causes	Unfair taxation War debt Lack of representation	Unfair taxation War debt Social inequalities Lack of representation	French Enlightenment Social and racial inequalities Slave revolt	Social inequalities Removal of peninsulares Napoleon's invasion of Spain
Key Events	Boston Tea Party Continental Congress Declaration of Independence Constitution and Bill of Rights	Tennis Court Oath National Assembly Declaration of Rights of Man Storming Bastille Reign of Terror 5 Man Directory	Civil war Slave revolt Invasion of napoleon	Peasant revolts Creole revolts Gran Colombia
Major Players	George III Thomas Paine Thomas Jefferson George Washington	Louis XVI Three Estates Jacobin Party Robespierre	Boukman Gens de Couleur Toussaint L'Overture Napoleon Bonaparte	Miguel Hidalgo Simón Bolívar José de San Martin Emperor Pedro I
Impacts	Independence Federal Democracy spreads—France, Haiti, Mexico	Rise of Napoleon Congress of Vienna Constitutional monarchy	Independence Destruction of economy Antislavery movements	Independence Continued inequalities Federal democracy (Mexico) Creole republics Constitutional monarchy (Brazil)

IV. INDUSTRY AND IMPERIALISM

The Industrial Revolution, which began in the mid-eighteenth century in Britain and spread rapidly through the nineteenth century, is inseparable from the Age of Imperialism, which reached its peak in the late nineteenth and early twentieth centuries. Industrial technology had two enormous consequences. First, countries with industrial technology by definition had advanced military weapons and capacity, and were therefore easily able to conquer people who did not have this technology. Second, in order to succeed, factories needed access to raw materials to make finished products and markets to sell those finished products. Colonies fit both of these roles quite well.

Because the bulk of the western hemisphere freed itself from European control by the early nineteenth century (a lot more on this later), the industrial imperialists turned their eyes toward Africa and Asia, where exploitation was easy and markets were huge.

A. The Industrial Revolution

The Industrial Revolution began in Britain, helping to propel the country to its undisputed ranking as the most powerful in the nineteenth century. But Britain wasn't the only country that industrialized. The revolution spread through much of Europe, especially Belgium, France, and Germany, as well as to Japan and ultimately to the country that would eclipse Britain as the most industrialized—the United States. Still, since most of the developments occurred in Britain first, and since the social consequences that occurred in Britain are representative of those that occurred elsewhere, this section will focus heavily on the revolution in Britain. References to other countries will be made where warranted.

Agricultural Revolution Part II

Hopefully you remember that early civilizations came about, in part, because of an Agricultural Revolution that resulted in food surpluses. This freed some of the population from farming, and those people then went about the business of building the civilization. In the eighteenth century, agricultural output increased dramatically once again. This time, it allowed not just some people, but as much as half of the population to leave the farms and head toward the cities, where jobs in the new industrial economy were becoming available.

Keep in mind that agricultural techniques had been slowly improving throughout history. Since so many developments happened so quickly in the eighteenth century, this period was considered a revolution. Agricultural output increased for a whole host of reasons. Potatoes, corn, and other high-yield crops were introduced to Europe from the colonies in the New World. Farmers began using more advanced farming methods and technology and increased their crop yields. Through a process known simply as **enclosure**, public lands that were shared during the Middle Ages were enclosed by fences, which allowed for private farming and private gain.

What really cranked up the efficiency and productivity of the farms was the introduction of new technologies. New machines for plowing, seeding, and reaping, along with the development of chemical fertilizers, allowed farmers to greatly increase the amount of land they could farm, while decreasing the number of people needed to do it. **Urbanization** was a natural outgrowth of the increased efficiencies in farming and agriculture. In short, cities grew. In 1800, there were only about 20 cities in Europe with a population of more than 100,000. By 1900, 150 cities had similar populations, and the largest, London, had a population of more than 6 million.

Cities developed in areas where resources such as coal, iron, water, and railroads were available for manufacturing. The more factories that developed in favorable locations, the larger cities grew. In 1800, along with London, the Chinese cities of Beijing (Peking) and Canton ranked in the top three, but just 100 years later, nine of the ten largest cities in the world were in Europe or the United States.

Technological Innovations: The Little Engine That Could

Prior to the Industrial Revolution, most Europeans worked on farms, at home, or in small shops. Even after Britain started importing huge amounts of cotton from its American colonies, most of the cotton was woven into cloth in homes or small shops as part of an inefficient, highly labor-intensive arrangement known as the **domestic system**. Middlemen would drop off wool or cotton at homes where women would make cloth, which would then be picked up again by the middlemen, who would sell the cloth to buyers. All of this was done one person at a time.

However, a series of technological advancements in the eighteenth century changed all this. In 1733, John Kay invented the **flying shuttle**, which sped up the weaving process. In 1764, John Hargreaves invented the **spinning jenny**, which was capable of spinning vast amounts of thread. When waterpower was added to these processes, notably by Richard Arkwright and Edward Cartright in the late eighteenth century, fabric-weaving was taken out of the homes and was centralized at sites where waterpower was abundant. In 1793, when **Eli Whitney** invented the **cotton gin**, thereby allowing massive amounts of cotton to be quickly processed in the Americas and exported to Europe, the textile industry was taken out of the homes and into the mills entirely.

Although industrialization hit the textile industry first, it spread well beyond into other industries. One of the most significant developments was the invention of the **steam engine**, which actually took the work of several people to perfect. In the early 1700s, Thomas Newcomer developed an inefficient engine, but in 1769, **James Watt** dramatically improved it. The steam engine was revolutionary because steam could not only be used to generate power for industry but also for transportation. In 1807, **Robert Fulton** built the first **steamship**, and in the 1820s, **George Stephenson** built the first **steam-powered locomotive**. In the hands of a huge, imperial power like Britain, steamships and locomotives would go a long way toward empire building and global trade. Because Britain had vast amounts of coal, and because the steam engine was powered by coal, Britain industrialized very quickly.

But Wait, There's More!

During the next 100 years, enormous developments changed how people communicated, traveled, and went about their daily lives. These changes are far too numerous to list entirely, but we've picked a few major inventions and listed them below. It's unlikely you'll need to know all of these for the exam, but an understanding of the impact of the Industrial Revolution is perhaps best grasped by looking at the details. There isn't one item on the list below that you can deny has changed the world.

- **The Telegraph**—Invented in 1837 by Samuel Morse. Allowed people to communicate across great distances within seconds.
- **The Telephone**—Invented in 1876 by Alexander Graham Bell. Don't answer it while you're studying.
- **The Lightbulb**—Invented in 1879 by Thomas Edison. Kind of a big deal: now factories can run all night.
- **The Internal Combustion Engine**—Invented in 1885 by Gottlieb Daimler. If you've ever been in a car, you've personally benefited from the internal combustion engine.
- **The Radio**—Invented in the 1890s by Guglielmo Marconi, based on designs by Thomas Edison.

At the same time, there were huge advances in medicine and science. Pasteurization and vaccinations were developed. X-rays came onto the scene. **Charles Darwin** developed the concept of evolution by means of natural selection. The developments of this time period go on and on and on.

Compare Them: The Scientific Revolution and the Industrial Revolution

Both changed the world, of course. One was about the process of discovering, learning, evaluating, and understanding the natural world. The other was about applying that understanding to practical ends. In both cases, knowledge spread and improvements were made across cultures and across time. Even though patents protected individual inventions, one scientist or inventor could build on the ideas of colleagues who were tackling the same issues, thereby leading to constant improvement and reliability. This same collaborative effort is used today. Universities and research organizations share information among colleagues across the globe. The Internet, of course, allows data to be analyzed almost instantaneously by people all over the world.

The Factory System: Efficiency (Cough), New Products (Choke), Big Money (Gag)

The Industrial Revolution permitted the creation of thousands of new products from clothing to toys to weapons. These products were produced efficiently and inexpensively in factories. Under Eli Whitney's system of **interchangeable parts**, machines and their parts were produced uniformly so that they could be easily replaced when something broke down. Later, Henry Ford's use of the **assembly line** meant that each factory worker added only one part to a finished product, one after another after another. These were incredibly important developments in manufacturing, and they made the factory system wildly profitable, but they came with social costs. Man wasn't merely working with machines; he was becoming one. Individuality had no place in a system where consistency of function was held in such high esteem.

The factories were manned by thousands of workers, and the system was efficient and inexpensive primarily because those workers were way overworked, extremely underpaid, and regularly put in harm's way without any accompanying insurance or protection. In the early years of the Industrial Revolution, 16-hour workdays were not uncommon. Children as young as six worked next to machines. Women logged long hours at factories, while still having to fulfill their traditional roles as caretakers for their husbands, children, and homes.

This was a huge change from rural life. Whereas the farms exposed people to fresh air and sunshine, the factories exposed workers to air pollution and hazardous machinery. The farms provided seasonal adjustments to the work pattern, while the factories spit out the same products day after day, all year long. The despair and hopelessness of the daily lives of the factory workers were captured by many novelists and social commentators of the time (for example, Charles Dickens).

Focus On: The Family

The biggest social changes associated with industrialization were to the family. Both women and children became part of the workforce, albeit at lower wages, and in more dangerous conditions than their male counterparts. Workers were often dependent on companies for food, personal items, and housing—in factory-run boardinghouses. These new living arrangements removed workers from families and traditional structures. In many ways, this lessened the restrictions on young women and men. They were able to live away from home, manage their own incomes, and pursue independent leisure activities—theatres, dance halls, recitals, dining out in restaurants—all of which developed to support the new urban working class.

The emergence of a middle class also brought changes to the family. Home and work were no longer centered in the same space. Middle- and upper-class women were expected to master the domestic sphere, and thus remain private and separate from the realities of the working world. This was a time of great consumption as desirable products were mass produced and women were expected to arrange parlors and dining rooms with fancy tea cups and serving trays.

New Economic and Social Philosophies: No Shortage of Opinions

Industrialization created new social classes. The new aristocrats were those who became rich from industrial success. A middle class formed, made up of managers, accountants, ministers, lawyers, doctors, and other skilled professionals. Finally, at the bottom of the pyramid was the working class—and it was huge—made up of factory workers in the cities and peasant farmers in the countryside.

The rise of the industrial class had its origins in the concept of private ownership. **Adam Smith** wrote in *The Wealth of Nations* (1776) that economic prosperity and fairness is best achieved through private ownership. Individuals should own the means of production and sell their products and services in a free and open market, where the demand for their goods and services would determine their

Contrast Them: Social Class Structures Before and After Industrialism

Keep in mind that throughout history, the wealthy class was small and the poorest class was huge, but industrialism gave it a new twist. Because of urbanization, people were living side by side. They could see the huge differences among the classes right before their eyes. What's more, the members of the working class saw factory owners gain wealth quickly—at their expense. The owners didn't inherit their position, but instead achieved success by exploiting their workers, and the workers knew it. In the past, under feudalism, people more readily accepted their position because, as far as they knew, the social structure was the way it had always been, and that's the way it was meant to be. If your dad was a farmer, you were a farmer. If your dad was the king, you were a prince. After industrialism, people saw for the first time the connection between their sacrifices and the aristocracy's luxuries.

prices and availability. A **free-market system** (also known as **capitalism**), Smith argued, would best meet the needs and desires of individuals and nations as a whole. When governments remove themselves entirely from regulation, the process is called **laissez-faire capitalism**.

Smith wrote his book in response to the Western European mercantilist practices that had dominated during the Age of Exploration. In the New World, monarchies—which were not only corrupt, but also highly inefficient—closely managed their economies. In the nineteenth century, European countries continued to develop their mercantilist philosophies (especially using colonies as a way of obtaining raw materials without having to import them from other countries and as a way of increasing exports). European countries also permitted and encouraged the development of private investment and capitalism. Hence the rise of factory workers and the rise of major investment firms like the British East India Company.

While Adam Smith believed that free-market capitalism would lead to better opportunities for everyone, **Karl Marx**, a German economist and philosopher who spent a good part of his adult life living in poverty, pointed out that the factory workers had genuine opportunities but were being exploited as a consequence of capitalism. In other words, the abuses weren't merely the result of the way in which capitalism was practiced, but an inherent flaw in the system. In *The Communist Manifesto* (1848), Marx and Friedrich Engels wrote that the working class would eventually revolt and take control of the means of production. All the instruments of power—the government, the courts, the police, the church—were on the side of the rich against the workers. Once the class struggle was resolved by the massive uprising of the exploited, Marx predicted that the instruments of power wouldn't even be needed. The impact of Marxism was enormous, and served as the foundation of **socialism** and **communism**.

Marx and Engels were not just theorizing, they were also observing, and there was much discontent to support their view. In England in the early 1800s, groups of workers known as **Luddites** destroyed equipment in factories in the middle of the night to protest working conditions and pitiful wages. The government unequivocally sided with the business owners, executing some of the workers, while also enacting harsh laws against any further action.

At the same time, however, a greater number of people with influence (the middle class and the aristocracy) began to realize how inhumane the factory system had become and started to do something about it. These reformers believed that capitalism was a positive development, but that laws were needed to keep its abuses in check. In other words, they believed that the government needed to act on behalf of the workers as well as the factory owners. By the mid-nineteenth century, there was a major split in thought among intellectuals and policymakers.

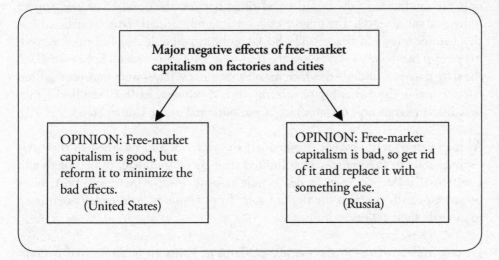

In Britain and the United States, where the impact of the Enlightenment was strong, democracy was developing, and the middle class was growing, reforms to the free-market system took root, lessening the negative impact of capitalism on workers. In other countries such as Russia, where absolute rule was strong and the peasant class extremely oppressed, reform was almost nonexistent. There, Marxist ideas grew popular among a small group of urban intellectuals—eventually including Vladimir Lenin—who believed they could lead a worker revolution and end the tyranny of the czars.

Elsewhere, Marxism impacted social thought and intermixed with capitalist thought to create economic systems that were partly socialist (in which the government owned some of the means of production) and partly capitalist (in which individuals owned some of the means of production). Most of Europe, including Britain after World War II, mixed socialist and capitalist ideas.

Capitalism and Enlightenment Combine: Reform Catches On

In the second half of the nineteenth century, after the abuses and social consequences of the Industrial Revolution became clear, a series of reforms occurred. The British Parliament passed laws, such as the **Factory Act of 1883**, which limited the hours of each workday, restricted children from working in factories, and required factory owners to make working conditions safer and cleaner. Meanwhile, **labor unions** were formed. The unions were vehicles through which thousands of employees bargained for better working conditions, or threatened to strike, thereby shutting down the factory. In addition, an increasing number of factory owners realized that a healthy, happy, and reasonably well-paid workforce meant a productive and loyal one.

All of these developments combined, though slowly and sporadically, to improve not only the conditions in the factories and cities, but also the standard of living on an individual family level. The middle class became substantially larger. Public education became more widely accessible. **Social mobility**—the ability of a person to work his way up from one social class to the next—became more commonplace. In 1807, the slave trade was abolished, which meant that no new slaves were transported from Africa, though the ownership of existing slaves continued. In 1833, the British outlawed slavery, and three decades later, it was outlawed in the United States.

As men earned more money, women left the factories and returned to their traditional roles in the home, which limited their social, political, professional, and intellectual influence, even as democratic reforms greatly increased most men's power, especially through the right to vote. In response, women began organizing to increase their collective influence.

Despite improvements in the overall standards of living in industrialized nations, by 1900 extreme hardships persisted. In many cases, Europeans dreamed of starting over somewhere else, or escaping cruelties at home. From 1800 to 1900, nearly 50 million Europeans migrated to North and South America. Millions fled from famine in Ireland, or anti-Semitism in Russia, or poverty and joblessness in general.

In Search of Natural Resources: Stealing Is Cheaper than Dealing

The factories of the Industrial Revolution created useful products, but to do so they required natural resources. Europe had its share of coal and iron ore used to provide power and make equipment for the factories, but raw materials such as cotton and rubber had to be imported because they didn't grow in the climates of Western Europe.

Industrial nations amassed incredible wealth by colonizing regions with natural resources, and then taking those resources without compensating the native peoples. The resources were sent back to Europe, where they were made into finished products. Then, the industrial nations sent the finished products back to the colonies, where the colonists had to purchase them because the colonial powers wouldn't let the colonies trade with anyone else. In short, the colonial powers became rich at the expense of the colonies. The more colonies a nation had, the richer it became.

Soon, Europe colonized nations on every other continent in the world. Europe became a clearinghouse for raw materials from around the globe while the rest of the world increasingly became exposed to Europe and European ideas. What's more, the need for raw materials transformed the landscape of the conquered regions. Limited raw materials depleted faster than at any time in human history. The Industrial Revolution, in addition to creating pollution, began to have an impact on the environment by gobbling natural resources.

The European Justification: Superiority Is a Heavy Burden

Even as progressives argued for an end to the slave trade and better working conditions in the factories, a huge number of Europeans—not just the industrialists—either supported or acquiesced in the colonization of foreign lands. Most Europeans were very ethnocentric and viewed other cultures as barbarian and uncivilized. Ironically, this ethnocentrism may have driven some of the social advancements within European society itself—after all, if you think of yourself as civilized, then you can't exactly brutalize your own people.

Two ideas contributed to this mindset. First, **social Darwinists** applied Charles Darwin's biological theory of natural selection to sociology. In other words, they claimed that dominant races or classes of people rose to the top through a process of "survival of the fittest." This meant that because Britain was the most powerful, it was the most fit, and therefore the British were superior to other races.

Second, many Europeans believed that they were not only superior, but that they had a moral obligation to (crassly said) dominate other people or (politely said) teach other people how to be more civilized—in other words, how to be more like Europeans. **Rudyard Kipling** summed it up in his poem "**White Man's Burden**." As European nations swallowed up the rest of the world in an effort to advance their economies, military strategic positioning, and egos, Kipling characterized these endeavors as a "burden" in which it was the duty of Europeans to conquer each "half-devil and half-child" so that they could be converted to Christianity and civilized in the European fashion. Never mind if the non-Europeans didn't want to be "civilized." The Europeans supposedly knew what was best for everyone.

"White Man's Burden"
This Kipling poem not only put forth the idea that European colonization and exploitation of other peoples was justified, it basically said that such actions were obligatory—a moral duty.

Contrast Them: Ethnocentrism in Europe and Elsewhere

To be sure, many cultures were ethnocentric. The Chinese, for example, believed their kingdom to be the Middle Kingdom, literally the "center of the world," and themselves ethnically superior to other races. Similar attitudes existed in Japan and in most major civilizations. The Europeans were hardly unique in their self-important attitudes. However, in their ability to act on those attitudes, they were dangerously unique. Armed with the most technologically advanced militaries and strong economic motives, the Europeans were quite capable of subjugating people whom they considered to be inferior, barbaric, or dispensable. Their success at doing so often reinforced the ethnocentric attitudes, leading to further colonialism and subjugation.

B. European Imperialism in India

As you know from the previous chapter, the Indian subcontinent had long been a destination for European traders eager to get their hands on India's many luxuries, such as tea, sugar, silk, salt, and jute (an extremely strong fiber used for ropes). By the early eighteenth century, the Mughal Empire was in decline after wars and religious conflict between Muslims and Hindus. Lacking a strong central government, India was vulnerable to influence from external powers.

In the 1750s, the rivalry between France and England reached a fever pitch. During the Seven Years' War (more on it later), the two countries battled each other in three theaters: North America, Europe, and India. England won across the board. The **British East India Company**, a joint-stock company that operated like a multinational corporation with exclusive rights over British trade with India, then led in India by **Robert Clive**, raised an effective army that rid the subcontinent of the French. During the next two decades, Clive successfully conquered the Bengal region (present-day Bangladesh), quite a feat given that the East India Company was a corporation. It wasn't British troops who conquered the region, but corporate troops!

Over the next hundred years, the company took advantage of the weakening Mughals and set up administrative regions throughout the empire. In 1798, the large island of Ceylon (present-day Sri Lanka) fell to the British. In the early 1800s, the Punjab region in northern India came under British control, and from there the Brits launched excursions into Pakistan and Afghanistan.

The Sepoy Mutiny: Too Little, Too Late

To help administer the regions under its control, the East India Company relied on Sepoys, Indians who worked for the Brits, mainly as soldiers. By the mid-1800s, the Sepoys were becoming increasingly alarmed with the company's insatiable appetite for eating up larger and larger chunks of the subcontinent. What's more, the company wasn't very good about respecting the local customs of the Sepoys, and respected neither Muslim nor Hindu religious customs. When, in 1857, the Sepoys learned that their bullet cartridges (which had to be bitten off in order to load into the rifle) were greased with pork and beef fat, thus violating both Muslim and Hindu dietary laws, the Sepoys rebelled. The fighting continued for nearly two years, but the rebellion failed miserably.

The consequences were huge. In 1858, the British parliament stepped in, took control of India away from the East India Company, and made all of India a crown colony. The last of the Mughal rulers, **Bahadur Shah II**, was sent into exile, thereby ending the Mughal Empire for good. Nearly 300 million Indians were suddenly British subjects (that's as many people as are currently living in the United States). By 1877, Queen Victoria was recognized as Empress of India.

Full-Blown British Colonialism: England on the Indus

In the second half of the nineteenth century, India became the model of British imperialism. Raw materials flowed to Britain; finished products flowed back to India. The upper castes were taught English and were expected to adopt English attitudes. Christianity spread. Railroads and canals were built. Urbanization, as in Europe, increased dramatically. All of this came at the expense of Indian culture and institutions. Still, as the upper castes were Anglicized, they gained the education and worldly sophistication to begin to influence events. Increasingly, they dreamed of freeing India from British rule.

In 1885, a group of well-educated Indians formed the **Indian National Congress** to begin the path toward independence. It would take the impact of two world wars before they would get it. In the meantime, Indians, especially those that lived in the cities, continued to adapt to British customs while trying to hold on to their traditions.

C. European Imperialism in China

As you know, for much of its history, China was relatively isolationist. It traded frequently, but it didn't make exploration a high priority. It also expanded by conquering its neighbors, but never took this expansion beyond its own region of the globe. Up until the 1830s, China allowed the European powers to trade only in the port city of Canton, and it established strict limitations on what could be bought and sold. As the European powers, particularly the British, gained industrial muscle, they came barging in, this time with weapons and warships.

The Opium Wars: European Drug Pushers Force Their Right to Deal

In 1773, British traders introduced opium to the Chinese. By 1838, the drug habit among the Chinese had grown so widespread and destructive that the Manchu Emperor released an imperial edict forbidding the further sale or use of opium. Consistent with this edict, the Chinese seized British opium in Canton in 1839.

The British would have none of it. From 1839 to 1842, the two countries fought a war over the opium trade. This was known as the first **Opium War**. Overwhelmed by British military might, China was forced to sign the **Treaty of Nanjing**, the first of what came to be known as the "**unequal treaties**," by which Britain was given considerable rights to expand trade with China.

In 1843, Britain declared Hong Kong its own crown possession, a significant development that went beyond trading rights because it actually established a British colony in the region. In 1844, the Manchu Dynasty was forced to permit Christian missionaries back into the country.

When China resisted British attempts to expand the opium trade even further, the two countries fought a second Opium War for four years beginning in 1856. The Chinese defeat was humiliating. It resulted in the opening of all of China to European trade. Still, other than in Hong Kong, European imperialism in China was quite different from what it was in India and what it would be in Africa. In China, Britain fought more for trading concessions than for the establishment of colonies.

The Word Is Out: China Is Crumbling

The Opium Wars had a huge impact on the global perception of China. For centuries, the world knew that China was one of the more advanced civilizations. With the clear-cut British defeat of China with relatively few troops, the world realized that China was an easy target. What's more, the Chinese themselves knew that their government was weak, and so they, too, started to rebel against it. Internal rebellion started at the beginning of the nineteenth century with the **White Lotus Rebellions** led by Buddhists who were frustrated over taxes and government corruption. It continued through the middle of the century with the **Taiping Rebellion**. The Taipings, led by a religious zealot claiming to be the brother of Jesus, recruited an army nearly a million strong and almost succeeded in bringing down the Manchu government. The rebels failed, but the message was clear. China was crumbling from within and unable to stop foreign aggression from outside.

In the 1860s, the Manchu Dynasty tried to get its act together in what became known as the **Self-Strengthening Movement**, but it did no good. In 1876, Korea realized China was weak and declared its independence. Later, in the **Sino-French War** (1883), the Chinese lost control of Vietnam to the French, who established a colony there called French Indochina. If that wasn't enough, a decade later the Chinese were defeated in the **Sino-Japanese War**, when the rising imperial power of Japan wanted in on the action. In the **Treaty of Shimonoseki** (1895), China was forced to hand over control of Taiwan and grant the Japanese trading rights similar to those it had granted the Europeans. Japan also defeated the Koreans and took control of the entire peninsula.

Meanwhile, the European powers were rushing to establish a greater presence in China. By establishing **spheres of influence**, France, Germany, Russia, and of course Britain carved up huge slices of China for themselves. These spheres were not quite colonies. Instead, they were areas in which the European powers invested heavily, built military bases, and set up business, transportation, and communication operations. The Manchu Dynasty was still the governmental authority within the spheres.

By 1900, the United States, which had its own trading designs on Asia, was worried that China would become another India or Africa, and that the United States would be shut out of trade if the Manchu government fell and the Europeans took over the government. (Let's not forget the irony that the U.S. had barred the immigration of all Chinese laborers in the **Chinese Exclusion Act** of 1882.) Through its **Open Door Policy**, the United States pledged its support of the sovereignty of the Chinese government and announced equal trading privileges among all imperial powers (basically Europe and the United States).

The Boxer Rebellion: Knocked Out in the First Round

By the twentieth century, nationalism among the Chinese peasants and local leadership was festering. Anti-Manchu, anti-European, and anti-Christian, the Society of Righteous and Harmonious Fists, or **Boxers**, as they came to be known, organized in response to the Manchu government's defeats and concessions to the Western powers and Japan. Infuriated, the Boxers' goal was to drive the Europeans and Japanese out of China. Adopting guerilla warfare tactics, the Boxers slaughtered Christian missionaries and seized control of foreign embassies. Ultimately, however, they were not successful in achieving their aims. Instead, their uprising resulted in the dispatch of foreign reinforcements who quickly and decisively put down the rebellion. The Manchu government, already having made great concessions to the Europeans and Japanese, was then even further humiliated. As a result of the rebellion, China was forced to sign the **Boxer Protocol**, which demanded that China not only pay the Europeans and the Japanese the costs associated with the rebellion but also to formally apologize for it as well.

Contrast Them: European Imperialism in China and India

Many European countries traded with India, but the British ultimately won out and established exclusive control. In China, the British dominated trade early on, and as they succeeded, more and more countries piled on.

In India, the British established a true colony, running the government and directing huge internal projects. In China, Europeans and the Japanese established spheres of influence, focusing on the economic benefits of trade with no overall governmental responsibilities. Therefore, when independence movements began in India, the efforts were directed against Britain, the foreign occupier. In contrast, when the people wanted to change the government in China, they targeted the Manchu Dynasty.

On its last legs, the Manchu Dynasty couldn't prevent the forces of reform from overtaking it from both within and without, and as a consequence, Chinese culture itself started to crumble. In 1901, foot binding was abolished. In 1905, the 2,000-year-old Chinese Examination System was eliminated. By 1911, the government was toppled and imperial rule came to an end. For the first time, under the leadership of Sun Yatsen, a republic was established in China. More on this in the next chapter.

D. Japanese Imperialism

During the seventeenth and eighteenth centuries, Japan succeeded in keeping European influences away from its shores. It consequently built a highly ethnocentric, self-involved society that didn't even allow its own citizens to travel abroad. By the nineteenth century and the Industrial Revolution, the Europeans and the United States became so powerful and so crazed for markets that Japan found it hard to keep the westerners at bay. In 1853, **Commodore Matthew Perry** from the United States arrived in Japan on a steamboat, something the Japanese had never seen before, and essentially shocked the Japanese, who quickly realized that their isolation had resulted in their inability to compete economically and militarily with the industrialized world.

For a time, the West won concessions from Japan through various treaties such as the **Treaty of Kanagawa** (1854). These treaties grossly favored the United States and other countries. As in China, the nationalists grew resentful, but unlike the Chinese, the Japanese were organized. Through the leadership of the samurai, they revolted against the shogun who had ratified these treaties, and restored Emperor Meiji to power.

The Meiji Restoration: Shogun Out, Emperor In, Westerners Out

The **Meiji Restoration** ushered in an era of Japanese westernization, after which Japan emerged as a world power. By the 1870s, Japan was building railways and steamships. By 1876, the samurai warrior class as an institution had been abolished, and universal military service among all males was established.

The relative isolation of Japan during the Tokugawa Shogunate and the deliberate attempt to Westernize while strengthening Japanese imperial traditions during the Meiji led to a period of increased cultural creativity with rituals aimed at developing national identity. Much of this new identity was centered on military pageantry that celebrated Japanese victories over China and Russia in the early twentieth century.

In the 1890s, Japanese industrial and military power really started to roll. It was now powerful enough to substantially reduce European and U.S. influence. It maintained trade, but on an equal footing with Western powers. Japan went through an incredibly quick Industrial Revolution. In 1895, Japan defeated China in a war for control of Korea and Taiwan. Japan was now an imperial power itself.

> **Compare Them: The Industrial Revolution in Europe and in Japan**
> The industrialization of Europe and Japan followed very similar paths, but Japan's was on fast forward. It managed to accomplish in a few decades what had taken Europe more than a century, in large part because it didn't have to invent everything itself—it just needed to implement the advances of Western industrialization. Still, the pattern was remarkably similar. Private corporations rose up, industrialists like the Mitsubishi family became wealthy, factories were built, urbanization increased dramatically, and reform was instituted. Japan learned from the Europeans quite well. If you can't beat an industrialized power, become one yourself.

E. European Imperialism in Africa

Unlike India and China, and to a certain degree Japan, Africa held little interest for most Europeans prior to the Industrial Revolution. To be sure, north of the Sahara, in Egypt and along the Mediterranean, Europeans had historical interest and impact. The vast interior of the continent remained unknown to the outside world. During the Age of Exploration, coastal regions of Africa became important to Europeans for limited trade, and also for strategic positioning, as stopping-off points for merchant ships en route to India or China. Most significantly, of course, Africa became the center of the slave trade.

The Slave Trade Finally Ends

As Enlightenment principles took root in Europe, larger and larger numbers of people grew outraged at the idea of slavery. Between 1807 and 1820, most European nations abolished the slave trade, although slavery itself was not abolished until a few decades later. In other words, no new slaves were legally imported from Africa, but those already in Europe or the New World continued to be enslaved until emancipation in the mid-nineteenth century. In some cases, former slaves returned to Africa. Groups of former American slaves, for example, emigrated to Liberia, where they established an independent nation.

The Slave Trade Ends, Oppression Does Not
It's a terrible irony that as the slave trade ended in the nineteenth century, Europeans turned their greedy eyes to the continent of Africa itself. Within fifty years, the Africans were subjugated again, but this time in their own homeland.

South Africa:
Gold Rings, a Diamond Necklace, and a British Crown

Prior to the discovery of gold and diamonds in South Africa in the 1860s and 1880s, South Africa was valuable to the Europeans only for shipping and military reasons. The Dutch arrived first and settled Cape Town as a stopping point for ships on the way from Europe to India. In 1795, the British seized Cape Town, and the South African Dutch (now known as Boers or Afrikaners) trekked northeast into the interior of South Africa, settling in a region known as the Transvaal. When the Boers later discovered diamonds and gold in the Transvaal, the British quickly followed, fighting a series of wars for the rights to the resources. After years of bloody battles, known as the **Boer War** (1899–1902), the British reigned supreme, and all of South Africa was annexed as part of the ever-expanding British Empire. Of course, throughout this entire process, Africans were not allowed claims to the gold and diamonds, and were made to work in the mines as their natural resources were sent abroad.

Egypt: A New Waterway Makes a Splash

In theory, the Ottomans ruled Egypt from 1517 until 1882, although throughout the nineteenth century, Ottoman rule was extremely weak. Local rulers, called *beys*, had far more influence over developments in Egypt than the rulers in Istanbul. When Napoleon tried to conquer Egypt during his tireless attempt to expand France into a mega-empire at the turn of the nineteenth century, **Muhammad Ali** defeated the French and the Ottomans and gained control of Egypt in 1805. Egypt technically remained part of the Ottoman Empire, but as viceroy, Ali wielded almost exclusive control. During the next thirty years, he began the industrialization of Egypt and directed the expansion of agriculture toward cotton production, which was then exported to the textile factories of Britain for substantial profit.

Ali's Westernization attempts were temporarily halted by his grandson, **Abbas I**, but were reinvigorated under subsequent rulers, who worked with the French to begin construction of the **Suez Canal**. The canal, when completed in 1869, connected the Mediterranean Sea to the Indian Ocean, eliminating the need to go around the Cape of Good Hope. Because Britain had a huge colony in India, the canal became more important to the British than to anyone else. As Egypt's finances went into a tailspin because of excessive government spending, Egypt started selling stock in its canal to raise money, stock that the British government eagerly gobbled up. By 1882, Britain not only controlled the Suez Canal, but had maneuvered its way into Egypt to such a degree that it declared it a British protectorate, which was essentially a colony except that Egyptians remained in political power.

Pushed out of Egypt, France focused on other parts of North Africa, particularly Nigeria. The Italians, once they had unified as a country, also became interested in North Africa. The race for control of Africa was on.

The Berlin Conference: Carving Up the Continent

In 1884, Otto von Bismarck hosted the major European powers at a conference in Berlin intended to resolve some differences over various European claims to lands in the African Congo. By the end of the conference, the delegates had set up rules for how future colonization rights and boundaries would be determined on that continent. With rules in hand, the Europeans left the conference in haste. Each country wanted to be the first to establish possession in the various parts of Africa. Within three decades, almost the entire continent of Africa was colonized by Britain, France, Germany, Italy, Spain, Portugal, and Belgium. Only Ethiopia and Liberia remained independent of European rule by 1914.

While the Europeans added substantial infrastructure to the continent by building railroads, dams, and roads, they stripped Africa of its resources for profit and treated the natives harshly. Every colonial power except Britain exercised direct rule over its colonies, meaning Europeans were put in positions of authority and the colonies were remade according to European customs. The British, having their hands full with the huge colony in India and massive spheres of influence in China and elsewhere, permitted the native populations to rule themselves more directly and to more freely practice their traditional customs (similar to how the Roman Empire handled its far-flung territories).

Because the Berlin Conference of 1884 encouraged colonialism solely based on bargaining for political and economic advantage, the boundary lines that eventually separated colonial territories were based on European concerns, not on African history or culture. Therefore, in some situations, tribal lands were cut in half between two colonies controlled by two different European nations, while in other situations two rival tribes were unwillingly brought together under the same colonial rule. For a time, the disruption of traditional tribal boundary lines worked to the Europeans' advantage because it was difficult for the native Africans to organize an opposition within each colony. It did much more than thwart opposition; it disrupted the culture. Add in European schools, Christian missionaries, and Western business practices, and traditional African culture, as elsewhere in the global colonial swirl, started breaking apart.

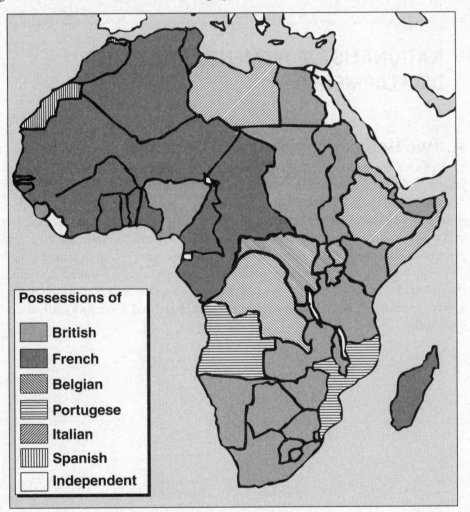

European Colonies in Africa, 1914

Compare Them: European Colonialism in Africa and Latin America
Colonialism in Africa was similar to that in the Americas in that boundary lines were determined by European agreements from abroad. In other words, there was total disregard for the societies that existed beforehand. Colonialism in Africa was similar to colonialism in America because multiple countries held claims to the land. Except for the colonies controlled by the British, the African colonies were governed by direct rule, similar to European rule of colonies in the Americas. This meant they sent European officials to occupy all positions of authority. Native traditions were overcome, not tolerated, and certainly not developed. This, of course, was in contrast to spheres of influence in China, for example, in which Europeans were generally more interested in making money rather than changing the entire culture.

V. NATIONALIST MOVEMENTS AND OTHER DEVELOPMENTS

A. Two Unifications: Italy and Germany

One of the consequences of the Napoleonic era was that it intensified nationalism, or feelings of connection to one's own home, region, language, and culture. France, Spain, Portugal, Britain, and Russia, of course, had already unified and, in some cases, built enormous empires. But the Italian and German city-states were still very feudal, and were constantly at the center of warfare among the European powers. In the second half of the nineteenth century, however, all of that changed. With the wave of industrialization and all the changes that it inspired, as well as the nationalist sentiments that were still lingering decades after Napoleon's defeat, a drive to unify Italy and Germany resurfaced. Italy and Germany unified and eventually altered the balance of European power.

The Unification of Italy:
Italians Give Foreign Occupiers the Boot

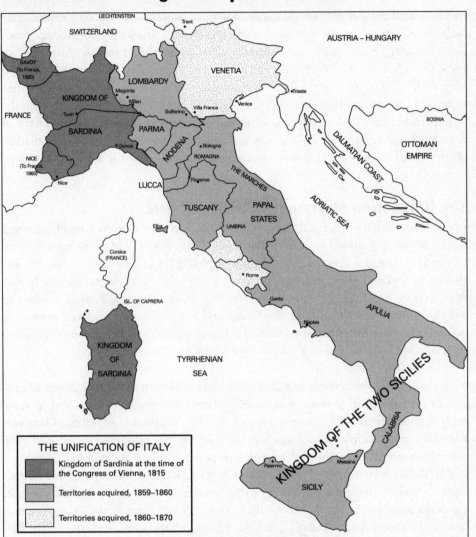

The Unification of Italy

In the mid-nineteenth century, Italy was a tangle of foreign-controlled small kingdoms. Austria controlled Venetia, Lombardy, and Tuscany in the north. France controlled Rome and the Papal States in the mid-section. Only the divided kingdom of Sardinia (part of which was an island in the Mediterranean) was controlled by Italians.

In 1849, the king of Sardinia, **Victor Emmanuel II**, named **Count Camillo Cavour** his prime minister, and nationalism in Italy took off. Both Emmanuel and Cavour believed strongly in Italian unification. Through a series of wars in which Cavour sided with European powers that could help him boot out Austria from Italy, he managed to remove Austrian influence from all parts of Italy (except Venetia) by 1859. Meanwhile, **Giuseppe Garibaldi**, another Italian nationalist, raised a volunteer army and in 1860 his army overthrew the kingdom whose citizens pledged allegiance to Sardinia. So, by 1861, a large chunk of present-day Italy was unified, and it declared itself a unified kingdom under Victor Emmanuel.

In the following decade, the Italians managed to gain control of Venetia after siding with Prussia in its war against Austria (which previously controlled Venetia) and finally won control of Rome in 1870 when the French withdrew. Still, even though Italy was essentially unified, the boundaries of Europe were still very shaky. Some Italians thought that southern provinces of Austria and France were far more Italian than not and that those provinces were rightly part of Italy. What's more, Italy had a hard time unifying culturally because for centuries it had developed more regionally. Still, now unified, Italy was more able to assert itself on the world stage, a development that would impact Europe in the next century.

The Unification of Germany: All About Otto

The provinces that comprised Germany and the Austrian Empire (the Hapsburgs) hadn't been truly united since the decline of Charlemagne's Holy Roman Empire in the Middle Ages. Since the Peace of Westphalia (1648), which asserted the authority of regional governments, two areas in the region of the former Holy Roman Empire had politically dominated it: Prussia and Austria. Prussia, under the enlightened monarch Frederick the Great and his successors, achieved economic preeminence by embracing the Industrial Revolution. They also strongly supported education, which created a talented work force.

Many in Prussia wanted to consolidate the German territories into a powerful empire to rival the great powers of Europe, particularly Britain, France, and increasingly Russia. So, in 1861, the new king of Prussia, **William I**, appointed **Otto von Bismarck** prime minister with the aim of building the military and consolidating the region under its authority. In order to achieve this consolidation, Bismarck had to defeat Austria, which he did in only seven weeks, after he won assurances from the other European powers that they would not step in on Austria's behalf. Through more war and annexation, Bismarck secured most of the other German principalities, except for heavily Catholic regions in the south. So, the crafty Bismarck formed an alliance with the Catholic German states against aggression from France, and then, in 1870, provoked France to declare war on Prussia, starting the **Franco-Prussian War**—a war which, once won, consolidated the German Catholic regions under Prussian control. In 1871, the victorious Bismarck crowned King William I as emperor of the new German Empire, which was also known as the Second Reich ("second empire," after the Holy Roman Empire, which was known as the First Reich).

After unification, Germany quickly industrialized and became a strong economic and political power. Otto was not popular with everyone, especially socialists. In 1888, Germany crowned a new emperor, **William II**, who wanted to run the country himself. In 1890, he forced Bismarck to resign as prime minister and re-established authority as the emperor. With the Industrial Revolution in Germany now running at full throttle, he built a huge navy, pursued colonial ambitions in Africa and Asia, and oversaw the rise of Germany into one of the most powerful nations in the world.

B. Other Political Developments

Russia: Life with Czars

In the nineteenth century, Russia consolidated power over its vast territory by giving absolute power to its Romanov czars. The vast majority of the citizens were serfs with no rights, living an almost slavelike existence. Alexander I and Nicholas I frequently used the secret police to quash rebellions or hints of reform, despite the fact that an increasing number of Russians demanded change.

By the 1860s, long after the Enlightenment had had an effect on most developments in the West, **Alexander II** began some reforms. He issued the **Emancipation Edict**, which essentially abolished serfdom. It did little good. The serfs were given very small plots of land for which they had to give huge payments to the government to keep, so it was difficult for them to improve their lot. Some peasants headed to the cities to work in Russia's burgeoning industries, but there, too, the reforms that softened some of the harsher working conditions in the West hadn't made their way eastward. Whether in the fields or in the factories, the Russian peasants continued to live a meager existence, especially when compared to many of their Western European counterparts.

Still, during the second half of the nineteenth century, a small but visible middle class started to grow, and the arts began to flourish. In a span of just a few decades, Russian artists produced some of the greatest works of all time: Tolstoy wrote *Anna Karenina* and *War and Peace*, Dostoyevsky authored *The Brothers Karamazov*, and Tchaikovsky composed *Swan Lake* and *The Nutcracker*. Meanwhile, an intellectual class well-acquainted with political and economic thought in the rest of Europe began to assert itself against the monarchy. In 1881, Alexander II was assassinated by a political group known as **The People's Will**.

Alexander III reacted fiercely by attempting to suppress anything that he perceived as anti-Russian. Through a policy known as **Russification**, all Russians, including people in the far-flung reaches of the Empire that did not share a cultural history with most of Russia, were expected to learn the Russian language and convert to Russian Orthodoxy. Anyone who didn't comply was persecuted, especially Jews. Meanwhile, terrible conditions in the factories continued, even as production capacity was increased and greater demands were put upon the workers.

The Ottoman Empire: Are They Still Calling It an Empire?

The Ottoman Empire began its decline in the sixteenth century and was never able to gain a second wind. Throughout the seventeenth and eighteenth centuries, the Ottomans continually fought the Russians for control of the Balkans, the Black Sea, and surrounding areas. Most of the time, the Russians were victorious. So by the nineteenth century, not only was the Ottoman Empire considerably smaller and less powerful, but it was in danger of collapse. Greece, Egypt, and Arabia launched successful independence movements. This worried Britain and France, who feared that if the Ottoman Empire fell entirely, the Russian Empire would seize the chance to take over the eastern Mediterranean. So, for the next century, Britain and France tried to keep the Ottoman Empire going if only to prevent Russian expansion, as they did in the Crimean War in 1853. At the same time, of course, Britain and France increased their influence in the region. In 1882, for example, Britain gained control of Egypt.

U.S. Foreign Policy: This Hemisphere Is Our Hemisphere

After the wave of independence movements swept Latin America in the early nineteenth century, Europe found itself nearly shut out of developments in the entire western hemisphere—even as European countries were swiftly colonizing Africa and Asia.

To ensure that Europe wouldn't recolonize the Americas, U.S. President Monroe declared in his 1823 State of the Union Address that the Western Hemisphere was off-limits to European aggression. The United States, of course, wasn't the superpower then that it is today, so it was hardly in a position to enforce its declaration, which became known as the **Monroe Doctrine**. Britain, whose navy was enormous and positioned all over the globe, was fearful that Spain wanted to rekindle its American empire, so it agreed to back up the United States. As a result, the European powers continued to invest huge sums of money in Latin American business enterprises but didn't make territorial claims. In 1904, after European powers sent warships to Venezuela to demand repayment of loans, President Theodore Roosevelt added what came to be known as the **Roosevelt Corollary to the Monroe Doctrine**, which provided that the United States would intervene in financial disputes between European powers and countries in the Americas, if doing so would help to maintain the peace. While Latin American nations have at times benefited from the protection and oversight of their North American neighbor, the Monroe Doctrine also angered some Latin Americans, who saw the United States as exercising its own brand of imperialism in the region. This became clear when the United States incited Panamanians to declare their independence from Colombia, so that the United States could negotiate the right to build the **Panama Canal** in the Central American nation.

In 1898, a European power was dealt another blow in its efforts to maintain its footing in the Western Hemisphere. Spain, which still controlled both Cuba and Puerto Rico, was embroiled in conflict with Cuban revolutionaries when the United States, which sympathized with the Cubans, intervened and launched the **Spanish-American War** of 1898. In a matter of a few months, it was all over. The United States quickly and decisively destroyed the Spanish fleets in Cuba and in the Philippines, and thereby gained control of Guam, Puerto Rico, and the Philippines. Cuba was given its independence, in exchange for concessions to the United States, including allowing the creation of two U.S. naval bases on the island. The United States, henceforth, was considered to be among the world powers.

VI. TECHNOLOGY AND INTELLECTUAL DEVELOPMENTS, 1750–1900

Economic, political, and social changes occurred so rapidly in this 150-year period that it is difficult to keep track of them all. The flow chart in "Pulling It All Together" (see page 336) of this chapter provides a good outline of the causes and effects of these changes. Advances in power and transportation drove the Industrial Revolution. Steam provided consistent power for new factories. In transportation news, millions of miles of rail lines were laid through out Europe, India, Africa, and throughout eastern Asia. This facilitated the movement of resources and manufactured goods. The new industrial world required large numbers of laborers. In the latter half of the nineteenth century, this need, along with the abolition of slavery, resulted in large-scale migrations around the world. Europeans and east Asians immigrated to the Americas, and south Indians moved into other British-controlled territories.

This rapidly transforming world also resulted in the creation of new forms of entertainment for the urban working class, new literature and revolutionary new ideas, exhibitions, fairs and amusement parks, professional sports, as well as the first department stores with widely available consumer goods. Both English and Japanese women published novels, some of which were indictments of working class life. The rapid industrialization also created the need for new forms of job protection including unions and new ideas about the relationships between the social classes.

With industrialization came new imperialism and interactions. The arts and culture of Europe were influenced by contact with Asia and Africa, resulting in the development of new art forms. Meanwhile, the Japanese started to integrate Western styles into traditional art forms. The seemingly radical Impressionist period in nineteenth-century European painting was based on depictions of real life, while the modernist art movements included cubism, surrealism, and art nouveau.

New industrialization and imperialism also resulted in new reasons and new ways to make war. This period saw the development of automatic weapons, including the Maxim gun of the 1880s. The assembly line allowed for mass production of gasoline-powered automobiles and eventually the first tanks, which led to the massive destruction wrought on the battlefields of World War I.

VII. CHANGES AND CONTINUITIES IN THE ROLE OF WOMEN

With all the dramatic transformations that took place in the nineteenth century, this was actually a low point in terms of women's rights. Education, real wages, and professional opportunities continued to be mostly inaccessible; however, the new intellectual and economic opportunities available to men did open doors for women, and movements began throughout the world to rally for women's political and legal rights.

Although women continued to be heavily restricted with few freedoms, political and legal barriers for men based on class or racial categories were mostly eliminated. However, women were not unaffected by the new Enlightenment ideals of freedom, equality, and liberty, and the earliest feminist writers emerged in Western Europe during this period. Both middle- and working-class women joined reform movements, labor unions, and socialist parties. Most important to these women was access to education, which was still denied to the majority of them due to ideas of mental inferiority based on social Darwinism.

Although most Western countries opened university education to women, literacy rates in China and India—countries with long histories of secluding women—remained shockingly low well into the twentieth century. However, male literacy in these regions was also low, and despite Christian missionary schools, it was not in the interest of the imperial powers to have a well-educated colonial populace.

VIII. PULLING IT ALL TOGETHER

From 1750 to 1900, so much happened in so many different places that it's easy to get lost unless you focus on major developments and trends. We suggest that you try to link up many of the events and movements in a flowchart. Once you start, you'll be amazed at how much is interconnected.

We've put together a sample flowchart for you. You may choose to connect developments quite differently from the way we have—there's certainly more than one way to link events together. That said, take a look at the chart and use it to help you begin to make your own.

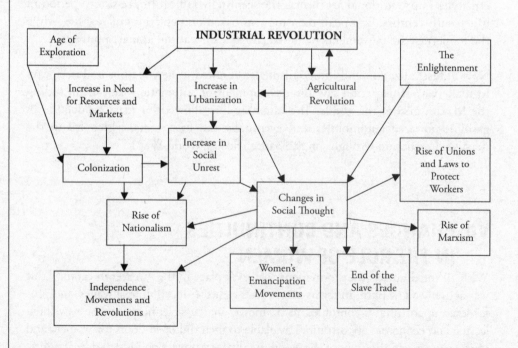

Of course, this chart doesn't begin to address many of the developments covered in this chapter. To include everything would require an enormous chart. In addition, developments were complicated and not entirely sequential. For example, there were two big rounds of independence movements and revolutions because there were two rounds of colonialism. The first round occurred after the Age of Exploration when the United States and Latin America declared their independence. The second round occurred after the Industrial Revolution and led to a race for new colonies in Asia and Africa. Those independence movements didn't occur until the twentieth century.

Notice also that there are arrows going in both directions between the Agricultural Revolution and the Industrial Revolution—they each led to more of the other. The greater the food surplus, the more a country could industrialize. The more it industrialized, the more it developed efficient machines and tools that could be used to increase agricultural production.

The Growth of Nationalism: Me, Myself, and My Country

Nationalism was an enormous force on all continents during the time period covered in this chapter. Nationalism, broadly defined, is the desire of a people of a common cultural heritage to form an independent nation-state and/or empire that both represents and protects their shared cultural identity. It drove movements in Germany and Italy to unify. It drove movements in the Americas to declare independence. It drove resistance against European colonialism in India, China, and Africa, while it drove Europeans to compete with each other to promote national pride and wealth by establishing colonies in the first place. In China, it even drove peasant movements against the Manchu government, which was targeted for not representing the Han majority. It drove the French to unite behind Napoleon to attempt to take over Europe, and it drove the British to unite to try to take over the world. Nationalism drove the Japanese to quickly industrialize and the Egyptians to limit the power of the Ottomans.

In short, people all over the world began to identify strongly with their nation, or with the dream of the creation of their own nation. Even in the European colonies, and perhaps especially there, nationalism was growing. The oppressors used nationalist feelings to justify their superiority. The oppressed used nationalistic feelings to justify their rebellion.

The Complex Dynamics of Change: Enough to Make Your Head Spin

During the time period covered in this chapter, there were many forces of change. Exploration. Industrialization. Education. The continuing impact of the Enlightenment. The end of slavery. Military superiority. Nationalism. Imperialism. Racism. Capitalism. Marxism. It's mind-boggling.

What's more, these changes were communicated faster than ever before. Trains and ships raced across continents and seas. Telegraph cables were laid and telephones were ringing. Think about how much faster Japan industrialized than England. Think about how much faster Africa was colonized than Latin America. Increases in transportation and communication had far-reaching consequences.

Urbanization, too, fueled change. As people came in closer contact with each other, ideas spread more quickly. Like-minded people were able to associate with each other. Individuals had contact with a greater variety of people, and therefore were exposed to more ideas. Increasingly, developments in the cities raced along at a faster pace than those in villages and on farms. In India, for example, British imperialism greatly impacted life in the cities. Indians learned to speak English and adopted European habits. In the countryside, however, Hindu and Muslim culture continued largely uninterrupted.

Of course, most change—even "revolutionary" change—didn't entirely supplant everything that came before it. For example, the Scientific Revolution challenged some assertions made by Catholicism, but both survived, and many sought to reconcile new scientific discoveries with traditional Christian teaching. Slavery was successfully outlawed, but that didn't mean that former slaves were suddenly welcomed as equals. Racism, both social and institutional, continued.

It's also important to keep in mind that individuals, even those who were the primary agents of change, acted and reacted based on multiple motives, which were sometimes at odds with each other. The United States declared its independence eloquently and convincingly, and then many of the signers went home to their slaves. Factory workers argued tirelessly for humane working conditions, but once achieved, happily processed raw materials stolen from distant lands where the interests of the natives were often entirely disregarded.

Change is indeed very complex, but it's also impossible to ignore. Life for virtually everyone on the globe was different in 1914 than in 1750. If you can describe how, you're well on your way to understanding the basics. If you can describe why, you're on your way to doing well on the exam.

CHAPTER 10 KEY TERMS

Estates-General
National Assembly
Declaration of the Rights of Man
Jacobins
Napoleonic Code
balance of power
neocolonialism
enclosure
urbanization
domestic system
flying shuttle
spinning jenny
cotton gin
steam engine
interchangeable parts
assembly line
free-market system (capitalism)
laissez-faire capitalism
socialism
communism
labor unions
social mobility
social Darwinism
"white man's burden"
British East India Company
unequal treaties
spheres of influence
Open Door Policy
Boxers
Russification
French and Indian War (Seven
  Years' War)
Thomas Paine
Maximilien Robespierre
Napoleon Bonaparte
Waterloo
Congress of Vienna
Pierre Toussaint L'Ouverture
Simón Bolívar
Miguel Hidalgo
Treaty of Cordoba
Mexican Revolution
Porfirio Díaz
Eli Whitney
Charles Darwin
Adam Smith
Karl Marx

Luddites
Opium War
Treaty of Nanjing
White Lotus Rebellions
Taiping Rebellions
Self-Strengthening Movement
Sino-Japanese War
Chinese Exclusion Act
Commodore Matthew Perry
Meiji Restoration
Boer War
Muhammad Ali
Suez Canal
Victor Emmanuel II
William I, William II
Otto von Bismarck
Franco-Prussian War
Emancipation Edict
Monroe Doctrine
Roosevelt Corollary
Panama Canal
Spanish-American War

Chapter 10 Drill

See the end of the chapter for the answers and explanations.

Questions 1–5 refer to the maps below.

Select World Empires, c. 1800

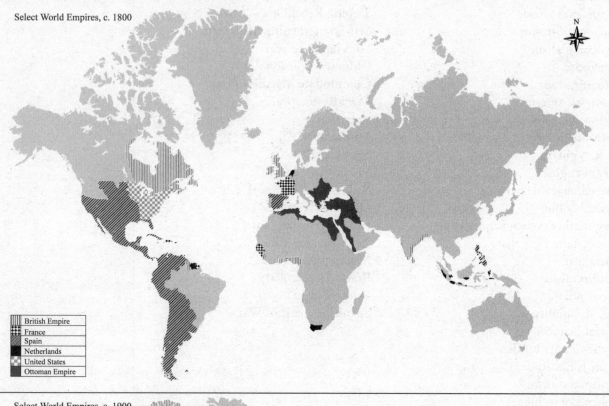

	British Empire
	France
	Spain
	Netherlands
	United States
	Ottoman Empire

Select World Empires, c. 1900

	Austria-Hungary
	France
	Germany
	British Empire
	Italy
	Netherlands
	Spain
	Ottoman Empire
	United States

1. Which of the following best explains the increasing extent of European empires during the eighteenth and nineteenth centuries, as indicated in the maps?

    (A) Increasing economic vitality generated by technological innovation resulted in population growth and allowed for larger, better-equipped armies.
    (B) Centuries of warfare in Europe led to European generals and soldiers becoming the best in the world.
    (C) Other states were generally weaker and more internally divided than they had been in the past, and European states capitalized on that advantage.
    (D) It was a purely cultural phenomenon; the European will to power overcame all obstacles.

2. Which of the following best summarizes the intellectual underpinnings of European colonialism?

    (A) Europeans believed that the divinely ordained order of things was for Europeans to rule the earth.
    (B) There were none; colonialism was the result of pure greed.
    (C) Europeans believed that resources belonged to those who could make the best use of them; thus, the factories of Europe had a claim to the resources of the world.
    (D) The most powerful societies (and races) were believed to be the most fit and therefore had an obligation to rule over inferior societies.

3. Which of the following best summarizes the driving impulses behind most movements of national unification?

    (A) Similar political structures and solidarity among the noble classes led to the imposition of national unification from above.
    (B) Popular feelings of similarity, driven by a shared language and culture, led to pressure for national unification from below.
    (C) Economic arguments about larger common markets and the value of currency unions swayed bourgeois opinion and brought about unification.
    (D) Nations, like empires, were conquered; national unification in Europe was driven primarily by warfare.

4. Which of the following most accurately characterizes the changes in the map of Europe between 1800 and 1900?

    (A) Increasing nationalist pressures drove the unification of German polities as well as the unification of Italian polities, while Poland was divided between Russia, Germany, and the Habsburg Monarchy.
    (B) The Habsburg Monarchy successfully united the German states behind its rule, while Poland agreed to unify with Russia and Italy became an independent state.
    (C) There were no substantial changes in the map of Europe between 1800 and 1900.
    (D) Following defeat by the Russians, the Habsburgs ceded much of the Balkan territories to the Ottoman Empire, while Germany and Italy became united, independent states.

5. Which of the following most accurately characterizes the changes in the map of North America between 1800 and 1900?

    (A) Canada's sale of Alaska to the United States complemented the results of the Louisiana Purchase and the Mexican-American War to lead to U.S. hegemony on the continent.
    (B) U.S. expansion to the west and south at the expense of France and Mexico led to the attainment of the present borders of the contiguous 48 states.
    (C) The collapse and disintegration of the Mexican Empire under Maximilian allowed Canadian and U.S. expansion into its former territories.
    (D) The Spanish-American War led to the United States occupying and annexing the bulk of Spanish imperial territories.

TIMELINE OF MAJOR DEVELOPMENTS, 1750–1900

	Americas	Europe	Africa	Mid East	South Asia	East Asia
		Enlightenment		Ottoman Empire		Manchu Dynasty
1750	French & Indian War (Seven Years' War)	Industrial Revolution			British in Bengal	
		Watt's Steam Engine				
1775	American Revolution	Louix XVI				
		French Revolution				
1800	Haitian Revolution / Mexican Independence		Slave Trade Abolished			
1825	Industrial Revolution	Congress of Vienna	British South Africa	Greece & Egypt Independence		
				French Algeria		Opium Wars
1850	Suffrage Movement / Mexican-American War	Communist Manifesto / Crimean War			Sepoy Revolt	Perry In Japan / French Indochina
		Emancipation of Serfs		Suez Canal		Meiji Restoration
1875	Civil War and Abolition	Italian & German Unification		Balkan Independence	Indian Nat'l Congress	Sino-Japan War
1900	Spanish-American War				Boxer Rebellion	

CHAPTER 10 DRILL EXPLANATIONS

1. **A**   Though this is a broad question, there are some straightforward ways to prune the answer choices. Choice (B) assumes that all other areas of the world had not experienced division and strife, which, while true for some areas over some times, does not describe this time period accurately. Similarly, (C) assumes that there was a novel and atypical degree of weakness and internal disunity across non-European states, which is an unwarranted assumption. Choice (D) makes an extreme claim—that it was only a cultural phenomenon. Extreme claims are typically incorrect, as, in this case, there are almost always multiple causes or influences on any historical phenomenon. Though cultural elements were likely relevant, the impact of the Industrial Revolution was far more relevant, so (A) is the best answer.

2. **D**   While European colonialism was certainly motivated at least in part by greed, that was not a core element in the intellectual underpinnings of the phenomenon, which would be important in determining against whom and to what extent such greed ought be exercised (among other things). So (B) doesn't work. Similarly, while religion was not irrelevant to colonialism, it was no longer the guiding principle of state policy in this era, if indeed it ever was. Therefore, (A) is incorrect. When comparing the last two answer choices, remember that the defining characteristic of European colonialism was the creation of a racial hierarchy. Only (D) speaks to the core issue and is thus the best answer.

3. **B**   Though commonalities of various kinds played a role in the rise of nationalism and ensuing national unification efforts, economics and political forms (whether a state was republican or monarchical in character, for example) were not substantial factors, and so (A) and (C) can be eliminated. Choice (D) may seem plausible, as many unification efforts did involve violence, but remember that the question is asking for what drove these movements, not how they were carried out. Thus, (B) is correct.

4. **A**   The most straightforward approach here is to use your knowledge of European history to eliminate incorrect answers. The map of Europe changed substantially over the nineteenth century, so (C) does not make sense. Though Poland did lose much of its territory to Russia, this was an involuntary process; similarly, Prussia united the German states, not Austria-Hungary. Therefore, (B) is incorrect. Choice (D) is partially right; Germany and Italy did become united independent states during this time, but the first clause flips the script. The Ottoman Empire lost much of its European territory to Austria-Hungary following a series of military defeats rather than the other way around, so (D) is incorrect. Choice (A) successfully accounts for the disappearance of Poland and the unifications of Germany and Italy, and is thus the best answer.

5. **B**   Be careful here; (A) is mostly correct, but remember that the U.S. bought Alaska from Russia, not from Canada. Choice (C) indicates that Mexico collapsed, which is incorrect. The Empire did end following Maximilian's execution, but the state itself neither collapsed nor disintegrated. While (D) is true in that the 1898 Spanish American War did lead to U.S. seizure of many of Spain's remaining colonial holdings, these were largely islands in Southeast Asia. There were no significant Spanish holdings on the North American continent by that time. Choice (B) correctly references the Louisiana Purchase and the Mexican-American War as leading to U.S. expansion in North America, and is therefore correct.

REFLECT

Respond to the following questions:

- For which content topics discussed in this chapter do you feel you have achieved sufficient mastery to answer multiple-choice questions correctly?

- For which content topics discussed in this chapter do you feel you have achieved sufficient mastery to discuss effectively in a short-answer response or essay?

- For which content topics discussed in this chapter do you feel you need more work before you can answer multiple-choice questions correctly?

- For which content topics discussed in this chapter do you feel you need more work before you can discuss effectively in a short-answer response or essay?

- What parts of this chapter are you going to re-review?

- Will you seek further help outside of this book (such as a teacher, tutor, or AP Students) on any of the content in this chapter—and, if so, on what content?

Chapter 11
Accelerating Global Change and Realignments, c. 1900 to Present

You've (Almost) Made It!
Now that you've made it all the way to the last period covered on the exam (1900 to present), you're in the home stretch! Reward yourself by taking a break before diving into this chapter.

I. CHAPTER OVERVIEW

From 1900 onward, everything seemed to have global significance. Wars were called "world wars." Issues were thought of in terms of their worldwide impact, such as "global hunger" or "international terrorism." Organizations formed to coordinate international efforts, such as the United Nations. Economies and cultures continued to merge to such a degree that eventually millions of people communicated instantaneously on the Internet, feeding a massive cultural shift known simply as "globalization."

It's a complex 116+ years. We'll help you sort through it. Here's how we organized this chapter.

I.   Chapter Overview

        You're reading it now.

II.   Stay Focused on the Big Picture

        This section will help you think about and organize the huge number of global events that have occurred over the past century.

III.   The Twentieth Century

        This is the largest section of the chapter. In it, we plow through historical developments in four massive chunks. If you're totally clueless on any part of this section, you might consider also reviewing the corresponding topic in your textbook. As you can see from the section titles, and as you hopefully remember from your history class, there were a bunch of very significant wars in the twentieth century. As you study, worry more about the causes and consequences than about particular battles, although with regard to World War II, it's important to understand the general sequence of military and political events, so we've included quite a bit. Here's how we've organized the information.

        A. The World War I Era
        B. The World War II Era
        C. Communism and the Cold War
        D. Independence Movements and Developments in Asia and Africa
        E. Globalization and the World Since 1980

IV.   Changes and Continuities in the Role of Women

        Finally, equal rights (in some places)

V.   Pulling It All Together

        Focus on big-picture concepts after you review the specific developments in the previous two sections.

II. STAY FOCUSED ON THE BIG PICTURE

As always, connections, causation, and big-picture concepts are important. As you review the details of the twentieth-century developments in this chapter, stay focused on the big picture, and ask yourself some questions, including the following:

1. How do nationalism and self-determination impact global events? As you review, notice how nationalism impacts almost every country that is discussed in this chapter. It serves as both a positive force in uniting people, and a negative force in pitting people against one another. Self-determination is closely linked with nationalism because it is the goal of most nationalists.

2. Are world cultures converging? If so, how? There's plenty of evidence that world cultures are, in fact, converging, especially with regard to technology, popular culture, and the Internet. On the other hand, there seems to be no shortage of nationalism or independence movements, which suggests that major differences exist. As you read the chapter, think about the forces that are making the cultures of the world converge and those that are keeping cultures separated.

3. How do increasing globalization, population growth, and resource use change the environment? Which resources are renewable and which are not? As the world grows ever more interconnected in trade and consumption of resources, think about what political, economic, and environmental decisions are made to maintain those trade relations.

III. THE TWENTIETH CENTURY

A. The World War I Era

At the beginning of the twentieth century, most of the world was either colonized by Europe, or was once colonized by Europe, so everyone around the world was connected to the instability on that small but powerful continent. This meant that when European powers were at war with each other, the colonies were dragged into the fight. To be sure, European rivalries had had a global impact for centuries, particularly during the colonial period. The Seven Years' War in the eighteenth century between the French and British, for example, impacted their colonial holdings everywhere. France, too, jumped in to help the U.S. in its revolution against the British. In 1914, a major fight among European powers had a far more substantial and destructive effect. The Industrial Revolution had given Europe some powerful new weapons plus the ships and airplanes that could be used to deliver them. Large industrial cities had millions of people, creating the possibility of massive casualties in a single bombing raid. A rise in nationalism fed a military build-up and the desire to use it. After the unifications of Germany and Italy, Europe simply had too many power-grabbing rivals. Not a good combination of factors if you like, well, peace.

Shifting Alliances: A Pre-War Tally of European Countries

In the decades leading up to World War I, the European powers tried to keep the balance of power in check by forming alliances. The newly unified Germany quickly gained industrial might, but it was worried that France, its archenemy since the Franco-Prussian War in 1870, would seek revenge for its defeat. So, before he resigned from office, Otto von Bismarck created and negotiated the **Triple Alliance** among Germany, Austria-Hungary, and Italy in the 1880s. On the side, Bismarck also had a pact with Russia. Otto played to win.

Over the next few decades, the major players of Europe became so obsessed with a possible war that their generals were already putting plans into motion in the event of an outbreak. After William II ousted Bismarck from power in 1890, he ignored Russia and allowed previous agreements between the two countries to wither. With Russia now on the market for friends, France jumped at the chance to make an alliance. With France to the west and Russia to the east, a Franco-Russo alliance helped keep Germany in check. Meanwhile, Germany's 1905 **Schlieffen Plan** called for a swift attack on France through Belgium, an officially neutral country that had a growing relationship with Britain. By 1907, Britain had also signed friendly agreements with France and Russia, creating what became known as the Triple Entente. Clearly, everyone was anticipating the possibility of war, which was a pretty safe bet considering the contentious climate.

Trouble in the Balkans

Remember the Ottoman Empire? In the first two decades of the twentieth century, it was still around, but it was in such bad shape that Europeans were calling it the "sick man of Europe." It kept losing territory to its neighbors. After Greece won its independence in 1829, the Slavic areas to the north of Greece, including Romania, Bulgaria, Serbia, and Montenegro began to win their independence as well. Bosnia and Herzegovina, however, were under the control of Austria-Hungary, as decided by the Berlin Conference of 1878, the same conference that led to the European scramble to colonize Africa. Serbia wanted Bosnia and Herzegovina for itself. To complicate matters, Russia was allied with Serbia, a fellow Slavic country.

It was in this political climate that **Archduke Franz Ferdinand** of Austria-Hungary visited Sarajevo, the capital of Bosnia, in 1914. While there, **Gavrilo Princip**, a Serbian nationalist, shot and killed the Archduke and his wife. In an age when Europe was so tightly wound in alliances, suspicion, and rivalry that a sneeze could have set off a war, the dominos quickly started to fall. Austria-Hungary declared war on Serbia. Russia, allied with Serbia, then declared war on Austria-Hungary. Because Russia and Austria-Hungary were on opposite sides of the Triple Entente–Triple Alliance divide, the pressure mounted on France, Italy, Germany, and Britain to join in. Britain was reluctant to honor its commitments at first, but when Germany implemented the Schlieffen Plan and stormed through Belgium toward France, Britain joined the fray in order to protect France. Italy, on the other hand, managed to wiggle out of its obligations and declared itself neutral, but the Ottoman Empire took its place, forming with Germany and Austria-Hungary an alliance called the **Central Powers**.

World War I: The War to End All Wars?

Europe on the Eve of World War I

Since the European powers had colonies or strong economic ties with most of the rest of the world, the original gunshot by a Serbian nationalist resulted in widespread casualties across the globe. More than 40 countries found themselves taking up arms, including Japan, which fought on the side of Britain, France, and Russia, now known as the Allies. In 1915, Italy managed to complete its about-face and joined the Allies as well.

The United States declared its neutrality at first, preferring to focus on its own internal affairs, a policy known as **isolationism.** When a German submarine (wow, technology came a long way quickly) sank the British passenger liner the *Lusitania* in 1915, killing more than 100 Americans who happened to be on board, public opinion in the United States shifted away from isolationism. The next year, as Germany tried to cut off all shipments to Britain, thereby starving the island country, it attacked U.S. merchant ships en route to Britain, further fueling American sentiment toward war. Then the **Zimmermann telegram**—a secret message sent between German diplomats suggesting that Mexico might want to join forces with Germany and thereby regain the territory it had lost to the United States in the Mexican-American War of 1846—was intercepted by Great Britain. U.S. President Woodrow Wilson learned of its contents soon after, and on April 2, 1917, America entered the war on the side of the Allies. On November 11, 1918, after brutal battles, trench warfare, and enormous loss of life, Germany and the Central Powers finally gave up.

The consequences of the war were staggering. Eight-and-a-half million soldiers were killed. Around 20 million civilians perished. The social impact on the home front was substantial as well. Most governments took over industrial production during the war, while instituting price controls and rationing of products that were needed on the front lines. With huge numbers of men taking up arms, women moved into the factories to fill empty positions. This experience revved up the women's suffrage movement, and became the basis for a successful push by women in Britain and the United States to gain the vote after the war.

Of course, World War II hadn't happened yet, so no one referred to the war as World War I. Instead, most people called it the Great War, mistakenly thinking that there would never again be one as big or bloody. Indeed, the war was so horrendous that commentators called it "the war to end all wars."

The "War to End All Wars"

At the time, commentators referred to the Great War (World War I) as "the war to end all wars." They never imagined that another war would ravage the continent in less than two decades—a war that was even more devastating.

The Treaty of Versailles

Signed in 1919, the **Treaty of Versailles** brought an official end to World War I. France and Britain wanted to cripple Germany economically, so that it could never again rise to power and threaten to invade other sovereign states of Europe. The resulting treaty was extremely punitive against Germany, which was required to pay war reparations, release territory, and downsize its military. It also divided Austria-Hungary into separate nations, and created other nations such as Czechoslovakia. The treaty was a departure from President Wilson's **Fourteen Points**, which were more focused on establishing future peace and a workable balance of power. However, Britain and France, for example, needed to justify the human and financial cost and duration of the war to their own demoralized populations and so found Wilson's proposal unacceptable. The victors blamed the war on Germany and then forced Germany to sign an extremely punitive treaty over the objections of the United States. The victors hoped that as a result, Germany would never threaten the security of Europe again. Instead, the treaty greatly weakened Germany's economy and bred resentment among the German population, laying the groundwork for the later rise of Adolf Hitler.

The League of Nations: Can't We All Just Get Along?

President Wilson was the voice of moderation at Versailles. He had hoped that the postwar treaties would be an opportunity to establish international laws and standards of fairness in international conduct. His Fourteen Points speech addressed these issues and called for the creation of a joint council of nations called the **League of Nations**. The leaders at Versailles agreed with the idea in principle, and they set out to create the organization to preserve peace and establish humanitarian goals, but when they got around to actually joining the league, many nations refused. England and France were tepid, while Germany and Russia initially scoffed at the idea (though later joined). Worse, the United States openly rejected it, a major embarrassment for President Wilson, who couldn't persuade the isolationist U.S. Congress that the league was a step toward lasting peace.

The Russian Revolution: Czar Out, Lenin In

By the time Nicholas II reigned (1894–1917), revolution was in the wind. The Socialists began to organize. Nicholas tried to rally Russians around the flag by going to war with Japan over Manchuria in 1904, but the Russians suffered a humiliating defeat. On a Sunday in 1905, moderates marched on the czar's palace in a peaceful protest, an attempt to encourage him to enact Enlightened reforms, but Nicholas felt threatened and ordered his troops to fire on the protestors. The day has since been known as Bloody Sunday.

For the next decade, resentment among the working classes festered. In 1906, the czar attempted to enact legislative reforms by appointing a Prime Minister, Peter Stolypin, and by creating the Duma, a body intended to represent the Russian people, but every time the Duma was critical of the czar, he immediately disbanded it. In the end, the attempts at reform were too little, too late. The Romanov Dynasty would soon come to an end.

The **Russian Revolution** occurred even before World War I had ended. Russia entered the war with the world's largest army, though not the world's most powerful one, because the nation was not nearly as industrialized as its Western neighbors. Very quickly, the army began to suffer large-scale losses and found itself short on food, munitions, and good leadership. In February 1917, in the face of rising casualties and food shortages, **Czar Nicholas** was forced to abdicate his throne. The Romanov Dynasty came to an end. Under **Alexander Kerensky**, a provisional government was established. It was ineffectual, in part because it shared power with the local councils, called soviets, which represented the interests of workers, peasants, and soldiers. Although the provisional government affirmed natural rights (such as the equality of citizens and the principle of religious toleration—changes that were inconceivable under the czar), it wanted to continue war against Germany in the hope that Russia could then secure its borders and become a liberal democracy. The working classes, represented by the soviets, were desperate to end the suffering from the war. The idealism of the provisional officials caused them to badly miscalculate the depths of hostility the Russian people felt for the czar's war.

By 1918, the soviets rallied behind the socialist party, now called the **Bolsheviks**. Amid this turmoil, **Vladimir Lenin**, the Marxist leader of the party, mobilized the support of the workers and soldiers. He issued his **April Theses**, which demanded peace, land for peasants, and power to the soviets. Within six months, the Bolsheviks took command of the government. Under his vision of mass socialization, Lenin rigidly set about nationalizing the assets and industries of Russia. In March 1918, the soviets signed an armistice with Germany, the **Treaty of Brest-Litovsk**, which ceded a huge piece of western Russia to Germany, so Russia dropped out of World War I. It therefore wasn't part of the negotiations during the Treaty of Versailles.

In the Baltic republics of what would soon be called the **Soviet Union**, and in the Ukraine, Siberia, and other parts of the former Russian Empire, counterrevolutionary revolts broke out. The Bolsheviks faced nonstop skirmishes between 1918 and 1921. To put down these struggles, the Bolsheviks created the **Red Army**, a military force under the command of **Leon Trotsky**. By 1918, the Red Army was a sizeable force, and with the support of the peasants, it defeated the counterrevolutionaries. The counterrevolution had two lasting implications. First, the prolonged civil war deepened the distrust between the new Marxist state and its Western neighbors, who had supported the counterrevolutionaries. Second, the Bolsheviks now had a very powerful army, the Red Army, at its disposal.

Here Come the Turks

The Ottoman Empire, already on its last legs, made a fatal mistake by joining the losing Central Powers of World War I. In the peace negotiations, it lost most of its remaining land, and was therefore ripe for attack from the Greeks, who picked up arms in 1919. **Mustafa Kemal**, who later became known as **Ataturk**, "the Father of the Turks," led successful military campaigns against the Greeks, and then overthrew the Ottoman sultan. In 1923, Ataturk became the first president of modern Turkey. He successfully secularized the overwhelmingly Muslim nation, introduced Western-style dress and customs (abolishing the fez), changed the alphabet from Arabic to Latin, set up a parliamentary system (which he dominated), changed the legal code from Islamic to Western, and set Turkey on a path toward Europe as opposed to the Middle East. However, he instituted these reforms against opposition, and sometimes was ruthless in his determination to institute change.

B. The World War II Era

The Great War Part II
Even though World War II didn't get started until 1939, its causes were already well underway in the 1920s. In some ways, World War II isn't a separate war from World War I, but instead the Great War Part II.

Stalin: The Soviet Union Goes Totalitarian

Once the Soviets removed themselves from World War I, they concentrated on their own domestic problems. Lenin first instituted the **New Economic Policy (NEP)** in the early 1920s, which had some capitalistic aspects, such as allowing farmers to sell portions of their grain for their own profit. The plan was successful in agriculture, but Lenin didn't live long enough to chaperone its expansion into other parts of the Soviet economy. When Lenin died, the leadership of the Communist Party shifted to **Joseph Stalin**.

Stalin believed the NEP was ridiculously slow, so he discarded it. Instead, he imposed his **Five Year Plans**, which called for expedient agricultural production by ruthlessly taking over private farms and combining them into state-owned enterprises, a process known as **collectivization**. The plans also advocated for the construction of large, nationalized factories. This process was achieved in the name of communism, but it was really totalitarianism. The people didn't share in the power or the profits, and had no choices regarding participation. Untold numbers died fighting to protect their farms. Even more died in famines that resulted when Stalin usurped crops to feed government workers at the expense of the farmers themselves.

Stalin's plans successfully industrialized the **USSR (Union of Soviet Socialist Republics)**, the formal name for the Soviet Union, and improved economic conditions for the country as a whole, but Stalin relied on terror tactics, such as a secret police force, bogus trials, and assassinations. These murders peaked between 1936 and 1938. Collectively, they are sometimes referred to as the "Great Purge" because the government systematically killed so many of its enemies. Stalin also established labor camps to punish anyone who opposed him.

The Great Depression: Capitalism Crashes, Germany Burns

World War I was shockingly expensive. Countries spent more than $180 billion on armaments, boats, and trench warfare. Europe spent an additional $150 billion rebuilding. The massive scale of the war meant massive spending, at a level that nations had never experienced previously, and in the years following World War I, capitalism financed most of the recovery. As a consequence, the financial headquarters of the world shifted from London to New York, which had become a major center of credit to Europe during and after the war. In other words, Americans lent Europeans money, and lots of it.

In particular, the economies of two countries relied on American credit: France and Germany. France had loaned huge sums of money to Russia, its prewar ally, but the Bolshevik government refused to honor the czar's debts, leaving France almost out of luck, except that Germany owed it a bunch of cash as well. Germany experienced extreme financial hardship because of the wartime reparations they were required to make under the Treaty of Versailles. Germany's answer was to use American credit to pay its reparations by issuing I.O.U.s to countries like France. France took these "payments," backed up by American credit and spent them on rebuilding its economy. From 1924 to 1929, this arrangement looked great on paper due to growth in both the United States and European economies. In many ways, the growth was artificial, based on loans that were never going to be repaid.

When the U.S. stock market crashed in October 1929, a spiral of monetary and fiscal problems called the **Great Depression** quickly escalated into an international catastrophe, and shattered the illusion of financial health in Europe. American banks immediately stopped extending credit. The effect was that Europe ran out of money, which it never really had in the first place. Germany couldn't pay its reparations without American credit, so France had no money either.

The depths of the depression were truly staggering. The United States and Germany were hit hardest. In both countries, almost one-third of the available workforce was unemployed. In the United States, out-of-work Americans rejected the dominant political party and in 1932 elected **Franklin Roosevelt** as president in a landslide election. Other countries had much more fragile political structures. In places where democracy had shallow roots, such as Germany and Italy, whose shaky elective assemblies had been created only a decade earlier after World War I, the crisis resulted in the triumph of a political ideology that was anathema to the very spirit of democracy: fascism.

It's hard to know for sure how many Soviet citizens were imprisoned or killed during the 1930s, especially because so many died as a result of famine during the collectivization process, but historians agree that millions of Soviets were slaughtered under Stalin's direction.

Fascism Gains Momentum

Between the First and Second World Wars, fascist parties emerged across Europe. They did not possess identical sets of beliefs, but they held a few important ideas in common. The main idea of **fascism** was to destroy the will of the individual in favor of "the people." Fascists wanted a unified society (as did the communists), but they weren't concerned with eliminating private property or class distinctions (the principal aim of communists). Instead, fascists pushed for another identity, one rooted in extreme **nationalism**, which often relied on racial identity.

Contrast Them: Fascism and Totalitarianism

Fascism is a subset of totalitarianism. A totalitarian dictator rules absolutely, attempting to control every aspect of life. Fascist rulers are a particular kind of totalitarian ruler, often regarded as extremely right-wing because they rely on traditional institutions and social distinctions to enforce their rule, and are extremely nationalistic. Their particular brand of nationalism is often based on racism. Communist totalitarian leaders like Stalin are often referred to as extreme left-wing because they seek to destroy traditional institutions and class distinctions, even as they retain absolute power themselves. Therefore, they're not referred to as fascist, but they're just as militaristic and controlling. Put another way, in their extreme forms, right-wing (fascist) and left-wing (communist) governments use the same tactics: totalitarianism. In both cases, all power rests in the hands of a single militaristic leader.

Fascism in Italy: Another Step Toward Another War

Italy was the first state to have a fascist government. The founder and leader was **Benito Mussolini**, who created the National Fascist Party in 1919. The party paid squads, known as **Blackshirts**, to fight socialist and communist organizations, an action that won over the loyalty of both factory owners and landowners. By 1921, the party seated its first members in the Italian parliament.

Although the fascists held only a few seats in the legislature, Mussolini demanded that King Victor Emmanuel III name him and several other fascists to cabinet posts. To rally support, Mussolini organized his paramilitary thugs to march to Rome and possibly attempt to seize power. If the king had declared martial law and brought in the army, most believe that the fascists would have scattered. However, the king was a timid man—facing economically troubling times—who was not unsympathetic to the fascist program. So, he named Mussolini prime minister, and the fascist march on Rome turned into a celebration.

As the postwar economy failed to improve, Italy was demoralized. Mussolini faced very little opposition to his consolidation of political power. He dabbled as a parliamentary leader for several months before completely taking over Parliament in 1922. He then implemented a number of constitutional changes to ensure that democracy no longer limited his actions, and, by 1926, Italy was transformed into a totalitarian fascist regime. To rally the people in a nationalistic cause, Italy started to focus on expansion, specifically in North Africa.

The Rise of Hitler

Immediately following the end of World War I, a revolt occurred in Germany when the emperor abdicated. Germany might well have become socialist at this point. Workers' and soldiers' councils (not unlike Russian soviets) formed in cities like Berlin. However, because the middle class in Germany was quite conservative and a large number of Germans had been relatively prosperous before the war, a socialist or communist system was rejected in favor of a fairly conservative democratic republic, called the **Weimar Republic**.

At the same time, Germany was in economic crisis, and Mussolini's success influenced Germany in many ways. The **National Socialist Party (Nazis)** rose to power in the 1920s, ushered in by the worldwide depression. As Germany's economy collapsed under the harsh reparations dictated by the Treaty of Versailles and the faltering world economy, German people increasingly rejected the solutions of the Weimar Republic's elected body, the **Reichstag**.

During this period **Adolf Hitler** rose to power as head of the Nazi Party. Like Mussolini's fascism, Hitler's Nazism inspired extreme nationalism and the dreams of renewed greatness for a depressed and divided country. Hitler's philosophies differed from Mussolini's in their emphasis on the superiority of one race over others. Well versed in social Darwinism, Hitler was convinced that the Aryan race was the most highly evolved race, and that "inferior" races, such as Slavs and Jews, had "corrupted" the German race. He argued that Jews should be deported (later that changed to "eliminated") and that Germans should take over Europe.

The Nazi Party gained political power in the 1920s with Hitler as its guide, or *führer*. At first, the Nazis received votes democratically and participated in the Reichstag. In the early 1930s, as the Great Depression devastated the German economy, Hitler received increasing support. In the election of 1930, the Nazi Party increased its seats in Parliament tenfold. By 1932, the Nazis dominated German government and many who disagreed with Hitler still backed him, thinking he was the country's only hope. In 1933, Hitler became chancellor, or leader of the Reichstag. He then seized control of the government, known under his fascist rule as the **Third Reich**, and set his eyes on conquering Europe.

Contrast Them: Nationalism in Europe and in Its Colonies

Nationalism was a driving force throughout much of the nineteenth and twentieth centuries, but it had a very different flavor in Europe and Japan than in most European and Japanese colonies. In Europe and Japan, nationalism fueled extreme racism, fascism, and domination. National pride became almost synonymous with national expansion and conquest of other peoples. In the colonies, nationalism meant self-determination, the ability to free the nation from rule by another and determine one's own destiny. National pride meant national sovereignty, not colonial or territorial expansion.

Appeasement: "Peace for Our Time," or Just Wishful Thinking?

EUROPE
AS of JUNE 6, 1944

■ GERMAN OCCUPIED AREAS
■ ALLIED AREAS
□ NEUTRAL COUNTRIES

In 1933, Hitler began to rebuild the German military. This was a clear violation of the Treaty of Versailles—which was specifically intended to limit future German aggression—but the other nations of Europe, especially Britain and France, chose not to object, fearing another war. Later that year, Germany again snubbed world opinion by withdrawing from the League of Nations.

Meanwhile, Spain, which had established a parliamentary democracy in 1931, was in turmoil following the fall of the Spanish monarchy. In the summer of 1936, a group of army officers under the leadership of General **Francisco Franco** took control of large parts of Spain. Democratic loyalists organized to defend the state, and a brutal and divisive civil war ensued. Germany and Italy supported Franco's troops, called "nationalists." Although Franco was not a fascist, the Germans and Italians believed that the defeat of democracy in Spain was a step in the right direction.

France and Great Britain, still scarred from the loss of life and money in the Great War, adopted a nonintervention policy and refused to aid the supporters of the Spanish democracy. By 1939, Franco's troops captured Madrid and installed a dictatorship in Spain that managed to stay neutral throughout the war that soon erupted in Europe. The message was clear: Germany and Italy were more than willing to exercise their influence and support antidemocratic uprisings.

Meanwhile back in Germany in 1935, Hitler continued his policy of restoring Germany to its former world-power status by taking back the **Rhineland**, a region west of the Rhine River that had been taken away from Germany after World War I. Still, the rest of Europe stayed quiet. In 1937, he formed an alliance with the increasingly militant Japan. Then, in 1938, he annexed Austria and moved to reclaim the Sudetenland from Czechoslovakia. At the **Munich Conference of 1938**, which included Hitler, Mussolini, and Prime Minister **Neville Chamberlain** of England, Hitler was given the Sudetenland, without the consent of Czechoslovakia, in return for the promise to cease his expansionist activities. This incredibly optimistic (some would say stupid) policy is known as **appeasement**. Chamberlain agreed to give Hitler what he wanted as a means of avoiding war, believing German claims that it would be satisfied with Austria and the northern half of Czechoslovakia and would not expand further. Hitler, in fact, did stop his expansion—for one whole year. In 1939, Hitler invaded the remaining territories in Czechoslovakia.

The rest of Europe was shocked but didn't do anything to kick the Nazis out of Czechoslovakia. Instead, in March 1939, while Italy was invading Albania, Britain and France signed a non-aggression pact with Greece, Turkey, Romania, and Poland that provided that if any one of them were attacked, they'd all go to war.

Meanwhile, the Germans signed the **Nazi-Soviet Pact** in August of 1939. Stalin and Hitler agreed that Germany would not invade the Soviet Union if the Soviets stayed out of Germany's military affairs. Furthermore, the countries determined how Eastern Europe would be divided among them, giving Lithuania and eastern Poland to Germany and the remainder of Poland and Finland and the Baltic States to Russia. Stalin got a measure of security, and Hitler got a clear path by which to take Poland. With a secure agreement with the Soviet Union, German forces marched into Poland. Two days later, Britain realized that all diplomacy had failed and declared war on Germany, and France reluctantly followed suit. World War II had begun.

Meanwhile, in Japan...

Remember in the last chapter, when we discussed the Meiji Restoration and how Japan defeated China in a war for control of Korea and Taiwan, thus making Japan an imperial power? Well, later on after the Russo-Japanese War of 1904, the victorious Japanese kicked Russia out of Manchuria and established its own sphere of influence there. As if demonstrating that Japan was now an equal among European states, the British offered them an alliance in 1905, a treaty the Japanese gratefully accepted. Japan was now not just an imperial power but a world power.

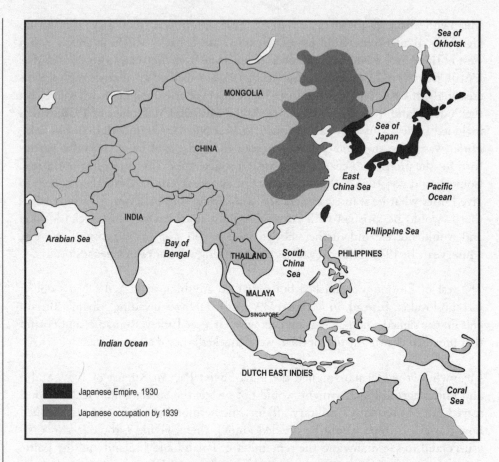

Japanese Territory by 1939

After World War I, in which Japan fought on the side of the Allies and was therefore one of the victors, Japan's economy and military really started to thrive. In 1915, during World War I, Japan sent a list of twenty-one demands to China, requiring China to give it trading rights and outright control over aspects of the government and economy, an act that was even more aggressive than some of the spheres of influence that had been established (and were still in effect) by the Europeans. In the 1920s, the country backtracked a little bit and focused on internal developments, softening its position toward China. By 1930, the Great Depression began to severely affect Japan and the Japanese militarists gained momentum, claiming that an empire would pull them out of the economic doldrums. In 1931, Japan invaded Manchuria, renaming it **Manchukuo** and establishing a colony there. After withdrawing from the League of Nations, Japan signed the **Anti-Comintern Pact** (against communism, specifically in Russia) with Germany in 1936, thereby forming the beginnings of an alliance that would eventually lead to a more formal one during World War II. In 1937, Japanese troops invaded China, pillaging towns and cities as they made their way down the eastern shore. One of the worst offenses was the aptly named "Rape of Nanjing," where in the city of Nanjing nearly 250,000 Chinese were slaughtered in a matter of a few weeks by occupying Japanese forces. Japan's war with China eventually merged into the global conflagration of World War II that later started to burn in Europe.

A Quick Review of World War II

Hitler's forces were devastating. Their war tactic, known as **blitzkrieg** (literally "lightning war"), destroyed everything in its path with historically unprecedented speed. Poland's flat open plains were tragically well-suited for the German run. The swiftly moving German forces acquired so much territory in the west of Poland that Stalin was forced to mobilize quickly lest he lose the entire country to the German Reich. Within ten days, Germany and Russia had divided Poland between them. Hitler then focused on the western front. In early 1940, Germany assaulted Holland and Belgium. Two days later, German forces entered France. Within a year, the Axis power controlled most of continental Europe.

Hitler assumed that Great Britain would crumble quickly after the fall of its ally, France. But a new leader, **Winston Churchill**, replaced Britain's more diplomatically minded Chamberlain. Churchill proved to be a resolute and fierce prime minister. He refused to cut a deal with Germany, so Hitler launched a massive air bombing campaign in 1940 known as the **Battle of Britain**, which pitted the superior numbers of the German air force against the smaller numbers of the Royal Air Force. The British succeeded in keeping the German army out, and with their newly devised handy tool known as radar, they managed a successful, though costly, defense of the island.

In the meantime, Italy attacked Greece but was unable to defeat the country until April 1941, when German armies rushed in to help out. The Nazi-Soviet Pact tacitly gave the Balkan state to Russia, so the takeover of Greece had serious consequences. Now that Germany had taken control of the Balkans, their previous agreement was moot, so they invaded the Soviet Union too for good measure, advancing quickly. The resulting movement of men and supplies into the Soviet Union relieved pressure on the desperate British, the only Allied nation still fighting (other than the Soviet Union, of course).

Meanwhile in the Pacific, Japan continued its expansion in China and invaded Indochina (Vietnam). For trade reasons, the United States viewed this action as hostile, but the United States still didn't want to get involved in the war, so it froze Japanese assets in the United States and imposed sanctions instead. At the same time, Japan entered into the **Tripartite Pact** with Rome and Berlin, ensuring worldwide implications for a war that had, up until that time, been two regional wars. Japan also planned to declare war against the United States if the U.S. refused to lift sanctions against Japan. The United States didn't, and on December 7, 1941, the Japanese bombed a U.S. naval station in Hawaii at **Pearl Harbor**. The United States was stunned, and promptly declared war against Japan, and in response, Germany declared war against the United States.

It took a while for the United States and Great Britain to coordinate a land attack against Germany because they needed a foothold in Europe from which to begin their assault. In the meantime, the Allies fought the Japanese in the Pacific and Germans and Italians in Africa while the United States also secretly worked on its **Manhattan Project**—the development of an atomic bomb. By 1943, the United States and Britain were ready for their European offensive, and they started it by taking control of Italy. The next year, English, American, and Canadian forces launched their biggest offensive, landing on the French beaches of Normandy on June 6, 1944, which is now known as **D-day**. With the help of French resistance forces, Allied Forces battled their way across northern France in the summer of 1944 and liberated France.

On the opposite side of Europe, the Red Army won a stunning victory against the Germans at Stalingrad in 1942 and advanced steadily west for three years. By May 1945, the Allied forces closed in on Hitler's troops from the eastern and the western fronts until they reached Berlin, ending the European theater of World War II. Hitler committed suicide.

The war in the Pacific continued to drag on for a few months. At great cost, the American forces defeated Japan from island to island in the South Pacific. But the Japanese refused to surrender, even though their fate was sealed. Believing that dropping an atomic bomb on Japan would end World War II quickly and result in fewer casualties than a prolonged war, **President Truman** of the United States ordered the dropping of an atomic bomb on the city of **Hiroshima** on August 6, 1945. The event marked the first time such a bomb had been used in warfare. The result was horrendous. More than 100,000 people were killed or injured and the city was completely leveled for miles. When the Japanese vowed to fight on, President Truman authorized the dropping of a second bomb on **Nagasaki** on August 9 with similar consequences. Japan finally surrendered and World War II was brought to a close.

The Consequences: So Much Changed!

The close of World War II brought with it enormous global changes. Since they are so numerous, it's best to think about them in broad categories.

The Holocaust Revealed

Outside of Germany, few knew just how horrible the Nazi regime was until after the war was over. In an ongoing slaughter known now as the **Holocaust**, but known in Nazi Germany as "The Final Solution," millions of Jews who lived in Germany and German-occupied lands were rounded up, blamed for every conceivable problem in society, and methodically killed in gas chambers and firing lines, their bodies disposed of in ovens and mass graves. As many as 6 million Jews were killed, making the Holocaust one of the largest acts of genocide in history (in addition, as many as 6 million Poles, Slavs, Gypsies, homosexuals, disabled people, and political dissidents were killed in the Holocaust). When the news of the atrocity spread after the war, public sympathy for the creation of Israel as a homeland for Jews rose sharply. More on that later.

The Peace Settlement

The United States and the Soviet Union became superpowers. Germany was occupied by the Allies—more on that later too. War crimes tribunals were established to prosecute and sentence Nazi officials. Japan was forced to demilitarize and establish a democracy. It did. It also embraced capitalism and became an economic powerhouse within a decade, but this time was friendly to the West.

Europe Torn to Shreds

In addition to a staggering loss of life (the Soviet Union alone lost more than 20 million soldiers and civilians), the infrastructure and communities of Europe were devastated. To help in the rebuilding effort, the United States instituted the **Marshall Plan** (named for George C. Marshall, the secretary of state who conceived of it) in 1947. The plan, in which billions of dollars of American money was made available for reconstruction, was offered to all European countries but only accepted by Western European nations. The plan worked: The economies of Western Europe recovered in less than a decade.

The Decline of Colonialism

European imperialism was already on the wane before World War II, but the war affected attitudes about empire, and inspired native populations to rise up against their oppressors. Much more on the decline of colonialism later in this chapter.

Big Changes for Women

Just as in World War I, in many countries, women worked outside the home during the war, raising money to support themselves or their families, while also helping the war effort. In Britain alone, more than three-fourths of adult women under age 40 were employed during the war. After the war, many women kept their jobs, or sought higher education, or otherwise began to broaden their horizons.

The Creation of International Organizations

After World War II, the Allies believed that a network of international organizations could reduce the probability that such a great war would break out again. The first of these international organizations was the **United Nations**, established in 1945 to replace the failed League of Nations. Given more muscle than the League of Nations, the primary goal of the UN was simple: to mediate, and if necessary to intervene in, international disputes between nations. As time passed, the UN expanded beyond the realm of political conflicts and increasingly involved itself in the monitoring of human rights and other social problems. In addition to the UN, the World Bank, the International Monetary Fund, and the General Agreement on Trade and Tariffs (now known as the World Trade Organization), were formed to create and manage a more integrated global economy. The Allies believed that countries that were more connected economically would be less likely to invade one another.

The Start of the Cold War

Although they were allies during the war, the United States and the Soviet Union had very different worldviews. One was democratic and capitalist, the other totalitarian and communist. Neither wanted the other to spread its influence beyond its borders, so even before the war ended, they were strategizing on how to contain each other. This strategizing lasted for nearly 50 years, and the following section in this chapter explains the consequences.

C. Communism and the Cold War

The Cold War in Europe

No One Saw It Coming
In 1945, no one would have predicted how polarized the world would become during the Cold War, or that a cold war would even develop in the first place.

The **Cold War** lasted from 1945 through the early 1990s. Very few areas of the globe were unaffected. The two superpowers that emerged after World War II, the United States and the Soviet Union, not only vied for global domination, but also tried to pull the rest of the world into their standoff. Every time a government in any country across the globe changed hands, the Americans and Soviets evaluated it based on its leanings toward one side or the other, and in many cases actually tried to militarily influence the position it would take. All of this took place in the context of an arms race between the two superpowers in which nuclear arsenals became so massive that a global holocaust became possible at the touch of a button.

Power Grab:
Soviets and Americans Want Everyone to Take Sides

After Germany was defeated, the U.S.-Soviet struggle immediately influenced the chain of events. The biggest conflict was over future security. Both superpowers wanted arrangements in Europe that made it more likely for their worldview to dominate. The U.S. promoted capitalism and variations on democracy. The Soviet Union promoted communism, which, as practiced by the Soviets at the time, also meant totalitarianism. A good chunk of Western Europe was solidly in the American camp, but the bigger question was Germany and parts of Eastern Europe.

According to plans drawn up by the Allies during conferences at **Yalta** and **Potsdam**, in February and July 1945 respectively, Germany and other parts of Eastern Europe were divided into temporary "spheres of influence," each to be occupied and rebuilt by respective members of the Allied forces. Germany was divided into four regions, each under the influence of one of four Allies: France, Britain, the United States, and the Soviet Union. Determined to protect its borders and ideology, the Soviet Union demanded that its neighboring states, places like Poland, Czechoslovakia, Hungary, Romania, and Bulgaria, be under its influence as well. The United States wanted those nations to have free elections. The Soviet Union refused and simply set up puppet states in those countries. This was the first hint of the beginning of the Cold War.

Meanwhile, in Germany in 1948, the French, British, and American regions merged into one, forming a democratic West Germany, while the Soviet Union's region became East Germany. The capital, Berlin, was on the eastern side, and within that city, an eastern and western zone were created. The Soviets wanted all of Berlin to be within its control, so they cut off land access to Berlin from the west, an action known as the **Berlin Blockade**. The West retaliated by flying in food and fuel to the "trapped" western half of the city, an action known as the **Berlin Airlift**. Eventually, the Soviets relented and Berlin was divided in half. In 1961, the Soviets built a wall between the two halves, preventing East Berliners access to the West until the wall fell in 1989 (more on that later).

East Versus West

By the late 1940s, Europe was clearly divided into East and West, each under the influence of their respective superpowers.

East Germany, Poland, Czechoslovakia, Romania, and Hungary became part of the Eastern bloc, also called the **Soviet bloc** or Soviet satellites. Yugoslavia was communist as well, but established its own path, having testy relations with Moscow. Western Europe, including Britain, France, Italy, Belgium, the Netherlands, Norway, West Germany, and eventually Greece and Turkey, became part of the **Western bloc**.

Under the **Truman Doctrine** of 1947, the United States explicitly stated that it would aid countries threatened by communist takeovers. This policy is known as **containment**, as in "containing" your enemy. To this end, the Western bloc formed a military alliance of mutual defense called **NATO** (the North Atlantic Treaty Organization). In response, the Eastern bloc formed a military alliance known as the **Warsaw Pact**. For more than 40 years, the two alliances loaded their borders with weapons, first conventional, then nuclear, and dared the other to strike first. Churchill called the line between East and West the **Iron Curtain** because Western influence couldn't penetrate it and Easterners were rarely allowed to go to the Western bloc.

As for the rest of the world, the two superpowers quickly tried to influence developments to tip the balance of world power in their favor. Some countries allied with one side or the other (more on this later), but other countries, such as India, refused to take sides and sometimes accepted investment from both, a policy known as nonalignment.

Focus On: Nuclear Proliferation

Ever improving weapons technology was the force behind political strength in the twentieth century. This was true from the devastated battlefields of World War I to the hot spots and standoffs of the Cold War. Beginning with the atomic bombs dropped on Japan in 1945, the Eastern and Western superpowers raced to develop superior weapons and defensive technologies. Despite attempts to limit nuclear technology to just five powers (China, Russia, U.S.A., Great Britain, and France) through the **Nuclear Nonproliferation Treaty** (1968) and the watchdog **International Atomic Energy Agency or IAEA** (1957), weapons development continued even after the collapse of the Soviet Union. Israel, India, and Pakistan chose not to participate in the treaty and now each has some nuclear weapons capacity. North Korea has continued to develop nuclear material in violation of treaty terms and both Iraq and Iran have attempted to build uranium enrichment programs. Only South Africa has voluntarily dismantled its nuclear weapons program.

The Cold War affected different countries in different ways. On the next several pages, you'll review how it impacted China, Korea, Vietnam, Cuba, and Europe.

China: Communists Make Huge Gains

China changed a lot after the fall of the Manchu Dynasty in 1911. Under the leadership of **Sun Yat-sen**, who led the **Chinese Revolution of 1911**, China became more Westernized in an effort to gain power and boot out the Europeans and Japanese, who had established spheres of influence in the country. Sun Yat-sen promoted his **Three Principles of the People**—nationalism, socialism, and democracy. It was hoped that nationalism would unite the people against foreign interests and give them a Chinese identity, state capitalism, or industrialization financed by the government, was useful in order to improve economic productivity and efficiency while not necessarily redistributing wealth, something Sun did not agree with. Although he advocated for a democratic system, Sun Yat-sen established a political party, the **Kuomindang (or KMT)**, which was dedicated to his own goals.

Sun Yat-sen didn't live long enough to see his plans implemented. His successor, however, **Chiang Kai-shek**, established the KMT as the ruling party of China, but only for a while. Throughout the 1920s and 1930s, two forces wreaked havoc on Chiang's plans. The Japanese Empire invaded Manchuria and made an effort to take over all of China in the late 1930s. Meanwhile, the communists, allied with the Soviet Union, were building strength in northern China. The communists joined the KMT in its fight against the Japanese, but at the same time were bitter rivals of the Kuomindang in the struggle to control the future of China.

During World War II, the United States pumped money into the KMT's efforts against Japan, while the Soviets weren't as active in their support for the communists' efforts against Japan, partly because they were focused on Germany. As you know, Japan was defeated. As in Europe, after the war, the powers of democracy and communism clashed, and the KMT and communists continued to fight the Chinese Civil War for the next four years.

By 1949, the communists under **Mao Zedong** had rallied millions of peasants in northern China and swept southward toward the Kuomindang strongholds, driving the Kuomindang farther and farther south until they finally fled to the island of Taiwan, where they established the **Republic of China**. The impact for mainland China was enormous. It became the **People's Republic of China**, the largest communist nation in the world under the leadership of Mao Zedong. The two Chinas have been separate ever since, and both claim to be the "real" China. Taiwan eventually developed into an economic powerhouse, but it lost its credibility as the true China when the United Nations and eventually the United States recognized the People's Republic of China as China in 1973. Taiwan has rejected China's efforts toward reunification, but nevertheless the two nations have grown close together, especially as the economies of both nations have grown stronger and stronger.

Mao Zedong: His Own Way

After the success of the Communist Revolution in China in 1949, its leader, Mao Zedong, collectivized agriculture and industry and instituted sweeping social reform using policies that were not unlike Stalin's five-year plans. Most of these plans were relatively successful, and China greatly increased its productivity, especially in the steel industry. By the late 1950s, Mao implemented his **Great Leap Forward**, in which huge communes were created as a way of catapulting the revolution toward its goal of a true Marxist state. In reality, however, the local governments that ran the communes couldn't produce the ridiculously high agricultural quotas demanded by the central government. These local governments did what any fearful local government would—they lied about their production, leading to the starvation deaths of nearly 30 million Chinese people. By all accounts, it was more like a Great Stumble Backward. The successes of Mao's initiatives in the early 1950s were erased, and agriculture and industry failed to produce results. Part of the problem was that the Soviet Union—up until that time the only foreign supporter of China—pulled away and eventually withdrew its support. The Soviet Union not only wanted the world to become communist, but it wanted the world to be communist under its control. China wasn't following orders, so Soviet support for China cooled. The Sino-Soviet split left China on its own with its communal system in disarray.

Mao stepped back to focus on building the military—something that was essential if the country couldn't rely on Soviet support—while more moderate reformers tried to turn the country around. The progress was quick and substantial; elements of capitalism were introduced into the economy and, in 1964, China tested its first atomic bomb, adding to the global arms race that was quickly building around the world. Mao was unimpressed, however. A purist, Mao was upset that the country was straying from its communist path, and so, in 1966, he jumped back to the forefront of his government and promoted his most significant domestic policy, the **Cultural Revolution**. Mao's goal in the Cultural Revolution was to discourage anything approaching a privileged ruling class, as it existed in the West as well as among the Soviet communist elite. To accomplish this, Mao instituted reforms meant to erase all traces of a Western-influenced intelligentsia. Many universities were shut down for four years. The students and faculty, along with other "elites" including doctors, lawyers, and classically trained musicians, were sent to work on collective farms for "cultural retraining." In addition, many political dissidents were either imprisoned or killed. When the universities were reopened, the curriculum was reorganized to include only communist studies and vocational training. During this time, Mao's *Little Red Book*, a collection of his teachings on communism, became a popular symbol of the forced egalitarianism of the Cultural Revolution.

The whole plan failed miserably in advancing China economically or socially. By the early 1970s, China realized it needed to open itself up to Western ideas. In 1976, the new leadership under Deng Xiaoping quickly changed the education policy and began to focus on restructuring the economic policies.

Note the Change: Dynastic China to Communist China

For more than 2,000 years, Confucianism and a class structure dominated China. With the Communist Revolution, however, all traces of a class-based system were nearly erased. Traditional Chinese society valued large families, both because children were able to help on the farm and because Confucian philosophy gave identity to people based on their relationships—the parent/child relationship was one of the most important. When the communists took over, however, their program of collectivization made family farms obsolete. In addition, communists were not sympathetic to traditional values based on religious or philosophical beliefs that competed with the authority of the state. As the population of China continued to grow dramatically through the late twentieth century, the communists took a practical approach to the overpopulation problem and began a propaganda campaign aimed at the use of contraception and abortion. By the late 1980s, faced with ever-increasing population figures, the Chinese government instituted a one-child-per-family policy. Reactions to the policy were severe. Many refused to abide by the policy in the first place. Others followed the law, but some of them killed their firstborn female infants in the hope of getting a male child the second time around. Opposition became more widespread and the government relaxed its policy.

The equality demanded in a classless society resulted in considerable advances for women. Husbands and wives were treated equally, at least as far as the law was concerned. Women gained the right to divorce their husbands. They obtained property rights. They received equal pay for equal work and were encouraged to pursue professional and vocational careers.

China Looks West: Likes the Money, Not So Sure About the Democracy

More recently, China's economy has been transformed from a strict communist command economy to one that includes elements of free-market capitalism. Deng Xiaoping's government entered into joint ventures with foreign companies in which the profits and business decisions were shared. In addition, Deng allowed for limited business and property ownership to stimulate hard work and innovation. The reforms have been wildly successful. China's economy is expanding faster than most of the economies of the world and reforms continue to be introduced slowly, which gives the economy time to adjust to the changes. However, despite the economic reforms, the government continues to remain strictly communist in the political sense, and has frequently resisted government and social reforms. In 1989, one million demonstrators converged on Tiananmen Square, calling for democratic reform. In an event known as the **Tiananmen Square massacre**, the government sent troops and opened fire. Hundreds were killed. Today, while China continues to reform its economy and is rapidly becoming a major economic power-house, the possibility for democratic reforms is still unknown.

Division of Korea: The Cold War Turns Hot and Now Possibly Nuclear

Prior to World War II, Korea was invaded by Japan and annexed as part of the expanding Japanese Empire. After Japan was defeated in World War II, Korea was supposed to be re-established as an independent nation, but until stability could be achieved and elections held, it was occupied by the Soviet Union and the United States in two separate pieces—the Soviet Union north of the 38th parallel and the United States south of it. This was very much like the way that Germany was split, and, similarly, the two superpowers couldn't agree on the terms of a united Korea.

In 1948, two separate governments were established—a Soviet-backed communist regime in North Korea and a U.S.-backed democracy in South Korea. Both superpowers withdrew their troops in 1949, but in 1950, North Korea attacked South Korea in an attempt to unite the two nations under a single communist government. The United Nations condemned the action and soon a multinational force, largely consisting of U.S. and British troops, went to the aid of the South Koreans. The UN forces made tremendous headway under **General MacArthur**, nearly reaching the Chinese border, but when it looked as if the North Koreans would be defeated, China entered the war on behalf of the communist North. The two sides battled it out along the 38th parallel, eventually leading to an armistice in 1953.

Today, the two nations remain separate and true to the political philosophies under which they were formed almost 70 years ago. The United States maintains a large military presence in South Korea, which has become an economic powerhouse. North Korea, meanwhile, has suffered through isolationist and just plain nutty rulers and massive food shortages, but has built up a huge military and acquired the technology to develop a nuclear bomb. It has already developed missiles capable of delivering those bombs to South Korea, Japan, China, or possibly even as far as the west coast of the United States. In October 2006, North Korea declared its first nuclear weapons test a success. Western scientists doubted its claims of success, but did confirm that some type of test had taken place. In response, the United Nations imposed additional, but largely symbolic, sanctions on North Korean imports (though China and Russia disagreed with the policy). Six-Party Talks (including

In May 2018, North Korea claimed that it would be dismantling its nuclear test site. Many experts remain skeptical about North Korea's commitment to denuclearize. At the time of publication, the future of diplomatic relations between the U.S. and North Korea remains uncertain, as does North Korea's alleged denuclearization.

the U.S., North Korea, South Korea, China, Russia, and Japan) resumed, for the fifth time, and concluded with the agreement that North Korea was to shut down its reactor in July 2007 in return for extensive fuel aid. As of 2009, North Korea pulled out of the Six-Party Talks for good and has continued its nuclear enrichment program; as of February 2013, the country has detonated three nuclear devices. The failure of the international community to reach a resolution on the Korean peninsula in the early 1950s has created a modern-day crisis of nuclear proportions. The secretive nature of the North Korean regime has made it harder for international observers to gauge the communist nation's intentions, an especially frightening prospect for foreign observers who feared the instability the transfer of power could bring when Kim Jong-Il passed away in December of 2011. However, their fears were not realized as his son Kim Jong-un seems to be pursuing similar militaristic and aggressive policies towards the West as his father did.

Vietnam: The Cold War Turns Ugly

After World War II, the French tried to hold on to their colony of **Indochina**, but nationalists known as the **Vietminh** fought them back. By 1954, the Vietminh's guerilla warfare techniques succeeded in frustrating the French, and an accord was signed in Geneva dividing the nation—you guessed it—into two pieces. The communists, under the leadership of **Ho Chi Minh**, gained control of the land north of the 17th parallel while **Ngo Dinh Diem** became the president of the democratic south. Under its new constitution, North Vietnam supported reunification of Vietnam as a communist state. Ho Chi Minh supported communist guerrillas in the south, and soon war broke out. France and the United States came to the aid of South Vietnam. Ho Chi Minh prevented them from taking over the north, but not before years of fighting led to hundreds of thousands of deaths. As United States forces finally withdrew in 1975, North Vietnamese Army and communist **Viet Cong** fighters took control throughout South Vietnam. A peace agreement eventually led to the reunification of Vietnam as a communist state under the leadership of Ho Chi Minh. The long-range impact was significant for the region, the world, and the United States. The world witnessed the defeat of a superpower by a small but determined nation. Communism took a major step forward in the region. For the United States, the defeat affected foreign policy for decades, as the American public remained fearful of involving itself in "another Vietnam."

Contrast Them: High-Tech Warfare and Guerilla Warfare

High-tech warfare, such as fighter jets, missiles, and tanks, are not only sophisticated and effective, but also costly and logistically complicated. Generally, nations that have mastered high-tech warfare, like the United States, take months to position their weaponry and put together a war plan. Once implemented, high-tech warfare can be devastatingly efficient. **Guerilla warfare**, on the other hand, is behind the scenes, stealthy, and much lower tech. Individuals or small groups fight site-to-site, disrupting their enemies' supply chains, or targeting seemingly random sites with small bombs and munitions. Each individual attack is generally less deadly, but since the attacks are flexible, random, and hard to predict, they can be very effective against a cumbersome, less flexible, high-tech opponent.

The Cuban Revolution: Communism on the American Doorstep

After Cuba won its independence from Spain during the Spanish-American War of 1898, the United States remained involved in Cuban affairs under the terms of the **Platt Amendment**, which also provided for the presence of U.S. military bases. During the following decades, the Americans invested heavily in Cuban businesses and plantations, but those investments generally only made the wealthy very rich with little or no benefit for the masses of peasants. From 1939 to 1959, the United States supported the **Batista Dictatorship** in Cuba, which continued the policies that benefited the wealthy landowners. In 1956, the peasants began a revolt under the leadership of **Fidel Castro**. Even the United States eventually withdrew its support of Fulgencio Batista. Using guerilla warfare techniques, the revolutionaries made tremendous advances, and by 1959, Batista fled. The **Cuban Revolution** was hailed as a great success against a dictator.

Castro, the great promoter of democracy, took control of the government, suspended plans for an election, and established a communist dictatorship. By 1961, he had seized the industries, nationalized them, and executed his rivals. The United States became increasingly concerned about this communist dictatorship and imposed an economic embargo on Cuba—a move that strengthened Castro's ties with the Soviet Union and thus heightened U.S. fears. In an attempt to overthrow Castro, the United States trained and supported a group of anti-Castro Cuban exiles living in the United States. The U.S. was convinced that an invasion by these exiles would lead to a popular revolt against Castro, but it didn't work out that way. In 1961, **President Kennedy** authorized the **Bay of Pigs Invasion**, not with the full force of the mighty U.S. military, but with the small force of Cuban exiles, who were quickly captured after they landed, their revolt over before it began.

After the Bay of Pigs debacle, Cuba and the Soviet Union realized the United States might try something bigger next time around, so they mobilized. In 1962, U.S. spy planes detected the installation of Soviet missiles in Cuba, and Kennedy immediately established a naval blockade around the island, refusing to allow any more shipments from the Soviet Union. Kennedy made it clear to the world that if missiles were launched from Cuba, the United States would retaliate against the Soviet Union itself. The standoff became known as the **Cuban Missile Crisis**. For three months the world waited to see who would back down, and on October 28, the Soviets said that they would remove the missiles in exchange for a promise from the Americans that they would not invade Cuba. The Americans agreed to the settlement. This was the closest brush the world has had with full-out nuclear war.

When the Soviet Union collapsed in the early 1990s, the Cubans lost their main financial backer. This was a huge loss because it amounted to billions of dollars of aid. Still, Castro managed to hang on to his power, but economic conditions in Cuba deteriorated sharply after the fall of communism in Europe. From 2006 to 2011, Fidel Castro transferred his powers and responsibilities to his younger brother, Raúl, in stages, handing over first the presidency and then his position as First Secretary of the Communist Party of Cuba, which he had held since 1965. The elder Castro stepped down due to illness but periodically resurfaced in videos, demonstrating his continued presence as a political force in his brother's regime up until his death in November 2016.

Conflicts with "Good Neighbors": Cold War Tensions and Democratization in Latin America

Despite independence movements, democratic elections, and developing economies, the United States maintained a heavy hand in Latin America whenever possible (remember the Roosevelt Corollary to the Monroe Doctrine?). Some of this was also the product of Cold War tensions. Marxism's anti-capitalist message had great appeal in less-developed countries and increased as U.S. investment in copper-mining and oil-drilling in the region intensified in the 1920s. Radical political parties developed in Mexico, Peru, Venezuela, Brazil, and much of Central America as complaints about imperial policies of the "**Good Neighbor**" to the north increased. As the U.S. confronted two world wars and the Great Depression, however, and Latin America became less of a priority, the region's nations took the opportunity to explore alternative paths to economic development. These took various forms: the stability of single-party rule (Mexico's **PRI**), the brutality of militaristic leaders (Argentina's Juan Peron) or the development of socialist democracies (Nicaragua and Guatemala). It was the latter that garnered the most attention from the United States—still in the midst of an ideological war with the Soviet Union—resulting in U.S.-backed coups, the use of Nicaragua as a staging ground for the Bay of Pigs invasion, and the targeting of the **Sandinista** guerillas in Nicaragua and El Salvador during the 1980s.

Perhaps the biggest issues Latin America continues to face are their **export economies**. Reliance on products such as coffee, fruit, sugar, and oil has resulted in weak domestic economies and tremendous debt. While there is a long history of democracy throughout the region, the lag in economic development, increasing debt payments from loans dating back to the 1970s and 1980s, and out-migration continue to challenge the region. However, at the beginning of the twenty-first century, there has been tremendous growth throughout Latin America. Some is based on rising oil prices, but much can also be attributed to the development of new industries and trade agreements, both within Latin America and with the U.S. and Canada. Both Chile and Brazil are among the fastest-growing economies in the world.

Democracy has also taken interesting turns in Mexico and Venezuela in the last decade. The year 2000 was the first time a true multi-party election was held in Mexico since the formation of the state under the 1917 Constitution. The opposition, **PAN** or **National Action Party** candidate won the presidency. Mexico had a second national election with an opposition slate in 2006 and again, the PAN candidate won, though the PRI won the most recent election in 2012. Venezuela, on the other hand, has amended its constitution to allow its Socialist president Hugo Chavez a third term as the country has nationalized a number of industries including telephone and steel. In 2013, Chavez died and was succeeded by Nicolás Maduro, who has continued many of Chavez's policies.

Europe: The Cold War Finally Ends

THE FALL OF COMMUNISM
IN EASTERN EUROPE,
1989

- Communist governments fall
- Unrest in Soviet republics

The Fall of Communism in Eastern Europe

During the Cold War, the standard of living in Western Europe improved dramatically, despite economic swings. In Eastern Europe, behind the iron curtain, the massive state-run industries couldn't keep up with the innovations in the West. A growing divide between the "rich" West and the "poor" East was becoming obvious, and as it became obvious to the people who lived within the Eastern bloc, they began to revolt.

The revolt was as much about democracy and self-determination as it was about the economy. The Soviet Union was a huge patchwork of many different nationalities, many of which wanted to control their own destinies. What's more, an increasing number of people in the Eastern bloc countries that were controlled by the Soviet Union, such as Poland, were also itching for democratic and economic reform. By the 1980s, groups of reform-minded individuals began scratching that itch.

Poland: Solidarity Grows in Popularity

The decline of communism brought sweeping reform to Poland and its government, which had been trying for years to prevent the spread of anticommunist sentiment. In 1980, more than a decade before the fall of communism in the Soviet Union, a group of workers began the Solidarity movement under the leadership of **Lech Walesa**. Thousands of workers joined a strike for reform of the communist economic system. The government reacted by imposing martial law and arresting Lech Walesa, as well as other Solidarity leaders. Throughout the early- and mid-1980s, the government tried to suppress Solidarity. In 1988, the reform-minded Rakowski became the Premier of Poland. Solidarity was legalized and in 1989, a member of Solidarity, **Tadeusz Mazowiecki**, became Prime Minister in the first open elections since the end of World War II. In 1990, the Communist Party fell apart in Poland, just as it was falling apart throughout Eastern Europe, and Lech Walesa was elected president. During the 1990s, the economy improved swiftly as Poland introduced market-based reforms and a new democratic constitution. Poland formally completed its integration into the West by joining NATO in 1999 and the European Union in 2004. Quite a change.

German Reunification: All This, Just to Be Back Where It Started

The decline of communism in the Soviet bloc directly led to the reunification of Germany as a free-market democracy. East Germany cut ties with the Soviet Union and began negotiations with West Germany. Many Western nations feared that a united Germany would lead once again to a nationalistic regime, but the prospect for peace, economic and political reform, and an improved standard of living for the people of East Germany outweighed the concerns. When the Berlin Wall was torn down in 1989, signaling the fall of East Germany, a mass exodus of East Germans fled to the West. Businesses in East Germany continued to struggle because their outdated corporate structures, equipment, and machinery could not compete with the more efficient businesses in the western half of the nation. Unemployment was high in both halves of the newly united nation. Nevertheless, the government did not abandon its ambitious reconstruction program aimed at the modernization of the former East Germany and the establishment of nationwide communication and transportation lines. Germany has therefore continued to press forward and has since emerged as a leading economy in Europe.

Germany's Journey

Just in case you haven't been keeping track, in the last 90 years Germany went from being crushed in World War I, to being built up under fascist Nazis, to being crushed in World War II, to being occupied by four former enemies, to being divided in two, to being at the epicenter of the Cold War, to being reunified as a modern, capitalist-leaning, democratic nation. That's some pretty extreme historical whiplash!

The Soviet Union Collapses: Glasnost, Perestroika, Kaput

When **Mikhail Gorbachev** came to power in the Soviet Union in 1985, he instituted policies of *glasnost* (openness) and urged a *perestroika* (restructuring) of the Soviet economy. He may not have realized it at the time, but he set in motion a tidal wave of change that he wouldn't be able to reverse. Legislation was passed to add elements of private enterprise to the economy. Nuclear arms treaties were signed with the United States. Gorbachev publicly and officially denounced the Great Purge, a huge deal because it showed that the Soviet Union was re-evaluating itself. The list of reforms and changes goes on and on, but the bottom line is that within six years, Poland and other former Soviet satellites declared their separation from the USSR. The Soviet Union itself disintegrated in 1991. Russia became its own country again, while the other parts of the old Soviet Empire, such as Ukraine, Belarus, and Georgia, became independent nations.

Some observers were shocked by the degree to which so many different nationalities within the former Soviet Union wanted to form their own countries, and further shocked that most of the shifts in power happened relatively peacefully.

But there were exceptions. In the same region that sparked World War I eighty years prior—the Balkans—nationalistic movements within the former Yugoslavia led to "**ethnic cleansing**" in which Bosnian and Albanian Muslims were raped and slaughtered by Christian Serbians in what was simply the latest horrific chapter in a centuries-long regional and ethnic conflict. The violence eventually led to the involvement of UN troops during much of the 1990s. Even in Russia itself, nationalists in different regions, especially in Muslim-dominated **Chechnya**, want to break away, and have used guerilla warfare and terrorist methods to advance their cause.

During the 1990s, most of the new countries in the former Soviet bloc, especially those in Eastern Europe, created constitutional democracies with economic systems based on variations of capitalism. Reform movements have occurred faster in some countries than in others, and adherents to communism have made themselves heard as the transition from state-owned to privately owned industries has resulted in high unemployment and corruption. Still, democracy seems to be taking a foothold in the region. Though much is uncertain about the future of the former Soviet bloc, a few things can be said for sure: by the end of 1991, the Cold War was over, the Warsaw Pact had disbanded, and the United States found itself as the world's only superpower.

Democracy and Authoritarian Rule in Russia

The new (old) country of Russia was (re)formed under a 1993 constitution. Although it had lost its Soviet satellite countries, this new Russian Federation was formidable in size, plentiful in natural resources, and full of corrupt Soviet bureaucrats looking to get rich under the new rules. On paper, the new Russia looks very much like a perfect **federal** state with three branches, checks and balances and an independent court. In reality, Russia's abrupt introduction to both democracy and capitalism resulted in a ten-year period of corruption, high unemployment, deep poverty, widespread crime and a nostalgia for Soviet-style control and discipline. The challenge for Russia's first president, **Boris Yeltsin**, was to reform the structures of both state and society. This was an enormous task, requiring completely new systems of government and trade.

Yeltsin resigned in 1999, and for the next eight years, former **KGB** agent **Vladimir Putin** headed the Russian state. He was elected president twice, in 2000 and 2004, and was appointed Prime Minister in 2008 by the newly elected president Dmitry Medvedev. This new style of Russian democracy has been marked by corruption and an authoritarian strengthening of the executive branch, limits on opposition candidates, and a crackdown on a free press. In a move that alarmed international observers, Putin announced in 2011 that he would run for a third presidential term in 2012, stretching his leadership to 16 years (and perhaps beyond?). Despite some protests in Russia, Putin defeated several challengers in March 2012 to return to the presidency. Russia's twenty-first-century economic growth has been considerable, but old habits die hard, and conflicts with the U.S. continue over plans for expansion of NATO, the placement of missiles in Eastern Europe, and the sale of technology to Iran.

Annexation of Crimea
In March of 2014, shortly after the successful Winter Olympic Games in Sochi, the Russian Federation annexed the region of Crimea in eastern Ukraine. Russia's continuing support of separatists within Ukraine and its military incursions into Ukrainian territory have led to the deaths of thousands of people and drawn widespread condemnation from the international community.

Contrast Them: "West" and "East"

During the Cold War, the two terms were frequently used to describe much of the world, especially the northern hemisphere. The "West," led by the United States, was generally democratic, generally capitalist, and generally prosperous. The "East," led by the Soviet Union, was communist, generally totalitarian, and generally substantially less prosperous in terms of per capita standard of living. Japan, incidentally, was part of the "West," because after World War II it developed along pro-Western, capitalist, generally pro-democracy lines. After the fall of communism in most of the world in the early 1990s, the terms began to lose their relevance. The West grew dramatically, but should Russia be considered part of the "West"? Clearly, most of its former satellites wanted to be considered as such. What's more, China, still communist, is transforming its economy and possibly irrevocably opening up its doors to the world, a movement called "Westernizing" but so far not leading to democratic reforms. As for the "East," nobody's sure what that refers to any more. Today, a new, perhaps overly general division between the "Western World" and the "Islamic World" is being used to describe world relations.

D. Independence Movements and Developments in Asia and Africa

After World War II, a wave of independence movements marked the beginning of the end of European imperialism. In an era when the United States and Western Europe were fighting a Cold War in part to defend people's right to choose their own futures (self-determination) under democratic systems, it became difficult for Western colonial powers to reconcile their post-World War II principles with their imperialist policies. More importantly, it was increasingly difficult for the subjugated peoples to tolerate their treatment, so they rose up and demanded independence.

The Indian Subcontinent

After the **Indian National Congress**, a mostly Hindu political party, was established in 1885 to increase the rights of Indians under colonial rule, and then the **Muslim League** in 1906 to advance the causes of Islamic Indians, it took years for momentum to build into an organized resistance to colonial power. In 1919, the **Amritsar massacre** catapulted the movement.

In Amritsar, 319 Indians, some Hindu and some Muslim, were slaughtered by British General Dyer during a peaceful protest in a city park. They were protesting the arrest of two of their leaders who also were doing nothing other than protesting, were unarmed, and entirely surprised by the attack. Because the park was walled, there was no way to escape from the attackers. By all accounts, the slaughter was unprovoked and entirely unwarranted. When news of the massacre spread, Indians joined the self-rule cause by the millions. It was now a full-fledged movement.

Cracking the AP World History Exam

During the 1920s, **Mohandas Gandhi** became the movement's most important voice and organized huge protests against colonial rule. Gandhi's philosophy of **passive resistance**, or civil disobedience, gained popular support in the struggle against British colonial rule. Instead of fighting with weapons, Gandhi's followers staged demonstrations and refused to assist the colonial governments. This included massive boycotts of British imperial goods as well as strikes, such as when hundreds of thousands of workers refused to act as labor for the British colonial government's salt factories. Gandhi's nonviolent teachings, and his success, became enormously influential.

At the same time, there was an increase in violence between Hindus and Muslims. While both groups worked together peacefully against the British, radical members of each group found it hard to tolerate the other. This disturbed Gandhi, who was raised Hindu but yearned for mutual respect among people of both religions. In the late 1920s, Gandhi began to call for Indian unity above religious considerations. Instead, the Muslim League actively pushed for the creation of a Muslim nation, and even bounced around a name for their future country: Pakistan.

Independence Won: Nations Two

After World War II, Britain finally granted independence to the Indian subcontinent. The long and relatively nonviolent struggle for independence had finally paid off. The terrible irony was that once independence was granted, the real bloodshed began. Radical Hindus and Muslims started killing each other.

There were two schools of thought regarding the newly independent subcontinent. The first, promoted by Mohandas Gandhi and, at first, the British, called for the establishment of a united India where both Hindus and Muslims could practice their religions. The second was a movement by **Muhammad Ali Jinnah**, whose aim was to partition the subcontinent and form a separate Muslim nation in the northern region, where Islam had become the dominant religion. The British eventually were convinced that a partition would save lives by separating people who seemed intent on killing each other, so when the British turned over the reigns to new leaders of independent India in 1947, it separated the country into thirds: India in the south and Pakistan in two parts, one to the northwest of India (Pakistan) and the other to the east (East Pakistan, currently Bangladesh).

Both parts of Pakistan were Muslim, while India was predominately Hindu, although officially secular. The result was chaotic. Millions of people moved or were forced to flee due to religiously motivated violence. Essentially, India and Pakistan exchanged millions of citizens, with practitioners of each religion moving to the nation where their religion was dominant. Nearly half a million people were killed as they migrated to their respective "sides." The move of so many people along religious lines only served to create an international conflict between Pakistan and India. Within a year, Gandhi himself was assassinated by a Hindu who was upset with Gandhi's secular motivations. Today, the two nations are still fighting, especially in Kashmir along their borders, where religious self-determination still remains the big issue. What's more, both countries have since become nuclear powers, and 2008 saw a significant increase in terrorism between the two nations as Pakistan became less stable.

Gandhi's Influence on U.S. History
Gandhi's teachings partly inspired the civil disobedience of the U.S. civil rights movements led by Dr. Martin Luther King Jr.

Africa

After World War II, African nations also began to assert their independence. They were partly inspired by events in India and the rest of the world, but they were also motivated by the war itself. Hundreds of thousands of Africans fought for their colonial powers during the war. Many of them felt that if they were willing to die for their governing countries, then they had earned the right to live free.

South Africa became a significant British colony, complete with extensive investment in infrastructure and institutions. In 1910, the colony established its own constitution, and it became the Union of South Africa, still part of the British Commonwealth, but exercising a considerable amount of self-rule. Under the constitution, only white men could vote, so the native Africans had few rights. In 1912, educated South Africans organized the African National Congress in an effort to oppose European colonialism and specific South African policies. This organization, of course, was similar to the Indian National Congress, which was established for similar ends.

After South Africa, the nations north of the Sahara were the next colonies to win independence. These nations had strong Islamic ties, and the mostly Muslim Middle East had already won its freedom in the decades prior (more on that later). Egypt, too, had won its independence early, in 1922, although it kept extremely close ties to Britain. In the 1950s, as the independence movement gathered steam in Africa, **Gamal Nasser**, a general in the Egyptian army, overthrew the king and established a republic. He nationalized industries, including the Suez Canal, and then became embroiled in Middle Eastern conflicts. Nasser's actions emboldened other Islamic nationalists to seek independence, and soon the African nations along the Mediterranean were free.

South of the Sahara, independence was a trickier issue. The problem was that while nearly everyone wanted independence, most of the colonies had been raped of their resources. There had been little investment in human beings. The vast majority of Africans were uneducated, or only educated through grammar school. Unlike in India, where a substantial number of upper-caste Indians were highly educated and even attended universities in Britain, many African nations had few natives who were skilled professionals: doctors, scientists, lawyers, diplomats, businesspeople. This meant that once the colonial powers left, there would be few people left with the education and skills to immediately take charge and begin to build a productive, self-sufficient society.

National unity among the natives was also difficult to foster because the boundaries of so many African colonies had been drawn according to European needs, and took no account of African history or needs. Africans within the same colony spoke different native languages and had differing, sometimes opposing, customs, histories, and loyalties. For all of these reasons, even after attaining their hard-won independence, many African nations struggled to build strong, stable, independent countries.

Decolonization and nation-building occurred in a variety of ways across Africa. The **Algerians** fought a bitter war for independence from France (1954–1962) while in the early 1960s Nigeria and **Ghana** negotiated their freedom into a Parliamentary governing style borrowed from England. After a series of military coups, they adopted presidential systems. **Kenya**, under the leadership of Jomo Kenyatta, negotiated its constitution with Great Britain after a brutal crackdown engineered by coffee planters unwilling to lose such profitable property. Others, such as **Angola** and **Belgian Congo**, overthrew colonial governments, only to become embroiled in civil wars or in Cold War tensions. **Zimbabwe** was among the last to establish African majority rule in 1980 (see following section on South Africa).

Fifty-three of Africa's 54 nations belong to the **African Union**, a political and economic confederation formed in 2001 to replace the **Organization of African Unity** or **OAU**. But success and stability is not guaranteed for any of these nations. **Chad**, **Sudan**, **Uganda**, **Somalia**, and **Rwanda** as well as the newly renamed **Democratic Republic of Congo** (former Zaire) have been wracked by ongoing and devastating civil wars since the turn of the twenty-first century. Attempts to form stable democracies have been thwarted by a reversion to "big man" politics, corruption, military coups, and escalating debt payments (to IMF and World Bank—see Alphabet Soup later in chapter). Even relatively stable governments such as Kenya's have seen political violence escalate in recent years.

Economically, most of Africa is still rich in natural resources, albeit different ones from those the colonial powers were interested in. Palm oil and rubber have given way to petroleum and metals including nickel, cadmium, and lithium—prized for batteries to power cell phones, laptop computers, and hybrid cars. So, the former colonial powers plus some new industrial players (China!) remain interested and invested in the nations of Africa.

Note the Change: Globalization and the Rise of NGOs

NGOs, or nongovernmental organizations, have become an ever-increasing presence in our modern world. NGOs are typically private, often nonprofit, agencies that provide relief services and/or advocacy for groups that are generally not serviced or represented by their governments. Some familiar examples of NGOs include the International Committee of the Red Cross (ICRC), Doctors Without Borders, Amnesty International, and even the American Civil Liberties Union. It is often NGOs that lead relief efforts following natural disasters and during wars, particularly to countries and people who cannot afford to pay for such efforts. Organizations such as the World Wildlife Fund provide advocacy for the world's animals, which of course do not have any representation in the world's governments. But why have most of these organizations formed only in the years since World War II? Well, the major international governmental organizations that formed after World War II, such as the UN and World Bank, were criticized for only representing the interests of the world's wealthier and more powerful nations (as they had been created by the victors of the war), and so many well-meaning individuals formed private companies to fill needs that were not being met by the world's governments. Globalization, which has increasingly made it easier to communicate and travel around the world, has not only made it easier for NGOs to provide their services on a global scale, but has also made it much easier for them to raise the money needed to fund their operations.

Rwanda: Ethnic Genocide

The difficulties of establishing stable nations in Africa are exemplified by the situation in Rwanda. Ethnic strife, genocide, and human rights violations in Rwanda stem from conflicts between two groups: the **Tutsi** (15 percent of the Rwandan population) who governed the **Hutu** (85 percent of the Rwandan population) during German and Belgian colonial occupation. Belgian rule in particular exacerbated interethnic tensions, setting the stage for bloodshed as soon as colonial authorities withdrew. Upon Rwanda's independence in 1962, the Hutu revolted against the Tutsi leadership, leaving thousands dead and the two groups locked in bitter, bloody conflict. In 1973, a military coup by Juvenal Habyarimana unseated the government and eventually established a one-party republic in 1981. The military government worked to keep peace but encountered only modest success. That, too, was destroyed when Habyarimana's personal airplane was shot down over his presidential palace in 1994, assassinating the Hutu general. Almost immediately, conflict escalated, with the Hutu needing little encouragement to exact revenge on the Tutsi population whose leadership they blamed for the assassination. One hundred days of genocide left as many as 800,000 Tutsi dead, and by the following year, more than 2 million mostly Hutu refugees were sent or fled to neighboring Zaire, where many died from disease. The genocide and displacement in Rwanda ranks among the most devastating in recent history.

Compare Them: Independence in Africa and India

Both India and Africa successfully gained independence in the years following World War II, and both areas were tragically torn apart by ethnic and religious strife shortly following independence. In India, the tensions between Hindus and Muslims, which existed before the British colonized the subcontinent, re-emerged as they departed. In many African nations, independence served only as an opportunity for long-held tribal hatreds to resurface in power struggles. The colonial powers, of course, were no better. They had been killing each other for thousands of years.

Developments in South Africa: The Rise and Fall of Apartheid

The year after the **South Africa Act** of 1909, the **Union of South Africa** was formed by combining two British colonies with two Dutch Boer republics, and although the British and Dutch colonists were given considerable rights to self-government, black people were entirely excluded from the political process. In 1923, residential segregation was established and enforced. In 1926, blacks were banned from work in certain skilled occupations that whites wanted for themselves. When South Africa won independence from Britain in 1931, the racial policies didn't improve. In fact, a system of **apartheid** ("separation of the races") was established in South Africa in 1948 as an all-encompassing way of dividing black (80 percent of the population) and white. By the late 1950s, apartheid was extended to the creation of homelands, areas of the country that were "set aside" for blacks. The homelands were in the worst parts of the country, and comprised less than 15 percent of the nation's land. The whites were given the cities, the resource-rich mines, and the best farmland. While many blacks were compelled to move to the homelands, others stayed in the cities, where they were segregated into black slums. If this starts to sound like *District 9* (2009), there's a reason a sci-fi movie about segregating aliens was set in South Africa.

In response, the black community organized. In the 1950s, **Nelson Mandela** became leader of the **African National Congress**, an organization determined to abolish apartheid. At first, he advocated peaceful protest, following the example of Gandhi. But in 1960, after the **Sharpeville massacre** in which 67 protesters were killed, the African National Congress supported guerrilla warfare. At Sharpeville, blacks were protesting a policy that forced them to carry passes to be in the cities in order to go to their jobs. The passes were issued at places of employment. This meant that if you worked and your wife didn't, you couldn't go into the city with her because she wouldn't have a pass. The massacre rallied the anti-apartheid movement. Mandela was arrested in 1964 for his role in anti-apartheid violence and sentenced to life imprisonment.

After decades of increasing pressure from the black majority and the international community, South Africa finally released Mandela in 1990 and agreed to negotiate on the policy of apartheid. The government more than negotiated, it crumbled. In 1994, after apartheid was abolished, Mandela was elected president in the first free and open election in the nation's history.

The Middle East

After the fall of the Ottoman Empire and the creation of the modern nation of Turkey at the close of World War I, the Middle East, which was largely comprised of old Ottoman lands, was temporarily put under the control of the League of Nations. As if the two European powerhouses didn't already control enough of the world, France was put in charge of Syria and Lebanon, while Britain got Palestine, Jordan, and Iraq. Persia (Iran) was already carved up into spheres of influence between Britain and Russia during the nineteenth century. As for Arabia, it united as a Saudi kingdom immediately following the fall of the Ottoman Empire.

The Middle East during the twentieth century is complicated stuff, but a good chunk of the essential information involves the creation of the modern nation of Israel, so that's where we'll start.

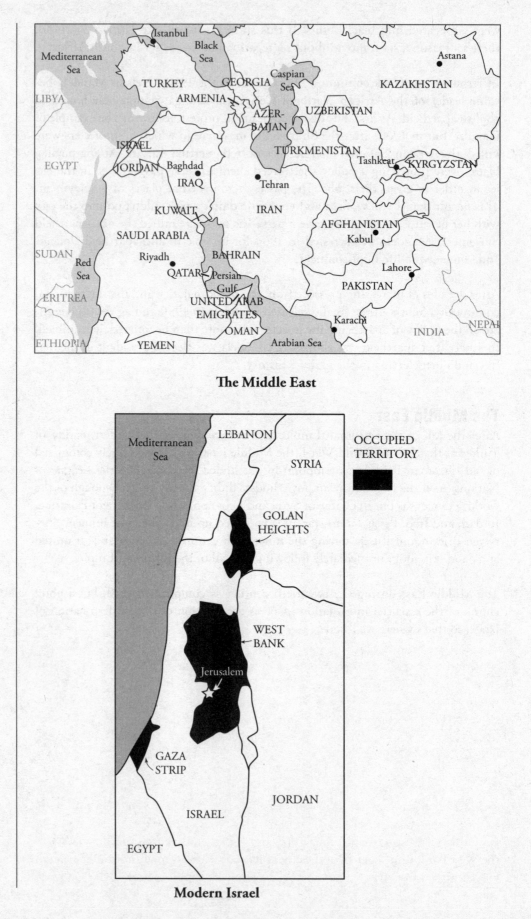

The Middle East

Modern Israel

Israel: Balfour Declares a Mess

If you remember way back four chapters ago, the Hebrews (Jews) occupied lands in Palestine at the time of the ancient Roman Empire. As is the case everywhere else on the globe, between that chapter and this chapter a series of conquests shifted power over the region a mind-numbing number of times. While a few Jews managed to stay in the region, most bolted for Europe or other areas as Palestine became increasingly entrenched in Islam. All the while, however, many Jews had wanted to return to what they believed was the "promised land." In the meantime, generation after generation of Muslim Palestinians had made that land home.

During World War I, **Zionists** (Jewish nationalists) living in Britain convinced **Arthur Balfour**, Britain's foreign secretary, that a Jewish homeland in Palestine was both desirable and just. He issued what became known as the **Balfour Declaration of 1917**, which explicitly stated the right for a home in Palestine for the Jewish people, but he also stated that it should in no way displace the Palestinians who currently lived there. As history would have it, Britain gained control of Palestine in 1920 as a mandate from the League of Nations—which meant that it was to govern on behalf of the League of Nations—and was therefore in a position to make good on its declaration.

The declaration was messy because it essentially provided that the Palestinians and Jews were to divide land that they both claimed. Not long after, many Jews, mainly Russian Jews fleeing violent, anti-Semitic mobs (**pogroms**), began streaming into Palestine. As their numbers grew, the Palestinians started to get uneasy. In the 1930s, huge numbers of Jews flooded the region to escape Germany as Hitler came to power. By the beginning of World War II, nearly 500,000 Jews had emigrated to Palestine. While Palestinians still outnumbered Jews, the Jewish population was now large enough to pull some serious weight, especially because money was pouring into the region from Jewish communities worldwide.

The Jewish Wait for a State Ends in 1948

In 1948, the United Nations (which had replaced the ineffectual League of Nations) officially created two Palestines, one for Jews and the other for Muslims (Palestinians). As soon as **David Ben-Gurion**, the first prime minister of Israel, announced the official creation of the Jewish homeland on May 14, 1948, Muslims from six Arab countries attacked Israel in what became known as the **1948 Arab-Israeli War**. However, the Israelis shocked and awed them with their quick organization and military capability. Within months, the Israelis controlled most of Palestine, including the Palestinian parts, while Jordan held the remaining portions (the **West Bank**). Suddenly, Palestinians were without a home. They had no land to call their own.

As Jews flocked to Israel from all over the world, Israel and Arab countries continued to have skirmishes. In 1967, the amazingly short **Six-Day War** resulted in total victory for the Israelis, who took control of the West Bank from Jordan, the Sinai Peninsula and **Gaza Strip** from Egypt, and the **Golan Heights** from Syria. With the West Bank came control of the city of Jerusalem, Judaism's historical homeland. However, Muslims throughout the region resented Israeli control of the Dome of

Sound Familiar?
The arrangement made between the Jews and Muslims in Palestine should sound familiar to you, as the same one was made between India and Pakistan. The Indians and Pakistanis have been fighting ever since.

the Rock, a revered Islamic shrine dating back to the Abbasid caliphate which is also the site of the Temple Mount, an important Jewish historical site. The territorial gains resulted in new waves of Palestinian refugees to Jerusalem. In 1977, Israeli **Prime Minister Menachem Begin** and Egyptian **President Anwar Sadat** signed the **Camp David Accords**, an agreement that did not mention Golan Heights, Syria, or Lebanon, but which led to Israel pulling out of the Sinai and Egypt becoming the only Arab country yet to recognize Israel's right to exist. This was a huge blow to the Palestinians and other Arab nations. Sadat was assassinated and the lands gained in the Six-Day War remain some of the most contested in the region.

In the years since, the Israelis and the Palestinians have been fighting over the Israeli occupation of the West Bank, Golan Heights, and Gaza Strip. The **Palestine Liberation Organization (PLO)**, a group dedicated to reclaiming the land and establishing a Palestinian state, has so far been unsuccessful in negotiating a homeland. The efforts are complicated by the *intifada* (uprising), an on-again off-again movement that sometimes uses terrorism against Israeli citizens in an attempt to either destroy Israel or force it into withdrawal from the occupied territories.

In 2000, a new intifada reignited violence between Palestinians and the occupying Israeli forces. As suicide bombings became more frequent, newly elected Israeli prime minister **Ariel Sharon** approved the construction of a wall to be built between the Palestinian West Bank and Israel in order to protect Israelis against suicide attacks. Often compared to the Berlin Wall, Israel's protective wall has been criticized by some in the international community for employing such a draconian measure to fight terrorist attacks. Many in Israel, meanwhile, have pointed to the wall as a successful way to prevent needless violence and terrorism.

Not limiting itself to criticism, however, in 2003 the international community, led by the United States, the European Union, the UN and Russia, proposed a "Roadmap to Peace," which outlined a set of goals to achieve peace in the region. Progress on the Roadmap remained stalled until the death of Palestinian president (and former PLO leader) **Yassir Arafat** in November 2004. Arafat had been consistently blamed by Israel and the United States for blocking such progress. Following his January 2005 election, Palestinian president **Mahmoud Abbas** quickly signed a cease-fire with Israel that effectively ended the *intifada* that began in 2000.

Under a "disengagement plan" adopted by the Israeli government, all Israeli settlers were supposed to have vacated the Gaza Strip by August 2005. Residents of the settlements who did not leave were forcibly removed by the Israeli army, a military action which greatly divided the Israeli public. Additional settlements were disbanded in the West Bank as part of the same plan. It is likely, however, that lasting peace will remain elusive until the Israelis and Palestinians can reach agreement on issues such as movement into and outside of the Palestinian Authority-controlled territories, the disarmament of militant groups, and the potential independence of a Palestinian state.

The situation is made even more complicated by limited financial stability and political divisions among Palestinians. The governing Palestinian Authority is divided into two factions: Fatah, a branch of the former Palestinian Liberation Organization, and Hamas. Translating to "Islamic Resistance Movement," Hamas was founded as an offshoot of the Muslim Brotherhood in 1987. Because of its open willingness to support terrorist tactics, Hamas is frequently the target of Israeli military attacks. Despite similar goals for a Palestinian state, Hamas and Fatah are deeply divided, and violent clashes occur with increasing frequency. After the creation of a unity government in 2006, Hamas led a coup in 2007 which concluded with a Hamas-imposed government in the Gaza Strip and a Fatah-run West Bank. Further complicating governance, in retaliation, President Mahmoud Abbas (Fatah) named Salam Fayyad prime minister. Hamas contended that Fayyad's appointment was illegitimate, as he was not voted into office. Israel's government—led by Prime Minister Benjamin Netanyahu—and the United States have shown willingness to work with Fatah. The United States and a number of European countries list Hamas as a terrorist organization and so do not negotiate with that party.

Israel's border with Lebanon and Syria remains another hotspot. Hezbollah, a militant Shia group backed by Syria and Iran, operates in the region. In 2006, Israel launched a major offensive against Hezbollah after two Israeli soldiers were captured in Israeli territory. These new hostilities threatened the stability of a country which had been the scene of intense fighting between Syrian, Israeli, and PLO forces throughout the 1980s and 1990s. Syria is widely seen to have a controlling hand in Lebanese politics. In 2005, when Prime Minister Rafiq Hariri was assassinated, fingers quickly pointed to Hezbollah and Syrian sources.

The Iranian Revolution: The Shah Gets Shooed

Reza Shah Pahlavi rose to power in 1925 by ousting the then-ruling shah, who had allowed Persia to fall under European spheres of influence. Taking a stance similar to the Japanese during the Meiji Restoration, Reza Shah decided that the best way to beat the Westernizers was to join them. Iran (formerly Persia) modernized slowly at first, but once the Europeans left after World War II, the Westernization efforts gained momentum, and in the 1960s, the shah instituted land and education reform, and increased the rights of women, including the right to vote. Women also pursued higher education and careers, and began to adopt Western dress. All of this infuriated many Islamic fundamentalists who wanted to make the teachings of the Qu'ran the law of the land. Believing that the influence of the West was too strong, they sought to reverse the economic and social changes. Others believed that the shah was not reforming enough, especially with regard to the political system, which lacked significant democratic changes.

The shah reacted violently against dissent from both sides, pressing forward with his own mix of social and economic reform even in the face of strong public opposition. When **President Jimmy Carter** of the United States visited Iran to congratulate it on its programs of modernization and Westernization, the Islamic fundamentalists had had enough. In 1979, the shah was ousted from power during the **Iranian Revolution**, which sent Iran back to a theocracy led by *Ayatollah* ("Mirror of God") **Khomeini**. Iran is primarily Shia, and the ayatollah is the Shiite caliph (this was important during the Iran-Iraq war, as Iraq was ruled by Sunni Muslims).

Immediately, modernization and Westernization programs were reversed, women were required to wear traditional Islamic clothing and to return to their traditional roles, and the Qu'ran became the basis of the legal system.

In 1980, soon after the revolution, Iraq invaded Iran following a series of border disputes between the two countries. Iran's position was further complicated by Iraqi leader Saddam Hussein's quiet support from the United States, which was still quite furious over Iran's taking of U.S. hostages during the revolution. Even with some U.S. support, the **Iran-Iraq War** turned into an eight-year war of attrition with neither side gaining much ground until a cease-fire was signed in 1988.

Since the Ayatollah Khomeini's death in 1989 (watch out—he was succeeded by the differently spelled **Ayatollah Khamenei!**), Iran has been characterized by a power struggle between powerful Islamic fundamentalist clerics and an increasingly vocal reform-minded and somewhat pro-Western minority. Most recently however, Iran has caused international concern (particularly in the United States) by pushing ahead with efforts to develop what they deemed "peaceful" nuclear technologies, claiming they have a right as an independent nation to develop such technology as they see fit. Along with the International Atomic Energy Agency and the European Union, the United States is currently calling on Iran to sign an international agreement limiting or even eliminating its nuclear programs.

From 2005 until 2013, Tehran's ultra-conservative mayor **Mahmoud Ahmadinejad** was president of Iran. He was succeeded by the more politically moderate leader Hassan Rouhani. The American-led war in Iraq that began in 2003, the relationship of Iran and Iraq's Shia populations, and Iran's development of weapons programs and nuclear research have only complicated matters further.

Compare Them: Role of Women After the Chinese Revolution and Before the Iranian Revolution

In the West, women have benefited from substantial societal and legal changes, but the change has been gradual, over many generations. In China and Iran, the changes were quick. Within a single woman's lifetime, she went from an extremely traditional, oppressive society to one in which she could vote (in the case of Iran), dress less traditionally, divorce her husband, become educated, and pursue a career. Of course, after the Iranian Revolution, those reforms were reversed immediately. At that point, women in China and Iran were in completely different situations.

Oil: Enormous Amounts of Goo

The Industrial Revolution was a huge bonanza for the Middle East. That's because they'd been sitting on over two-thirds of the world's known oil reserves since the beginning of civilization. Prior to the Industrial Revolution, it was goo. After the Industrial Revolution, it was fuel. As multinational corporations rushed to the Middle East throughout the twentieth century to obtain drilling and production rights, Middle Eastern governments such as those of Saudi Arabia, Kuwait, Iran, and Iraq started to earn billions of dollars annually. The oil also meant that the rest of the world had become very, very interested in the Middle East, because oil allowed the West to do one of its favorite things: drive. This world interest sometimes led to intervention and war.

Once the oil-producing nations of the Middle East realized how much power they wielded, they organized. In 1960, the region united with a few other oil-exporting nations, such as Venezuela, to form a petroleum cartel known as **OPEC** (Organization of Petroleum Exporting Countries). With three-quarters of the world's petroleum reserves, OPEC members collectively cut supply dramatically in the 1970s, sending the price of oil through the roof. Billions of extra dollars flowed into OPEC member nations' coffers. Nations such as Saudi Arabia used the extra money to modernize their infrastructures and spent billions on attempts to improve their agricultural sectors. Since the 1970s, OPEC hasn't been able to keep its members in line, and is therefore a much less powerful organization, but the individual members who make up the organization continue to wield huge power over the world economy.

E. Globalization and the World Since 1980

International Terrorism and War

Since World War II and the formation of the United Nations, there has been increased interest in maintaining international security. Some of the organizations that are charged with this task are from the Cold War era: NATO, the United Nations, and the International Atomic Energy Agency. Others, such as the International Criminal Court in The Hague (formed in 2002) were formed to prosecute war crimes and crimes against humanity, no matter who committed them. Still others, including NGOs such as Amnesty International, Human Rights Watch, and Doctors Without Borders, serve to publicize issues that threaten human health and safety and provide aid to those in need.

War in the Gulf: Oil and Saddam Hussein

Iraq invaded Kuwait in August 1990 under the leadership of **Saddam Hussein** because Iraq wanted to gain control of a greater percentage of the world's oil reserves. Iraqi control of Kuwait would have nearly doubled Iraq's oil reserves to 20 percent of the world's total, and would have put it in good position to make advances on Saudi Arabia and the United Arab Emirates, actions that would have given Iraq control of more than half of the world's oil reserves. The world, especially the industrialized West, reacted immediately. In January 1991, the United Nations, and particularly the United States, sent forces to drive the Iraqis out of Kuwait in what we now call the **Persian Gulf War**. The immediate impact of their success was the liberation of Kuwait and the humiliation of Iraq, which was subjected to UN monitoring, severe limitations on its military activities, and economic sanctions. Nevertheless, Hussein remained in power, and the UN forces left the region without moving forward to oust him. Hussein held on to his brutal dictatorship for another ten years while also, many argue, ignoring key elements of the peace treaty that allowed him to keep his power after his invasion of Kuwait.

In April 2003, a coalition of countries consisting primarily of the United States and Great Britain invaded Iraq to oust Saddam from power. Saddam's government quickly fell to coalition forces but Hussein himself was not captured until December of that year. Sovereignty was returned to a transitional government in June of 2004, and a new democratically elected government was formed in May 2005. However, since the initial invasion, Iraq has been increasingly plagued with sectional conflicts among Sunni, Shiites, and Kurds, the conflicts defined by suicide bombings against coalition forces and more and more against Iraqi forces and civilians of rival sects. Even amidst the violence, the Iraqi government ratified a new constitution in October 2005, followed by a general election in December 2005, with legislative seats distributed according to "proportional representation." This system allotted percentages of seats to women, Sunni Muslims, Kurdish Iraqis, as well as to the Shia majority. Despite delays in certifying the results of the December 2005 election, the newly elected government took office in May 2006, with **Jalal Talabani**, who is Kurdish, as president, and **Nouri al-Maliki**, who is Shia, as prime minister. The government has faced a number of challenges, and it remains to be seen whether it can successfully bring a violent insurgency to peaceful engagement in the political process. Even with the end of U.S. combat operations and the withdrawal of most coalition troops by the end of 2011, Iraq must also still contend with a number of opposing domestic and international interests as it tries to find stability in its new incarnation.

Taliban, Al Qaeda, Osama bin Laden

During the early 1980s, the Soviet Union sent thousands of troops to Afghanistan at the request of Marxist military leader **Nur Muhammad Taraki**, who had engineered a military coup against the previous government. Many Afghans opposed communism and Soviet intervention, however, and soon a massive civil war raged. Some of the resistors called themselves "holy warriors" and, with the aid of weapons from the Western powers who supplied the Cold War on every front, launched guerilla attacks against the superior military might of the Soviet Union. As internal problems escalated in the Soviet Union, Gorbachev agreed to withdraw Soviet troops from the region and a peace accord was signed. While communism fell apart in the Soviet Union and Eastern Europe, the problems in Afghanistan continued. The decline of communism removed the Soviet threat, but warring factions vied to fill the power void.

The power that finally triumphed after 14 years of fighting and more than 2 million deaths was called the **Taliban**, an Islamic fundamentalist regime that captured the capital of Kabul in 1996. The new government imposed strict Islamic law and severe restrictions on women. It also provided safe haven for **Osama bin Laden**, the Saudi leader of an international terrorist network, known as **Al Qaeda**, which has a serious distaste for Saudi Arabia and the United States. It's believed that Al Qaeda's main issue with Saudi Arabia is that the ruling family is too cozy with the United States and that they have allowed U.S. troops to remain in the country since the Persian Gulf War, which amounts to the presence of infidels in a kingdom that is home to Islam's most holy sites. Al Qaeda despises the United States for what many believe are at least three reasons. First, the United States supports Israel, which the organization would like to see removed from the planet. Second, it has troops stationed in Saudi Arabia, and third, the United States is the primary agent of globalization, which Al Qaeda believes is infecting Islamic culture.

On **September 11, 2001**, Al Qaeda operatives managed to take control of four American passenger jets and fly two of them into the **World Trade Center** in New York City, one into the Pentagon in Washington, D.C., and one into a field in Pennsylvania. The towers of the World Trade Center fell to the ground, killing more than 2,500 civilians. The deaths of the people on all four planes and those killed at the Pentagon bring the total number of casualties to almost 3,000. The United States immediately launched a war on terrorism, targeting Al Qaeda and the Taliban. Within months, the Taliban was removed from power and U.S. and UN forces occupied the country of Afghanistan. Al Qaeda, on the other hand, still survives, though its leadership is being directly attacked and eliminated, most notably with the death of Osama bin Laden in May of 2011.

Although smaller in scale, suicide bombing and terrorist attacks (many linked to Al Qaeda and similar groups) continue regularly. They are a problem throughout the Israeli territories, between Sunni and Shia factions in Iraq, targeting tourists in the cities of Saudi Arabia, Egypt, and Turkey, and among Muslim separatists in Russia. Coordinated attacks occurred throughout Lebanon in 2004 and 2005, killing the former Prime Minister Rafiq Hariri (among others), while larger-scale attacks occurred in March 2004 on commuter trains in Madrid, Spain, in July 2005 on the London subway system, and the following July on trains in Mumbai (Bombay), India. Many of these attacks were linked to Islamic fundamentalists, who have also attacked Jewish and Christian minorities throughout Europe and the Middle East.

The Rise of ISIS

The recent rise of so-called Islamic State (also known as IS, ISIL, or ISIS) in Iraq and Syria has led to constant instability in that region. ISIS has been especially effective at broadcasting its terrorist methods through online videos. The extremely graphic videos, which feature beheadings, shootings, and other executions, have led to nearly universal condemnation from the international community. The stated goal of ISIS is to revive a caliphate that unifies the entire Islamic world under ISIS's rule. Similarly, the terrorist group Boko Haram, whose name means "Western education is forbidden," has led to conflict and violence in West African countries such as Nigeria, Chad, Niger, and Cameroon. An alliance between ISIS and Boko Haram, which was formalized in 2015, will only worsen the terrorist problem in the Islamic world over the coming years.

World Trade and Cultural Exchange

The end of the Cold War removed the last obstacles to true global interaction and trade. Currencies were no longer tied to old alliances, and new business opportunities emerged. This deregulation, along with the development of systems of instantaneous communication such as the Internet, resulted in globally integrated financial networks. Commercial interdependence intensified in the 1980s as eastern Asia began to flex its industrial and commercial muscles.

Competition further drove global developments, and regional trading blocks such as the **North American Free Trade Agreement (NAFTA)** were created in the early 1990s. The European Economic Community (EEC), originally formed in 1957, transformed into the modern **European Union** (EU) tied to a single currency, the euro. The ease with which goods and ideas are transported across the world has resulted in cultures being more homogenous and integrated. This does not mean that local culture is lost, but it does mean that one can satisfy a craving for a Starbucks latte inside Beijing's Forbidden City. It also means almost instantaneous access to a wider range of music, art, literature, and information. Much of this is facilitated by the spread of English as the language of business and communication across the globe. This began in the eighteenth century with the far-flung colonies of the British Empire and continued with the emergence of the United States as a global power after World War II.

The **European Union** or EU was formed to give the United States some economic competition by banding Europe together in a single market. The real impetus to expand the powers of the EU came in the early 1990s when the collapse of the Soviet Union simultaneously opened Europe and left the U.S. unchallenged as the world's superpower. In 1989, the EU had 12 members; by 2011, it had 27, of which 10 were former Soviet satellite nations. The EU has three branches: executive, legislative, and judicial. Elections are held throughout Europe every five years. The formation of a monetary union, the **Eurozone**, in 1999, led all but three nations (UK, Sweden, and Denmark) to adopt a unified currency, the euro, in 2002.

While economic integration initially seemed relatively easy and produced a few boom years, in the crisis of the late 2000s (which began slightly earlier in Europe than in the U.S.), it became clear that stronger economies such as Germany's had borne the freight of weaker, over-extended economies such as Greece's, and by 2010, economic collapse in states such as Greece, Ireland, and Portugal threatened to destabilize the entire Eurozone. This has provoked sharp debates about economic integration that have now piled onto existing concerns about political and judicial integration, putting national interests and questions of sovereignty at stake.

Note the Change: The Threat of "McDonaldization"

Consider for a moment just how far and wide fast food culture has spread since the first McDonald's restaurant opened in California in the late 1930s. Take a quick jump over to McDonald's website and you can view the list of over 100 countries in which McDonald's has restaurants today, including Saudi Arabia, Pakistan, and Egypt. But why point out these Muslim countries? The so-called "McDonaldization" of the world can be used as both an example and a metaphor for the spread of what is predominantly a Western popular culture to the rest of the world. Many countries, such as India and even China, have embraced the fruits of Westernization, integrating and assimilating aspects of Western culture into their own. Other groups however, including fundamentalist movements in some Muslim countries, have rejected this "invasion" of modern Western culture, which they see as a threat to their traditional Islamic ways. Responses to the perceived threat of globalization have included many acts of international terrorism in an effort to fight encroachment as symbolized by the international spread of such Western cultural icons as Starbucks, Walmart, and Disney.

To Be Rich Is Glorious: The Rise of China and India

"Socialism with Chinese Characteristics" or "To Be Rich Is Glorious" sum up Deng Xiaoping's plans for China after the death of Chairman Mao. Since normalized trade relations with the United States in the 1990s and acceptance into the World Trade Organization in 2001, China has become an industrial and economic juggernaut. What began with the creation of **special economic zones** exempt from the strict controls of communism in the late 1980s has become the world's warehouse and discount store! In the last ten years, China's imports have increased from $82 billion (1999) to $338 billion (2008) built on a wide array of everyday consumer goods, toys, and apparel. This new and profitable industrial revolution has funded a building boom throughout China, brought the 2008 Olympic games to Beijing, and contributed to a rising and educated middle class who now shop and eat at 300 Starbucks and 800 McDonald's restaurants. Economic success has also led to a crackdown on Internet freedom. Politically, it is pretty much the same old China. The CCP allows some local elections and the *New York Times* is available online, but one party is clearly in charge and watching what you Google.

India, the world's largest democracy and one of its fastest growing economies, has spent the past two decades making itself indispensible to the globally connected world. In 1991, India was broke, the leading contender for prime minister had been assassinated, and the country desperately needed a way to reinvent its economy and industries. Since loans from the IMF required economic reforms and austerity measures, major industries were privatized and others were publicly traded. India's greatest advantage is its highly educated and skilled population, yet the focus on traditional industry advocated by Gandhi had left India isolated and unable to compete globally. The desperation of 1991, at a time when technology and computer chip industries were developing in the United States, was a moment of opportunity for Indian investors and workers, many of whom had migrated to Silicon Valley. Indian entrepreneurs brought these new ideas back to Indian companies such as Infosys and Tata, developed technology to route global calls, and built on the global demand for software, new technology, and support.

Both India and China are nuclear powers with two of the world's largest armies. Both are currently dealing with belligerent neighbors (Pakistan and North Korea), both have complicated relationships and history with Western powers, both have yet to deal with tremendous economic inequality and poverty within their borders, and as members of the G20 (see Global Alphabet Soup) both have figured out a way to keep growing while much of the industrialized world is in an economic slowdown.

Global Alphabet Soup

With globalization of trade come many agencies and organizations designed to protect and facilitate trade. The earliest of these were the International Monetary Fund or IMF (1945), with 185 members and the World Bank (also founded in 1945), with 188 members. Both organizations were formed to stabilize world economic relationships and to loan financial assistance when needed. At the same time, the General Agreement on Tariffs and Trade, or **GATT**, was agreed upon to reduce barriers to international trade. GATT became the World Trade Organization, or WTO, in 1994. The WTO boasts 153 member states—most of the world's active trading nations—who adhere to the WTO's rules and regulations regarding trade relationships.

An organization of note is the **Group of Six**, or **G6**, created in 1975 as a forum for the world's major industrialized democracies. Its original members included the U.S., Great Britain, West Germany, Italy, Japan, and France. They have since been joined by Canada in 1977, and by Russia in 1997, and are now know as the **G8**. Recently, Russia was excluded from the forum by the other members in March 2014 as a result of its involvement in the 2014 Crimea crisis in Ukraine. The group has changed yet again and now meets as the **G7** group of nations. This informal summit of the world's most powerful leaders meets annually to discuss issues of mutual or global concern such as climate change, terrorism, and trade.

In addition to the G8, a group of 19 nations plus EU representatives make up the **G20** or the Group of 20 Finance Ministers and Central Bank Governors. Beginning with the financial crises of the late 1990s, this group represents key industrialized as well as developing economies.

Environmental Change

Until the 1980s, environmental issues focused on localized pollution or waste management, but along with global integration in every sector came global environmental concerns. Most recently, these concerns have focused on food; as suppliers become ever more distant from their consumers and trade agreements open up supply routes, safety regulations may not follow.

The "green revolution" of the 1950s and 1960s led to increased agricultural productivity through industrial means—chemical fertilizers and pesticides, biologically engineered foods, more efficient means of harvesting, and more marginal lands available for agriculture. While this resulted in inexpensive and plentiful food supplies, it destroyed traditional landscapes including rainforests in Indonesia and South America, reduced species diversity, and fostered social conflicts that might not have otherwise existed. As has been true throughout history, marginal lands cannot sustain the population increases they initially produce with new industrial technologies. This is especially notable in eastern and sub-Saharan Africa, where political and financial mismanagement contributed to widespread famines in the 1970s and 1980s.

Alternative Advances
Although some progress has been made in developing alternative fuel options like ethanol, there are big drawbacks to them as well. Clearly, much more research into viable alternatives to fossil fuel is needed.

Bottled water has become ubiquitous, but water is a crucial natural resource that is often carelessly managed by cities at the expense of their hinterlands. This is not a rapidly renewable resource and needs to be regulated for drinking and for agriculture. A similar pattern is seen with industrialized countries' consumption of oil—they want more and they want it cheap! Oil fuels industry, transportation, and heating of homes and businesses. The insatiable appetite for oil reserves on the part of industrialized democracies has led to strange political and economic alliances (see the previous section on the Middle East).

Finally, a quick note on global warming. It's getting warmer and human activities, including fuel consumption, heating, and cooling, are contributing to this. The outcome of these warming trends is uncertain. On the positive side, there will be longer growing seasons in temperate parts of the world, but the negative effects are more extreme conditions in marginal areas—longer periods of drought in some, flooding and disappearance of coastlines in others. The first Earth Summit on global climate change was held in 1992 in Rio de Janeiro. Five years later, the Kyoto Protocol was an attempt to make a global agreement on ways to reduce environmental damages, but because the United States has refused to ratify the Protocol (and Canada denounced it in 2011), it remains controversial and unable to function to its full potential. Industrialized nations continue to struggle with balancing potential damage to the environment with the growth potential of their business sector, and it is the business of production and consumption that has been of primary importance to policymakers.

Global Health Crises

Within globalization efforts, the relief of health crises is a primary focus. Non-profit organizations such as the WHO (World Health Organization) work to lower infant mortality as well as to combat various diseases, such as influenza, which kill millions in third-world countries due to a lack of appropriate medical care and medicine. This problem has existed as far back as 1918, when a flu epidemic killed millions across the globe, but is still important today. Recent outbreaks of bird flu and swine flu, two strains of influenza passed from animals to humans, show that such epidemics, especially in countries without the U.S.'s high level of sanitation, are still an issue.

AIDS is another notable global health crisis, especially in sub-Saharan Africa, where almost 25 percent of adults in some countries live with HIV (the virus that causes AIDS). While AIDS treatments can help those with the disease to live relatively normal lives, there is no cure as yet for this fatal illness, and only those in wealthier countries tend to have access to the most advanced treatments. Currently, global efforts to combat this health crisis are focused on prevention, and the WHO and other organizations are working on changing the social norms and behaviors of at-risk populations, particularly in Africa where the AIDS crisis is at its worst.

Other notable global health issues today include diseases that, in developed countries, are not a threat, such as cholera. New treatments for cholera, such as oral rehydration therapy, have drastically lowered mortality rates associated with the disease in Bangladesh, India, and neighboring countries. A severe outbreak of the Ebola virus in West Africa received global attention throughout 2014. As of this writing, the virus has claimed more than 10,000 lives, mostly in Liberia, Sierra Leone, and Guinea. When a few high-profile (but isolated) cases of Ebola appeared in Europe and the United States, strong national debates emerged about forced quarantines and open borders. Global health issues highlight the disparities that, despite the ongoing process of globalization, still exist between first-world, industrialized countries and those that are not.

Another AP, Perhaps?
Much of what you are learning in your AP World History class could prepare you for the AP Human Geography Exam as well. Check out AP Central for further information about that exam and pick up a copy of *Cracking the AP Human Geography Exam* for detailed review.

The Age of the Computer

The single most important technological advance since the 1980s has been the rise of computers and, in turn, the Internet. Beginning in the 1970s, American companies such as Compaq and IBM developed new hardware, which allowed computers to shrink radically in size (by using a silicon chip to store data). The PC, or personal computer, became a reality, since this advance meant that computers no longer took up entire rooms. By the late 1980s, an early version of the Internet existed, though only those with advanced technical knowledge had access.

In the 1990s, more homes got computers; commercial software, such as web browsers and the services and programs offered by America Online, introduced the Internet to the American population at large, transforming both the home and the workplace. The Y2K scare, which involved a possible glitch in computers caused by the switch of dates to the new millennium, pointed out how dependent industry and society were on computers and the Internet. Y2K did not cause an actual crisis, and personal computers and similar technologies, including cell phones, are all the more crucial today to the personal and global business lives of many.

More recently, social media and the spread of the Internet have had huge ramifications worldwide. Social media platforms such as Twitter and Facebook have changed the way news is reported and have played a huge role in political developments in Middle Eastern countries, for example. During the "Arab Spring" of 2011, oppressive regimes in several nations were toppled due in part to the exposure—via social media—of the problems in those countries. Internet censorship exists in many nations, notably India and China, but overall this technology has served to bring people together both in business and in other aspects of life, changing the way we receive our news, take classes, and even shop. One current concern, however, is the growing gap in access between those in developed and those in undeveloped countries. The importance of the Internet and computer technology may serve as a barrier to globalization in countries without the infrastructure to join this "digital revolution."

The Internet has also raised the important issue of government surveillance and individual privacy. In 2013, Edward Snowden, an American computer specialist with access to classified documents, leaked information about the government's anti-terrorism measures to journalists. His revelations were astonishing. According to Snowden and the documents he released, the U.S. government had been collecting information from all of its citizens—not just terrorists or potential terrorists—and storing it in massive data centers. Such a surveillance system is considered by many privacy experts to be unconstitutional and unnecessary. Some in the government have denied the existence of such programs or claimed they are both legal and necessary to stop future terrorist attacks. For his part, Snowden fled the country and has been formally charged with crimes by the U.S. government for leaking the information. The problem was not limited to the United States, however. Similar revelations have sparked loud international debates in Europe, Asia, and Latin America and reveal the complicated nature of a world in which so much private information is accessible online.

IV. CHANGES AND CONTINUITIES IN THE ROLE OF WOMEN

Finally, the upheavals and changes of the twentieth century resulted in really dramatic changes in women's social, political, and economic roles. The integration and global connectedness of the world made access to education and political freedoms far more widespread, especially among the middle and upper classes. Change came more slowly to the lower and working classes, but still it came.

Politically, women gained the right to vote in many parts of the world by the first quarter of the twentieth century. By 1930, that right had been gained by women in much of Latin America, India, China, Japan, and most of Europe. After World War II, most of the newly independent African countries included women's suffrage in their constitutions, and it is only in the most fundamentalist of the Middle Eastern countries that women still do not have the right to vote. However, having the right to vote differs significantly from having the education and opportunity to vote. In most Asian and African countries, female access to formal political power continues to be limited.

Contradictions also exist between theory and practice in communist and formerly communist countries. Under communism, everyone was equal, women played key roles in the Communist Revolutions in Russia, China and Cuba, and educational opportunities were opened especially in professions such as medicine. Women were also generally given equal legal rights including those of inheritance, divorce, and child rearing. However, in reality, discrimination and gender issues continue. Almost all key positions within the Communist parties were and are held by men. In China, the one-child policy and mandatory sterilization disproportionately impact women and female children. State-sponsored sterilization was also common in Puerto Rico and India. Additionally, the end of communism and the loosening of economic restrictions seems to present more opportunities for men than for women.

Family structure changed dramatically in the twentieth century, especially in the industrialized world. Birth rates dropped, birth control was widely available, and marriage rates declined as divorce and second marriages became more common. The twentieth century also saw dramatic changes in the role of women at work. Beginning with wage labor in factories during the World Wars, women's presence in the workforce has become more widely accepted. A shift to profitable industries in chemicals, textiles, and electronics, has provided further economic opportunities for women. By the mid-1980s, education and access in Westernized and industrialized countries allowed women to participate fully in the work force. Women in agricultural economies, however, continued to have their labor under-enumerated. Throughout the world, women's pay has yet to fully equal that of male counterparts, nor are women compensated for the time they spend on a "second shift" as primary caregivers of young children.

V. PULLING IT ALL TOGETHER

You've read about a lot of stuff in this chapter. Two world wars. A cold war and all its consequences. The end of European imperialism. The rise of the United States as a superpower. Islamic fundamentalism in the Middle East. These are all huge issues. It's hard to discern immediately how you can connect them all together other than to say that there were a lot of wars and a lot of hatred. Nevertheless, beyond the morbidity and feelings of helplessness that a careful study of history can engender, there are also a lot of ways to think about history that can help you evaluate how people and the world function.

In the last chapter, we talked a lot about nationalism, and it certainly didn't stop in the twentieth century. Nationalism not only led to fascism in Nazi Germany, but also to independence movements after World War II in India and Africa, and in Europe and Asia after the fall of the Soviet Union. Sometimes it was based on broad cultural characteristics—Gandhi, for example, unsuccessfully wanting everyone to look at themselves as Indians, not as Hindus or Muslims—and other times it was very narrowly defined—Serbs, for example, or Nazis.

Regardless of its forms, nationalism affected all of the major global events in the twentieth century. In both World War I and World War II, the aggressors were highly nationalistic. The independence movements following World War II were nationalistic. And the Cold War, because it pitted two opposing worldviews that were so strongly identified with the nations of the Soviet Union and the United States, was arguably a nationalist struggle as well. National pride was on the line. In the end, superpower status was on the line, too.

By the late twentieth century, whether because of nationalism or not, there was a huge number of independent nation-states. Each former colony in Africa was independent. Lots of new countries formed from the old Soviet Union. What's more, most of the countries were developing along democratic lines—though some along militaristic or Islamic theocratic lines—and capitalism seemed to be making huge gains after the fall of the Soviet Union, which leads us to the next question.

Is There Currently a Convergence of Cultures?

If you study history enough, you can argue for both sides. On the one hand, globalization is clearly occurring and has for a long time. It's just that now it's happening a lot faster and penetrating more and more hidden parts of the globe. Centuries ago, trade, conquest, and exploration were forms of globalization because they brought people together, essentially "making the world smaller." Major movements like the Scientific Revolution, the Enlightenment, and the Industrial Revolution can certainly be categorized as shifts toward globalization because they weren't culturally specific, but rather could be applied nearly anywhere around the globe. They brought people closer together because they led to certain ways of thinking that were attractive and accepted by different kinds of people. If people start to agree on how the universe is organized or how governments should be organized, that is most certainly a convergence of cultures.

In the twentieth century, globalization really took off. Aided by transportation, communication, and imperialism, anything produced in one country could be received in another. Popular examples of globalization are the appearance of the same multinational companies everywhere (seeing a McDonald's in Istanbul) and certainly the use of the Internet, but globalization is much broader than even these examples. Globalization has led to an interconnectedness of entire economies. The Great Depression in the 1930s proved that the economies of most industrialized nations were heavily intertwined. Today, the economies are so connected that a fall in stock prices in Tokyo will have an instantaneous impact on the stock market in the United States.

As more and more countries start to look the same (independent, democratic, constitutional), their economies function in similar ways (stock market, low barriers to trade, strong banking system), and their cultures look the same (educated people who know English, cell phones in their hands, Hollywood movies playing at theaters), it can be strongly argued that there is a convergence of cultures.

On the other hand, globalization doesn't necessarily mean convergence; it just means that everything is spread all around the globe all the time. It doesn't mean that people accept, like, or want what's being hurled at them. It just means that it's available. Some argue that globalization will lead to an increase in the number of people who lash out against it, sometimes aggressively or violently. Globalization isn't well received in Islamic fundamentalist countries, or in countries that are trying hard to maintain a historical cultural identity, like France.

More significantly, it can't be denied that the biggest movements of the twentieth century were rooted in self-determination and nationalism. The whole point of self-determination is for nations to chart their own course. If self-determination and nationalism mean that a country is going to use its independence to do what every other country does, then why be independent in the first place? Clearly, people want to chart their own course. They fought wars for the right to do so. They must have done so for a reason. So it makes sense that globalization will have its limits. Moreover, isn't the world a whole lot less consolidated today than it was under European imperialism, when that small continent ruled the world? Doesn't that suggest the opposite of global convergence?

In the end, there's no right answer to this question. The challenge is not to accurately predict the future, but to have an understanding of history to make a reasonable, defendable argument about the direction that history seems to be taking. If you can discuss globalization, nationalism, and self-determination in the same essay or conversation without totally losing your mind, you have command enough of the issues and complexities to be confident in yourself. Keep reading, keep studying, and keep thinking.

CHAPTER 11 KEY TERMS

Triple Alliance
Central Powers
Schlieffen Plan
isolationism
Zimmermann telegram
Fourteen Points
League of Nations
April Theses
Red Army
New Economic Policy
  (NEP)
Five Year Plans
collectivization
Great Depression
fascism
totalitarianism
blackshirts
Reichstag
nationalism
appeasement
Manhattan Project
the Holocaust
genocide
Marshall Plan
Cold War
spheres of influence
Soviet bloc
Western bloc
NATO
Iron Curtain
Three Principles of the
  People
Westernization
guerilla warfare
Platt Amendment
"Good Neighbor"
export economy
glasnost
perestroika
ethnic cleansing
passive resistance
NGOs
apartheid
pogroms
OPEC
special economic zones

Archduke Franz
  Ferdinand
Gavrilo Princip
Treaty of Versailles
  (1919)
Russian Revolution
Czar Nicholas
Alexander Kerensky
Bolsheviks
Vladimir Lenin
Treaty of Brest-Litovsk
Soviet Union
Leon Trotsky
Ataturk (Mustafa
  Kemal)
Joseph Stalin
USSR
Franklin Roosevelt
Benito Mussolini
Weimar Republic
National Socialist
  Party (Nazis)
Adolf Hitler
Third Reich
Francisco Franco
Rhineland
Munich Conference
  (1938)
Neville Chamberlain
Nazi-Soviet Pact (1939)
Manchukuo
Anti-Comintern Pact
Winston Churchill
Battle of Britain
Tripartite Pact
Pearl Harbor
D-Day
Harry Truman
Hiroshima and
  Nagasaki
Berlin blockade
Berlin Airlift
Yalta and Potsdam
Warsaw Pact
Nuclear Nonprolifera-
  tion Treaty (1968)

International Atomic
  Energy Agency (1957)
Chiang Kai-shek
Mao Zedong
People's Republic of
  China
Cultural Revolution
Tiananmen Square
  massacre
Ho Chi Minh
Ngo Dinh Diem
Fidel Castro
Cuban Revolution
Bay of Pigs Invasion
Cuban Missile Crisis
National Action Party
  (PAN)
Mikhail Gorbachev
Boris Yeltsin
Muslim League
Amritsar massacre
Gandhi
Muhammad Ali Jinnah
Gamal Nasser
Tutsi and Hutu
Nelson Mandela
Sharpeville massacre
Zionists
Balfour Declaration of
  1917
Arab-Israeli War (1948)
Palestine Liberation
  Organization (PLO)
Yassir Arafat
Ariel Sharon
Iranian Revolution
Ayatollah Khomeini
Iran-Iraq War
Persian Gulf War
Saddam Hussein
North American Free
  Trade Agreement
  (NAFTA)
Group of Six (G6)
West Bank
September 11 attacks
European Union

Chapter 11 Drill

See the end of the chapter for the answers and explanations.

Questions 1–4 refer to the passage below.

"At present, we are concerned with a question which has immense importance for the party now and for the future—with how the cult of the person of Stalin has been gradually growing, the cult which became at a certain specific stage the source of a whole series of exceedingly serious and grave perversions of party principles, of party democracy, of revolutionary legality...Stalin originated the concept of 'enemy of the people.' This term automatically rendered it unnecessary that the ideological errors of a man or men engaged in a controversy be proven; this term made possible the usage of the most cruel repression, violating all norms of revolutionary legality, against anyone who in any way disagreed with Stalin, against those who were only suspected of hostile intent, against those who had bad reputations."

Nikita Khruschev, Special Report to the 20th Congress of the Communist Party of the Soviet Union, 1956

1. Which of the following most clearly describes the "cruel repression" referenced in the passage?

    (A) Economic discrimination and severe social pressures
    (B) Mob violence initiated and directed by state officials
    (C) Persecution through the use of secret police, summary execution, and work camps
    (D) Exile or deportation out of the country for periods up to twenty years

2. Which of the following best characterizes the impact of the document from which this passage is drawn?

    (A) It marked an important thaw in social and political tensions.
    (B) It marked the beginning of a purge of the Communist Party under Stalin.
    (C) It marked the beginning of the end for McCarthyism.
    (D) It marked the de-Stalinization of the Chinese Communist Party.

3. Based on the passage and your knowledge of world history, which of the following offers the most accurate contrast between Stalin's mode of rule and that of Khruschev?

    (A) Stalin governed through fear, while Khruschev relied on revolutionary zeal among the workers to bring about true communism.
    (B) While Khruschev established a democratic system of policy deliberation in the Soviet Union, Stalin ruled as a tyrant without input from the Party or the people.
    (C) Khruschev restored the Party to the center of Soviet government under the so-called Nomenklatura system, while Stalin sidelined the Party through a tyrannical cult of personality.
    (D) Both Stalin and Khruschev relied primarily on repression and terror to carry out their policies.

4. Which of the following best characterizes the Cold War in the 1950s?

    (A) U.S. economic and technological advances had led to a decisive U.S. advantage in the Cold War.
    (B) Infighting between China, Yugoslavia, and the Soviet Union over leadership of the communist bloc paralyzed the Warsaw Pact.
    (C) Advances in Soviet rocket technology gave the Soviet Union a clear advantage over the United States.
    (D) A combination of technological, industrial, and diplomatic factors interacted to generate a situation where two evenly matched political blocs struggled for advantage over the other.

TIMELINE OF MAJOR DEVELOPMENTS SINCE 1900

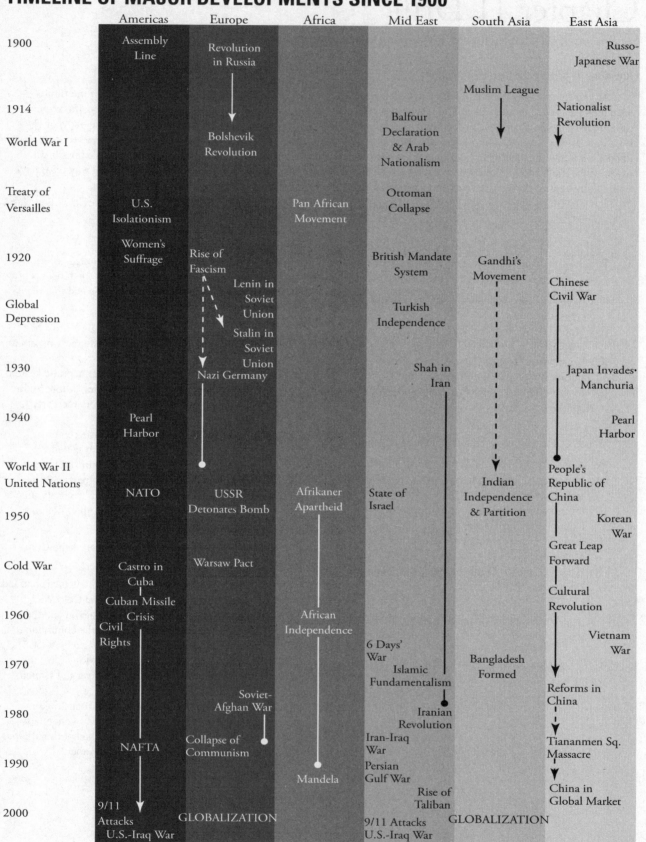

	Americas	Europe	Africa	Mid East	South Asia	East Asia
1900	Assembly Line	Revolution in Russia				Russo-Japanese War
1914				Balfour Declaration & Arab Nationalism	Muslim League	Nationalist Revolution
World War I		Bolshevik Revolution				
Treaty of Versailles	U.S. Isolationism		Pan African Movement	Ottoman Collapse		
1920	Women's Suffrage	Rise of Fascism		British Mandate System	Gandhi's Movement	Chinese Civil War
Global Depression		Lenin in Soviet Union		Turkish Independence		
		Stalin in Soviet Union				
1930		Nazi Germany		Shah in Iran		Japan Invades Manchuria
1940	Pearl Harbor					Pearl Harbor
World War II United Nations	NATO	USSR Detonates Bomb	Afrikaner Apartheid	State of Israel	Indian Independence & Partition	People's Republic of China
1950						Korean War
Cold War	Castro in Cuba	Warsaw Pact				Great Leap Forward
	Cuban Missile Crisis		African Independence			Cultural Revolution
1960	Civil Rights					Vietnam War
1970				6 Days' War	Bangladesh Formed	
				Islamic Fundamentalism		Reforms in China
1980		Soviet-Afghan War		Iranian Revolution		
	NAFTA	Collapse of Communism		Iran-Iraq War		Tiananmen Sq. Massacre
1990			Mandela	Persian Gulf War		China in Global Market
				Rise of Taliban		
2000	9/11 Attacks	GLOBALIZATION		9/11 Attacks	GLOBALIZATION	
	U.S.-Iraq War			U.S.-Iraq War		

CHAPTER 11 DRILL EXPLANATIONS

1. **C** This question is essentially getting at a characterization of Stalinist repression. Use POE. Choice (A) is far too mild; this best describes the consequences suffered by those accused of Communist Party affiliations in the United States during the McCarthy era. Choice (B) does not match the legalism or the structure of Stalinism, being instead a good description of the repressive practices of Maoist China. Choice (D) does not accurately describe any repressive system used in any Communist state in the first half of the twentieth century, and thus is incorrect. Choice (C) does speak to the use of secret police as the main instrument of state repression, while also incorporating a description of the most common punishments; summary execution and sentencing to terms in the Gulag. Therefore, (C) is correct.

2. **A** Knowledge of important dates in Soviet history will help you here. This "Secret Speech," as it is known, took place in 1956, while Stalin died in 1953. Therefore, (B) cannot be correct, as Stalin had been dead three years before anyone in the Soviet Union summoned the courage to criticize him. Similarly, the Army-McCarthy hearings were in 1954, so McCarthyism was well on the decline before this speech was given; eliminate (C). Choice (D) is half-right: it did mark the beginnings of de-Stalinization, but only in the Soviet Union and its satellites. Stalin's legacy lasted much longer in Maoist China, and indeed Khruschev's repudiation of Stalin was a driver of the Sino-Soviet split. Therefore, (A) is the best answer.

3. **C** For comparison questions, make sure both parts of the answer are correct. Look at (A), for example: while it is true that Stalin ruled by fear, Khruschev did not return power to the workers and peasants of the Soviet Union. His government also relied on administrative repression and government action, though in a much different way; therefore, eliminate (A). Choice (B) is more difficult: although it is true that Khruschev restored a measure of deliberative authority to Party bodies, governance did not become democratic; instead, it became oligarchic, so (B) is incorrect. Choice (D) mischaracterizes Khruschev's government in the other direction: although the Soviet Union remained authoritarian, the atmosphere of terror that Stalin used to implement policy was dismantled under Khruschev. Choice (C) accurately characterizes both the shift to an oligarchic system centered around the Party (the Nomenklatura system) and the tyrannical character of Stalin's cult of personality, so (C) is the correct answer.

4. **D** Choice (A) describes the Brezhnev era, which began much later in the Cold War. Choice (B) mischaracterizes the import of the lack of unity in the Communist bloc: though Yugoslavia did break away, it was a minor state and, broadly speaking, this did not affect the Cold War. The Sino-Soviet split was more momentous but also came later (1961). Choice (C) may sound plausible due to Sputnik and related developments, but this was a public-relations measure rather than one that substantially shifted the balance of power in the Cold War one way or the other. Choice (D) best conveys the stalemate of the early Cold War, and is thus the correct answer.

REFLECT

Respond to the following questions:

- For which content topics discussed in this chapter do you feel you have achieved sufficient mastery to answer multiple-choice questions correctly?

- For which content topics discussed in this chapter do you feel you have achieved sufficient mastery to discuss effectively in a short-answer response or essay?

- For which content topics discussed in this chapter do you feel you need more work before you can answer multiple-choice questions correctly?

- For which content topics discussed in this chapter do you feel you need more work before you can discuss effectively in a short-answer response or essay?

- What parts of this chapter are you going to re-review?

- Will you seek further help outside of this book (such as a teacher, tutor, or AP Students) on any of the content in this chapter—and, if so, on what content?

Part VI
Practice Test 2

- Practice Test 2
- Practice Test 2: Answers and Explanations

Practice Test 2

The Princeton Review®

Completely darken bubbles with a No. 2 pencil. If you make a mistake, be sure to erase mark completely. Erase all stray marks.

1.

YOUR NAME: _____
(Print)   Last   First   M.I.

SIGNATURE: _____ DATE: __ / __ / __

HOME ADDRESS: _____
(Print)   Number and Street

_____
City   State   Zip Code

PHONE NO.: _____

IMPORTANT: Please fill in these boxes exactly as shown on the back cover of your test book.

2. TEST FORM

3. TEST CODE

4. REGISTRATION NUMBER

5. YOUR NAME

First 4 letters of last name				FIRST INIT	MID INIT

6. DATE OF BIRTH

Month	Day	Year
JAN		
FEB		
MAR		
APR		
MAY		
JUN		
JUL		
AUG		
SEP		
OCT		
NOV		
DEC		

7. GENDER

MALE
FEMALE

The Princeton Review®

1. (A) (B) (C) (D)
2. (A) (B) (C) (D)
3. (A) (B) (C) (D)
4. (A) (B) (C) (D)
5. (A) (B) (C) (D)
6. (A) (B) (C) (D)
7. (A) (B) (C) (D)
8. (A) (B) (C) (D)
9. (A) (B) (C) (D)
10. (A) (B) (C) (D)
11. (A) (B) (C) (D)
12. (A) (B) (C) (D)
13. (A) (B) (C) (D)
14. (A) (B) (C) (D)
15. (A) (B) (C) (D)

16. (A) (B) (C) (D)
17. (A) (B) (C) (D)
18. (A) (B) (C) (D)
19. (A) (B) (C) (D)
20. (A) (B) (C) (D)
21. (A) (B) (C) (D)
22. (A) (B) (C) (D)
23. (A) (B) (C) (D)
24. (A) (B) (C) (D)
25. (A) (B) (C) (D)
26. (A) (B) (C) (D)
27. (A) (B) (C) (D)
28. (A) (B) (C) (D)
29. (A) (B) (C) (D)
30. (A) (B) (C) (D)

31. (A) (B) (C) (D)
32. (A) (B) (C) (D)
33. (A) (B) (C) (D)
34. (A) (B) (C) (D)
35. (A) (B) (C) (D)
36. (A) (B) (C) (D)
37. (A) (B) (C) (D)
38. (A) (B) (C) (D)
39. (A) (B) (C) (D)
40. (A) (B) (C) (D)
41. (A) (B) (C) (D)
42. (A) (B) (C) (D)
43. (A) (B) (C) (D)
44. (A) (B) (C) (D)
45. (A) (B) (C) (D)

46. (A) (B) (C) (D)
47. (A) (B) (C) (D)
48. (A) (B) (C) (D)
49. (A) (B) (C) (D)
50. (A) (B) (C) (D)
51. (A) (B) (C) (D)
52. (A) (B) (C) (D)
53. (A) (B) (C) (D)
54. (A) (B) (C) (D)
55. (A) (B) (C) (D)

The Exam

AP® World History Exam

DO NOT OPEN THIS BOOKLET UNTIL YOU ARE TOLD TO DO SO.

At a Glance

Time
55 minutes
Number of Questions
55
Percent of Total Score
40%
Writing Instrument
Pencil required

Instructions

Section I, Part A of this exam contains 55 multiple-choice questions. Fill in only the ovals for numbers 1 through 55 on your answer sheet.

Indicate all of your answers to the multiple-choice questions on the answer sheet. No credit will be given for anything written in this exam booklet, but you may use the booklet for notes or scratch work. After you have decided which of the suggested answers is best, completely fill in the corresponding oval on the answer sheet. Give only one answer to each question. If you change an answer, be sure that the previous mark is erased completely. Here is a sample question and answer.

Sample Question   Sample Answer

Chicago is a   Ⓐ ● Ⓒ Ⓓ
(A) state
(B) city
(C) country
(D) continent

Use your time effectively, working as quickly as you can without losing accuracy. Do not spend too much time on any one question. Go on to other questions and come back to the ones you have not answered if you have time. It is not expected that everyone will know the answers to all the multiple-choice questions.

Your total score on the multiple-choice section is based only on the number of questions answered correctly. Points are not deducted for incorrect answers or unanswered questions.

At a Glance

Time
40 minutes
Number of Questions
3 (Questions 1 and 2 are required. Then, choose EITHER Question 3 or Question 4.)
Percent of Total Score
20%
Writing Instrument
Pen with black or dark blue ink

Instructions

Section I, Part B of this exam consists of 4 short-answer questions, of which you will answer 3. Answer all parts of Questions 1 and 2, and then choose to answer EITHER Question 3 or Question 4. Write your responses on a separate sheet of paper.

After the exam, you must apply the label that corresponds to the last short-essay question you answered—Question 3 or 4. For example, if you answered Question 3, apply the label ③ . Failure to do so may delay your score.

WORLD HISTORY

Section I, Part A

Time—55 minutes

55 Questions

Directions: Each of the questions or incomplete statements below is followed by either four suggested answers or completions. Select the one that is best in each case and then fill in the appropriate letter in the corresponding space on the answer sheet.

Questions 1–4 refer to the excerpt below.

> This ruler of Syria made me spend many years as commander of his army,
> Every land to which I turned
> I overcame.
> I destroyed its green fields and its wells,
> I captured its cattle, I took captive its inhabitants, I deprived them of their provisions,
> and I slew [many] people...by my sword, my bow, my marchings, and my good devices.
> Thus my excellence was in his heart; he loved me and he knew my valor;
> ...he set me at the head of his sons, when he saw the success of my handiwork.
>   There came a champion of Syria
> to defy me in my tent;
> a bold man without equal, for he had vanquished all his rivals.
> He said, "Let Sanehat fight with me."
> He thought to overcome me; he designed to take my cattle, thus being counseled by his tribe.

The Tale of Sanehat, Egyptian poem written during the Middle Kingdom, circa 1800 B.C.E.

1. Which of the following developments in early urban societies in Mesopotamia and Egypt is most directly supported by the passage?

   (A) The militarism of early Mesopotamian polities
   (B) The creation of long distance trade routes
   (C) The specialization of labor
   (D) The stratification of the population along social lines

2. The text of this passage is best seen as evidence of which of the following in Egyptian society?

   (A) Meritocratic appointments by rulers to their bureaucracies
   (B) Long-distance contact between Egypt and other lands
   (C) The clan as the basic political unit
   (D) A lack of emphasis on martial ability

GO ON TO THE NEXT PAGE.

3. Which of the following best describes foreign policy followed by the Egyptian New Kingdom, which existed between 1550 and 1069 B.C.E.?

   (A) A gradual withdrawal from the Nubian lands in Sudan conquered during the Middle Kingdom

   (B) Peaceful coexistence with Libyan peoples who lived along the Mediterranean coast

   (C) War with the successor kingdoms of Alexander the Great's empire for hegemony of the Eastern Mediterranean

   (D) War with the Hittites over control of Syria and the Levant

4. Which of the following best expresses the goal of conflict, according to the passage?

   (A) To earn love and respect

   (B) To defeat threats to the political order

   (C) To gain property

   (D) To gain excellence by displaying valor

GO ON TO THE NEXT PAGE.

Questions 5–8 refer to the passage below.

"After the Tencteri came, in former days, the Bructeri; but the general account now is, that the Chamavi and Angrivarii entered their settlements, drove them out and utterly exterminated them with the common help of the [neighboring] tribes, either from hatred of their tyranny, or from the attractions of plunder, or from heaven's [favorable] regard for us. It did not even grudge us the spectacle of the conflict. More than sixty thousand fell, not beneath the Roman arms and weapons, but, grander far, before our delighted eyes. May the tribes, I pray, ever retain if not love for us, at least hatred for each other; for while the destinies of empire hurry us on, fortune can give no greater boon than discord among our foes."

Germania, Publius Cornelius Tacitus, circa 98 C.E.

5. Which of the following conclusions about imperial treatment of "barbarian" (foreign) peoples in the period 600 B.C.E. to 600 C.E. is most directly supported by the passage?

   (A) Empires encouraged rival tribes to destroy one another to reduce threats to the state.
   (B) Empires welcomed migrations of barbarian peoples as sources of military manpower or economic productivity.
   (C) Empires used military force against all neighboring barbarian peoples as a means of expanding their influence.
   (D) Empires used religion to convert barbarian peoples so that they might become friendlier to the state.

6. The views expressed in the excerpt are best seen as evidence of which of the following in Roman society?

   (A) Disgust for barbarian peoples
   (B) Concern about barbarian attacks
   (C) Absence of Stoicism among the aristocracy
   (D) Maintenance of large armies

7. Which of the following contributed LEAST to the decline of the Roman Empire?

   (A) Civil wars between rivals for the throne
   (B) Incursions of barbarian peoples into the empire
   (C) The persistence of the senate as a body of government in the empire
   (D) Demographic weakness on account of diseases and epidemics

8. Which of the following is a treatment of barbarian peoples by civilized societies in the period 600–1450 C.E. that is similar to the treatment of barbarian peoples by civilized societies between 600 B.C.E. and 600 C.E.?

   (A) Barbarian peoples were converted to the religions of their host societies.
   (B) Barbarian peoples were utilized as soldiers in their host societies.
   (C) Barbarian peoples were uniformly relegated to a servile status through the laws of their host societies.
   (D) Barbarian peoples were often invited by their host societies to rule instead of the societies' own ruling classes.

GO ON TO THE NEXT PAGE.

Questions 9–12 refer to the map below.

Spread of Buddhism circa 500 B.C.E. to 600 C.E.

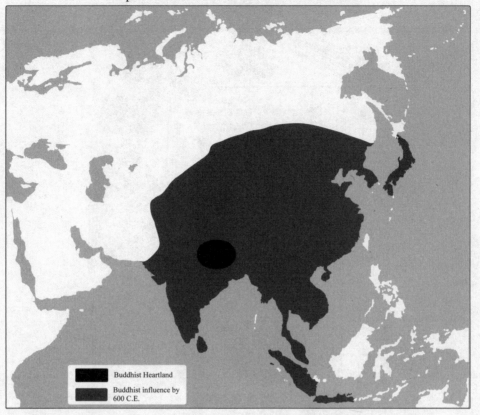

Buddhist Heartland

Buddhist influence by 600 C.E.

9. Which of the following was a direct result of the spread of Buddhism shown on the map?

(A) Indian princes and kings largely ceased their support of Buddhist monasteries by 600 C.E.

(B) Merchant activity between India and Southeast Asia increased.

(C) Missionaries brought Buddhism outside of India via major trade routes.

(D) Chinese emperors under the T'ang Dynasty passed decrees banning Buddhist practices.

10. Which of the following led directly to the extent of Buddhist influence indicated on the map?

(A) Invasions of Northern India by the Kushanas and Hunas

(B) Royal edicts declared by Emperor Asoka and his successors

(C) Japanese Imperial sponsorship of monasteries and monks

(D) Strong trade routes linking South, Central, and East Asia

11. Which of the following contributed most to the decline of Buddhism in India after 600 C.E.?

(A) The strengthening of the influence of the caste system across the subcontinent

(B) The domination of Indian Ocean trade routes by Arab merchants

(C) The collapse of centralized rule and rise of regional powers on the Indian subcontinent

(D) The rise of the Gupta Empire

12. Which of the following most inspired the emergence of Buddhism?

(A) The strength of Indian rulers

(B) The strict adherence to Hindu castes and their legal restrictions

(C) The penetration of Greek philosophies into India

(D) The strength of trade routes between India and the rest of the world

GO ON TO THE NEXT PAGE.

Questions 13–17 refer to the image below.

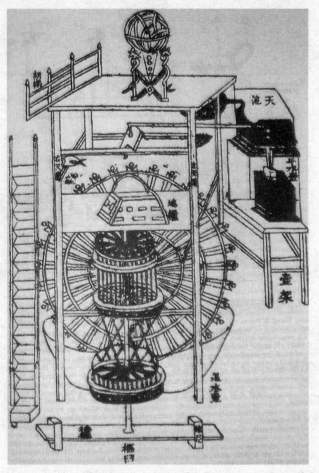

Clock tower design by Song-era mathematician and scientist, Su Song, 1094 C.E.

13. The design of this clock tower by Su Song was indicative of the Song Dynasty's renewed focus on developing

    (A) government reform
    (B) a civil service exam
    (C) an industrial society
    (D) the Grand Canal

14. The Song Dynasty proved itself valuable to international trade due to its prolific production of

    (A) silk
    (B) iron
    (C) gold
    (D) coffee

15. The focus on education during the Song Dynasty can be linked to

    (A) mandated school attendance under Legalist rule
    (B) the invention of moveable type
    (C) increased rights for women
    (D) a decreased focus on military development

GO ON TO THE NEXT PAGE.

16. The preceding T'ang Dynasty differed from the Song in that

    (A) the Song abolished the Confucian civil service exams

    (B) the Song sponsored Buddhism to the detriment of Taoism and Confucianism

    (C) the Song pursued a less expansive foreign policy

    (D) the Song dynasty was originally from outside of China

17. The Chinese population increased dramatically under the Song Dynasty due to

    (A) improved sanitation technology

    (B) a large rurally based population

    (C) vast military conquests

    (D) more efficient food production techniques

GO ON TO THE NEXT PAGE.

Questions 18–20 refer to the image below.

Inca *quipu* from the Larco Museum in Lima

18. The use of the quipu in the image above best illustrates which of the following features of pre-modern civilizations?

    (A) Rulers used bureaucracies to administer their empires.
    (B) Rulers relied on religious authority to justify their rule.
    (C) Rulers used military force to impose their rule on other peoples.
    (D) Rulers relied on feudal arrangements to administer their domains.

19. Ancient Mesoamerican and Andean civilizations most commonly used which of the following activities to demonstrate their religious authority?

    (A) The sponsoring of production of religious literature
    (B) The performance of elaborate sacrifice rituals
    (C) The creation of record keeping implements
    (D) The sponsorship of astronomical research

20. Which of the following best describes the significance of urban centers for pre-modern civilizations?

    (A) They provided surplus manpower for armies.
    (B) They reflected and reinforced the stratification of society along class lines.
    (C) They were centers of trade and commercial activity.
    (D) They were exclusively religious centers for pilgrimages.

GO ON TO THE NEXT PAGE.

Questions 21–24 refer to the passage below.

"Al-Zawawi also said 'This sultan Musa told me that at a town...he has a copper mine from which ingots are brought to [another town]. "There is nothing in my kingdom, Musa said, on which a duty is levied except this crude copper which is brought in. Duty is collected on this and on nothing else. We send it to the land of the pagan Sudan and sell it for two-thirds of its weight in gold, so that we sell 100 measures of this copper for 66 2/3 measures of gold.' He also stated that there are pagan nations in his kingdom from whom he does not collect the tribute (jizya) but whom he simply employs in extracting the gold from its deposits. The gold is extracted by digging pits about a man's height in depth and the gold is found embedded in the sides of the pits or sometimes collected at the bottom of them."

From N. Levtzion & J.F.P. Hopkins, eds. *Corpus of Early Arabic Sources for West African History*. Cambridge University Press, 1981. Reprinted with permission of Cambridge University Press.

Al' Umari, Arab historian, circa 1300–1384

21. Based on the passage and your knowledge of world history, Mansa Musa's assertion about the lack of duties levied on goods in his kingdom most strongly reflects which of the following about the kingdom of Mali?

    (A) Mali's wealth came in large part from its exploitation of minerals.
    (B) Mali's wealth came in large part from its conquest of pagan neighbors.
    (C) Mali's wealth came in large part from large agricultural estates.
    (D) Mali's wealth came in large part from the exploitation of the slave trade.

22. Which of the following best accounts for the spread of Islam to the lands of the kingdom of Mali?

    (A) Muslim missionaries who came from Southern Africa
    (B) Trade contacts who came from the north across the Sahara
    (C) Berber armies who conquered the former kingdom of Ghana
    (D) Pressure from Christian Ethiopia caused the king of Mali to seek Muslim allies

23. Which of the following inferences is most supported by the discussion of copper and gold in the passage?

    (A) Mali was able to forge advanced bronze tools from its mineral resources.
    (B) International trade with sub-Saharan Africa involved the exchange of mineral resources.
    (C) The jizya could only be collected on unbelievers who had minerals to exploit.
    (D) Mali's relatively advanced mining technologies accounted for its mineral wealth.

24. Which of the following statements about the period 600–1450 C.E. is supported by the passage?

    (A) Religions were often spread through warfare during the period.
    (B) International trade connections were still being developed in the period.
    (C) Diseases spread along trade routes.
    (D) Nomadic migrations created powerful empires during the period.

GO ON TO THE NEXT PAGE.

Questions 25–28 refer to the passage below.

"At least one of the [world's] societies would have to somehow enormously increase its productivity [in order to achieve global hegemony]. That quantum jump would have to be made *before* the various scientific, technological, agricultural, and industrial revolutions on which our post-quantum-leap world rests. It could only be accomplished by exploiting the ecosystems, mineral resources, and human assets of whole continents outside the lands of the society making the jump. Western Europe did just that by means of its brutality and guns and, more important, by geographical and ecological luck."

Copyright © 2015 Cambridge University Press. Reprinted with the permission of Cambridge University Press.

Alfred Crosby, historian, *Ecological Imperialism*, 2004

25. Crosby's argument in the passage is most likely a response to which of the following developments of the period 1450–1750 C.E.?

   (A) The development of direct trade links between Western Europe and India
   (B) The beginning of the Industrial Revolution
   (C) The colonization of North and South America by Western Europeans
   (D) The increasing development of seafaring technologies

26. Which of the following would best support the author's assertion regarding the "quantum jump" that would help Western Europe achieve global hegemony between 1450 and 1750 C.E.?

   (A) The colonization of the interior of Africa
   (B) The conquest of the Aztec Empire
   (C) The reformation of Catholic Christianity
   (D) The isolationism of Tokugawa Japan

27. Based on your knowledge of world history, which of the following contributed LEAST to Western European global hegemony between 1450 and 1750 C.E.?

   (A) The exchange of food sources between the Americas and Europe
   (B) Refinement of gunpowder technologies
   (C) The development and application of steam-powered technologies
   (D) The implementation of joint-stock companies

28. The "quantum jump" mentioned in the passage most directly contributed to which of the following developments in the period 1450–1750 C.E.?

   (A) A breakdown in trade routes through the collapse of the established state structure
   (B) An increase in the population of the world through more plentiful supplies of food
   (C) The spread of Chinese and Indian belief systems across the world
   (D) An increase in social unrest

GO ON TO THE NEXT PAGE.

Questions 29–33 refer to the passage below.

"Thereupon it was declared by the above-mentioned representatives of the aforesaid King and Queen of Castile, Leon, Aragon, Sicily, Granada, etc., and of the aforesaid King of Portugal and the Algarves, etc.:

[I.] That, whereas a certain controversy exists between the said lords, their constituents, as to what lands, of all those discovered in the ocean sea up to the present day, the date of this treaty, pertain to each one of the said parts respectively; therefore, for the sake of peace and concord, and for the preservation of the relationship and love of the said King of Portugal for the said King and Queen of Castile, Aragon, etc., it being the pleasure of their Highnesses, they, their said representatives, acting in their name and by virtue of their powers herein described, covenanted and agreed that a boundary or straight line be determined and drawn north and south, from pole to pole, on the said ocean sea, from the Arctic to the Antarctic pole. This boundary or line shall be drawn straight, as aforesaid, at a distance of three hundred and seventy leagues west of the Cape Verde Islands, being calculated by degrees, or by any other manner as may be considered the best and readiest, provided the distance shall be no greater than abovesaid. And all lands, both islands and mainlands, found and discovered already, or to be found and discovered hereafter, by the said King of Portugal and by his vessels on this side of the said line and bound determined as above, toward the east, in either north or south latitude, on the eastern side of the said bound provided the said bound is not crossed, shall belong to, and remain in the possession of, and pertain forever to, the said King of Portugal and his successors. And all other lands, both islands and mainlands, found or to be found hereafter, discovered or to be discovered hereafter, which have been discovered or shall be discovered by the said King and Queen of Castile, Aragon, etc., and by their vessels, on the western side of the said bound, determined as above, after having passed the said bound toward the west, in either its north or south latitude, shall belong to, and remain in the possession of, and pertain forever to, the said King and Queen of Castile, Leon, etc., and to their successors."

Treaty of Tordesillas between Spain and Portugal, 1494

29. Which of the following historical developments provides the best context for the treaty?

(A) European maritime exploration
(B) European engagement in the African slave trade
(C) The Scientific Revolution
(D) The Protestant Reformation

30. Which of the following inferences best explains the reason the King of Portugal insisted on Portuguese control of territory east of the demarcation line?

(A) Portuguese explorers were convinced that the route to the New World was easier traveled by going east.
(B) The Portuguese desired to continue the crusades against the Mamelukes who controlled the Holy Land.
(C) The Portuguese desired control of the wealthy lands of Mexico.
(D) The Portuguese knew of a route to India via the Cape of Good Hope in the south of Africa.

31. Which of the following inferences best explains the reason the King and Queen of Castile and Aragon insisted on Spanish control of territory west of the demarcation line?

(A) The Spanish desired to convert the Barbary states to Catholicism.
(B) The Spanish believed Portugal did not know about their discovery of the New World.
(C) The Spanish wanted to preserve the independence of Native states in the New World as a buffer against Portuguese expansion.
(D) The Spanish thought India would be harder to conquer than the New World.

GO ON TO THE NEXT PAGE.

32. The treaty provides evidence for which of the following historical developments?

   (A) Monarchs were involved in and interested in voyages of discovery.
   (B) Joint-stock companies sponsored colonization efforts in the western and eastern hemispheres.
   (C) Trade of guns and slaves between Europe and sub-Saharan Africa.
   (D) The Scientific Revolution and the discovery of heliocentricity.

33. Which of the following technologies most directly caused the treaty to be signed?

   (A) Gunpowder weapons
   (B) The compass
   (C) Steel
   (D) Germ Theory

GO ON TO THE NEXT PAGE.

Questions 34–38 refer to the passage below.

"When the Portuguese go from Macao in China to Japan, they carry much white silk, gold, musk, and porcelain: and they bring from Japan nothing but silver. They have a great carrack which goes there every year and she brings from there every year about six hundred coins: and all this silver of Japan, and two hundred thousand coins more in silver which they bring yearly out of India, they employ to their great advantage in China: and they bring from there gold, musk, silk, copper, porcelains, and many other things very costly and gilded.

When the Portuguese come to Canton in China to traffic, they must remain there but certain days: and when they come in at the gate of the city, they must enter their names in a book, and when they go out at night they must put out their names. They may not lie in the town all night, but must lie in their boats outside of the town. And, their time expired, if any man remains there, he is imprisoned."

Ralph Fitch, an account of his travels to the Far East, 1599 C.E.

34. The description of the route Portuguese sailors took in the first paragraph most directly supports which of the following historical developments?

(A) Chinese merchants' domination of East Asian trade

(B) Competition between Dutch and Portuguese traders for markets in Japan

(C) European participation in East Asian trade patterns

(D) Jesuit missionary work in Japan and China

35. In addition to the sources of silver mentioned in the first paragraph, the greatest volume of additional silver came to China from which of the following regions?

(A) Central Asia

(B) Europe

(C) The Middle East

(D) The New World

36. The description in the second paragraph of the procedures that Portuguese and other foreigners followed when trading in China supports which of the following inferences about trade policy in the later Ming Dynasty?

(A) The Ming Dynasty was very supportive of and welcoming to all commercial enterprise.

(B) The Ming Dynasty sought to regulate trade strictly to limit contact with foreigners and ease collection of taxes.

(C) The Ming Dynasty was too busy battling pirates along its coast to pay any attention to regular merchant activity.

(D) The Ming Dynasty only allowed Portugal to trade with China through Canton, permitting only one boat a year.

37. Which of the following developments from the period 1750–1900 C.E. most directly undid the trade patterns mentioned in the first paragraph?

(A) The discovery of certain goods that the Chinese were interested in purchasing from European merchants

(B) Enlightenment revolutions in Europe and the Americas

(C) The Industrial Revolution

(D) The colonization of Africa

38. Which of the following developments from the period 1450–1750 C.E. most directly undid the trade patterns mentioned in the first paragraph?

(A) The eastward expansion of Russia

(B) The Portuguese conquest of India

(C) The establishment of the Tokugawa Shogunate

(D) The Spanish conquest of Mexico

GO ON TO THE NEXT PAGE.

Questions 39–42 refer to the map below.

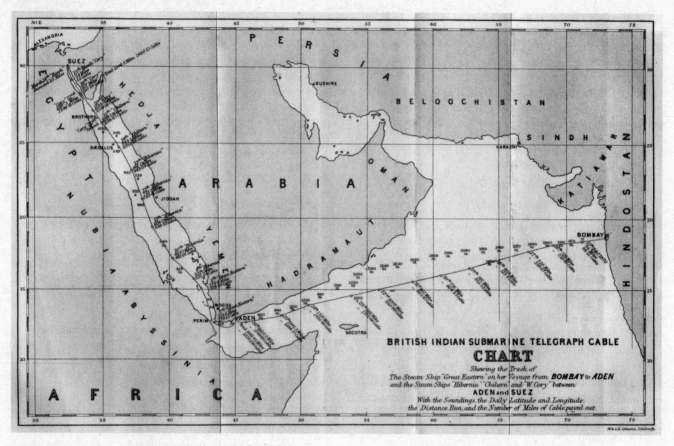

Reprinted with permission of Atlantic-Cable.com.

Map of British undersea telegraph cable, circa 1870

39. Based on the map and your knowledge of world history, which of the following likely accounts for the western-most end of the cable in Egypt?

    (A) The Suez Canal was a strategic outpost for communications with Europe.

    (B) The French garrison in Egypt needed to communicate with the British in India.

    (C) The Ottoman Empire demanded that the cable from India be built through Egypt.

    (D) The Italian investors in the undersea cable instructed that the cable go through the Italian colonies in Egypt.

40. Technologies like the telegraph cable depicted in the map above had which of the following effects on empires in the period 1750–1900 C.E.?

    (A) Empires were slow to take up advanced communications technologies until the end of the nineteenth century and did not benefit much from them.

    (B) Empires were able to grow much larger as messages and information could travel at very rapid speeds.

    (C) Empires only used technology like telegraph cables for military purposes, as they were too expensive for daily public use.

    (D) Empires found expansion more difficult as communications technologies like the telegraph diffused quickly all over the world.

GO ON TO THE NEXT PAGE.

41. Which of the following best characterizes this area of the Indian Ocean in the period 600–1450 C.E.?

    (A) Roman and Persian merchants competed with one another over the trade coming to and from India.

    (B) Arab merchants dominated the Indian Ocean region for the entire period.

    (C) Indian merchants founded enclaves in Persia and Egypt.

    (D) Mongol traders facilitated the development of seaborne trade to carry the produce of Central Asia.

42. Based on the map and your knowledge of world history, which of the following best characterizes British involvement in the Indian Ocean between 1750–1900 C.E.?

    (A) The British constructed an undersea cable connecting India to Arabia to facilitate communications among the Islamic world.

    (B) The British invested in strategic infrastructure and occupied territories in order to protect their interests in the region.

    (C) The British dominated the entire Indian Ocean region by virtue of their powerful navy.

    (D) The British largely left existing powers in control of their domains, content to monopolize trade in the region.

GO ON TO THE NEXT PAGE.

Questions 43–46 refer to the tables below.

MANUFACTURING AS A PERCENTAGE OF
GROSS DOMESTIC PRODUCT (GDP)

Table 1

	Argentina	Brazil	Chile	Colombia	Mexico
1945	24.7	17.2	23.1	10.5	19.1

Table 2

	Argentina	Brazil	Chile	Colombia	Mexico
1980	24.7	30.2	22.3	18.2	24.1

43. Which of the following conclusions is best supported by the data in Table 1?

(A) Latin American societies had to import vast quantities of industrial materials from abroad to satisfy internal demand.

(B) Participation in World War II did not impact Latin American industrial capacity as much as it did North American.

(C) Trade with the United States turned Latin American states into producers of raw materials.

(D) Industrialization had not taken firm root in Latin American economies by 1945.

44. A historian researching the economic history of Latin America from 1900 to the present day would most likely find the two tables useful as a source of information about which of the following?

(A) The successful industrialization of Latin America over the course of the twentieth century

(B) The impact of Cold War politics on Latin American economic development

(C) The relative effectiveness of import substitution industrialization strategies in Latin America

(D) The spread of industrial technologies across Latin America between 1945 and 1980

45. The data presented in the two tables best support which of the following comparative comments about Latin American manufacturing between 1945 and 1980?

(A) Argentina's economy did not grow between 1945 and 1980.

(B) Brazil had the wealthiest economy among the countries listed in the tables by 1980.

(C) Colombia's rate of urbanization almost doubled between 1945 and 1980.

(D) Industrial production remained a less significant economic activity across Latin America than other economic activities.

46. Which of the following from the period 1450–1750 C.E. best explains the relatively under-industrialized nature of Latin American economies in the twentieth century?

(A) The policies of mercantilism followed by the colonial powers

(B) The focus on the exploitation of precious metals in Mexico and Brazil

(C) The demographic collapse endured by the population of Latin America after the arrival of Europeans

(D) The weakness of haciendas and other plantation-based elites in the administration of Latin America

GO ON TO THE NEXT PAGE.

Questions 47–51 refer to the passage below.

"The spontaneous forces of capitalism have been steadily growing in the countryside in recent years, with new rich peasants springing up everywhere and many well-to-do middle peasants striving to become rich peasants. On the other hand, many poor peasants are still living in poverty for lack of sufficient means of production, with some in debt and others selling or renting out their land. If this tendency goes unchecked, the polarization in the countryside will inevitably be aggravated day by day. Those peasants who lose their land and those who remain in poverty will complain that we are doing nothing to save them from ruin or to help them overcome their difficulties. Nor will the well-to-do middle peasants who are heading in the capitalist direction be pleased with us, for we shall never be able to satisfy their demands unless we intend to take the capitalist road. Can the worker-peasant alliance continue to stand in these circumstances? Obviously not! There is no solution to this problem except on a new basis. And that means to bring about, step by step, the socialist transformation of the whole of agriculture simultaneously with the gradual realization of socialist industrialization and the socialist transformation of handicrafts and capitalist industry and commerce; in other words, it means to carry out co-operation and eliminate the rich-peasant economy and the individual economy in the countryside so that all the rural people will become increasingly well off together. We maintain that this is the only way to consolidate the worker-peasant alliance."

Mao Zedong, *On the Question of Agricultural Co-operation,* 1955

47. Mao's quotation is best understood in the context of which of the following?

   (A) Governments in communist countries implementing liberal political and economic reforms to mitigate social unrest

   (B) Governments promoting collectivization of the land to reduce inequality between sectors of the population

   (C) Governments promoting policies intended to hasten industrialization

   (D) Governments promoting capitalist policies to reduce inequality between sectors of the population

48. The developments described in the speech regarding the cooperation of the peasant economy contributed most directly to which of the following global processes?

   (A) The decline of Chinese influence in Asia and globally

   (B) The expansion of multinational corporations and globalization

   (C) The decline of Soviet-style communism and the rise of Maoism

   (D) The Green Revolution and development of more efficient agricultural techniques

49. Which of the following best explains Mao's concept of the "socialist transformation of the whole of agriculture" in China?

   (A) Agriculture fueled industrialization in cities as excess labor flowed from the countryside to urban centers.

   (B) Agricultural surpluses allowed the state to invest more heavily in modernizing agricultural production.

   (C) Agricultural efficiency reduced prices of basic commodities, raising the standard of living across the whole of China.

   (D) Agriculture was collectivized, with the result that entire communities shared fields instead of individuals owning the land as private property.

GO ON TO THE NEXT PAGE.

50. Mao's view of the cooperation of peasant labor most directly reflects the influence of which of the following?

    (A) The ideals of communism as stated by Joseph Stalin

    (B) The ideals of the Enlightenment as stated by political revolutionaries such as Maximilian Robespierre

    (C) The ideals of classical liberalism as stated by Adam Smith

    (D) The ideals of globalization as evidenced by multinational trade blocs such as NAFTA or the European Union

51. Which of the following later developments would most undermine the hopes expressed by Mao in the second-to-last line of the passage?

    (A) The development of special economic zones along the Chinese coast brought economic growth to China.

    (B) Political friction with the Soviet Union pushed China into the orbit of the United States during the Cold War.

    (C) The cooperatives of peasants on the farmland and an emphasis on countryside steel production brought famine and poverty to the Chinese peasantry.

    (D) Opposition voices in the Communist Party led by men such as Deng Xiaopeng were rooted out and silenced during the Cultural Revolution.

GO ON TO THE NEXT PAGE.

Questions 52–55 refer to the passage below.

"This government represents a regime, whose leader and his father were illegally in power. This government is therefore illegal…How can anyone appointed by the Shah be legal? We are telling all of them that they are illegal and they should go. We hereby announce that this government, which has presented itself as a legal government is in fact illegal. Even the members of this government before accepting to be ministers, were considering the whole establishment to be illegal…Only America is backing him and has ordered the army to support him. Britain has backed him too and had said that he must be supported. If one were to search among the nation, one would not find a single person among all strata of the nation, who accepts this man, but he is saying that one country cannot have two governments. Well of course, it is clear that this country does not have two governments and in any case, the illegal government should go."

From Arshin Adib-Moghaddam, *Psychonationalism: Global Thought, Iranian Imaginations.* Cambridge University Press, 2017.

Ayatollah Khomeini, addressing the subject of the shah of Iran, 1979

52. Which of the following provides the best context for this passage?

(A) The Industrial Revolution
(B) Decolonization
(C) Regional Free Trade Associations
(D) Autarky

53. Which of the following is referenced by the mention of "America"?

(A) Iranian revolutionaries appeal for a western ally
(B) Opposition to transnational trade agreements
(C) Tacit approval of the Iranian military
(D) Western support for the shah

54. Which of the following most directly resulted from the existence of "two governments"?

(A) A nationalist revolution that deposed of the shah
(B) A reform movement that yielded a democratic constitution
(C) Popular denunciation of the Ayatollah
(D) The emergence of the Iran-Iraq War

55. Which of the following most inspired this speech?

(A) Fascism
(B) Social Darwinism
(C) Pan-Islamism
(D) Classical liberalism

GO ON TO THE NEXT PAGE.

WORLD HISTORY

SECTION I, Part B

Time—40 minutes

3 Questions

Directions: Answer all parts of Questions 1 and 2, and then choose to answer EITHER Question 3 or Question 4. Read each question carefully and write your responses on a separate sheet of paper.

Use complete sentences; an outline or bulleted list alone is not acceptable. On test day, you will be able to plan your answers in the exam booklet, but only your responses in the corresponding boxes on the free-response answer sheet will be scored.

1. Use the image below to answer all parts of the question that follows.

Portrait of Sultan Mahmud II of the Ottoman Empire, painted after his clothing reform in 1826

a)   Identify and explain ONE reason Mahmud II embarked on reforms such as the clothing reform depicted in the painting.

b)   Identify and explain ONE way in which the painting illustrates the creation of new cultural identities in the nineteenth century.

c)   Identify and explain ONE way in which Ottoman expansionism affected international relations in the period from 1520–1700.

GO ON TO THE NEXT PAGE.

2. Answer all parts of the question that follows.

a) Identify and explain TWO ways in which rulers legitimized or consolidated their power during the period 600 C.E. to 1450 C.E. Use specific examples from one or more states or empires.

b) Identify and explain TWO ways that nation-states increased their power through cultural assimilation.

GO ON TO THE NEXT PAGE.

Choose EITHER Question 3 OR Question 4.

3. **Use the map below to answer all parts of the question that follows.**

Major Mediterranean and Near Eastern Trade Routes, 200 C.E.–600 C.E

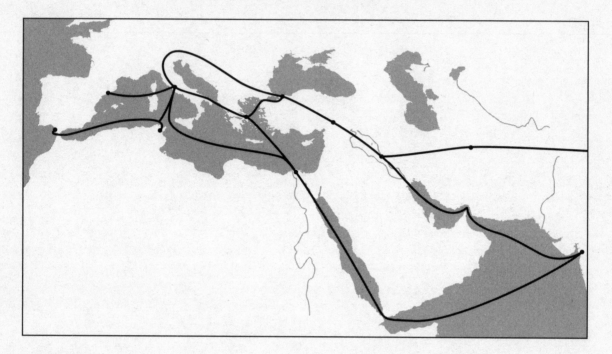

a) Identify and explain TWO factors from 600 B.C.E to 600 C.E. that account for the development of the routes shown on the map.

b) Identify and explain ONE reason that the land-borne routes displayed on the map declined in significance between 600 C.E. and 1450 C.E.

GO ON TO THE NEXT PAGE.

4. Use the two passages below to answer all parts of the question that follows.

Source 1

"The voyages of Columbus in 1492 can rightly be said to have begun the discovery and settlement of the New World, as scores of European migrants settled open lands in the Americas and constructed exclaves of Europe on distant shores that lacked much sense of advanced civilization before their arrival. Their task was the settlement and development of wide open continents."

Source 2

"While the bounty of the New World enriched the whole world through trade and transmission once it was finally connected to the Old World in 1492, this bounty came at the cost of the blood of its inhabitants. Europeans neither 'discovered' nor 'settled' the Americas for humans had done just that for thousands of years before the arrival of the Spaniards. Instead, the Europeans conquered the Americas for God, gold, and glory."

a) Identify and explain ONE piece of historical evidence that would support Source 1's interpretation of Europe's interaction with the Americas.

b) Identify and explain ONE piece of historical evidence that would support Source 2's interpretation of Europe's interaction with the Americas.

c) From the two evaluations above, select the one that, in your opinion, is more accurate to the actual nature of Europe's interaction with the Americas. Briefly explain your choice using additional evidence beyond that used to answer (a) or (b).

STOP
END OF SECTION I
IF YOU FINISH BEFORE TIME IS CALLED, YOU MAY CHECK YOUR WORK ON THIS SECTION.
DO NOT GO ON TO SECTION II UNTIL YOU ARE TOLD TO DO SO.

AP® World History Exam

SECTION II: Free Response

DO NOT OPEN THIS BOOKLET UNTIL YOU ARE TOLD TO DO SO.

At a Glance

Total Time
1 hour, 40 minutes
Number of Questions
2
Percent of Total Score
40%
Writing Instrument
Pen with black or dark
blue ink

**Question 1 (DBQ):
Mandatory**

**Suggested Reading and
Writing Time**
60 minutes
Percent of Total Score
25%

**Question 2, 3, or 4 (Long
Essay): Choose ONE
Question**

Answer either Question
2, 3, or 4
Suggested Time
40 minutes
Percent of Total Score
15%

Instructions

The questions for Section II are printed in the Questions and Documents booklet. You may use that booklet to organize your answers and for scratch work, but you must write your answers in this Section II: Free Response booklet. No credit will be given for any work written in the Questions and Documents booklet.

The proctor will announce the beginning and end of the reading period. You are advised to spend the 15-minute period reading the question and planning your answer to Question 1, the document-based question. If you have time, you may also read Questions 2, 3, and 4.

Section II of this exam requires answers in essay form. Write clearly and legibly. Circle the number of the question you are answering at the top of each page in this booklet. Begin each answer on a new page. Do not skip lines. Cross out any errors you make; crossed-out work will not be scored.

Manage your time carefully. The proctor will announce the suggested time for each part, but you may proceed freely from one part to the next. Go on to the long essay question if you finish Question 1 early. You may review your responses if you finish before the end of the exam is announced.

After the exam, you must apply the label that corresponds to the long-essay question you answered—Question 2, 3, or 4. For example, if you answered Question 2, apply the label [2]. Failure to do so may delay your score.

This page intentionally left blank.

GO ON TO THE NEXT PAGE.

WORLD HISTORY

SECTION II

Total Time—1 hour, 40 minutes

Question 1 (Document-Based Question)

Suggested reading period: 15 minutes

Suggested writing time: 45 minutes

<u>Note:</u> You may begin writing your response before the reading period is over.

Directions: Question 1 is based on the accompanying documents. The documents have been edited for the purpose of this exercise.

In your response you should do the following.

- **<u>Thesis/Claim:</u>** Respond to the prompt with a historically defensible claim that establishes a line of reasoning.

- **<u>Contextualization:</u>** Describe a historical context relevant to the prompt.

- **<u>Evidence:</u>** Support an argument in response to the prompt using at least **six** documents. Use at least one additional piece of specific historical evidence (beyond that found in the documents) relevant to an argument about the prompt.

- **<u>Analysis and Reasoning:</u>** For at least **three** documents, explain how or why the document's point of view, purpose, historical situation, and/or audience is relevant to an argument. Demonstrate an understanding of the historical development that is the focus of the prompt, using evidence to support or modify an argument that addresses the question.

GO ON TO THE NEXT PAGE.

Question 1: Using the following documents and your knowledge of world history, explain some of the major social and political challenges facing Latin American countries in the period from 1875 to 1950.

Document 1

Source: Painting by Thomas Somerscales, sinking of the *Esmeralda*, a Chilean wooden vessel, by the Peruvian Ironclad *Huascar* in the battle of Iquique during the War of the Pacific, 1879.

GO ON TO THE NEXT PAGE.

Document 2

Source: Maria Eugenia Echenique, Argentine feminist, *The Emancipation of Women,* 1876.

When emancipation was given to men, it was also given to women in recognition of the equality of rights, consistent with the principles of nature on which they are founded, that proclaim the identity of soul between men and women. Thus, Argentine women have been emancipated by law for a long time. The code of law that governs us authorizes a widow to defend her rights in court, just as an educated woman can in North America, and like her, we can manage the interests of our children, these rights being the basis for emancipation. What we lack is sufficient education and instruction to make use of them, instruction that North American women have; it is not just recently that we have proclaimed our freedom. To try to question or to oppose women's emancipation is to oppose something that is almost a fact, it is to attack our laws and destroy the Republic. So let the debate be there, on the true point where it should be: whether or not it is proper for women to make use of those granted rights, asking as a consequence the authorization to go to the university so as to practice those rights or make them effective.

Document 3

Source: United States Recognition of Cuba's Independence, Resolution of the U.S. Congress, April 11, 1898.

Joint Resolution for the recognition of the independence of the people of Cuba, demanding that the Government of Spain relinquish its authority and government in the Island of Cuba, and to withdraw its land and naval forces from Cuba and Cuban waters, and directing the President of the United States to use the land and naval forces of the United States to carry these resolutions into effect. Whereas, the abhorrent conditions which have existed for more than three years in the Island of Cuba, so near our own borders, have shocked the moral sense of the people of the United States, have been a disgrace to Christian civilization, culminating, as they have, in the destruction of a United States battleship, with two hundred and sixty-six of its officers and crew, while on a friendly visit in the harbor of Havana, and can not longer be endured, as has been set forth by the President of the United States in his message to Congress of April eleventh, eighteen hundred and ninety-eight, upon which the action of Congress was invited: Therefore, Resolved, by the Senate and House of Representatives of the United States of America in Congress assembled, First. That the people of the Island of Cuba are, and of right ought to be, free and independent. Second. That it is the duty of the United States to demand, and the Government of the United States does hereby demand, that the Government of Spain at once relinquish its authority and government in the Island of Cuba, and withdraw its land and naval forces from Cuba and Cuban waters. Third. That the President of the United States be, and he hereby is, directed and empowered to use the entire land and naval forces of the United States, and to call into the actual service of the United States, the militia of the several States, to such extent as may be necessary to carry these resolutions into effect. Fourth. That the United States hereby disclaims any disposition or intention to exercise sovereignty, jurisdiction, or control over said Islands except for the pacification thereof, and asserts its determination, when that is accomplished, to leave the government and control of the Island to its people. Approved, April 20, 1898.

GO ON TO THE NEXT PAGE.

Document 4

Source: Photograph of Plantation in Cuba, circa 1900.

Document 5

Source: Pierre Denis, *The Coffee Fazenda of Brazil*, 1911.

Each *fazenda* constitutes a little isolated world, which is all but self-sufficient and from which the colonists rarely issue; the life is laborious. The coffee is planted in long regular lines in the red soil, abundantly watered by the rains, on which a constant struggle must be maintained against the invasion of noxious weeds. The weeding of the plantation is really the chief labor of the colonist. It is repeated six times a year. When the coffee ripens, towards the end of June, the picking of the crop commences. Sometimes, in a good year, the crop is not all picked until November. The great advantage enjoyed by Saõ Paulo is that the whole crop arrives at maturity almost at the same moment. The crop may thus be harvested in its entirety at one picking… This entails a great reduction in the cost of production and of labor. At the time of picking the colonists are gathered into gangs. They confine themselves to loading the berries on carts, which other laborers drive to the *fazenda*; there the coffee is soaked, husked, dried, and selected, and then dispatched to Santos, the great export market. All these operations the colonists perform under the supervision of the manager of the *fazenda*. A bell announces the hour for going to work; another the hour of rest; another the end of the day; the laborers have no illusions of independence. What really enables the colonists to make both ends meet is the crops they have the right to raise on their own account, sometimes on allotments reserved for the purpose set apart from the coffee, and sometimes between the rows of the coffee-trees. They often think more of the clauses in their contract which relate to these crops than to those which determine their wages in currency… It even happens at times that the colonists produce more maize than they consume. They can then sell a few sacks at the nearest market, and add the price to their other resources. In this way crops which are in theory destined solely for their nourishment take on a different aspect from their point of view, yielding them a revenue which is not always to be despised.

GO ON TO THE NEXT PAGE.

Document 6

Source: George M. McBride: *Haciendas from The Land Systems of Mexico,* 1923.[1]

The Haciendas of Mexico are the most conspicuous feature of the land system of the country. They give to agricultural Mexico its distinctive cast, and, by their great size, create the impression that the entire land is divided into vast rural estates. These properties, indeed, are the only type of agricultural holding immediately visible to the traveler in many parts of Mexico, just as the *hacendado* is the only type of agriculturist whose interest reach beyond the immediate neighborhood of his home...Many of the haciendas are of very great extent; it is estimated that 300 of them contain at least 25,000 acres each...The Mexican hacienda seldom contains less than 2,500 acres—whether situated in the arid plains of the north, where land is worth little or nothing, or in the densely settled areas of the Mesa Central. The haciendas are settlements complete in themselves. Indeed, few of these estates have less than a hundred, while many of them have as many as a thousand inhabitants...Furthermore, the haciendas are all named; they appear on the maps; and they are important units of public administration, often being incorporated as *municipios*. They include all the customary accessories of an independent community, such as a church, a store, a post office, a burying ground, and sometimes a school or hospital. Workshops are maintained, not only for the repair but even for the manufacture of machinery and of the numerous implements on the estate. The permanent population consists of an *administrador*, one or more majordomos, a group of foremen, and the regular peons, together with the families of these individuals.

[1] Reprinted with permission of the American Geographical Society.

Document 7

Source: Annual Message of the President of the United States Transmitted to Congress December 3, 1912.

In Central America the aim has been to help such countries as Nicaragua and Honduras to help themselves. They are the immediate beneficiaries. The national benefit to the United States is twofold. First, it is obvious that the Monroe Doctrine is more vital in the neighborhood of the Panama Canal and the zone of the Caribbean than anywhere else. There, too, the maintenance of that doctrine falls most heavily upon the United States. It is therefore essential that the countries within that sphere shall be removed from the jeopardy involved by heavy foreign debt and chaotic national finances and from the ever-present danger of international complications due to disorder at home. Hence the United States has been glad to encourage and support American bankers who were willing to lend a helping hand to the financial rehabilitation of such countries because this financial rehabilitation and the protection of their customhouses from being the prey of would-be dictators would remove at one stroke the menace of foreign creditors and the menace of revolutionary disorder.

GO ON TO THE NEXT PAGE.

Question 2, Question 3, OR Question 4 (Long-Essay Question)

Suggested writing time: 40 minutes

Directions: Choose ONE of EITHER Questions 2, 3, or 4.

In your response you should do the following.

- **Thesis/Claim:** Respond to the prompt with a historically defensible thesis/claim that establishes a line of reasoning.

- **Contextualization:** Describe a broader historical context relevant to the prompt.

- **Evidence:** Support an argument in response to the prompt using specific and relevant examples of evidence.

- **Analysis and Reasoning:** Demonstrate an understanding of the historical development that is the focus of the prompt, using evidence to support or modify an argument that addresses the question.

> **Question 2:** Evaluate the extent to which the emergence of Taoist philosophies in the fifth century B.C.E. can be considered a turning point in world history. In the development of your argument, explain what changed and what stayed the same from the period before the emergence of Taoism in the fifth century B.C.E. to the period after the emergence of Taoism in the fifth century B.C.E.

> **Question 3:** Evaluate the extent to which the Mongol sack of Baghdad in 1258 C.E. can be considered a turning point in world history. In the development of your argument, explain what changed and what stayed the same from the period before the Mongol sack of Baghdad to the period after the Mongol sack of Baghdad.

> **Question 4:** Evaluate the extent to which the Berlin Conference can be considered a turning point in world history. In the development of your argument, explain what changed and what stayed the same from the period before the Berlin Conference to the period after the Berlin Conference.

STOP

END OF EXAMINATION

Practice Test 2: Answers and Explanations

PRACTICE TEST 2 ANSWER KEY

1.	A		29.	A
2.	B		30.	D
3.	D		31.	B
4.	C		32.	A
5.	A		33.	B
6.	B		34.	C
7.	C		35.	D
8.	B		36.	B
9.	B		37.	A
10.	D		38.	C
11.	C		39.	A
12.	B		40.	B
13.	C		41.	B
14.	B		42.	B
15.	B		43.	D
16.	C		44.	C
17.	D		45.	D
18.	A		46.	A
19.	B		47.	B
20.	C		48.	A
21.	A		49.	D
22.	B		50.	A
23.	B		51.	C
24.	B		52.	B
25.	C		53.	D
26.	B		54.	A
27.	C		55.	C
28.	B			

PRACTICE TEST 2 EXPLANATIONS

Multiple-Choice Questions

1. **A**   The passage discusses an Egyptian exile leading armies into battle in Syria. Eliminate (B), (C), and (D) because they do not mention hostility or militarism.

2. **B**   The passage discusses Syria, which is an independent land from Egypt at this point in time, as stated in the passage with the line "this ruler of Syria." Thus, eliminate answers that aren't supported by the passage. Choice (A) can be eliminated because there's no mention of a formal bureaucracy in the text. Choice (C) can be eliminated because the question asks about Egyptian society, which was based on a pharaoh. Choice (D) can be eliminated because it is a reversal based on the passage.

3. **D**   Egypt constantly tried to subjugate Nubia throughout its history, so eliminate (A). If you're not certain about Libyan peoples, leave (B) alone. Choice (C) is much too far ahead into the future for this question, but (D) is demonstrably true; historically, ancient Egypt always tried to rule over the Levant and Syria. Therefore, you can safely choose (D) as the answer.

4. **C**   Choice (A) could be a side effect of conflict, but it is not the main goal. Even though the phrase appears in the passage, in context there is no evidence that this is a goal; eliminate (A). Choice (B) is plausible, but it is not justified by the passage; eliminate (B). Like (A), (D) is a side effect of conflict rather than the main goal, so it is incorrect. Choice (C) is the stated goal of both the author of the passage and his challenger, and therefore it is the correct answer.

5. **A**   The passage discusses tribes destroying each other for the benefit of Rome. Eliminate (B), (C), and (D), as they are not supported by the passage.

6. **B**   The passage expresses relief that tribes are destroying each other instead of fighting Rome, indicating some relief that they are not fighting Rome. Eliminate (A), as it is too extreme. Eliminate (C) because stoic tones are present in the passage. Choice (D) is also not supported by the passage, so (B) is the correct answer.

7. **C**   The Senate persisted throughout Roman history and beyond. Choices (A), (B), and (D) are all serious issues that the Romans encountered in the imperial period and all are arguably far worse than the existence of the Senate. Therefore, you can eliminate those three choices and choose (C).

8. **B**   Eliminate (A), as religious uniformity was less important to societies before 600 C.E. than afterwards. Choice (C) can also be eliminated, as the word *uniformly* is too strong for this choice to be valid. Eliminate (D); tribes in both periods seized control of their host societies (such as Rome and the Abbasid Caliphate), but in both instances, the tribes arguably seized control on their own accord.

9. **B**   A geographic map such as this does not show political history, so the political acts of princes, kings, and emperors (though they may be true) would not be supported by this source; eliminate (A) and (D). The map does show, however, that Buddhism originated in northeastern India and eventually was present in most of East and Southeast Asia. This is consistent with (B) and (C). However, (C) is a factor that led to the spread of Buddhism, while (B)—increased merchant activity between India and Southeast Asia—is a result of its spread. The correct answer is (B).

10. **D** Buddhism spread out of India by means of merchants trading between India and its neighbors. Eliminate any answer choices that do not match this. Choice (A) helped the decline of Buddhism in India, so eliminate (A). Choice (B) is too limited, as the royal edicts supported India, not Buddhism specifically; get rid of (B). Choice (C) happened after 600 C.E., so eliminate it, as it does not work chronologically. Choice (D) is correct; strong trade routes linking south, central, and east Asia helped spread Buddhist influence as shown on the map.

11. **C** You're looking for the answer choice that describes the most logical reason for Buddhism's declining influence in India after 600 C.E. A strengthened, more influential caste system would probably inspire converts to Buddhism (in an effort to escape the caste system), so eliminate (A). The nationality of merchants in the Indian Ocean was not necessarily relevant to the spread of Buddhism, so eliminate (B). The Gupta Empire ruled in India between 320 and 550 C.E., which is outside the time period of the question, so eliminate (D). The decline of Buddhism is generally attributed to the collapse of centralized rule and rise of regional powers in India, so (C) is correct.

12. **B** Buddhism's main attraction was that it offered an escape from the strict caste system imposed by Hindu beliefs, which best aligns with (B). Eliminate (A) because Buddhism emerged before kings like Asoka converted to it. Eliminate (C) because Greek philosophies did not inspire Buddhist beliefs. Eliminate (D) because Buddhism was only spread over trade routes, not created by them.

13. **C** The Song concentrated on developing an industrial society. Choice (C) is correct. The Song continued much of the same government structure (civil service, etc.) as the T'ang. Eliminate (A) and (B). The Grand Canal was completed during the Sui Dynasty in the sixth and seventh centuries, so eliminate (D) as well.

14. **B** Between 800 and 1100 C.E., iron production increased tenfold to about 120,000 tons per year. Choice (B) is correct. Silk had long been associated with China, but this question seems to be looking for a product closely associated specifically with the Song, so silk does not seem like a likely choice. Eliminate (A). Gold production was far more associated with Africa, so (C) is incorrect. Coffee was a product of the islands of Southeast Asia and Africa, though not closely associated with the Chinese mainland. Eliminate (D).

15. **B** An early form of moveable type resulted in an increase in literacy and bureaucrats among the lower classes. This best aligns with (B). The Song Dynasty had renewed focus on Buddhism, with Daoism and Confucianism still present. This was not a dynasty characterized by Legalism. Eliminate (A). The Song saw further subjugation of women (foot binding comes to mind), so (C) is incorrect. While Chinese expansion slowed during the Song, there were still significant military technologies being developed, such as gunpowder. Choice (D) is incorrect.

16. **C** The Song might have revitalized China to new and impressive heights, but Song emperors were not nearly as interested in territorial expansion as the T'ang emperors were. Eliminate (A) because the civil service exams were halted during the Yuan Dynasty, not the Song. Eliminate (B) because the Song Dynasty fostered the intellectual movement that would eventually culminate in Neo-Confucianism. Eliminate (D) because the Yuan Dynasty, the dynasty Kublai Khan founded, was Mongolian in origin.

17. **D** The introduction of Champa, a fast-ripening rice from Vietnam, linked with new agricultural techniques, increased food supplies. The increased food supplies allowed for the sustenance of a larger population. Choice (D) is correct. While the Song Dynasty was known for its technological gains, the world saw no significant sanitation technology for some time after this period. Eliminate (A). The Song Dynasty saw an increase in urban centers, which has a closer link with population increases than does a rurally-based population. Eliminate (B). Song China was smaller than the T'ang, as its military focus decreased in favor of trade relationships. Choice (C) is incorrect.

18.   **A**   The question asks about the image of a quipu, which was an Incan device for record keeping and bureaucratic function. Therefore, eliminate answer choices that do not involve bureaucracy or record keeping. Choice (A) does, so keep it. Choices (B) and (C) do not fit this description, so eliminate them. Choice (D) does discuss administration, but bureaucracies are not usually feudal in nature. Choice (A) is stronger than (D), so eliminate (D) and choose (A).

19.   **B**   The question asks about a common practice of Mesoamerican and Andean civilizations to demonstrate religious authority. Choice (A) discusses state-sponsored religious literature, which was more of a tenet of Old World civilizations, so eliminate it. Choice (B) discusses sacrifices, which were indeed widely practiced by Andean and Mesoamerican civilizations, so keep it. Choice (C) discusses record keeping, which is the purpose of the quipu in the image and not primarily a device used for religious expression, so eliminate (C). Choice (D) discusses the sponsorship of astronomical research, which is a notable scientific achievement of the ancient Mayans but not a focus of all Mesoamerican and Andean civilizations, nor done primarily out of expressing religious authority. Therefore, eliminate (D) and choose (B).

20.   **C**   The question asks about the significance of cities for pre-modern civilizations. Cities historically have been centers of commerce and religion, among other things, and often were the source of great wealth for states. Eliminate choices that do not reflect this focus. Choice (A) discusses manpower for armies—in pre-modern states most armies were furnished from the countryside and the peasantry, not the urban populations, so eliminate (A). Choice (B) discusses further stratification of society, which does not make sense given that cities were the source of mercantile wealth, and that wealth often allowed merchants to transcend social barriers, not reinforce them. Eliminate (B). Choice (C) discusses the very merchant activity that cities are historically known for, so keep (C). Choice (D) does feature a known function of cities: religious centers. But this choice uses the word *exclusively,* and that extreme language precludes any other function of cities, which is not correct. Eliminate (D) and choose (C).

21.   **A**   If a king boasts that he does not need to exact taxes (duties) in his kingdom, it means that his kingdom is rich. The passage discusses in large part Mali's mineral wealth so eliminate answer choices that do not discuss mining: (B), (C), and (D). Choice (A) is the answer.

22.   **B**   Mali's position below the Sahara desert meant that it was not easy for outsiders to conquer. However, because it sat astride the north-south trade routes to the Mediterranean, it was definitely frequented by Muslim merchants. Eliminate (A) because the missionaries are coming from the wrong direction. Eliminate (C) because Berber tribes did not conquer Ghana. Eliminate (D) because Ethiopia and Mali were not rivals. Choice (B) is the best answer.

23.   **B**   The discussion of copper and gold is in the middle of the passage in which Mansa Musa claims that Mali sells copper for gold. Choices (A), (C), and (D) do not mention trade in any way, so they can be eliminated for this reason. Choice (B) is correct.

24.   **B**   The passage's focus on international trade demonstrates how links between nations were still being developed but they were present. Therefore, you should be looking for an answer choice that involves international commerce. Choices (A), (C), and (D) are not related to this idea, so you can eliminate them and choose (B).

25.   **C**   Crosby's argument is essentially that Europe achieved a position of global hegemony by discovering and exploiting the New World. Eliminate (A) and (B) because they do not discuss the New World. Eliminate (D) because it does not explicitly refer to the settlement of the New World. Choice (C) is the best answer.

26.   **B**   Only through the conquest or colonization of the New World, Crosby argues, was Europe able to achieve global hegemony. Choices (A), (C), and (D) do not involve the New World and therefore are not related to his argument. Eliminate those choices and choose (B).

27. **C** Rely on the contextualization offered in this question: 1450–1750 C.E. Choices (A), (B), and (D) all largely occurred during 1450–1750, but since you're looking for the choice that contributed the LEAST, choose (C), which developed a little after this time period.

28. **B** The "quantum jump" in the passage refers to the Columbian Exchange and the settlement and conquest of the New World by Europeans. Choices (A) and (C) are historically false and can be eliminated. Choice (D) is a possible answer, but not as supportable as (B), which is the answer.

29. **A** The Treaty of Tordesillas split the world and the territories discovered by Spain and Portugal in half. Eliminate (B) because the treaty mentions nothing about slaves. Eliminate (C) because the Scientific Revolution refers to a more systematized procedure for scientific discovery that the passage does not discuss. Eliminate (D) because the passage does not discuss Protestantism at all. Therefore, (A), European maritime exploration, is correct.

30. **D** The Portuguese ensured that they would own the lands to the east of the demarcation line to maintain their hold on India. Eliminate (A) because Portugal knew that India was not the same land mass as the New World. Eliminate (B) because Portugal was not interested in waging war against the Mamelukes in Egypt. Finally, eliminate (C) because the Portuguese never expressed any imperial interest in Mexico. Choice (D) is the best answer.

31. **B** The Spanish were interested in preserving their stranglehold over the whole of the New World. Eliminate (A) because the Barbary States would actually be east of the line. Eliminate (C), as the Spanish *conquistadores* ended up conquering the natives who were in their way. Eliminate (D) because the relative ease of conquest played very little role in the diplomatic negotiations for the Treaty of Tordesillas. You're left with (B), which is the answer.

32. **A** The treaty is a clear sign that monarchs were willing both to wage war and settle disputes over land exploration, which aligns with (A). Eliminate (B) because neither Portugal nor Spain used joint-stock companies in their colonization efforts. Eliminate (C) because the treaty does not discuss the trading implications with Africa. Eliminate (D) because the treaty makes no mention of formal scientific research, only exploration. Choice (A) is the answer.

33. **B** The Treaty of Tordesillas principally involved negotiations over exploration, so eliminate technologies that did not help European navigation—namely (A), (C), and (D). Choice (B), the compass, is the only choice that is related to exploration, so it is the best answer.

34. **C** Eliminate (A) because the passage does not state whether Chinese merchants dominated the East Asian trade networks. Eliminate (B) because the passage does not discuss the presence of Dutch ships in Japan. Finally, get rid of (D) because the passage does not discuss Jesuits. The first paragraph does relate to the idea of Europe's participation in East Asian trade patterns, so (C) is the best answer.

35. **D** New World silver powered the Chinese economy, as Spanish treasure galleons brought it over in massive quantities from Mexico, so (D) is correct. Eliminate (A) and (C), as Central Asia and the Middle East are not immediately recognizable as silver exporting regions. Choice (B) can be eliminated as well since the production of silver in Europe proper did not match that of the New World.

36. **B** The Ming Dynasty in its later years tried to enact measures to control foreign merchants' endeavors in China, as the last paragraph details the Ming Canton system. Eliminate (A) because it is not supported by the passage. Eliminate (C) because the system of controlling trade is clearly present in the passage, so the Ming had to have had some interest in it. Eliminate (D) because it conflates China with Japan's later restriction of foreign merchants. Choice (B) is the answer.

37. **A** The trade pattern in question is the acquisition of silver from India and Japan to purchase goods from China. Opium would eventually be a deal-breaker, as Chinese merchants and customers would come to crave the drug and pay silver for it! Eliminate (B), (C), and (D), as these developments did not nearly create a reversal of the balance of trade as much as the export of opium to China did.

38. **C** The trade pattern in question is the acquisition of silver from India and Japan to purchase goods from China. The Japanese government under the Tokugawa Shogunate would close Japan off to all foreign merchants save the Dutch who had to operate under severe limitations, limiting the amount of silver that could be drawn out of Japan. Eliminate (A) because Russia's eastward expansion made little impact on silver flows in East Asia. Eliminate (B) because the Portuguese never conquered India. Eliminate (D) because Spanish silver from Mexico strengthened the trade system more than weakened it. Choice (C) is correct.

39. **A** The cable line ends in Egypt at the spot labeled Suez. This obviously invokes the Suez Canal, so (B), (C), and (D) can be eliminated on the basis that they do not mention the canal. Choice (A) is correct.

40. **B** The telegraph allowed communications to travel over the world near instantly, bridging gaps that would have taken weeks or months to traverse and effectively "shrinking" the world. This also allowed empires to grow larger to accommodate their expanded reach. Eliminate (A); this is the opposite of what actually occurred. Eliminate (C) because common people used telegraphs just as often as governments. Eliminate (D) because only the most modern nations had access to the technology required to set up telegraph connections. Choice (B) is the answer.

41. **B** The map focuses on the western end of the Indian Ocean, centering on Arabia. The period 600–1450 C.E. should strike you immediately as the era of Islam in Arabia. Eliminate any answer choices that do not pertain to Islam. Choices (A), (C), and (D) can be eliminated for this reason, so you're left with (B), which is correct.

42. **B** The Suez Canal in the west, India in the east, and the cable spanning the distance between the two should all remind you that the British were heavily involved in the Indian Ocean. Choices (A) and (D) do not support this idea, so eliminate them. Eliminate (C) as well; although the British navy was powerful, the British did not control the entire Indian Ocean area. Therefore, (B) is the answer.

43. **D** The tables show the percentages of manufacturing out of the total economic output of several countries. Table 1 is from 1945, and it shows that no country had more than a quarter of its economy coming from manufacturing. Eliminate answer choices that are not supported by the table. Choice (A) can be eliminated, as the table does not present information about goods and their sources. Eliminate (B) because there is no information about North America in the tables. Eliminate (C) because the table does not present any data about trade with the United States.

44. **C** The tables show the relative proportion of industry in the total economies of several Latin American states. Eliminate (A) because Latin American states by and large did not successfully industrialize in the twentieth century. Eliminate (B) because the tables do not contain any information related to governments or Cold War politics. Eliminate (D) because the tables do not suggest any sort of spread of industrial technology.

45. **D** Choices (A) and (B) can be eliminated because the values for Argentina and Brazil are percentages, not actual quantities. Eliminate (C) because industrialization does not necessarily entail urbanization. Choice (D) is the correct answer.

46.   **A**   Eliminate (B) because exploitation of precious metals in Mexico and Brazil would not alone explain the lack of industrialization in other Latin American countries. Eliminate (C) because the population losses suffered by the natives were made up by immigration from Europe and Africa. Eliminate (D) because the haciendas and provincial elites were very strong in Latin American society, not weak. The mercantilist policies followed by colonial powers, however, does explain why Latin American economies were under-industrialized, so (A) is the answer.

47.   **B**   The passage discusses Mao's plan to collectivize agriculture in China, which is mentioned in (B). Eliminate (A) because the passage doesn't discuss political reforms. Eliminate (C) because the passage does not discuss industrialization. Finally, eliminate (D), as the passage does not advocate capitalism. The answer is (B).

48.   **A**   You can eliminate (B) because collectivization does not involve globalization or corporations. Eliminate (C) because the collectivization regime in the speech actually damaged Chinese prestige, not Soviet prestige. You can also get rid of (D) because the collectivization program did not involve adoption of the Green Revolution. Therefore, (A) is the answer.

49.   **D**   The "socialist transformation" described in the passage is the collectivization of farms that would eventually culminate in the Great Leap Forward. Eliminate (A), (B), and (C), as they do not discuss collectivization.

50.   **A**   The collectivization program discussed in the source seeks to abolish private agricultural property, so eliminate answers that would retain it. Choices (C) and (D) both advocate capitalism, so eliminate them. Eliminate (B) as well because the ideals of the Enlightenment put forth by Robespierre are political, not economic, by nature. The answer is (A).

51.   **C**   Mao's hopes in the second to last sentence in the passage are that the peasantry will enjoy increased prosperity on account of his collectivization regime. Eliminate (A) because the special economic zones were introductions of capitalism into China. You can also eliminate (B) and (D), as the reforms in the passage are economic, not political. Choice (C) is the best answer.

52.   **B**   The Ayatollah Khomeini made this speech at a time when much of the world had decolonized, yet formerly colonized countries faced a phenomenon known as neocolonialism. Iran was officially independent, though the United States aided in the 1953 coup d'état of the democratically elected prime minister and installed the shah, a man many Iranians saw as a tool of the West. Therefore, the context of the speech best aligns with (B). The Industrial Revolution occurred a couple centuries before this speech, so eliminate (A). Eliminate (C) because Free Trade Associations are not supported by the passage. Eliminate (D) because autarky, or the complete absence of foreign trade, is not supported by the passage.

53.   **D**   The United States and Great Britain helped with the 1953 coup d'état, installing the shah as leader of Iran. Khomeini is referencing the United States' continued support of the shah. Choice (D) is correct. Since Khomeini resented the American support for the shah, (A) is incorrect. Choice (B) is also incorrect, as the passage does not mention trade agreements. And (C) is incorrect since Khomeini connects the Iranian army with the United States, which would not gain the military approval from Khomeini.

54.   **A**   Ultimately, the people of Iran rejected the shah (one of the governments) in favor of the theocracy represented by Ayatollah Khomeini. Choice (A) aligns with that event. The 1979 constitution was technically democratic, but that was not the purpose of the reform movement (an Islamic state was), and Iran has not had fair and open elections under this constitution. Eliminate (B). Choice (C) is incorrect, as the fallout of the 1979 revolution put the Ayatollah in power. The Iran-Iraq War did not begin until 1980, a year after one of the governments of Iran came to an end. Eliminate (D).

55.	**C**	Khomeini espoused an Islamic state, first and foremost. Choice (C) is correct. Eliminate (A) because fascism was widely discredited in the years following World War II. Eliminate (B) because social Darwinism has little to do with economics at a fundamental level. Eliminate (D) because classical liberals believe the state should be involved in the economy as little as possible.

Short-Answer Questions

Question 1

a)	Your answer should discuss how the portrait reflects attempts made by the Ottoman Empire to reform itself along Western lines. A good response must include ONE reason of the following:

- Ottoman military defeats at the hands of European powers in the previous century

- Ottoman economic weakness and decline

- The weakness of the position of the sultan with respect to the Janissary corps or the Grand Viziers

- Ottoman technological backwardness with respect to Europe

b)	A good response must include ONE discussion of Ottoman efforts to Westernize themselves as supported by the painting. Responses can discuss Mahmud's military uniform or the Western column and draperies in the background as definite evidence of the acceptance of Western culture and art forms. Mahmud's stylish fez indicates some Ottoman conservatism.

c)	Your answer should discuss one of the many wars the Ottomans waged against European or Muslim powers in the time period. Responses may discuss the Ottoman wars against the Hapsburgs of Spain, Austria, or Portugal, Ottoman wars against Russia, Ottoman wars against Safavid Persia, or even the Ottoman alliance with France.

Question 2

a)	A good answer to this question must address the period from 600 to 1450 c.e. and major developments within this period, accompanied by specific historical examples. A successful answer must include TWO of the following:

- **Religion:** Empires like the Umayyad or Abbasid Caliphates, the Holy Roman Empire, and the Byzantine Empire all strongly relied on religion as a cohesive force and a way to legitimize the ruler in the eyes of the subjects.

- **Conquest and Warfare:** Empires like the Caliphates, the Mongols, the Aztecs, and many others relied on victory in war to build internal strength as well as legitimize the ruler in the eyes of the people.

- **Trade and Commerce:** The period saw the further formation of international trade routes and commerce. States like the Italian cities, the Hanseatic League, Song China, and many others stimulated commerce, which inspired cultural golden ages and generally high levels of prosperity that kept people content.

- **Technological Change:** Technologies like gunpowder helped states, especially Europe, strengthen their military power, while other technologies like the three-field system helped agricultural output grow.

- **Feudalism:** The period of time specified by the question is situated in the age of feudalism, a system of government in which rulers delegated land to vassals in exchange for the obligations of loyalty and military service. Feudal societies stretched from Europe to China, and the power dynamics between the ruler and his vassals swung from either extreme throughout the time period. A good example of this is France, where the nobility was more powerful than the King and caused a significant headache to ruling that realm. Only through powerful monarchs in later periods were nobles' ambitions curtailed.

b) Some examples of cross-cultural assimilation include the following. (Remember, you need to cite TWO examples.)

- Western Europe acquired new scientific and medical knowledge from Islamic civilizations during the Crusades.

- New technologies entered Europe from the Islamic world through al-Andalus.

- The Mongols acquired Islamic scientific knowledge.

- The Swahili Coast became wealthy due to its participation in Indian Ocean trade.

Question 3

A successful response to this question must address the fact that these trade routes are the westerly ends of the Silk Roads and track their development throughout the periods mentioned in the question.

a) Your answer should include TWO of the following:

- Consolidation of empires such as Persia, Greek states, and Rome to facilitate trade

- Economic development of the Mediterranean basin in order to stimulate demand for Asian goods

- Development of vessels suitable for trade between the Red Sea and the Indian Ocean.

- Consolidation of steppe empires like those of the Parthians to protect overland trade to India through central Asia.

b) Your answer should include ONE of the following:

- Empires became politically fractured (for example, Rome and the conquest of the Sassanid Empire of Persia by the Arabians).

- Attacks by steppe peoples such as the Hunas in India, White Huns in Persia, and the Huns or Avars in Roman lands disrupted international trade routes.

- Arab mastery of Indian Ocean trade increased seaborne trade's volume relative to overland trade.

Question 4

a) You need to discuss ONE way European colonists developed and exploited the lands of the Americas. Possible topics would include the plantation colonies of the Caribbean, the English Thirteen Colonies, or the Portuguese colony of Brazil.

b) A successful response must discuss the violent relationship that marked certain European relationships with the natives of the New World. Possible topics would include the Spanish conquest of the Aztecs, Incans, and other such civilizations, the English wars against natives such as the Pequot War, or the eradication of native resistance in the Caribbean.

c) To successfully answer (c), you need to justify your answer to either (a) or (b), but add evidence beyond what is presented in (a) and (b), and explain how your examples typify European interaction with the natives of the New World.

Document-Based Question (DBQ)

A strong essay will discuss some of the various issues that Latin America confronted between the period 1875 and 1950 C.E., ranging from territorial disputes that resulted in all-out war between nations, as in Document 1; to European colonialism and American hegemony, as in Documents 3 and 7; to the agrarian nature of Latin American economies, as described in Documents 4, 5, and 6; to gender inequality, as described in Document 2. To earn the maximum number of points, you need to use only six of the seven documents. A strong essay will include discussion of global politics during the period—neocolonialism through commercial domination of Latin America, World Wars I and II, and the beginnings of the Cold War—and how these affected Latin America (or did not!). A good essay might therefore touch on Latin America's lack of industrialization and make a claim that this comparative disadvantage in its economics led the region to geopolitical instability and maintained the strong plantation culture that had existed in the continent since its colonial days, with all its various disadvantages such as backbreaking labor, strong regional tendencies, and gender inequality. There is no one right answer, though, so long as your thesis is supported by the documents, you are on the right track!

Long Essay

Question 2

A strong essay will discuss Taoism and its rise to prominence in tandem with Confucianism. It will also explain how Taoism is functionally a reaction to Confucianism in that Confucianism stresses an orderliness to the world and prescribes proper behavior in order to achieve harmony for the state and, therefore, for the world. Taoism instead espouses a harmony with nature and a search for inner peace within the natural confines of the world.

An essay that contends that Taoism is an important development should discuss Taoism as it relates to Confucianism as well as the strength of the Chinese dynasties at the time. Recall that China was not unified during the fifth century B.C.E.; instead it was suffering its centuries-long period of civil war called the Warring States period, but would eventually be unified under the Qin Dynasty by Qin Shi Huangdi in 221 B.C.E. Consequently, an essay that stresses the importance of Taoism would show that its rise is indicative of the chaotic political nature of China during the fifth century B.C.E. and also relate it to the reaction against the increasing strength of the central Qin and Han governments following 221 B.C.E.

An essay that seeks to downplay the importance of Taoism would instead focus on the lack of state support that Taoism received compared to Confucianism or Legalism in the same historical period. Such an essay would probably make the assertion that Taoism remained a religion of the common people and did not influence government officials to the degree that the Confucian classics did. It might also note Taoism's lack of global success, as its influence remained limited to East Asia.

Question 3

A strong essay will discuss the Mongol sack of Baghdad in its historical context. It is generally accepted that this sack allows modern historians to date the end of the golden age of Islam, but its long-term ramifications are arguable. An argument in favor of the sack as a significant moment in history would contend that the unity of Islamic civilization centered on the authority of the Abbasid Caliph in Baghdad was forever shattered by the Mongol invaders. Such an argument would contend that the Abbasids managed to hold onto their religious authority and primacy in the Muslim world even under Seljuk "protection," but following the sack, the Abbasids retained none of that authority and the various regions of the Islamic world, such as Egypt, Anatolia, Spain, North Africa, India, and Southeast Asia definitely split and went their own ways.

An argument contending that the sack was not an important moment in history would instead state that the Abbasids did not retain much authority while they were under the thumb of the Seljuk Turks and that Islamic civilization was largely fragmented by the year 1258. Therefore, when the Mongols crushed the Seljuks and the rather limited power base the Abbasids retained in Mesopotamia, the cities of the Muslim world in Iran and Mesopotamia traded one nomadic suzerain for another.

Question 4

A strong essay will develop the historic context of the Berlin Conference before evaluating the importance of the event as a turning point. The Conference was called by Otto von Bismarck in order for the European powers to develop criteria for establishing colonies in Africa. The years following the conference saw European nations— Britain, France, Germany, Italy, Spain, Portugal, and Belgium—carve up the African map into a series of colonies, with the exception of Liberia and Ethiopia.

An essay that argues the Berlin Conference was a turning point would point to the impact that colonial holdings had on the start of World War I. European tensions and the race for colonial holdings were exasperated by the meeting in Germany. Further, the imprecision with which colonial borders were created, in terms of the division of tribal lands, brought internal warfare to African nations. Finally, without control of its own natural resources, African economic development was stalled by the European colonial powers.

If one were to argue that the Berlin Conference were not a significant turning point, the essay would need to play up the inevitability of the colonizing of Africa, with or without the Berlin Conference. Further, the essay would claim that the tensions that led to the First World War existed without the Berlin Conference. While this claim may be more difficult to argue, it is possible with appropriate analysis that claims how little the Berlin Conference altered the events that proceeded it due to their inevitability and myriad other factors at play.

8000 BCE – 600 BCE

Neolithic Revolution

1st

Mesopatamia, Egypt
- cuniform
- UR
- trade w/ Egypt
- Hamarabi's code
- City states
- Ziggurats
- priest — top

- Pyrimads
- hyroglifics
- phero
- Nile
- Mummification
- Priest

Indus
- Mochen Jo Dara, Harapa (City states)
- Aryan Invasions
  - Caste system
  - Horses
  - Hinduism

oldest modern religion

China
- Shang
- Zhou → LAW mandate of Heaven

Olmec: head
Chavin

Classical 600 BCE – 600 CE

Rome
- 12 tables
- Senate - Ceasar
- Aquaducts
- Roads
- Archs
- Colisium
- Republic - first 500 years
- Empire - Next 500 years
- Patricians + Plebeians
- pater familias
- Weakend after Han fell
  = 2nd to fall
  = Christianity

Persia
- Royal Road
- Zoroastrianism
-

Greeks
- Alexander
  - Helenism

a poor person's Religion (catholic) higher

Han
- Confusionism
- Emperor
- Civil Service Exam
- Silk Road
- they make silk
- Filial piety
- 1st to fall

All 1000 years

BR Connected them together

Gupta   1-2 set
- last to fall
- Maritime
- Mansoon winds
- Hinduism (polythestic)
- Judaism
- Christianity — Mono.
- Buddhism
- Confusionism

Post-Classical 600 – 1450

Main Change: ISLAM

BUT: spread disease
1200.. Mongols
Baghdad 1250
- positive on Religion - Yuan Ied 62 bring trade v easy
on SR Ideas spread

Byzantine
- East Rome
- Constantinople
- Hagia Sophia
- Justinian's code
- Great Schism
- Orthodox
- Walls
- Greek Fire
- lasted 500-1453
- Not powerful in the last 500
- Mediteratanian
- Halas

S/T/S
- paper money
- flying cash
- junk
- magnetic compass
- steri-postrva.
- gun powder
- Neo Confusionism
- Tang didn't like Buddhists
- Brought back silk Road → Abbasid

Abbasid / Ummay
- Golden Age
- 711 - India + Spain
  - Dar Al-Islam
- Trading (main reason for converting)
- Sub-trans Saharan trade route
- brought Islam to West Africa
- lowest classes converted
- Shariah law - caliphs
- Sufis - Religios
- Jizya - Political
- Sunni/Shia
- Haij/Mecca

RVC 8000^BCE – 600^BCE 1 set

classical 600^BCE – 600^CE 1-2 sets
3-4 sets

pr. classical 600 – 1450

porch on -SSS 1450 – 1750   4 sets

IIR 1750 – 1900   4 sets

modern 1900 – Present   3-4 sets

East vs West
– Society/States } – Laws

~~~~~~~~~~~~~~~~~~~~~~~~~~~~~~~

1450 – 1750:

Europe	Portugal	Spain
– Futual	– Diaz	– Columbus
– they became very violent	– De gama	– discovers a new hemisphere
– Nation State	–	– Columbian Exchange
– Crusades		– DISESE, DISESE
– Rerasance		– Cash crop
– Charlamagne:		– Sugar → Rum
– tries to centerlize Europe		– Slave trade
– Cathalisism		– Went mostly to Brazil and the carribean
		– Silver
		– Silk

3 S's

Exploration (SSS)

Empires
– British
– French
– Portugal
– Spain
– Dutch
VOC

will end up controlling Indian Ocean trade

All Maritime

Ming/Qing
Richest in the beginning to the end
– Ottomans
– Mongols

Capitilism in this period

NOTES

1750-1900

IIR

Industrial   Revolutions
              -American
              -French --> Nationilism
              -Haiti
              -Creole

1900-Present   WWI: -caused by Nationilism
                     -No one lost
                     -Treaty of Versilles
                WWII: -started by ↑
                      -Fasicism
                      -Hitler
                      -America comes out most power
                      -Russia (USSR) - 2nd ↑

Modern   Cold War - Nuclear Weapons

                De-Colonization-

                Globalization-US-LEADER

NOTES